ISBN: 9781313441841

Published by:
HardPress Publishing
8345 NW 66TH ST #2561
MIAMI FL 33166-2626

Email: info@hardpress.net
Web: http://www.hardpress.net

MEMOIRS OF THE
COMTESSE DE BOIGNE

MEMOIRS OF THE COMTESSE DE BOIGNE

1781–1814

EDITED FROM THE ORIGINAL MS.

BY

M. CHARLES NICOULLAUD

WITH PORTRAIT

CHARLES SCRIBNER'S SONS

NEW YORK :: :: :: :: :: :: 1907

INTRODUCTION

THE Comtesse de Boigne, *née* Charlotte Louise Eléonore Adélaide d'Osmond, " had for her own name [to use her own expression] a passion which finds no counterpart in this age." This sentiment, which she has depicted as dominant in the heroine of a novel which appeared in the year of her death,[1] was paramount throughout the life of Mme. de Boigne, and inspired her last wishes. As she had no children, from her many nephews and nieces she chose as her general heir her grand-nephew Osmond, the future Marquis d'Osmond, with whom, against all human foresight, became extinct this illustrious family name, the arms of which appear in the Salle des Croisades at Versailles. He was ten years of age when his great-aunt died in 1866, at the age of eighty-five.

In accordance with her will, when he attained his twenty-fifth year, in the month of August 1881, he came into possession of a fortune which had been considerably increased by the wise and prudent administration of faithful executors. I was at that time his most intimate friend, and we had numerous interests in common. Together we made an inventory of the legacy of Mme. de Boigne. Among a number of valuable objects of art, dispersed in a famous sale in 1884, we found a certain number of family papers and some memoirs in manuscript. Our first idea was to publish them in common.

[1] *Une passion dans le grand monde*, by the Comtesse de Boigne. 2 vols. Paris, 1866.

But attentive reading forced us to recognise the fact that the immediate publication of these interesting recollections was impossible. There were too many private interests and personal rights to be considered, and before these obstacles we were forced at that time to yield.[1] The same motives doubtless obliged M. Taine to quote these memoirs as he has done in the third volume of the *Régime Moderne,* " Mémoires inédits de Mme. de . . . (I am not permitted to mention the author's name)." [2] To our great regret, it was necessary to wait, and to wait probably for many years, for the publication of the attractive recollections written by the Comtesse de Boigne for her nephews. For this reason, Osmond, who readily resigned his interests in these distant hopes, gave me, at my request, the original manuscript which his great-aunt had left him, together with numerous papers belonging to the estate and likely to be of historical interest, while urging upon me the duty of publication as soon as I saw any possibility. I proposed, while awaiting the moment when this publication could appear in its entirety, to make use of the information for other works which I had then in hand.

For twenty-five years these important documents, destined in the thought of their author to sleep upon the shelves, at first of the library in the Château de Pontchartrain, and afterwards in the Château d'Osmond, have remained in my possession, and have been communicated to no one.

---

[1] The Duc d'Audiffret Pasquier had received a copy of her memoirs from the Comtesse de Boigne, with permission to publish them if he thought fit. He was never willing to avail himself of this permission, and his heirs have observed the same reserve. His family is thus entirely unconnected with this present publication.

[2] Taine, *Les origines de la France contemporaine*, vol. xi. p. 98, 18mo edition.

Three articles which have appeared at different dates in the *Gaulois*,[1] and some notes inserted in a volume of history [2] with the reference *mémoires inédits*, have been the only hint to the initiated of the existence of these interesting recollections, or of the name of their actual possessor.

During this long period time had performed its work. The last Marquis d'Osmond, my friend, had gone to join his father, his grandparents, his great-aunt de Boigne, and all his relatives, in the little memorial cemetery of Aubrey le Pathou in Normandy. The family name is extinct. The estate of Osmond has been sold piecemeal. The castle has passed into other hands, and the archives are dispersed.

Other burial vaults also have been opened and closed by deaths which have further modified the position.

Moreover, those political conditions which had forced us to hold our hands in 1881 have been fundamentally altered by death and by the progress of events: various questions, then of burning interest, can now be examined with historical calm and serenity. The same passions no longer exist, and the present generation is less stirred by certain great problems which keenly interested their predecessors. The struggle has been transferred to other ground.

For this reason I think the time has come to fulfil my friend's commission by the publication of the manuscripts of the Comtesse de Boigne.

These papers will, I believe, throw many side-lights upon a long period extending from the reign of Louis

[1] Of July 12 and August 12, 1890, and April 28, 1893.
[2] *Casimir Périer, député de l'opposition 1817–30*, by Charles Nicoullaud, 1 vol. 8vo, with portrait. (Plon-Nourrit & Co., Paris, 1894.)

XIV. to the Revolution of 1848, and this rather by means of the special details which are narrated than by any generalisations from a wider outlook. This period was in every respect one of the most troubled and extraordinary in our national history, and is fertile in events and changes, important though not always fortunate.

At the same time, the reader must never lose sight of the fact that the Comtesse de Boigne, as she very modestly states, had no intention of writing a history, and wished merely to be a chronicler. " I have said nothing," she writes, " except that which I believe to be the truth," and she adds in the sixteenth chapter of this volume, " I am amusing myself in these scattered notes by reviving, like a series of shadows, without order or consecution, the different recollections which recur to memory; I am more inclined to enlarge upon minor circumstances which are striking enough to remain in my memory, but are not of sufficient importance to be mentioned elsewhere. Historical personages do not come within my view except as personally connected with myself or when I have collected detailed information concerning them upon the accuracy of which I can depend."

With these restrictions, she relates all the gossip which went round the *salons* of her time. Her narrative is marked by all the freedom of eighteenth-century speech, and with a wit sustained by touches of keen criticism,[1]

---

[1] Mme. Lenormand, speaking of the affection of her aunt, Mme. Récamier, for the Comtesse de Boigne, writes: "She liked that strong and charming mind, that archness full of reason, the perfect distinction of her manners, and even the slight shade of disdain which made her friendliness rather exclusive and her approbation more flattering."—*Madame Récamier*, by Edouard Herriot, vol. i. p. 142. (Wm. Heinemann, London, 1906.)

although she claims impartiality. These *salons* were numerous, and their importance is well known. " Remember," says Taine, " that during this century women were queens, set the fashion and the social tone, led the conversation, and therefore guided ideas and public opinion. When they appear in the vanguard of political progress, we may be certain that the men are following; each of these women is bringing with her the whole of her *salon*." [1]

Mme. de Boigne held this delightful position after her return from exile, and for nearly sixty years we see almost every person of importance visiting her or joining the special circle over which she presided with so much tact and graceful foresight. Many rising talents in politics or in literature were able, through her benevolent support, to traverse the first and often the most painful stages upon the road to fame. Celebrities recognised as such were happy to secure the approbation of an appreciative mind and of a judgment always accurate and informed. The two following letters selected from many others are adequate proofs of the fact.

Friday.

Madame,—

As you have with you to-morrow the poet Jasmin, permit me to offer you as *libretto* an article which I wrote long ago upon him, and of which his translated poetry forms the main part; it is only for this reason that I venture to bring to your notice this volume of archaisms.

Faithfully yours,

Sainte-Beuve.[2]

---

[1] *Les origines de la France contemporaine*, vol. ii. p. 149, 18mo edition.

[2] Letter hitherto unpublished.

MADAME,——

On Monday evening I am to read my poor *Judith* to some friends, and venture to inform you of this fact, without hope of further consequences. You cannot be permitted to leave your *salon*, where so many distinguished minds come daily to seek inspiration from yourself. I am not so presumptuous as to think that these advantages can be sacrificed for my sake, and merely wish to let you know that I shall be thinking of you on that day of my trial, and shall regret your absence as that of one of my most benevolent and enlightened critics.

Yours very truly,
D. GAY DE GIRARDIN.[1]

Saturday.

Born at Versailles before the Revolution,[2] brought up, so to speak, at the knees of the royal family, her mother

[1] Letter hitherto unpublished.

[2] In 1781, not in 1780, as Mme. Lenormand states in error in the delightful preface which she wrote to *Une passion dans le grand monde.* In any case we can quote the certificate of baptism of the Comtesse de Boigne, which the archivist has kindly extracted for us from the register of the parish of St. Louis at Versailles:——

Ville de Versailles.
Paroisse Saint-Louis.

Registre de 1781.   Folio 14. *Verso.*
Baptêmes.

L'an mil sept cent quatre-vingt un, le vingt février, Charlotte-Eléonore-Louise-Adélaide, née hier, fille légitime de haut et puissant seigneur Mgr. Eustache René d'Osmond, mestre de camp de cavalerie du régiment d'Orléans, et de haute et puissante dame Eléonore Dillon, a été baptisée par nous soussigné curé de cette paroisse. Le parein messire Charles-Antoine-Gabriel d'Osmond, évêque de Comminges, représenté par messire Jean Joseph-Eustache d'Osmond clerc du diocèse de Comminges; la mareine haute et puissante dame Marie-Louise-Mauricette-Elizabeth de Montmorency-Luxembourg, éspouse de haut et puissant seigneur Mgr. le marquis de Montmorency-Laval, lesquels et le père ont signé avec nous.

MONTMORENCY-LUXEMBOURG-LAVAL.
JACOB, *curé.*

LE MARQUIS D'OSMOND.
L'ABBÉ D'OSMOND.

being one of the ladies of Madame Adélaide, daughter of Louis XV., a friend in her youth during exile of Princesse Marie Amélie of Naples, who was to be Duchesse d'Orléans and Queen of France, Mlle. d'Osmond completed her education in England.

She came back with a keen taste for politics, marked by a wider liberalism than was in conformity with the *émigré* environment in which her parents lived. Wise guidance, open-mindedness, and a healthy and straightforward judgment enabled her to avoid the unfortunate exaggerations of that society to which she was attached by her birth; while she was also able to shun the revolutionary tendencies, more or less openly avowed, but always dangerous, to which many of her friends, and those by no means unimportant, were but too inclined before they succeeded in attaining to power.

It has been said that the Comtesse Osmond de Boigne was a complete embodiment of the transition between the old and the new *régime*. We must add that the statement was true even in respect of those foibles which are natural to every human character, and from which no one, whatever his nature, is entirely exempt; the statement will be proved by the reading of these pages, where the writer's character can be easily and openly divined. Her severity in some cases, and her indulgence in others, would be difficult of explanation in the case of a mind so highly gifted and well balanced, if we do not take into full consideration the conditions of her environment . . . and the affections of a heart which will always remain entirely womanly, perhaps even in spite of efforts to the contrary. Her stay with her father, the Marquis d'Osmond, at the Embassy of Turin in the first instance, and at the London Embassy afterwards, helped her to preserve the golden mean of political opinion, long before the phrase became a party label, manufactured perhaps in the political *salon* of the Comtesse de Boigne.

This *salon* exerted such a charm upon all who have frequented it that its attraction was irresistible, and if unavoidable conditions prevented a renewal of visits, the recollection none the less remained in the visitor's mind. It was an institution, almost a moral force, by which no one wished to be forgotten. "I press your hands," writes the Comte de Saint-Aulaire, then Ambassador at Vienna. "All my friends wish to be remembered to you, and do not forget me, I beg of you, in your *salon*." [1] Xavier Marmier, when forced to leave Paris, expresses a similar feeling. "I am leaving next Monday . . . Believe me, Madame, that, little as I have seen, to my great regret, of your kindly house, I have none the less appreciated it, and when far away I shall think more than once with affection of the charming *salon* in the Rue d'Anjou and of the beautiful trees of Chastenay." The Comtesse de Boigne had a European acquaintance, and distinguished foreigners were unable to escape the magnetic force of her brilliant parties. The same regret and sadness at the thought that he could not see as much of them as he would have liked, is apparent in this letter from the Count Nesselrode, First Minister of Russia: " . . . to secure a place in the recollection of one's friends is certainly one of the greatest happinesses of life. And your recollection is too precious for me not to attach the keenest interest to anything which may recall the delightful hours which I have spent at your house. . . . You have been able to preserve a charming *salon* throughout the political confusion which you have been forced to traverse. . . ." [2] It is true, if we should believe the rumours mentioned by the Duc de Laval, Adrien

---

[1] Unpublished letter.   [2] Ibid.

de Montmorency, to Mme. Récamier, that we might read between the lines and see a hidden reference to a deeper feeling for the " little Adèle," experienced long previously and not forgotten.[1] General Pozzo, her constant friend, who is often mentioned in the memoirs, wrote when leaving the Russian Embassy at Paris to join that at London: " You do well to think of me in these last parting moments. Our friendship is of such long standing that it is always ready to help us in difficult moments. The impulse which obliges me to leave so many agreeable habits and friends is hard to obey, but I shall do my best, irksome as it may be, to grow accustomed to it. . . ."[2]

All opinions were welcomed in Mme. de Boigne's *salon,* and the doors were ever opened to talent and good education. Lamartine, whose poetry was certainly more popular in this cultured meeting-place than his political ideas, was a constant visitor, and the greyhounds, before they appeared at the foot of the great poet's statue, sent one of their number to this hospitable house. The two following autograph letters, interesting and as yet unpublished, leave no doubt upon the subject.

" M. de Lamartine has the honour of sending to Mme. la Comtesse de Boigne the friend which she has desired, which he has reared for her and which he can recommend with feelings entirely paternal. It is the most sensitive and intelligent animal that he has ever known, and he feels more grief at separation from it than he can venture to admit.

" It is not yet entirely trained, and requires patience for some time longer. A gentle word of reproach is the

[1] *Madame Récamier*, by Edouard Herriot, vol. i. p. 259.
[2] Unpublished letter.

only punishment needed for this kind of dog; to do more is to destroy for ever the freshness of its character.

" It has had the distemper, but should it cough, a little mallow water is all that is required, never anything more. Veterinary surgeons kill dogs invariably, because they forget that these are not dogs, but four-footed birds.

" The first few days the dog will be rather downcast, and it will be better to have another dog to keep it company. It is fed on bread, with vegetables and a little chicken, but no other meat.

" I must ask pardon for all these details, but in six months Mme. de Boigne will understand their necessity, and I ask her to accept, together with this information, my kindest regards.

"LAMARTINE."

" A teaspoonful of olive oil with sugared mallow water, or the water mixed with honey to drink; vegetables, spinach, &c., to be eaten with bread only twice a day; this is the medicine and the diet.

" It should be taken out in the garden for a little, and should eat dog's grass.

" I greatly regret that I have not been able to avail myself of the kind permission of Mme. la Comtesse de Boigne to call, but from eight o'clock in the morning until midnight there is not an hour's time for pleasure when one is so doubly occupied as to be both deputy and poet.

" With kindest regards,
"LAMARTINE."

Guizot, the austere Guizot himself, whose time was no less occupied, though he was not a poet, adds his high and valuable testimony to this rapid sketch : [1]

[1] Unpublished letter.

" . . . I know no house anywhere so pleasant as yours; for some time past I have been spending my evenings in an unavoidable and wearisome manner.

" Certainly I much prefer the Rue d'Anjou to Châtenay [1] or Pontchartrain. [2]

" . . . I hope that notwithstanding the wind and dull weather, I shall return once more to perform my social duties to Châtenay. But you will soon be coming back, I hope. Châtenay can only be an agreeable interlude; the Rue d'Anjou is a very agreeable custom.

" With all kind regards,

" GUIZOT.

" *Saturday, October 2, 1841.*"

These quotations might easily be multiplied from the letters that have reached our hands. All testify to the attraction of those meetings which were held for more than half a century at the house of the Comtesse de Boigne. It only remains to add for the sake of accuracy that the reputation of the dining-room in no way impaired that of the *salon*, and, to the great satisfaction of the guests, the dinners in the Rue d'Anjou, at Châtenay, or at Trouville were an agreeable prelude to the evening's conversation. As a careful hostess, with a full knowledge of men, Mme. de Boigne took trouble to find unusual delicacies for them, as appears from the following letter from the chief of the palikars:

" MADAME LA COMTESSE,—

" As I have already had the honour to announce to you, I now take the liberty of sending all the honey from Mt. Hymettus which has reached me. I had ordered it

---

[1] Country house of Mme. de Boigne.

[2] Estate of the Marquis Rainulphe d'Osmond, brother of the Comtesse de Boigne.

for you, and little as there is of it, it will serve as a token of my respect and admiration, and also of my gratitude for the sympathy which I know you feel for the country where the bees have made this honey, which country is my beloved fatherland.

"Believe me, Madame la Comtesse,

"Yours faithfully,

"J. COLLETIS.[1]

"*February* 10, 1838."

I cannot resist the pleasure of quoting some further extracts from unedited letters of Mme. Récamier, which will show more exactly the seductive charm exerted by the Comtesse de Boigne upon all with whom she came in contact.

"*Tuesday the Seventeenth.*

"I write to thank you, dear Madame, for your charming hospitality, and to say how much I regret the fresh foliage of Châtenay, and especially the hours which I have spent alone with you; never have I felt more keenly the attraction of your mind, the inexhaustible charm of your conversation, the sole disadvantage of which was to spoil my natural kindliness by making me regard as disagreeable whatever happened to separate us. . . .

"I will give your message to M. de Chateaubriand; you are one of the very few persons for whose society he still cares, for he has once more become very exclusive, much to my regret, though he is as good and kind as ever to his friends.

". . . How I should like to walk with you again by the seaside and to talk with you of other times; in any case, your conversation is one of the greatest pleasures

---

[1] Greek statesman and minister, member of the provisory government; representative of Greece at Paris. (1788–1847.)

that I know, one of the only pleasures that I can still appreciate. . . ."

Mme. Récamier was an authority upon this subject, for " the worship of talent was part of her character." In this letter she shows us the secret which made the society of the Comtesse de Boigne so attractive : she was able to converse and to arouse conversation about her; this agreeable tradition is gradually dying out, and but few ladies of the present day have learnt the art of preserving it. There is plenty of talking in modern *salons*, but scant listening and no conversation. Conversation is a forgotten art which our ancestors practised until they were able to be bored wittily. Mme. de Boigne possessed in the highest degree this delicate and charming science of good society. To be convinced of the fact we have only to read the definition which her quick and dainty pen has given in one of the two novels which she has published.

" Conversation," she writes, " like all other pleasures, must not be abused : it should arise by chance, impromptu and naturally, under favourable conditions, when the participators meet without set purpose; then it is that they produce attractive conversation, as trees bear fruit in good season; . . . conversation is both the most tenacious and the most elusive thing in the world : sometimes it secures a firm footing in spite of all interruptions or obstacle; at other times the movement of a fly or a chair pushed back will break the thread; must we then feel any excess of grief? Certainly not. At the proper time it will begin once more, it may be to-morrow or presently, and the movement of the same fly or armchair will perhaps have provided another theme; they will revivify it and inform it with fresh grace. The necessary ingredients for conversation are distinguished people who take a pleasure in it, together with some men of learning, and a certain proportion of women and people who may seem futile, but are intelligent. Given these elements, allow things to take their course, and the less conversation is guided the sooner it will proceed." [1]

These high qualities, together with an intelligent application of the principles which she defines with so much wit and exactitude, enabled the Comtesse de Boigne to keep about her a circle which cheered the evening of her life, composed of people who had a definite place in contemporary society by birth, fortune, position, or talent. Until extreme old age she preserved, if not beauty, at any rate all the brilliant faculties of her youth, as appears in the delightful portrait drawn by the niece of Mme. Récamier.

" For many years Mme. de Boigne could not walk or even take a step: she was carried to her carriage, to her garden, from her room to the *salon*, from her *salon* to her dining-room, and was only carried into the latter when the guests were already assembled. Great was the surprise of some new guest to discover the incredible contrast between the swathed and hooded figure carried in by two footmen and the keen, fine intellect which appeared beneath these coverings as she sat at table and talked and charmed the company as though she were but thirty years of age. . . . Mme. de Boigne had lost none of her teeth, or her beautiful hair, or her pretty features, and if the conversation amused and animated her, a gleam of her youthful beauty would rise above the surface of her more than eighty years." [2]

[1] *La maréchale d' Aubemer*, by the Comtesse de Boigne, one vol. 18mo.
[2] *Une passion dans le grand monde*, by the Comtesse de Boigne. Preface by Mme. Lenormand.

Mme. de Boigne was not content to be an accomplished hostess and to dominate by her charm and intelligence all who were admitted to her *salon;* she was also a remarkable musician, gifted with a beautiful voice, and an author. I have already mentioned two novels published by her, the last of which was in the press at the moment of her death. In accordance with her wishes, Mme. Lenormand undertook the task of final revision. The Comtesse de Boigne has also left another work of fiction yet unpublished, and finally the narratives to which these lines are introductory, and which are by far her most important and remarkable work. She read certain passages to her intimate friends as they were written, and some of her friends, no less strange than herself to the world of letters, did not disdain to use their social leisure to follow her example, if we may believe the unpublished correspondence of Mme. Récamier. These special readings have their place side by side with the famous meetings of the Abbaye aux Bois, where a certain number of privileged persons were permitted to hear before publication the *Mémoires of Chateaubriand,* the *Premières Méditations* of Lamartine, the *Peau de Chagrin* of Balzac, the *Prométhée* of Edgard Quinet, the works of Ballanche, J. J. Ampère, Sainte-Beuve,[1] &c.

" . . . I am impatiently awaiting," writes Juliette, " my return to the Abbaye aux Bois, to come and see you and to be able to spend the whole evening with you; M. Pasquier will perhaps read us some chapters of his memoirs,[2] and you will not forget that you have also

[1] Cp. *Madame Récamier*, by Edouard Herriot, vol. ii., chaps. 15, 21, 22, and 23.

[2] *Histoire de mon temps: Mémoires du chancelier Pasquier*, published by the Duc d'Audiffret-Pasquier, of the French Academy. 6 vols. in 8vo. (Plon-Nourrit & Co., Paris, 1894.)

made *a promise* to me. This is an agreeable prospect to charm the present solitude."

PASSY, *Wednesday.*

" I am expecting on Friday at one o'clock that you will be so kind as to give me a delightful amusement; you know what I think of what you call your *papcrasses,* and I claim to be an excellent critic; I therefore thank you a thousand times for a reading, which is a real kindness in my position."

It would be a pity to pass over this praise, which was as delicately offered as it was fully deserved:

" Have you read the *Revue des deux mondes?* What M. Sainte-Beuve says of authors unsuspicious of their powers has made us think so naturally of you that I am certain he had the same thought." [1]

" The author unsuspicious of her powers," was not insensible to the compliment, and the number of the periodical having been asked for, Mme. Récamier, with her usual kindness, replied, " I send you the *Revue des deux mondes;* I could not send it earlier, as Amélie [2] had lent it to Mme. Guizot." [3]

Thus it appears that a literary critic of high importance, but not usually considered to possess the " natural benevolence " of the gentle Juliette, not only appreciated the intellect and judgment of Mme. de Boigne, but also thought well of her literary powers. This fact, in addition to the high and dominant social position which she so long occupied, lends a special interest to the narrative which she wrote for her nephew Comte

[1] Mme. Récamier, unpublished letter.
[2] Mme. Lenormand.   [3] Unpublished letter.

Rainulphe d'Osmond, the father of the man who entrusted to my friendship the full custody of these interesting papers.

In publishing these documents I am obeying the formal
desires which have been entrusted to me by the sole heir
of Mme. de Boigne, his great-aunt.   Had I been personally unable to perform this commission, which I execute
with the utmost pleasure, I should have placed the original manuscript in some public library, at the disposal of
any one who cared to use it.   An editor under these conditions would probably not have felt the same reasons
for performing his delicate task with the prudent reserve and the scrupulous care which I have attempted to
bring to it.
My task is confined to these limits, and it is not my
business to criticise the thought, to correct, alter, or mod-
ify the text.   It will be understood that these memoirs
represent the opinions of the Comtesse de Boigne, not
those which I have known her great-nephew and heir,
the Marquis d'Osmond, to entertain.   We have often
spoken of the reserve with which we should be obliged to
publish these narratives, had we been able to collaborate.
At the present day and under present conditions, I do
not think there can be any general interest in an account
of the restrictions to which I have been subject.   I have
contented myself with adding a certain number of historical or biographical notes, and with quoting from the
papers handed to me with the manuscript such docu-
mentary evidence as might attest the facts with which
the narrative deals.   The former will be found as foot-
notes, and the latter in the Appendix at the end of the
volume.   It was impossible to avoid a few omissions of
no great length; the full stops in the text represent the

length of the suppressed passages, and suppressions are indicated in the notes.[1]

The proposal conceived by Osmond and myself in common twenty-five years ago had now been realised, but it is no longer possible, as I had always intended, to place his name before mine upon the cover of these volumes. Since Providence has so willed it, my name stands alone, but I wish that the memory of my friend the Marquis d'Osmond should be associated as closely with my name as it is vivid in my recollection.

CHARLES NICOLLAUD.

NEUILLY-SUR-SEINE,
February 2, 1907.

[1] For this edition of the memoirs I have used nothing but the original manuscript and the papers bequeathed by the Comtesse de Boigne to her grand-nephew Osmond. To these I have merely added the result of my personal researches in the public archives. None of the special archives belonging to families related by birth or friendship to the Comtesse de Boigne have provided any documents for the purpose of this book; consequently the book stands apart from outside influence.

TO MY NEPHEW

RAINULPHE D'OSMOND

I pray you . . . when you shall these . . . deeds relate
Speak of me as I am; nothing extenuate,
Nor set down aught in malice.

SHAKESPEARE (*Othello*).

I HAD never thought of giving a title to these disconnected pages until the binder to whom I entrusted them
wished to know what title he should place upon the back
of the volume. I did not know what to reply. Memoirs
seemed too solemn; as for souvenirs, Mme. de Caylus
has made this title her own, and recent publications have
somewhat debased it. I therefore replied, " I will think
of it." With this idea in mind, I dreamt during the
night that my nephew was asked what those two clasped
volumes were. " Those are the stories of my aunt."
" Here goes for the stories of my aunt! " I cried when
I woke up, and hence the book has been baptised

STORIES OF AN AUNT.

TO THE READER, IF ANY READER BE FOUND

AT the beginning of 1835 I underwent a terrible misfortune. A child of fourteen years, whom I had been
bringing up for twelve years, and whom I loved as a
mother, perished in a dreadful accident which the least
precaution might have avoided, but the most tender care
could not have foreseen. I shall never recover from
so cruel a blow.[1] After this catastrophe the saddest
hours of my sad days were those which I had been wont
to spend in developing a keen and youthful mind, which
I had hoped would soon be able to support my growing
weakness.

Some months after this event, when talking to a friend
whose kindness of heart was devoted to soothing my own
sorrow, I mentioned a detail concerning the old-time
etiquette of Versailles. "You ought to write these
things down," he said: "the traditions are disappearing,
and I assure you that they even now possess real interest."
This advice was supported by the necessity of living in
the past when the present is joyless and the future without hope. I attempted to cheat my grief with this task,
undertaken during the painful moments which had once
been pleasantly employed. At times I was obliged to
struggle with my grief without success; at times, again,
I found some distraction. The following pages are the
result of these efforts, and their object was to drive away
the thoughts which I could hardly bear.

[1] See in the Appendix the letters of the Queen Marie Amélie and of
General Pozzo.

My first object, so far as I had an object, was merely to recall what I had learnt from my parents about their youth, and the court of Versailles. The idleness and uselessness of my present existence stimulated me to continue the narrative by the addition of more recent recollections; I have spoken of myself possibly too much, and certainly more than I should have wished; but it was necessary to use my life to form the thread to my story, and to show how I was able to learn what I have related.

A considerable amount of paper had already been covered with handwriting more or less illegible, when a person in whose taste I have full confidence secured a knowledge of my task, and strongly advised me to have a copy made and to revise it. The making of a copy was no difficulty, but the revision is a complete impossibility; I do not know how to write, and at my age I cannot learn, and if I were to try to correct my sentences these pages would lose the only merit which they can claim, and which rests upon the fact that they have been written without premeditation and without claim to permanent value. If I had been obliged to undertake any researches elsewhere than in my memory, I should have given up my project, for I desired a distraction and not a laborious work.

Hence, if my nephews should ever glance at these writings, they must not expect to find a book, but merely the chatter of an old woman and the piecing together of the conversation of her *salon;* I regard the result as of no more importance than a piece of fancy work. I have successively used my pen to rest my needle, and my needle to rest my pen, and my heirs will receive my manuscript as they might receive an old armchair.

As I have consulted no document, there are probably many errors in dates, places, and possibly in facts. I affirm nothing, except that I sincerely believe what I say. I have but little confidence in absolute impartiality, but I think that any one may lay claim to perfect sincerity; we are truthful when we say what we believe.

As I go over the past, I have found that there is always some good to be said of the worst people, and something bad to be said of the best. I have attempted not to be led by my personal predilections, though I admit that this is difficult, and if I have been unsuccessful, I can at any rate affirm my good intentions.

Living as we do in a calmer period, it will perhaps be interesting to observe how in the times in which I have lived the force of circumstance has always drawn me into partisanship, whereas my instincts, my tastes, and my intellect gave me a hatred of partisanship, and I had a healthy judgment for the faults and absurdities to which it leads.

I trust that my nephews will be saved from this false situation, and I wish this in their interests and also in the interests of my country and of the world, which must need a little rest. As for myself, I shall probably rest long enough before the idleness of some rainy morning or some long autumn evening possibly induces some one to open this volume, which is intended for the library of Pontchartrain.

OSMOND DE BOIGNE.
(In *facsimile*).

CHÂTENAY, *June*, 1837.

NOTE OF 1860

Death, cruel death, has changed all my proposals. This manuscript will be placed in the library of the Château d'Osmond, in the department of Orne, the cradle of my ancestors and my own tomb.

CONTENTS

CHAPTER I

CHAPTER II

CHAPTER III

CONTENTS

CHAPTER VIII

CHAPTER IX

CHAPTER X

CHAPTER XI

CHAPTER XII

CHAPTER XIII

CHAPTER XIV

CHAPTER XV

CHAPTER XVI

CHAPTER XVII

CHAPTER XXII

CHAPTER XXIII

CHAPTER XXIV

CHAPTER XXV

CHAPTER XXVI

MEMOIRS OF THE
COMTESSE DE BOIGNE

CHAPTER I

THE generation preceding your birth was filled with
occurrences so momentous and so entirely absorbing that
family traditions would be lost in that ocean of events,
were not some old woman like myself to attempt their
reproduction from the memories of her childhood. Some
of them I shall try to gather for your benefit, my dear
nephew.

Gianoni in his *Histoire de Naples* will tell you the more
splendid of our family claims. Moréri will expound your
right to claim descent from those successful Norman adventurers who conquered Apulia, a right quite as well
established as are the majority of these old family claims.
The cathedral of Salisbury contains the dust of an Archbishop, St. Osmond, with whom our traditions are connected, and the arms of the county of Somerset contain quarterings to be found in yours, and derived from

Osmond, the lord of the county and a compatriot of William the Conqueror. These arms were given by the Duke of Normandy to his Governor Osmond, who had removed him from the vengeance of Louis d'Outremer.

The English branch has long since become extinct, but the name has remained native to the country, and is constantly to be found in English poetry and novels. The Norman branch was impoverished by equal divisions of inheritance; the heads of the family, during the three generations preceding that of my father, had only daughters, and those in such number that they made exceedingly poor marriages. Thus it was that one of my great-aunts, lady canon of Remiremont, when her sister's husband, M. de Sainte-Croix, asked her if she had never regretted her maiden state, was able to reply, " No, brother; the ladies of the house of Osmond have been in the habit of marrying too poorly." So much for our family.

Should you place any value upon these traditions of former grandeur when you make your appearance in society, you will find it easier to recover the traces of this distant past than to gain a detailed knowledge of events but a century old. I am myself without any special skill for narratives of this kind. I never placed any high value upon advantages of birth; in my girlhood they were not disputed, I have had no right to them in womanhood, and it may be that this obvious fact has prevented me more than others from considering their nature. Hence I propose to tell you none but such details as I can remember, and as I have personally known and seen : they will be somewhat disconnected, and I regard them merely as anecdotes which will interest you on account of my connection with the personages concerned ; the result will be a somewhat patchwork production, valuable only for its sincerity.

My grandfather was a sailor; while still young he was in command of a corvette during the war of 1746, and was ordered to accompany a convoy from Rochefort to Brest. A terrible storm scattered the vessels and drove him to put in at Martinique, where his vessel arrived in a somewhat shattered condition. My grandfather found the colony in high festivity, with illuminations and celebrations in progress. As soon as he disembarked, he was asked whether he brought despatches for his Highness.

" What Highness? "

" The Duke of Modena."

" I never heard of him."

A summons arrived from his Highness, and my grandfather was shown into a room which the governor had given up to a very handsome man, bedizened with orders and decorations, and of highly imposing appearance. " How is it, Chevalier d'Osmond, that you have no despatches for me? Your vessel is surely the one that was to have been sent for that purpose." My grandfather explained that he had started from Rochefort for Brest, and had been driven out of his course to Martinique.

The Duke then overwhelmed him with kindness, and required him to start at once with his despatches. The corvette was not seaworthy, but fortunately a little schooner was in the harbour. The Duke gave my grandfather the command of this vessel, authorised him to leave his corvette, and, showing him a letter in which he requested M. de Maurepas to make him a captain, explained that he was a cousin german to the King *par alliance*. He was ceding to the King his state of Modena, a transaction which was then a great secret; in exchange he was offered the sovereignty of the island of Martinique,. but had been unwilling to agree until he had

personally examined his new residence : he was highly
pleased with the island, and was now sending my grandfather with the ratification of the treaty, which was
awaited at Versailles with such impatience that the bearer
of the good tidings might expect all kinds of favours.
Consequently he added a postscript to his letter, requesting that the cross of St. Louis might be conferred upon
the Chevalier d'Osmond in addition to his nomination as
full captain.   My grandfather mentioned a vessel, the
captaincy of which was to fall vacant.

" This vessel pleases you, then ? "

" Indeed it does."

" Then I give you command of it.   I will write to
Maurepas and explain that this is an essential condition."

The Duke of Modena was surrounded by the court
and the household which he had brought with him, a
Lord High Chamberlain, chief equerry, *valet de chambre,*
&c.   The whole colony, from the governor to the smallest negro, was at his disposal; and though my grandfather had been highly incredulous at the moment of his
arrival, he was eventually convinced that a man who
distributed orders and crosses could be nothing but a
real sovereign.   He started off, crowded on all sail at
the risk of a catastrophe, and made an extremely rapid
passage, jumped into a boat as soon as he saw land,
mounted a post-horse, and rode to Versailles to M. de
Maurepas without a moment's delay.   The minister was
not at home, but he would not leave the residence without seeing him, and was therefore shown into a study
to wait.   An old *valet de chambre,* whose interest was
aroused by his anxiety, got him something to eat.   After
the meal, fatigue and youth won the day; he dropped
into an arm-chair and went sound asleep.

The minister came in, but no one remembered the

Chevalier d'Osmond. While his master was undressing, the *valet de chambre* mentioned the young naval officer who was so anxious to see the minister. M. de Maurepas had heard nothing of him. Inquiries were made, and he was found asleep in his arm-chair. He woke up with a start, and presented a large packet to the minister.

" My lord, here is the treaty signed."

" What treaty?"

" The treaty of Martinique."

" Martinique?"

" I come from the Duke of Modena."

" The Duke of Modena? Ah! I begin to understand. You go to bed and have a good sleep, and come back to-morrow."

The minister was highly amused by the dream of the young officer, which apparently continued even while he was speaking; but as he proceeded to read these extraordinary despatches, he began to wonder in his turn whether he were not dreaming also. All the authorities of the island were under the same delusion, and the " Duke " had written with full seriousness in his supposed character. The letter that he had shown to my grandfather was in the packet.

Next morning M. de Maurepas received him with extreme kindness, and informed him that his Duke of Modena was an adventurer who had probably been anxious to get him out of his way. It was, in any case, not surprising that a young man should have fallen a victim to a deception shared by the whole colony, and he was therefore acquitted of all blame in leaving his corvette. The vessel which his Highness had promised him had already been filled up, but out of consideration for the recommendation of his " cousin german," and even more in view of the fact that he was an excellent

officer, the King gave my grandfather the command of
a frigate, and M. de Maurepas expressed a hope that
his new command would soon enable him to deserve the
cross. My grandfather, ashamed of himself and entirely
disillusioned, returned to Brest, well pleased, however,
that he had so easily escaped the consequences of leaving
his corvette. As for the Duke of Modena, he was so
entangled in the honours he had appropriated that he was
unable to escape. He was arrested at Martinique, identified as a swindler, and sent to the galleys.

A few years later my grandfather visited St. Domingo
and married a certain Mlle. de la Garenne; she was a
distant relation (their respective mothers were daughters
of the family of Pardieu), and was considered enor-
mously rich. She possessed, in fact, magnificent estates,
but so overwhelmed with debt and in so miserable a
condition that my grandfather was obliged to leave the
service and settle in the colony, to try and bring affairs
into some order. Various unfortunate circumstances detained him in the colony, which he never left. In the
course of the following years he sent six boys to Europe,
one after another, though the fate of the last consign-
ment proved disastrous. The boy was sitting on a cable
coiled on deck, and was suddenly hurled into the sea by
a manœuvre which necessitated the employment of the
cable, and was drowned.

The other five had reached their destination. The first
was my father, the Marquis d'Osmond; then came the
Bishop of Nancy, the Vicomte d'Osmond, and the Abbé
d'Osmond, who was massacred at St. Domingo during
the Revolution; finally the Chevalier d'Osmond, who was
killed while serving as a naval lieutenant in the American War.

All these children were received with paternal kindness

by a brother of my grandfather, who was then the Comte
de Lyons and shortly afterwards Bishop of Cominges.
The eldest of this generation, the Comte d'Osmond, married Mlle. de Terre, who bore him only daughters, according to the custom of the family, and in further
pursuance of this custom the said daughters made very
poor marriages. They succeeded in diverting from the
name of Osmond the whole of the ancient patrimony
which had belonged to it from time immemorial and included the properties of Ménil-Froger and Médavy.

This Comte d'Osmond was Chamberlain to the Duc
d'Orléans, grandfather of King Louis Philippe; he was
on terms of the greatest intimacy in the Palais-Royal,
especially with the King's mother, who treated him like
a son. Contemporary memoirs speak of him as famous
for his extravagances, though at the same time he was a
lovable character, excellent company, and highly obliging.
I shall have an opportunity of recurring to this point. I
have just said that he was Chamberlain to the King's
grandfather, but he could not have held that position
under the son, and for these reasons; they are court
details which seem ridiculous to our generation, but their
tradition is vanishing, and for that very reason they are
at least curious.

Louis XV. had reserved to the Duc d'Orléans, then
known as the *gros duc d'Orléans,* grandson of the Regent,
the rank of first prince of the blood, though his right to
the dignity had disappeared; as, however, in the elder
branch the sons of the Dauphin could alone rank as " fils
de France," this favour had been granted to the Duc
d'Orléans. Now the honorary household of the first
prince of the blood was appointed and paid by the King,
and the nobility were always ready to take positions in
it. In the case of the other princes of the blood, the first

gentleman and the first equerry were alone appointed and paid by the King, and a member of court society was unable to accept any other positions in the households of the inferior princes.

On the death of the Duc d'Orléans,[1] his son [2] earnestly begged that the rank might be continued in his case. A reason for refusal was found in the birth of the children of the Comte d'Artois, and as the court was disinclined to grant the wishes of the Duc d'Orléans, he was unable to secure his object. He would thus have been obliged to recruit his household from some other social class than that which his father had employed, and this fact induced him, under pretext of reform, not to appoint a household, and to abandon state of every kind; this again largely contributed to increase the bad temper which brought misfortune upon him, and eventually a death which he too well deserved.

I return to our family. My grandfather had also a sister, who lived with her brother, the Bishop of Cominges, at Allan in the Pyrenees. There she married one M. de Cardaillac, a man greatly respected in the district, owner of a beautiful castle, and bearing a name as old as his mountains. The family name is now extinct, but not through the fault of our aunt, for within three years of marriage she had had seven children, two sets of twins and triplets. The Bishop of Cominges was in Paris when the triplets were born, and as soon as he heard the news a lady who was present said to him, " My Lord, write at once and tell them to keep the prettiest for you." This same Mme. de Cardaillac fell from top to bottom of a precipice, being carried over by the fall of a cart which was loaded with blocks of cut stone, in company with

[1] In 1785.
[2] Louis Philippe Joseph, known as Philippe Égalité.

which she reached the bottom. The rescuers imagined
that she must be in fragments, but she came off with a
broken leg, and had several more children afterwards.

My father and uncles were educated with the greatest
care under the supervision of the Bishop of Cominges:
they attended the best college in Paris. There they were
under the personal supervision of a tutor who was a
highly intellectual man, but whose form of instruction
was to kick them in the stomach. The result was that
when a uniform was put on my father at the age of
fourteen, he found courage to announce to the Bishop
that he had been completely miserable for the last six
years, and had learned nothing whatever. This revelation proved advantageous to his brothers, but he was
placed upon a post-horse and sent to join his regiment at
Metz. Fortunately, he avoided the attractions of the
café, and during the first years of his garrison life he
completed by his own efforts an education which the
Bishop piously considered as admirable as it was inex-
pensive.

Having reached the age of nineteen, his father sent
him a present of 2000 crowns from St. Domingo, in
addition to his allowance, that he might amuse himself
during his first six months of freedom, which would
probably be spent in Paris. The young man spent the
money in travelling to Nantes and taking his passage on
the first boat that he could find, in order to devote his
spare time to his father and to make his acquaintance, for
he had left St. Domingo at the age of three years. This
proof of affection completely won his father's heart, and
the father and son were henceforward devoted friends.
My grandmother was nothing more than a creole, for
whom her children felt no greater affection than duty
demanded.

Several years passed; my father pursued his military
career, spent his winters at Paris with his uncle and in
the society of the Palais-Royal, where he was treated as
a son of the house, in remembrance of the Comte d'Osmond. He was appointed lieutenant-colonel of the regiment [1] as soon as his age allowed him to profit by the
kindness of the Prince, while Mme. de Montesson, who
was even then married to the Duc d'Orléans,[2] overwhelmed him with kindness.   Much of his spare time
was spent with the Bishop of Cominges; he accompanied
him to the watering-place of Barèges in 1776.   There
they met Mme. and Mlle. Dillon, and with the latter the
Bishop fell almost as deeply in love as his nephew.   He
made the ladies promise to come to Allan, the castle in
the Pyrenees which was the residence of the Bishops of
Cominges, where he wished the marriage to be celebrated
at once, in order that his pretty niece might do the
honours of the house and establish herself in Paris for
the winter.   But my father would not marry without
the consent of his parents, and the ceremony was put
off until the spring.

I must now speak of my mother's family.   Mr. Robert
Dillon, of the Dillons of Roscommon, was an Irishman
and a Catholic, possessed of a handsome fortune; Roman
Catholics then being incapacitated by law, one of his
brothers undertook to increase this fortune in business.
Mr. Dillon had married a rich heiress, by whom he had
a daughter, Lady Swinburne.   Upon the death of his
wife he married Miss Dicconson, the youngest of three
sisters of famous beauty, who had been brought up at
Saint-Germain by their father, the tutor of the Prince
of Wales (the son of James II.).   At the time of the

---

[1] In 1776.   He was born December 17, 1751.
[2] The secret marriage took place in 1773.

marriage their parents had returned to England, and were established upon a fine estate in Lancashire.

Mr. Dillon and his charming wife settled in Worcestershire, where my mother and six elder children were born. The brother who was in charge of the Irish business died, and his affairs were found to be highly involved. Mr. Dillon was obliged to undertake their management. As the centre of the business was at Bordeaux, he decided to move thither, and took his family with him; he liked the country, and his wife, who had been brought up in France, preferred it to England. He took a fine house at Bordeaux, bought land in the neighbourhood, and lived as a wealthy man, when one day on rising from the table he clapped his hand to his head, called out, " My poor wife, my poor children! " and fell down dead.

His exclamation was but too well founded. He left Mrs. Dillon at the age of thirty-two years, and expecting her thirteenth child, in a foreign country without a single relative or a single intimate friend, though the excessive jealousy of her husband would hardly have tolerated such friends in any case. This isolation aroused interest and brought forth helpers. Her affairs, of which she was totally ignorant, were examined: it was discovered that Mr. Dillon had been living on the capital, which was running low, and she was left with thirteen children, and as her sole property a piece of land about three leagues from Bordeaux, which might be worth some £160 a year.

Mrs. Dillon was still extremely beautiful and an attractive and prudent character; the beauty of her children was also striking, and this group of nestlings aroused general interest. Everybody wished to help them, with the result that without even leaving her castle of Terrefort, my grandmother was able to keep up her position, to educate thirteen children, and to establish them in professions which promised brilliant careers, when these hopes were cut short by the Revolution. At the time of which I speak she had but one unmarried daughter left, a beautiful and amiable girl, but without a farthing of her own.

My father's marriage being thus fixed for the spring, the Bishop went away to Paris. No sooner had he arrived than the spell of the enchantress was broken, and there was no difficulty in pointing out to him the absurdity of the marriage, and in making him understand that my father ought to use his name and position to marry money. He had no property in Europe; the colonial property was of uncertain value, and when it was equally divided between the heirs to the estate he would never have a sufficient income to marry a penniless wife, while if the Bishop took them into his house it would be nothing more than a temporary relief; Mlle. Dillon, besides, might be an admirable young lady, but had no connections in the country. The Comte d'Osmond in particular, who was very proud of his nephew, and thought him capable of anything, loudly raised his voice against this proceeding, which he called putting a rope round his neck.

The Bishop was easily induced to subscribe to these ideas, but at that moment the answer came from St. Domingo, entirely in the affirmative. My father, who knew nothing of what was going on, arrived from his garrison to receive his uncle's final orders before proceeding to Bordeaux. He learnt that the Bishop had changed his views and wished to hear no more of the marriage; he had already closed his correspondence with Terrefort. There was a lively scene between my father and the Bishop, who told him that he and his wife could not expect to find a resting-place with him.

My father informed his own parent of the change in his uncle's views, and wrote to Mlle. Dillon describing his position. She proceeded to break off the engagement, released him and herself from all obligations, and began to trust she might die of grief, after the manner of a heroine in a novel. My father had been somewhat hurt by a decision to which he could hardly object, as his prospects had been greatly diminished by the Bishop's ill-temper, but learning by chance of Mlle. Dillon's despair, and hearing that she was supposed to be dying, he did full justice to the nobility of feeling which had directed his conduct. His father's reply was as sympathetic as he could desire: he expressed his approval, told him to go through with the marriage, as his happiness depended upon it, and promised to provide for the needs of the household at any sacrifice to himself. He stated that he had sent off sugar barrels to the value of 20,000 francs to meet the first expenses of the household.

Armed with this letter, my father started off at full speed, surmounted all obstacles, and made his way to Mlle. Dillon, who became his wife a week later.

As soon as her health was restored, he brought her to Paris, but the Bishop refused to see them. The Comte d'Osmond, who had raised the strongest objections to the marriage, was extremely anxious to make the best of it since it was an accomplished fact. He introduced my mother to the Palais-Royal as if she had been his daughter-in-law, and there she soon became intimate. Mme. de Montesson was enchanted with her, and would have liked to secure her a position about the person of the Duchesse de Chartres,[1] but the Comte d'Osmond flatly

[1] Louise de Penthièvre, wife of Philippe Joseph Égalité.

refused the proposal.   He did not wish his nephew's wife
to be the lady of a princess who was not *famille royale;*
moreover, he perceived that Mme. de Montesson wished
to monopolise her, and he did not wish her to become
the confidant of this lady.

The Archbishop of Narbonne (Dillon) had been somewhat shocked by the objections which the Osmond family
had raised to a marriage with a daughter of his name,
whom he recognised as a near relation.   He therefore
came forward to help the young couple, invited them to
his country residence of Hautefontaine, an estate in
Picardy, where he led a life of a character more delightful than episcopal.   My mother's social triumph was
immense: she was extremely beautiful, of a proud and
even haughty bearing, and could receive admiration to
perfection, though any tokens of admiration were
straightway reported to my father, for whom her passion remained undiminished until her death.   The arrival of this beautiful personage and the romantic incident of her marriage was quite an event at the court,
where events were somewhat rare.   She was presented
by Mme. de Fleury, who, like Mlle. de Montmorency,
was related to my father, and by Mme. Dillon, niece of
the Archbishop.   She was greatly admired.

A few months afterwards, by the joint influence of
the Archbishop of Narbonne and of the Comte d'Osmond, my mother was appointed lady-in-waiting to Mme.
Adélaide, daughter of Louis XV.   The Duchesse de
Chartres was by no means dissatisfied with this arrangement, but Mme. de Montesson considered herself deeply
insulted by the Comte d'Osmond, and remained on ill
terms with my relatives in consequence, especially with
the Comte, whose intimacy with the Duchesse de Chartres
increased accordingly.   It was an entirely paternal feel-

ing, which never became a subject of gossip, although the Duc de Chartres would jestingly speak of him as "my wife's husband." He died at the outbreak of the Revolution, unfortunately for that princess, whom he might have saved from many misfortunes and mistakes. I remember him as a tall, thin man of distinguished appearance, with a waistcoat generally well powdered with snuff. I was very fond of him, although he preferred my brother to myself, and always filled my eyes with snuff when he stooped down to kiss me; I was therefore careful to close them as I ran to him, a precaution which amused him greatly.

My father had a strong objection to court life; like all men who have not been brought up in that atmosphere, he found himself out of his element and entirely ill at ease. He was at that time a man of very attractive appearance, extremely companionable, an excellent soldier, devoted to his profession and adored in his regiment. My mother was fond of royalty and endowed with court instincts; her post obliged her to spend one week in every three at Versailles. This separation from my father was painful to them both, while the modest extent of their income made the maintenance of a double establishment a heavy burden.

My mother induced my father to establish himself permanently at Versailles, a reasonable proceeding in their position, but unusual except in the case of high court officials. My father often told me that no resolution ever cost him more, and that this was the greatest sacrifice he could have made my mother. There is no doubt that his tastes, his habits, his intellectual power, and his independence of character made him singularly unfitted for the profession of courtier. It was a profession, however, by no means difficult under Louis XVI., apart from cer-

tain forms of etiquette, and his honourable character gave
him so strong a hold upon the King that his majesty
speedily appreciated qualities akin to his own.

It was shortly after the establishment of my parents
at Versailles that I came into the world [1]; I had been
preceded by a still-born child, and was therefore received
with extreme joy, and pardoned for being a girl. I was
not wrapped in swaddling clothes, as was still customary,
but dressed in English style and nursed by my mother
at Versailles. I speedily became the plaything of the
princes and of the court, the more so as I was a good
baby, and as a child at that period was an object as rare
in a drawing-room as it is customary and tyrannical at
the present day.

My father grew accustomed to Versailles, and was
eventually reconciled to court life.

Saturday evening and Sunday were court days in full
dress, and were numerously attended. All the ministers
and all those known as *les charges*—that is to say, the
First Captain of the Guard, the First Gentleman of the
Ante-Room, the Chief Equerry, the Governess of the
Children of France, and the Keeper of the Queen's Household—gave a supper on Saturday and a dinner on Sunday. Arrivals from Paris were invited to be present,
and those who had households carried the guests off almost by force.

There was also a table of honour, served at the expense
of the King for the common benefit, but no courtier
would have cared to appear there. If it should have
happened by way of exception that a courtier had received no invitation to any of the houses that I have
mentioned, he would have preferred to send out for a

---

[1] February 19, 1781. She was baptised the next day. See the
baptismal certificates in the Introduction.

chicken rather than to sit down at this table, which was regarded as an inferior place, although it had originally been instituted for the lords of the court, who made no difficulty in using it until the middle of Louis XV.'s reign. At that time, however, the household officers had no establishments of their own, and dined at the common table. It was now occupied by officers in a kind of subaltern rank, who formed a class from which emergence was impossible as long as they remained at court; these were men who took orders from officials not possessing the title of " grand." Thus the ordinary groom of the chamber, as he took orders from the First Groom, was of very inferior rank, whereas the First Equerry, who took his orders from the Grand Equerry, was a man at court; but equerries who took orders from him belonged to the inferior class, and this distinction formed an impassable line of demarcation. There was no means of surmounting this obstacle, and thus it was, for example, that M. de Grailly, being an equerry, found that the door of every courtier proper was closed against him.

These secondary dwellers in the castle of Versailles formed a society apart, the queen of which was Mme. d'Angivillers, the wife of the court architect. It was a highly agreeable and well-informed society, but a full courtier could not have frequented it habitually. My father often regretted this fact. Artists, scholars, and literary men were to be met there; in fact, everybody who was not a courtier, and who came to Versailles on business or pleasure.

The Prince de Poix, who was in love with one of the Queen's women of the chamber (these were very beautiful ladies of the upper class), often visited this society under the excuse that his position as governor of Versailles necessitated constant communication with the architect d'Angivillers. His action was regarded as highly improper, but nevertheless a number of young men followed his example, and brought back excellent accounts of the beauty of the women and the cordiality of the men. By this means a breach might have been made in the barrier, but the ladies of the court showed a keen and angry opposition to any such possibility.

When my parents set up house at Versailles, the officers of the Life Guard formed members of this secondary division. They were known as the *Messieurs bleus*. It was only a short time since they had begun to wear their uniform, and I believe that the captains of the body-guard had no uniform before the Revolution. They wore plain clothes, the only distinguishing mark being a large black walking-stick with an ivory knob. The Queen, Marie Antoinette, invited these officers to her balls, and thus changed their social status. However, they never dined with the royal family. For instance, I well remember that at Bellevue, where the princesses were staying, an officer of the body-guard did not dine at their table. The rule was so strict that M. de Béon, the husband of one of Mme. Adélaide's ladies in waiting, dined at the second table when he was on duty, and the next day would sit down with his wife at the table of the princesses. This, however, was an innovation and a relaxation of etiquette, which had been a great concession on the part of the good princesses. More extraordinary still, the bishops were in the same predicament, and never dined with the King or with the princes of the royal family. I never learnt the reason for their exclusion.

Among other points of etiquette, there was one to which my father never became reconciled, and which I have often heard him describe: this was the manner in which invitations were distributed to what was known

as the *souper dans les cabinets.* These supper parties
were composed of the royal family and of some thirty
guests. They were given in the King's private apartments, in rooms so small that the billiard-table was covered with planks to form a sideboard, and that the King
was obliged to hurry over his game that these preparations might be made.

The ladies received their invitations in the morning or
the evening before, and wore an old-fashioned dress,
entirely out of use for any other ceremony, a dress with
tucks, and a head-dress with drooping pinners. They
made their way to the small theatre-room, where places
were reserved for them, and after the performance followed the King and the royal family to the *cabinets.*

The fate of the gentlemen was less agreeable. There
were two rows of seats opposite those reserved for the
lady guests. Courtiers who wished to be invited took
their seats there; during the performance the King, who
was alone in his box, surveyed these seats through a
large pair of opera-glasses, and could be seen writing a
certain number of names in pencil. The occupants of
these seats (and to take a seat was known as *se présenter
pour les cabinets*) then waited in an ante-room to the
cabinets.

Shortly afterwards an usher, candlestick in hand, and
holding the slip of paper written by the King, half opened
the door and pronounced a name; the fortunate man then
bowed to the remainder, and entered the holy of holies.
The door reopened, another name was called, and so on
until the list was finished. At the last name the usher
closed the door with a customary bang.

This sound informed the remainder that their hopes
were vain, and they went off somewhat downcast, though
they had been well aware that there were more candi-

dates than invitations. My mother told me that she had spent years in inducing my father to take one of these seats; he eventually went from time to time, and was frequently invited; but the procedure was always extremely distasteful to him. He saw a certain man come from Paris ten years running, merely to hear the door slammed upon his aspirations. Excessive perseverance possibly exasperated the King, or he may have grown accustomed to see faces without inviting them, as princes may easily acquire the habit of putting the same questions to the same people.

The Queen's balls were well ordered, and all who had been presented at court were informed of their occurrence; anyone might come who wished, and many wished to come because they were delightful. The balls were given on the terrace at Versailles, in wooden structures which were left standing throughout the carnival; but these entertainments, notwithstanding the Queen's charm of manner, tended to accentuate the unpopularity of the court.

The increase of wealth among the middle classes had induced all of inferior rank to adopt the manners and customs of high society, and, notwithstanding the absurd regulation which demanded proof of nobility in the case of any would-be officer, anyone who had wealth and education could enter the service. Rank and wealth were thus hand-in-glove, both in garrison and in all Paris society, but the balls of Versailles restored the line of demarcation in the most uncompromising manner. M. de Dussón, a young man of charming appearance, immense wealth, an excellent officer, and frequenting the best society, was so imprudent as to go to one of these balls; he was turned out with such harshness that he committed suicide on arriving in Paris, in despair at the ridicule to which he was exposed in an age when ridicule was the worst of calamities. Such action seemed a matter of course to members of the court, but was hateful to the wealthy middle classes.

It was not only wealth that furnished victims for the Queen's balls. M. de Chabannes, of high birth, handsome, young, rich, and almost the man of the hour, in making his first appearance was so clumsy as to fall down while dancing, and was so tactless as to cry " Jésus Maria! " as he fell. It was a fall from which he never rose again; the designation clung to him permanently, to his complete despair. He volunteered for the American wars, and distinguished himself in action, but he came back " Jésus Maria," as he went out. Thus the Duc de Coigny observed to his daughters on the day they were presented at court: " Remember that in this country vice is immaterial, but ridicule is fatal."

M. de Lafayette did not, however, succumb to the epithet of *Gilles le grand,*[1] which M. de Choiseul had given him upon his return from America. On the contrary, he aroused so much enthusiasm that society undertook to secure his success with Mme. de Simiane, to whom he had been paying attentions before his departure. She was considered the prettiest woman in France, and had had no affairs as yet. Everyone conspired to throw her into the arms of M. de Lafayette, and a few days after his return he was by her side in a box at Versailles, while an air was being sung from some opera, " Love beneath the laurels finds ladies kind." The moral was pointed in a manner which clearly showed the sympathy and approval of this privileged audience.

I have heard my mother say that her sister, the wife

[1] The fool's part on the eighteenth century stage.

of the Président de Lavie, happened to come to Paris, and that she procured her a seat that she might look on at the Queen's ball; the sisters were talking, when the Queen approached and asked her who that beautiful woman was.

" It is my sister, Madame."

" Has she seen the apartments? "

" No, Madame; she is here as a spectator; she has not been presented."

" Then you must show them to her; I will take the King away." And with her gracious kindness she actually took the King's arm and led him into another room, while my aunt examined the ballroom. The Queen had intended to be extremely obliging, but Président de Lavie regarded the matter from another point of view. He was of a very ancient family, extremely touchy upon the question of his rank, and a personage of high importance at Bordeaux, where a president in the *parlement* was a public character; he was indignant that the King and Queen should feel obliged to leave a room in order that his wife might enter it. He went back to Bordeaux a yet more vigorous *frondeur* than he had left it, was appointed a deputy, and displayed strong revolutionary leanings; to humiliate the court nobility soothed his feelings. Wounded vanity has made more enemies than one may suppose.

The etiquette in custom for extraordinary festivities and for journeys would seem intolerable to us to-day. It was necessary to put down one's name; that is to say, ladies and gentlemen betook themselves to the First Groom of the Chamber. They wrote their names with their own hands, and guests were chosen from this list; those who were not to be invited were eliminated in a manner which was tantamount to the slight of a refusal.

The Dauphine [1] would have liked to revive this etiquette during the restoration, in the case of the somewhat infrequent court entertainments. But it was impossible to restore the custom when nobody considered it a duty to go and put down his name with the possibility of receiving a refusal. It was considered much less disagreeable not to be invited than to be rejected.

As for journeys, customs varied with the destination. At Rambouillet, where the King never went for more than a few days, and only with a bachelor party, guests were received as at the house of some rich friend, and provision made for them in every respect. At Trianon, which was also visited by the Queen only at long intervals and for a few days, with but few attendants, things were the same. At Marly, board and lodging were provided. The guests in residence were distributed among different tables, kept by the princes and princesses in their respective houses at the expense of the King. Afterwards all returned to the *grand salon* where the whole court was to be found.

At Fontainebleau the guests were given nothing more than a bare *apartement*. They were obliged to find their own furniture, linen, &c., and to provide their own food. As it happened, all the ministers and chief officials had their own houses, and the princes kept a table for their suites, so that it was easy to secure an invitation to dinner or supper. But no effort was made to provide anything beyond lodging. If the castle was full, and a large portion of it was in such bad repair as to be uninhabitable, the guests (or rather those who were admitted, for names had to be put down) were distributed throughout the

[1] Marie Thérèse, Duchess of Angoulême, daughter of Louis XVI., did not become the Dauphine until the death of Louis XVII.

town; their names were written in chalk upon the doors, as though an army were halting upon the march.

I do not know if any payment was made for these lodgings, but the advantage of these visits to Fontainebleau was so great to the inhabitants that no complaints of the imposition were ever heard. It is well known that the French court never appeared in greater magnificence than at Fontainebleau. In its little theatre were given the first and most carefully rehearsed performances, and it was practically admitted that ministerial intrigues were unravelled at Fontainebleau for the apparent object of continuing the historical existence of this fine residence. The last journey was made in 1787. Notwithstanding the apparent lack of hospitality, these journeys were a heavy expense to the crown, and the King abandoned them, though he had a great liking for Fontainebleau, being ever ready to sacrifice his own desires; he displayed greater cordiality there than anywhere else, and at greater expense.

This excellent prince had much trouble in overcoming a certain timidity, which was conjoined with a manner apparently unpolished, the result of his early training, and presented him in an unfavourable light to those who could only see the rude exterior. With the best intention of being courteous, he would walk towards a man until he had pushed him back to the wall; and if no remark occurred to him, as often happened, he would burst into a loud laugh, turn on his heels, and walk off. The victim of this public performance was always offended, and if he were not accustomed to the manners of the court would take his leave in fierce anger, persuaded that the King had wished in some way to insult him. In private life the King would complain bitterly of the way in which he had been brought up. He would say that the only man for whom he felt any real hatred was the Duc de La Vauguyon, and he quoted in support of this feeling instances of low servility towards his brothers and himself which justified his opinion. The prince had less aversion to the memory of the Duc de La Vauguyon.[1]

The Comte d'Artois was also an object of the King's repugnance. His happiness of character, his accomplishments, and perhaps even his easy morals had made him the Benjamin of the whole family; he committed folly after folly, while the King scolded him, pardoned him, and paid his debts. But what he unfortunately could not overcome was the injury which he did to his own reputation and to that of the Queen.

The King never played any game except tric-trac and *petits écus*. He said to a man one day who was playing for high stakes, " I can understand your playing for high stakes if that amuses you; you are playing with money which belongs to you, but I should be playing with other people's money." But even while he was making speeches of this kind, the Comte d'Artois and the Queen played so highly that they were obliged to admit to their society. every damaged reputation in Europe, to be able to make up a game. This disastrous habit—for it was by no means a passion in either case—was the origin of those calumnies which brought a flood of vexations upon our unfortunate Queen even before her historical misfortunes had begun.

Who would have dared to accuse the Queen of France of selling herself for a necklace, if she had not been seen before a table piled with money, attempting to win it from her subjects? No doubt she set but little value upon the stakes, but people who gamble play to win, and

[1] Lieutenant-general and tutor of the three sons of the Dauphin, fl. 1706 to 1772.

it is impossible to conceal some show of eagerness. Princes, moreover, accustomed to meet with submission everywhere, are almost always bad gamblers, an additional reason for them to avoid high stakes. If, then, the Queen did not care about play, why did she gamble? The reason was that she was absorbed by another passion, that of fashion. She dressed to be fashionable, ran into debt to be fashionable, gambled to be fashionable, was a free-thinker to be fashionable, and was a flirt for the same reason. To be a pretty woman entirely in the fashion seemed to her the summit of ambition, and this caprice, unworthy of a great queen, was the sole origin of the improprieties which have been cruelly exaggerated. The Queen wished to be surrounded by all the most agreeable young men of the court, and accepted the compliments addressed to the woman far more readily than those offered to the sovereign. The result was that empty-headed youths were treated with greater favour and distinction than men of discretion and value to their country. Envy and jealousy were ever ready to calumniate this foolishness. The most culpable feature no doubt was the fact that the Queen allowed this band of careless young men to speak lightly of the King and to make fun of his boorish manners, in which amusement she very wrongly joined.

An excessive desire to please involved her in faults of another kind, which created enemies. She had great influence, wished the fact to be known, and was glad to use it, but she was extremely unbusinesslike, and her influence was only employed as a means to social success. She wished to have posts at her disposal, and was unfortunately in the habit of promising the same nomination to several different people. There was hardly a regiment the colonel of which had not been appointed at the Queen's request, but as she had promised the vacancy to ten different families, she merely made nine discontented men and sometimes one ungrateful man. The stories related of her love affairs by various libels are so many calumnies. My parents, who had every opportunity of seeing and knowing the nature of her private life, always declared these rumours to be without foundation.

The Queen was never strongly attracted but once, and displayed perhaps only one weakness. The Comte de Fersen, a Swede, an extremely handsome and distinguished man, appeared at the French court. The Queen began to flirt with him, as she did with all foreigners, for foreigners were then the fashion: he fell sincerely and passionately in love, and she was certainly touched by his devotion, but none the less obliged him to take his departure. He went to America and stayed there for two years, during which he was so ill that he returned to Versailles, ten years older in appearance and having almost entirely lost his good looks. It was supposed that this change touched the Queen's heart; whatever was the reason, there was practically no doubt among her intimate friends that she yielded to her passion for M. de Fersen.

He justified the sacrifice by boundless devotion and an affection as sincere as it was respectful and discreet; he lived only for her, and his life was arranged with the express purpose of compromising her as little as possible. Thus, though the connection was guessed, it never became a subject of scandal. Had the friends of the Queen been as discreet and as disinterested as M. de Fersen, the life of this unfortunate princess would have been less calumniated.

Mme. de Polignac was a more dangerous influence.

She was not a bad character, but was indolent and slow-witted. She intrigued by means of her weakness. She was under the influence of her sister-in-law, the Comtesse Diane, an ambitious woman, as avaricious as she was immoral, who was anxious to monopolise all favours for herself and her family; she, again, was dominated by her lover, the Comte de Vaudreuil, an utterly immoral character, who used the Queen as a key to unlock the public treasury for himself and his boon companions.

Whenever the fulfilment of his demands was delayed he vented his wrath upon Mme. de Polignac. The Queen would find her favourite in tears, and forthwith set herself to discover the means of drying them. As regards her own fortune, Mme. de Polignac asked nothing, and confined herself to a careless acceptance of the favours prepared by the intrigues of the Comtesse Diane, and the poor Queen praised her disinterested character. She believed in her unselfishness, and her affection was sincere; her confidence had been unlimited for some years.

The appointment of M. de Calonne somewhat restricted this intimacy: he was one of Mme. de Polignac's close friends, and the Queen would not have a member of the King's council in her sanhedrin. She had expressed herself loudly on this subject, but the clique, anxious to have a high financial official at their disposal, induced the Comte d'Artois to accede to their wishes. It was through his efforts that M. de Calonne was nominated in spite of the Queen's objection. She continued her displeasure; her intimacy with Mme. de Polignac cooled, and M. de Calonne made vain efforts to secure her good graces. One day, however, when she preferred a request, he replied, " If what the Queen desires is possible, it is already done; if it is impossible, it will happen."

Notwithstanding the official nature of this language, the
Queen never pardoned him.

If this desire to please was disastrous, it had also certain advantages: it gave the Queen a certain charm;
whenever she could forget her part as a fashionable
woman, which completely absorbed her, she was full of
grace and dignity. She might easily have become an
accomplished princess if any one had had the courage to
speak to her boldly. But those about her realised the
saying of the English poet:

> All who approach them, their own ends pursue.

In her domestic circle the Queen was loving and beloved, and was occupied solely with the task of composing
the little differences which troubled her family life. Unfortunately, she lent too ready an ear to the foolishness
of the Comte d'Artois, and prejudiced the King in his
favour, for the King was so entirely captivated by her
charms that he would have adored her, had fashion suffered her to permit his adoration.

Monsieur,[1] an ambitious and cunning courtier, did not
like the Queen. He foresaw that when she became more
serious she would secure that real importance to which
he himself aspired, and he was afraid of compromising
himself if he manifested his designs too clearly. He stood
somewhat aloof from current events, laying the foundation of his reputation as a man capable of useful work.

The Comte d'Artois[2] then made his entry upon that
fatal destiny which was to ruin his family and his country. His tastes and his caprices were merely those of
the young men of his time, but he displayed them upon
a stage sufficiently high to make them visible to the mob,

[1] Louis Stanislas Xavier, Comte de Provence, born at Versailles
in 1755.
[2] Born at Versailles, 1757.

while merit, that well-worn resource of the man of the world, did not sufficiently obscure his deficiencies.

At the siege of Gibraltar,[1] at which caprice had led him to be present, his bearing was so miserable that the general in command had resolved to warn the English batteries, and firing ceased when the prince visited the works. It is said that this was done without his knowledge, but these are facts which can always be learnt, if it be not thought preferable to ignore them. I know that M. de Maillebois was reproached in consequence, and replied, " Better that, than the faces he made the first day." The ridiculous ostentation of his duel with the Duc de Bourbon was a further proof of the nature of a character only too well confirmed by the rest of his conduct.

Madame [2] the wife of Monsieur was a woman of some intellect and of a certain grace of manner, though extraordinarily ugly. She had lived very happily with her husband during the first years of their marriage, but after his attachment to Mme. de Balbi he scarcely ever saw her, and she consoled herself in the intimacy of her ladies in waiting and, it is said, by drinking to such an extent that the consequences were obvious in public.

Her sister, the Comtesse d'Artois, was even uglier, a stupid, surly, clumsy woman. She consoled herself for her husband's infidelity with members of the life-guards. The arrival of a daughter under somewhat suspicious circumstances, who died soon after birth, decided the Comte to take steps which precluded any further increase of his family, which then consisted of two princes.

[1] In 1782, during the American War.

[2] Marie Joséphine Louise de Savoie, daughter of King Victor Amédée, and sister of the last three kings of the elder line, Charles Emmanuel IV., Victor Emmanuel I., and Charles Félix. Another sister, Marie Thérèse, was the Comtesse d'Artois.

None the less, her condition soon obliged the Comtesse to take the Queen into her confidence and request her intercession with the King and the prince. The Queen was much disturbed by the imposition of this unpleasant duty, sent for the Comte d'Artois, and in a private interview informed him of the situation with much circumlocution. Her brother-in-law stood before her, hat in hand. When he realised the position he dropped his hat and held his sides with laughter, crying:

"Ah, poor man, poor man; I am sorry for him; he is well punished."

"Indeed," said the Queen, "as you look at it in that light, I am sorry that I ever felt any sympathy with you. Go and find the King, and tell him that you pardon the Comtesse."

"Why, with all my heart. Poor man, poor man!"

The King was more severe, and the supposed culprit was banished to colonial service. But, as Mme. Adélaide said to my sister when telling the story, "But, my dear, every company of them should be sent to the colonies." The Comtesse went to take the waters, I believe; in any case, nothing was heard of the child.

Mme. Elisabeth [1] played no part at court before the Revolution, but after that time she deserved the title of saint and martyr. Her household had been composed of incongruous elements. The Comtesse Diane de Polignac, who was scandal incarnate, was her lady of honour, as also was Mme. de Canillac, concerning whom had originated the duel between the Comte d'Artois and the Duc de Bourbon. Her intimacy with the Comte d'Artois was well known, but was dignified by her great unselfishness. She loved him for himself, and having no means, lived in great humility, not to say poverty, without condescend-

[1] Born in 1764.

ing to accept the smallest present from him. There was some distinction in such conduct, but she was none the less unsuitable as a companion to a young princess, though by no means immoral.

The taste of the court for foreigners was turned to advantage in an extraordinary manner by two illustrious characters exiled from their country by the Mussulman persecution, the Prince of Chios and Justiniani his son, who were directly descended from the Eastern emperors, and begged hospitality from Louis XVI. at the outset of his reign. This was granted to them in full measure as became a king of France. Until the claims that he was making at the Seraglio for the restitution of his property should have been admitted, the Prince of Chios was begged to accept a handsome pension, while Prince Justiniani entered the French service and took the command of a crack regiment.

These Greek princes lived for some years on the royal bounty, and were well received by the best company at Paris and Versailles. Their accent and a somewhat pronounced foreign bearing assured their success. One day, when they had been dining for the hundredth time with the Comte de Maurepas, the Comte saw the Prince of Chios, who was sitting by him, growing pale and agitated.

" You are not feeling well, Prince? "

" It is nothing; it will pass away."

But his indisposition increased until he was obliged to leave the table, and to call his son to accompany him. M. de Maurepas had spent the ten years of his exile upon his estate of Châteauneuf in Berry. When he left his estate, one of his *valets de chambre* was left in charge: as he happened to be at Versailles, he was now waiting at table, and was in his master's room the next day when he received orders to go and inquire after the health of the Prince of Chios. M. de Maurepas saw him stifle a burst of laughter, glancing at his companions.

" What are you laughing at, Dubois? "

" You know, sir; it is the Prince of Chios."

" And why should he amuse you? "

" You are making fun of me, sir; you know him quite well."

" Of course I do; I see him every day."

" Have you really failed to recognise him, sir? But it cannot be."

" Come, now, you weary me with your mysteries. Tell me plainly what you mean."

" Well, my lord, the Prince of Chios is fat Guillot."

" And whom do you call fat Guillot? "

" Well, my lord, I cannot understand how you have forgotten fat Guillot. He used to come up to the castle pretty often to work. He lived in a little white house near the bridge; and then his son—your lordship cannot possibly have forgotten little Pierre, who was so polite and quick that my lady would always have him hold the bridle of her donkey. I see now that your lordship remembers him; I recognized him at once, and fat Guillot recognised me."

M. de Maurepas bound his servant to silence; but once on the track, it was immediately discovered that the heirs to the empire of the East were simply two peasants from Berry, who had been mystifying, to their own advantage, the King of France, his government and his court, for the last few years. How had they conceived this plan, whence did they come, and whither did they go? To these questions I have no answer, and know only this episode in the life of these two clever adventurers.

CHAPTER II

FROM Sunday to Saturday life at Versailles was terribly quiet and monotonous to people who were forced to
leave their usual society, to enter less comfortable quarters
and perform their court service. It was, however, a life,
not without interest for those who had a definite position,
and was a kind of country house existence with important
subjects of gossip. The majority cared nothing for the
fate of the country in their interest in the intrigue which
was to end in the dismissal of M. de Malesherbes or in the
appointment of M. de Calonne. But the more intelligent
characters, such as my father, found interests wider than
a musical quarrel or a breach between J. J. Rousseau and
the wife of the Marshal of Luxembourg, which were then
great social events.

No one thought of national politics, or if they did, their
attention was attracted involuntarily and by interests connected with finance or with party. The cabinets of foreign
governments were as unknown to us as that of China probably is to-day. My father was thought somewhat pedantic for following the history of Europe and reading the

34

only newspaper which gave any foreign news. Mme.
Adélaide asked him one day :

" M. d'Osmond, is it true that you take in the *Gazette
de Leyde?* "

" Yes, Madame."

" And you read it ? "

" Yes, Madame."

" It is incredible! "

Notwithstanding this incredible eccentricity, Mme. Adélaide afterwards conceived a great liking for my father,
and in the years immediately preceding the Revolution he
was constantly at her house, though he had no official
status there. The Comte Louis de Narbonne, her *ché-
valier d'honneur*, an intimate friend of my father, was
delighted that he should be willing without title or remuneration to perform those functions which he himself
was glad to be able to neglect.

My mother was a kind of favourite. I have mentioned
that she nursed me herself, and instead of dispensing with
her services during this period, Mme. Adélaide authorised
her to bring me to Bellevue; a special apartment was to
be reserved for this nursery business. My father was with
his regiment, and Mme. Adélaide wished my mother to
take up her quarters at Bellevue for the whole summer.
Either from apprehensions of monotony or with a courtier's instinct, my mother refused, and the proposal was
not executed until long afterwards.

During the first years of my parents' stay at Versailles
they divided their summer between the houses of the Duc
d'Orléans, Sainte Assisse and le Raincy; Hautefontaine,
belonging to the Archbishop of Narbonne; Frascati, to the
Bishop of Metz; and Esclimont, to the Marshal de Laval.

I am wrong in saying that Hautefontaine belonged to
the Archbishop of Narbonne; it was the property of his

niece, Mme. de Rothe, daughter of his sister, Lady For-
ester. Her husband had been a General Rothe; she had
been a beauty in her time, retained her domineering manners and did the honours of her uncle's house, with whom
she lived for years in an intimacy the closeness of which
they took no pains to conceal.

The Archbishop had an income of some $40,000 from
ecclesiastical property: he went to Narbonne for a fortnight every two years, and acted as president of the estates at Montpellier for six weeks. Throughout this time
he lived in full episcopal state, and displayed considerable
administrative capacity as president of the estates. When
the last meeting was over, he put his papers in his port-
folios and banished all thoughts of administrative or di-
ocesan business until the date of the next assembly.

Hautefontaine was his usual residence. Mme. de Rothe
was the owner, but the Archbishop had set up his household there. He had married his nephew, Arthur Dillon,
son of Lady Dillon, to Mlle. de Rothe, an only daughter
and his great-niece. She was a very pretty woman and
very fashionable, one of the Queen's ladies in waiting,
and continued a somewhat pronounced intimacy with the
Prince de Guéméné, who spent the whole of his life at
Hautefontaine. He had organised a pack of hounds in a
neighbouring village in conjunction with the Prince de
Lauzun and the Archbishop, whose identity was concealed
behind that of his nephew Arthur.

Hautefontaine was always full of visitors, and hunting
went on three times a week. Mme. Dillon was a good
musician. The Prince de Guéméné brought down the
famous virtuosi of the day; excellent concerts were given,
plays were acted, horse-races were held, and every kind
of distraction was pursued.

The social tone was so free that my mother has told me

that she was often embarrassed to the point of tears. During the first years of her marriage the sarcasms and jests to which she was exposed often made her very unhappy, but the patronage of the Archbishop was too valuable to be rejected by the young couple. An old *grand vicaire,* who happened to be in the midst of this cheerful company, seeing her very sad one day, remarked: " Marquise, do not worry; one of your faults is your beauty, but that will be pardoned. But if you wish to live peaceably, take more pains to conceal your love for your husband; it is the one kind of love which is not tolerated here."

The fact is certain that every one else allowed himself full freedom, but this under certain regulated formalities which deceived no one, but which no one could omit without *se perdre,* as the phrase then ran. There were certain established rules which could only be neglected by a lady of unusually high position, or by one who had secured a special position in virtue of effrontery or unusual talent. Mme. Dillon belonged to neither of these categories, but her transgressions were conducted with such taste that my mother often said, " On arriving at Hautefontaine it seemed certain that she was the mistress of the Prince de Guéméné, and after a stay of about six months we began to suspect it."

On the whole, if the language of this society was free, its actions were extremely restrained. A man who placed his hand on the arm of a chair occupied by a lady would have been considered excessively rude. Only the greatest intimacy could justify a walk arm in arm, and that was unusual, even in the country. Gentlemen never offered their arms or their hands to take a lady in to dinner, and a man would never have sat down on a sofa together with a lady; but language, on the other hand, was free to the point of licentiousness.

At Hautefontaine, in respect for the episcopal master of the house, the company attended mass on Sunday. No one brought a prayer-book, but all were provided with volumes of light and even scandalous literature, which were left in the castle pews for the inspection of chapel cleaners, who might thus edify themselves at their leisure.

I have dealt with life at Hautefontaine in some detail, because I have an accurate knowledge of the facts. I do not assert that every archbishop of France led a similar life, but merely that such a life was possible for a bishop without any damage to his reputation. The most noble, brilliant, and fashionable members of the court, with the highest and most distinguished of the clergy, were constantly to be found at Hautefontaine, and thought themselves honoured by an invitation. The Bishop of Montpellier, whose family name I do not know, was the only ecclesiastic whose lofty virtue at all impressed the Archbishop, and when this prelate was following the hunt in his carriage, the Archbishop would say to his fellow-huntsmen, " By the way, gentlemen, no swearing to-day." As soon as the excitement of the chase came over him, he was the first to drive in his spurs and to forget his admonition.

In any case, our prelates were by no means the only ecclesiastics in Europe who united a taste for country sport and good cheer. A short time ago the Comte Théodore Lameth related to me the following story :

To enter into possession of ecclesiastical benefices, the Knights of Malta were obliged to take the tonsure. The French bishops were disinclined to perform this ceremony, as the claims of the knights absorbed a considerable proportion of ecclesiastical property. Théodore de Lameth, being a Knight of Malta and a cavalry captain at the age of twenty, had good prospects and even better desires of

obtaining a living. He attempted to arrange to receive
the tonsure, and met with obstacles. Being in garrison
at Strasburg, he opened negotiations in Germany and induced the sovereign Bishop of Paderborn for a moderate
remuneration to perform this service, which the ecclesiastics of his own country declined. On the evening before the day of the ceremony he arrived at the house of
the Bishop of Paderborn. The cavalry captain found
champagne and cheerful stories in progress, and a supper
of the most animated description. The next day he appeared in church in his uniform, in a flowing cloak which
allowed his epaulets and breast-straps to be seen, and was
turned back over his sword hilt, while he carried his sur-
plice over his arm; his hair, which was then worn in a
pigtail, was hanging down upon his shoulders.

He found the Bishop before the altar, supported by a
numerous body of clergy. The ceremony was conducted
with great solemnity, pomp, and magnificence. The
Bishop seized a large pair of scissors in one hand and
grasped the locks of the neophyte with the other. The
young man trembled, and feared that he would be so
shorn as to be unable to show his face to his garrison.
But as the anthem continued, the Bishop allowed the hair
to pass through his fingers until he held only one or two
locks, the ends of which he clipped.

At the conclusion of the ceremony the neophyte knelt
down to receive the episcopal benediction, and was much
astonished to hear these words pronounced in a low voice
at the most solemn moment : " Be quick and get that uniform off. Come round to my house at once ; we will have
a cup of chocolate and go out hunting."

A fine conclusion, and one worthy of the beginning.

The story of this strange ceremony was amusingly re-
counted by a man eighty-two years of age, and seemed to

me to be a humorous reflection of the customs in vogue during his youth.

The Princesse de Guéméné, governess of the Children of France, was unable to pass a night away from Versailles without a written permission in the King's own hand. This she never asked except in order to go to Hautefontaine; it was in consequence of this general politeness that the Queen was induced to show particular attention to her favourite lady.

This brilliant if somewhat unecclesiastical life was brought to an end by the death of Mme. Dillon and by the financial ruin of the Archbishop. Notwithstanding his enormous income, he was overwhelmed with debt, and Hautefontaine was abandoned some time before the Revolution. My mother did not go there so frequently after my birth. Children were not wanted, and the middle class sentiment of family life was regarded as out of place.

Frascati, the residence of the Bishop of Metz, was situated at the gates of this great town. The Bishop was a brother of the Marshal de Laval. He had a passionate affection, entirely honourable, for his niece, the Marquise de Laval, and a Montmorency like himself. He wearied her to desperation by his continual shower of attentions and presents, and she would only grant his desire to see her reigning in the magnificent residence of Frascati at such times as my mother was able to accompany her. To this plan my mother was the more inclined, as for some years my father's garrison was stationed in Lorraine.

The Bishop lived in the greatest state, and kept open house for the vast garrison at Metz and for all the higher officials who passed through the town on the way to their regiments. This half clerical, half military household was

governed with far greater regularity and severity than
that of Hautefontaine. However, not to be entirely out
of keeping with the age, it was well known that the abbess
of the chapter of Metz and the Bishop had entertained a
warm affection for each other for years past, but this long-
standing connection was entirely proper.

The intimacy of my mother with the Marquise de Laval
often brought her to Esclimont, to the house of her father-
in-law, the Marshal. There all was peace, and family life
proceeded undisturbed. The old Marshal spent his time
in the detestable musical performances to which he was
devoted, and his wife, a woman entirely good and indulgent, though a scrupulous pietist, occupied her time in
tapestry work.

The Marquise de Laval,[1] when she left the school of
Sainte Marie, was transported to this family life, whence
she derived principles of conduct which may have been
modified, but were not fundamentally changed, by the distractions of society. She was united to my mother by a
boundless devotion, and consequently to my father, whose
relative she was, and she was delighted to find in them
the principles that she appreciated, accompanied with less
monotonous severity of life than at Esclimont, where an
intimacy of this kind was highly approved.

At Versailles the house of the Princesse de Guéméné
was that chiefly frequented by my parents. The Princesse overwhelmed them with kindness, and with her my
father had some family connection. She was a very extraordinary person, and though endowed with considerable intellectual power, spent her time in pursuing the follies of spiritualism. She was always surrounded with a
multitude of dogs, to which she paid a kind of worship,

---

[1] Marie Louise Mauricette Elizabeth de Montmorency Luxemburg,
Marquise de Laval, was the godmother of Adèle d'Osmond.

asserting that by their means she was in communication with intermediary spirits. In the midst of a conversation, where her intellect and good sense were prominent, she would stop short and fall into a trance. She sometimes related to her intimate friends what she had then learnt, and was offended at any display of incredulity.

One day my mother found her in her bath with tears streaming down her face.

" You are ill, Princesse."

" No, my dear, I am sad and terribly tired; I have been fighting all night for this poor child " (pointing to the Dauphin), " but I have been defeated, and they have won the day. There will be nothing left for him, alas! and what will be the fate of the others? "

My mother, accustomed to the wanderings of the Princesse, paid no great attention to these words; afterwards she remembered them and repeated them to me.

The Queen often came to visit Mme. de Guémené, but not so often as she afterwards went to Mme. de Polignac. Mme. de Guémené was too great a lady to descend to the post of favourite.

Her duties obliged her to sleep in the room of the Dauphin. She had had a room made where her bed could be placed against a glass aperture looking into the room of the little prince. After the process known as the *remuer*, that is to say, the swaddling of the child before the doctors each morning, thick curtains were drawn across this glass and Mme. de Guémené began her sleep, having previously gone to bed very late, and spent her time in reading and writing. She had an enormous quantity of jewellery, which she never wore, but which she was glad to lend for show. There was no great ceremony at which the jewellery of Mme. de Guémené was not to be seen. In the summer she often dined in her little house in the

Avenue de Paris. The children were brought thither. One day when they were going back under the escort of the life-guards, some one ventured to express astonishment at all this ceremony for a child in long clothes. Mme. de Guémené replied very dryly, " Nothing is more obvious when I am the governess."

Madame, the daughter of the King, who was known by the title of La Petite Madame, was even then of so sad a countenance that people of her acquaintance used to call her Mousseline la Sérieuse.

The Princesse de Guémené bore with admirable courage the reverses of fortune brought about by the great bankruptcy of the Prince de Guémené. My parents went to see her in an old castle which had been lent her by her father, the Prince de Soubise. There she lived in circumstances which bordered upon penury, and there they found her a greater lady, if possible, than she had been amid the splendours of Versailles. She was much touched by this visit, as she found herself deserted by all.

The Queen, who was anxious to give her post to Mme. de Polignac, had shown greater severity than she would have done in other circumstances. The resignation of Mme. de Guémené had been accepted with joy, and her retirement had been hastened in a manner almost harsh. My mother, who loved her as a daughter, was greatly vexed in consequence, and never visited Mme. de Polignac. It must be said at once to the honour of the Queen that, far from bearing her any grudge on that account, she treated her with greater kindness.

The little court of the princesses was a separate organisation, known as the old court. Their habits were regular in the extreme. They spent the whole summer at Bellevue, where their nephews and nieces were constantly coming to ask them to dinner without ceremony or attendants.

They were announced by a courier, who preceded them by some minutes. When it was a courier of the Prince, afterwards Louis XVIII., verbal information was given, and a more elaborate and longer dinner was provided. In other cases nothing was said, not even in the case of the King, who had a large appetite, but was not nearly so fastidious as his brother.

At Bellevue the royal family dined with everyone who happened to be there, the people in attendance on the princesses, their families and some guests, generally forming a company of twenty or thirty persons.

Madame Adélaide was undoubtedly the cleverest of the daughters of Louis XV.; she was pleasant and easy in family life, though extremely haughty. If a stranger happened to address her as " Royal Highness " she would grow angry, scold the person who introduced the ambassadors, even the Minister of Foreign Affairs, and discuss the incredible carelessness of this gentleman for a long time to come. She wished to be known as Madame, and would not permit the Sons of France to assume the title of Royal Highness.

She hated wine, which she never drank, and those who sat near her at table turned away from her to drink it. Her nephews were always careful in this respect. If anyone neglected her wish she would say nothing, but the offender would not have found himself in her neighbourhood again at table, and the lady of honour would have requested him to move away from the Princess. If due consideration were given to some of her weak points, especially by not spitting on the floor, which roused her almost to the point of brutality, nothing could have been pleasanter than her company.

Madame Adélaide was the eldest of five princesses. She had not cared to marry, preferring her position as a

Daughter of France. She had been head of the court until the death of King Louis XV. She was the friend and adviser of the Dauphin, her brother, whose memory was afterwards very dear to her, and of which she often spoke as the most cherished recollection of her heart. One of her sisters, Madame Infante, reigned in somewhat gloomy state at Parma; another, Madame Louise, was a Carmelite sister.

Of these five princesses, the latter seemed the most worldly, beyond comparison. She was passionately fond of every pleasure, was something of a glutton, very fond of dress, incapable of living without every new invention of luxury, had a lively imagination and great leaning to coquetry. So that when the King came into the room of Madame Adélaide and told her that Madame Louise had gone away in the night, her first cry was, " With whom ? "[1]

The three sisters who were left never pardoned Madame Louise for concealing her intentions, and though they went to see her sometimes, it was with no feelings of pleasure or friendship. Her death was no grief to them. The death of Madame Sophie was a very different matter. Her sisters Adélaide and Victoire regretted her deeply; and their intimacy would have been even closer had not the two ladies of honour, Mme. de Narbonne and Mme. de Civrac, done their best, though never with complete success, to separate them.

---

[1] Beneath this apparent frivolity, assuming it to be as real as Mme. de Boigne seems to assert, Madame Louise is now known to have concealed the austerity of life and the heroic virtues of the Venerable Mother Thérèse of St. Augustine. There is reason to suppose that she offered herself, before entering the Carmelite sisterhood on April 11, 1770, as an expiatory victim to redeem the soul of the King her father (cp. "Madame Louise de France," by Léon de la Brière, Paris, 1900).

Madame Victoire was by no means clever, though extremely kind. It is said of her that during a famine, when the conversation turned upon the sufferings of the poor for want of bread, she said with tears in her eyes, " But why cannot they put up with pie crust ? " [1]

At Bellevue all lived together, and met for dinner at two o'clock, retiring to their rooms at five o'clock until eight. They then came back to the drawing-room, and after supper the evening was spent in various amusements. People came in from Paris and Versailles, and played at loto both then and after dinner.

It will hardly be believed that at this game of loto, the score was never accurate, or that in such a gathering many people were notorious for such inaccuracy. Among others there was a reverend bishop, the most charitable of men, an old marshal's wife, and in short so many people that my mother told me that she decided to stake invariably upon the same numbers, so that everybody knew her game beforehand. After the game the princesses and their ladies worked in the drawing-room, and intercourse was entirely informal.

At Versailles life was entirely different, and the princesses heard Mass separately, Madame Adélaide in the chapel, Madame Victoire at a later hour in her oratory. They met in one another's rooms during the morning in a manner wholly informal, and dined together. At six o'clock the princesses began their game in the apartments of Madame Adélaide, and then held their court. The other princes and princesses often took part in the game, which was always loto.

At nine o'clock the whole royal family met for supper

[1] To appreciate this anecdote, often quoted and so often made a basis of reproach, it must be added that the good princess had an extreme dislike to pie crust, which she could not eat.

in the apartments of Madame. It was entirely a family
party, and it was but rarely that they failed to be present
at this supper. Some positive reason had to be given, or
the King was displeased. The Comte d'Artois himself,
much as he was bored by it, did not venture to demand his
enfranchisement. Court gossip was retailed and family
affairs discussed. The party was on familiar terms and
often very cheerful, for as soon as they were lifted out
of their oppressive environment these princes were the best
company in the world. After supper everyone went his
own way.

The King went to bed.

This process of going to bed, *le coucher*, as it was
known, took place every evening at half-past nine. The
courtiers met in the room of Louis XIV. (which was not
that in which Louis XVI. slept). I believe that anybody
who had been presented at court could go.

The King came in from an inner room, followed by his
attendants. His hair was tied up and he had taken off
his orders. Without paying attention to anybody, he
walked inside the balustrade of the bed, and the almoner
of the day took from the hand of the *valet de chambre* a
prayer-book and a large candlestick with two lights. He
followed the King within the balustrade, gave him the
book, and held the candle during the prayer, which was a
short one. The King then came back into that part of the
room where the courtiers were standing. The almoner
handed the candlestick to the first valet, and he to a person
indicated by the King, who continued to hold it while the
King was undressing. This was a much-envied mark of
distinction, and at every reception in the court all those
who were coming down from the *coucher* were asked,
" Who held the candlestick? " and the choice, as happens
everywhere and at all times, was but seldom approved.

The King's coat, waistcoat, and shirt were taken off; he stood there naked to his waist, scratching and rubbing himself as if he had been alone, in the presence of the whole court and often of many strangers of distinction.

The first valet handed the night-shirt to the most highly qualified person, to one of the princes of the blood if any were present; this was a right and not a favour. When the person was one with whom he was on familiar terms, the King would often play tricks while putting it on, stepping on one side to make the holder run after him, accompanying these charming jokes with loud guffaws, which greatly vexed those who were sincerely attached to him. When his shirt was on he put on his dressing-gown, while three valets unfastened his waist-belt and knee-breeches, which fell down to his ankles, and in that garb, scarcely able to walk with these ridiculous fetters, he would shuffle round the circle of those in waiting.

This reception was of no fixed duration, and might continue for a few minutes or for an hour; its length depended upon those who were present. If there were no *releveurs,* as the courtiers called those of their number who could draw the King into conversation, the reception lasted little more than ten minutes. Among the *releveurs* the cleverest was the Comte de Coigny; he was always careful to discover what the King was reading, and was very clever at turning the conversation upon points which he foresaw would please his majesty. The candle was thus given to him constantly, and his presence was objectionable to those people who wished the ceremony to be cut short.

When the King had had enough of it, he shuffled backward to an arm-chair which was pushed into the middle of the room, and dropped into it, lifting up his legs; two pages on their knees immediately seized his legs, pulled off the King's shoes, and let them drop with a crash, which was a point of etiquette.   As soon as he heard the noise, the usher opened the door, saying, " Gentlemen will please pass out."   Those present went away, and the ceremony was finished.   However, the person who was holding the candlestick was allowed to stay if he had anything special to say to the King, and hence the value that was attached to this strange favour.

The courtiers then returned to Paris or made their way to the various *salons* of Versailles, where they were awaited by the ladies, bishops, and by those who were not presented at court, often for the purpose of continuing games that had been interrupted.   In this court life there were numerous antechamber intrigues, and positions to which all the nobility of France aspired.

One evening while the King was going to bed, M. de Créqui happened to lean against the balustrade of the bed, and the usher on duty said to him, " Sir, you are profaning (*vous profanisez*) the King's bedroom."

" Sir, I will confirm (*je préconerai*) your accuracy," replied the other without hesitation.

This prompt retort was much applauded.

The Queen on leaving the apartments of the Princess was accustomed to go to Mme. de Polignac or Mme. de Lamballe on Saturday.   The Prince would be with Mme. de Balbi, the Princess at home with her ladies in waiting, the Comte d'Artois in society at Versailles or Paris, and the Comtesse d'Artois at home with the body-guard, while the princesses were with their respective ladies of honour.

Mme. de Civrac held a *salon* for Madame Victoire, quite respectably filled with courtiers.   Mme. de Narbonne made little addition to the retinue of the Princess, except in the way of dining companions ; her haughty temper did not permit other relations.   Current scandal asserted that Comte Louis de Narbonne was a son of

Madame Adélaide, a rumour utterly false and absurd, though it is true that the Princess made enormous sacrifices to his caprices. Mme. de Narbonne, imperious as she was, was entirely dominated by the whims of Comte Louis. When he had committed any foolishness and was in want of money, her ill-temper was unbearable, and she vented it chiefly upon Madame Adélaide, making her house intolerable. After a few days the poor Princess would buy back her peace of mind in hard cash. In this way the Comte de Narbonne became possessed of enormous sums, which he procured without the least trouble and accepted as easily. In other respects he was the most amiable and the least ill-tempered of men ; a bad character, doubtless, but merely because he had been spoiled.[1]

Madame Adélaide felt the burden of this yoke, and complained whenever she dared. One evening when my mother was taking her home, and Mme. de Narbonne had been more ill-tempered than usual, she conceived the idea of not returning to her house the next day. Pleased with the plan, she proceeded to imagine what Mme. de Narbonne would say, how she would act, and how her character would develop, &c.

" You do not answer, Mme. d'Osmond. You are wrong ; I am a weak woman, a Bourbon, and I need guidance, but I am never treacherous."

[1] Comte Louis de Narbonne Lara, born at Colorno in the duchy of Parma in 1755, a son of the Duc de Narbonne Lara, lord in waiting to the Duc de Parme, Philippe de Bourbon (son of Philippe V. of Anjou), and of the Duchesse de Narbonne Lara, lady of honour to the Duchesse de Parme, Madame Elisabeth of France (daughter of Louis XV.). On the death of the Princess, Mme. de Narbonne returned to France and became lady of honour to Madame Adélaide. Comte Louis de Narbonne was a constitutional Royalist, and Minister of War in 1791. He emigrated after August 10. On Brumaire 18 he returned to France, took service with Bonaparte, occupied different positions, and died in 1813.

"I do not suspect Madame of the smallest indiscretion, but I know that to-morrow you will be a little more gracious than usual towards Mme. de Narbonne, and recompense her for this small treachery of thought."

"Alas! I much fear that you are right."

In fact, the next day the explanation demanded by the Princess produced a request for money, which was given, and Mme. de Narbonne was charming throughout the evening. The good Princess attempted to excuse her weakness, and told my mother as she withdrew that Mme. de Narbonne had apologised for her rudeness of the evening before; she did not explain how she had soothed her, but this was an open secret. Comte Louis was the first to laugh at the proceeding, whereby his position was simplified, for in that age every extravagance, every vice, and every cowardice was sure to meet with indulgence, provided it was admitted and recognised with some show of humour.

Custom demanded that her lady of honour should accompany the Princess from Mme. de Narbonne's rooms to her own within the castle, but she often dispensed with her escort, especially in the cold weather, as she was accustomed to walk on foot, while her ladies traversed the corridors and antechambers in sedan chairs. These chairs were extremely handsome, gilded with coats of arms on the side. The chairs of the duchesses were covered with red velvet, and they were allowed to have bearers in their own livery; the other ladies employed special bearers, wearing the King's livery, and known in court phraseology as *porteux bleus* (the latter, *porteux*, and not porters, being the correct term).

For nearly a year Madame Adélaide had been accustomed to ask my mother, and often my father, to go into her rooms when she left Mme. de Narbonne. She took pleasure in their talk upon serious topics. But the lady of honour was informed of this habit, the Princess was scolded, and frankly admitted that she could no longer venture to invite them.

It was in one of these conversations that she told my father in what way her curiosity had been checked on the subject of the Iron Mask. She had persuaded her brother, the Dauphin, to question the King upon the subject, and to bring her the information. The Dauphin put the question to Louis XV., who replied, " I will tell you, my son, if you wish, but you will have to swear, as I have done, to reveal the secret to no one."

The Dauphin admitted that his sole reason for wishing to know was to tell the secret to his sister Adélaide, and said he would not press the matter. The King replied that his action was the more advisable, as the secret had never been of any great importance and had lost its interest at that time, although he kept it because he had sworn to do so. He added that the only men now living who knew it were himself and M. de Machault.

The Princess also told my father how M. de Maurepas had secured his ministry.

On the death of Louis XV. his daughters, who had nursed him through the smallpox, were separated from the new King by the inexorable laws of etiquette. The latter had been recommended by his father, the Dauphin, to take the advice of his aunt Adélaide at all times, and now wrote to her to ask to whom he should entrust the care of this kingdom for which he was suddenly responsible. Madame Adélaide replied that the Dauphin would not have hesitated to summon M. de Machault, and to him a courier was immediately sent.

The King sent a second note, asking what arrangements should be made for the funeral, what etiquette was

customary, and to whom he should apply. Madame Adélaide replied that experience and connection made no one
more fitted to undertake these details than M. de Maurepas.

The courier for M. de Machault had not yet started.
M. de Machault's estate was three leagues beyond that of
Ponchartrain, and the roads were in a dreadful condition
at that time. He was ordered to deliver the letter to M.
de Maurepas as he passed.

The old courtier, weary of his exile, arrived without
delay. The King was impatiently awaiting him, and summoned him forthwith. While they were talking the King
was informed that the council had assembled. Custom
demanded that each minister should be informed on each
occasion by the usher. The omission of this formality
excluded from the council, and was equivalent to a dismissal. The usher of the council, seeing M. de Maurepas
thus intimate with the new King, and knowing that he
had been summoned, looked at him with hesitation, while
the King said nothing, but appeared confused. M. de
Maurepas bowed as if he had received a message, and the
King walked out without venturing to say good-bye. M.
de Maurepas followed, took his seat in the council, and
governed France for ten years.

When M. de Machault arrived some hours afterwards,
the position was filled up. The King uttered a few com-
monplaces, paid him some compliments, and left him to
make his way home. Madame Adélaide was greatly
vexed, and complained; but she and her nephew were
Bourbons, as she used to say, and had not the energy
to resist the wills of others, or to support them by co-
operation.

If Toirée had been nearer to Paris than Ponchartrain,
there might have been no Revolution in France. M. de

Machault was a prudent man, who would have been able to turn the virtues of Louis XVI. to better account than the witty but unprincipled and immoral courtier to whom he entrusted his fate. It was not that M. de Maurepas better suited his taste, but merely supplied his momentary needs.

I have mentioned that in this age ready wit could atone for all things, and occupied the position which talent now holds. I propose to relate certain anecdotes which I have heard from my mother, whose morality reached the point of prudery, though many years afterwards these events seemed to her nothing more than ironical witticisms.

The Vicomte de Ségur, the most fashionable man of his time, used to write pretty society verses, the chief merits of which were his own social position. M. de Thiard, irritated by his success, and possibly jealous, also composed a poem, in which he advised M. de Ségur to send his works to the confectioner, having discovered, he said, that they contained no more spirit than could be put into a sweet.

M. de Ségur pretended to laugh at this epigram, but resolved on vengeance.

Now there was in Normandy a certain Mme. de Z., a lady of great beauty, living quietly in her own castle with her own husband, and highly respected, notwithstanding her connection with M. de Thiard, which continued for several years and was said to be extremely intimate. He was supposed to be passionately in love with her. The Vicomte used his influence with his father, who was Minister of War, and secured the transference of his regiment to a town near the castle of Mme. de Z. He played his part admirably, feigned a devouring passion, and after he had continued his attentions for several months, secured the favour of the lady.

Mme. de Z. soon found herself *enceinte;* her husband was away from home, and so also was M. de Thiard. She informed the Vicomte of her misfortune. The evening before he had protested his fervent adoration, but he then replied that he had attained his object, and had never cared for her. He had merely wished to avenge himself for the sarcasms of M. de Thiard, and to show him that his intellect was above the manufacture of confectionery. He therefore bowed himself out, and she heard no more of him. In fact, he went to Paris immediately, and repeated the story to any one who would listen.

Mme. de Z., scorned by her husband, a subject of scandal in her province, and on bad terms with M. de Thiard, died in childbirth. M. de Z. was obliged to recognise the unfortunate child, who has been seen in society as Mme. L. de X.; her intriguing character showed her worthy of her father. The Vicomte de Ségur boasted everywhere of this exploit, and could never understand that it would shock any one who heard it.[1]

Here is an anecdote of another kind. M. de Créqui was anxious to secure favour at court, and consequently did his best to win the good graces of M. and Mme. de Maurepas. One form which his obsequiousness took was to play a game every evening with Mme. de Maurepas, an ancient and wearisome lady; she therefore took his part, and her importunity induced her husband to support his claim. On the day when the favour was secured, M. de Créqui came to the house of Mme. de Maurepas. Mme. de Flamarens, a niece of M. de Maurepas, who did the honours of the house, offered the cards to M. de Créqui as usual. He bowed, and replied with a face of stone,

[1] Mme. de Boigne wrote in full the names here replaced by Z. and X., the names of two high families whose descendants still survive. The reasons for suppression will be readily understood.

" I beg your pardon, I never play cards." Nor did he again play with Mme. de Maurepas. The pointed character of this meanness removed its offence, and no one laughed more heartily than the old minister.

M. de Maugiron was the colonel of a magnificent regiment, but he hated, or rather was bored by, all military details, and was reputed not to be particularly courageous. One day the French Grenadiers, in whose ranks he had formerly served, made a charge at a critical moment. M. de Maugiron voluntarily joined their ranks, and distinguished himself. The next day at dinner the officers of his regiment complimented him on his conduct. " Well, gentlemen, you see that I am as capable as any one else when I please. But it seems to me so disagreeable and stupid an occupation, that I have resolved not to be drawn into it again. You have seen me under fire, and I advise you not to forget it, for it is for the last time."

He kept his word. When his regiment charged, he stood on one side, wished his officers a pleasant journey, and said loudly, " Look at those idiots rushing on to death." None the less, M. de Maugiron was not a bad officer. His regiment was in excellent order, and his business admirably conducted, so that he was popular and even respected in spite of his eccentricity. It was he who received this famous letter from his wife, a very clever woman :

" I am writing to you because I do not know what to do, and I am ending my letter because I do not know what to say.

" SASSENAGE DE MAUGIRON,
" Very sorry that I am."

No one could deny himself the pleasure of a smart retort. The Marshal de Noailles had by no means distinguished himself in the war, and his reputation for courage had remained somewhat doubtful. One day, when it was raining, the King asked the Duc d'Ayen if the Marshal would come hunting. " Oh no, Sire; my father fears water as much as he does fire." This reply was in every-body's mouth.

My only reason for repeating these incidents, which might be easily multiplied, is to show that during an age commonly represented as more moral than our own, and during a time when society is thought to have been a tribunal before which everybody must pass, wit or effrontery sufficed to avert sentences which would prob-ably have been passed upon misdemeanours less brill-iantly admitted.

I have observed that Mme. de Civrac was lady of hon-.our to Madame Victoire. Her life is a romance.

Mlle. Monbadon, daughter of a notary of Bordeaux, had reached the age of twenty-five. She was tall, beauti-ful, clever, and in particular ambitious. She was asked in marriage by a country squire of the neighbourhood, called M. de Magnac. He was in service in the Life Guards, a poor man and a boorish character, incapable of appreciating his wife's qualities, but anxious to share the small fortune which she was to inherit from her father.

The person who was negotiating the marriage laid much stress upon the good birth of M. de Magnac, who belonged to the family of Durfort. Mlle. Monbadon de-manded the documents, and, satisfied with her inspection, married M. de Magnac.

With some scanty luggage and the portfolio containing these genealogical documents, she started for Paris with her husband. There she first called upon Chérin, handed him her papers, and begged him to examine them most carefully. After some days she came back for them, and was assured that the connection of M. de Magnac with the branch of Durfort-Lorge had been completely made out. She procured a certificate of this fact, and began to style herself Magnac de Civrac. She wrote to the old Marshal de Lorge and asked for an interview, telling him in very modest terms that she happened to be passing through Paris, and thought her husband had the honour of belonging to his family; distant as the connection might be, it was so great an honour and happiness that she could not return to her provincial obscurity without claiming the connection, and if she could venture so far as to make a call once only upon the Marquis's wife her gratitude would be infinite.

The Marshal was deceived by these honeyed words, without entirely recognising the relationship, upon which she did not insist. She was allowed to pay her call, and behaved very adroitly. She received permission to return for a farewell visit, and came back again. Her departure was postponed, and she returned once more; at length she remained definitely. The Marshal's wife was soon enchanted with her; sitting on a little stool at her feet, she would work on the same piece of tapestry, and became an inmate of the house. Her husband remained in the background. One day, when her influence was established, she heard some contemptuous words upon the position of life-guardsmen, and raised her head in astonishment.

When she was alone with the Marshal and his wife she said, " I fear that in our provincial ignorance we must have been treating you very badly, for one of your relatives is a life guardsman. Is that entirely as it should be? " M. de Lorge replied in friendly terms, but gently refused any ackowledgment of the relationship. " Well," said she, " I know nothing of all that, but I will bring you my husband's papers." She brought the papers in due order and the certificate from Chérin. It was impossible to dispute the facts, nor did any one wish to contest them.

The husband was removed from his service, given a regimental appointment, and sent into garrison. His wife had a little *apartement* in the residence of de Lorge. The Marshal de Lorge had no son. The Marshal de Duras had one only, who promised to develop into an extremely bad character. Soon her condition demanded attention, and the footstool became an arm-chair. She soon was known only as Mme. de Civrac, the second title of the branch of de Lorge. Eventually, at the end of a few months, she was so entirely installed that she governed the household, though she preserved an attitude of the greatest respect towards M. and Mme. de Lorge. The Duras family shared this infatuation.

When the household of Madame Victoire was organised, she was appointed lady in waiting, and soon became her favourite and her lady of honour. On this occasion she was given the title of the Duchesse de Civrac.

She had always preserved most friendly relations with her husband, whom she overwhelmed with proofs of her kindness, though he was too great a blockhead to make use of his advantage when he was present. She succeeded in getting him appointed Ambassador to Vienna, and he was kind enough to die without delay, this being the sole proof of intelligence that he had displayed throughout his life. He left her with three children: a son, who afterwards became Duc de Lorge and heir to the fortune of this branch of the Durfort family; and two daughters, Mme. Donissent and Mme. de Chastellux.

Mme. de Civrac was as clever as she was lively. She wished to patronise others as soon as she had reached the summit of her ambition, and constituted herself patron of

the town of Bordeaux. Every one who came from that
town was certain to meet with her support, and she eventually succeeded in changing the status of her own family.
The Monbadon family became by degrees de Monbadon.
Her nephew entered the service, was appointed colonel,
and almost became a personage at court.

After this success, when she was at the height of her
grandeur, she happened to be visiting a Pyrenean watering-place, and there received a list of promoted colonels.
She proceeded to enlarge upon the unsuitable appointments that had been made. An old lady of high standing
in the provinces replied, " What do you expect, Duchesse?
Chacun a son badon."

The ambitious Mme. de Civrac had been entirely successful, but she was still unsatisfied. Though very ill, she
thought she had brought negotiations to a conclusion for
the marriage of her son, the Duc de Lorge, with Mlle. de
Polignac, whose mother was then all-powerful ; one of her
conditions was a captaincy of the Guards for this young
son. At this moment Mme. de Gramont, a no less skilful
intriguer, crossed her path. She owed her influence with
the Queen to the fact that she had been exiled by the King
for some rudeness to Mme. Dubarry. Her claims were
supported by the Choiseul party. The Queen gave the
preference to her, and thus turned the balance.

Mme. de Civrac was suddenly informed that young Gramont,[1] a regimental subaltern, had arrived at Versailles,
had been made Duc de Guiche, captain of the Guards, and
that his marriage to Mlle. Polignac was announced. Her
anger in consequence threw her into a fever, and in forty-

[1] Louis Antoine, Duc de Gramont, general and peer of France at
the Restoration (1755–1836); nephew of the Duchesse de Gramont,
a sister of the Duc de Choiseul. The Duchess was guillotined in
1794 (1730–94).

eight hours she expired, though her disease had not threatened so rapid a conclusion.

Madame Victoire, who was much distressed by this loss, promised the mother to appoint Mme. de Chastellux her lady of honour. Mme. de Donissent was already her lady of the bedchamber.

This Mme. de Donissent, who is still alive at the age of ninety-two, is the mother of Mme. de Lescure. Both ladies acquired an honourable and melancholy celebrity in the first war of La Vendée, in which they both took an active though not an unfeminine share. The memoirs of Mme. de Lescure, dealing with those events, relate in a touching and realistic manner the glory and the misfortunes of this campaign. They were edited by M. de Barante from the narrative of Mme. de Lescure (who became Mme. de la Rochejaquelein) while he was prefect of Morbihan.

CHAPTER III

My childhood—A beautiful doll—Kindness of the King—Commencement of the Revolution—Opening of the States General—Departure of the Comte d'Artois—October 6, 1789—The journey to England—Mrs. Fitzherbert—The buckles of the Prince of Wales—A country visit—The English princesses.

I was brought up literally upon the knees of the royal family. The King and Queen especially overwhelmed me with kindness. It was a time, as I have already said, when children were put out to nurse, then weaned and sent to a convent, or dressed up like little ladies and gentlemen, and appeared only to be wearied and made peevish and ill-tempered; in my cambric frock, a profusion of fair hair framing a pretty little face, I was extremely striking. My father had taken pains to develop my intelligence, and I was honestly regarded as a little prodigy. I had learnt to read with such facility that at the age of three I could read and repeat the tragedies of Racine for my own pleasure, and, it is said, for the pleasure of others.

My father often took me to the theatrical performances at Versailles. After the first piece I was taken away, that I might be sent to bed, and I remember that the King sometimes called me into his box and made me tell him the story of the play that I had just seen. I generally added my reflections on it, which were usually highly appreciated. On one occasion, in the middle of my literary observation, I told him that I very much wanted to ask him a favour, and encouraged by his kindness, I admitted my desire for two of the smallest glass drops from the chandeliers, to use as ear-rings, as my ears were to be bored the next day.

I remember, from the pleasure I received, a story of the same kind. Madame Adélaide, who spoilt me with all her heart, made me tell her one day a fairy tale of my own invention. The fairy had given the princess a palace of diamonds with appointments to match, and by way of culmination the heroine had discovered in a carbuncle writing case a treasure of one hundred six franc pieces.

Madame Adélaide turned this story to account, and after using all her influence to obtain my mother's permission, she enabled me to find in my little writing case, which was not, however, of carbuncle, a hundred six franc pieces. There was a piece of paper on which was written, " One hundred six franc pieces for Adèle," precisely as had happened to the princess of the story. I am not quite sure that I could count up to a hundred, but I still remember my astonishment at this sight.

My parents had eventually come to spend the whole summer at Bellevue, and my room was on the ground floor, looking into the courtyard. Madame Adélaide took long walks every day to supervise her workmen. She used to call me as she passed; my hat was put on, I got out of the window, and went off with her without any nurse. She was generally followed by a number of servants, and a little carriage drawn by one led horse, which she never entered, but which I often occupied. I preferred, however, to run by her side, and to carry on what I called a conversation.

My rival and friend was a large white spaniel, a very intelligent dog, who shared these walks. If the road happened to be very muddy, he was put into a large white linen bag and carried by two of the servants on duty. I was extremely proud of being able to pick my steps without getting muddy as he did.

When we came back to the castle, I fought with Visir for his red velvet cushion, which he abandoned more readily than he did the cakes which were broken up for us on the floor. The good Princess would often go down on all fours and join in our romps, to restore peace or to obtain the prize of the race. I can still see her tall, thin figure, her tucked violet dress (which was the uniform at Bellevue), her butterfly hat, and two large teeth, which were the only ones she had. She had been very pretty, but at this time was extremely ugly, and so I thought her.

Madame Adélaide had made for me, at great expense, a magnificent doll, with a complete wardrobe, basket, and jewels, including a watch by Lépine,[1] which I still possess, and a duchesse bed, in which I slept at the age of seven, so that the size of the doll can be imagined. The presentation of this doll was a festival for the royal family. The family went to dine at Bellevue; they sent for me when they rose from the table. The folding doors were opened, and the doll arrived, dragged forward upon her bed and escorted by all her property. The King held me by the hand.

" Who is that for, Adèle? "

" I believe it is for me, Sire."

Everybody began to play with my new property. They wished to put me in the bed instead of the doll, and the Queen and Madame Élisabeth on their knees, on either side of the bed, amused themselves in making it, with much delight at their cleverness in turning the mattresses.

---

[1] The King's watchmaker. This very pretty gold watch belonged to the Marquis d'Osmond; he inherited it from his great-aunt.

The poor princesses, alas! did not think that a very few years later, in 1788, they would be reduced to making their own bed. How extravagant such a prophecy would then have seemed!

I often met the King in the gardens at Versailles, and would run from whatever distance I saw him. One day when I did not go he called me, and I arrived in tears.

" What is the matter, little Adèle? "

" It is your naughty gardeners, Sir, who want to kill my dog because he runs after your fowls."

" I promise you that he shall not be hurt."

And, in fact, orders were given that Mlle. d'Osmond's dog was to be allowed to run after the poultry.

I was no less a favourite with the younger generation. The Dauphin,[1] who died at Meudon, was very fond of me, and was continually asking that I might play with him, while the Duc de Berry [2] got himself into disgrace because he would not dance with any one but myself at a ball. Madame [3] and the Duc d'Angoulême [4] showed me less attention.

The misfortunes of the Revolution ended my successes at court. I cannot say if they acted upon me as homœopathic medicine, but it is certain that, in spite of my early childhood, I never possessed the instincts of the courtier or any taste for the society of princes. Events had become too serious, and the affectations of a child no longer had interest; the year 1789 had begun.

My father was well aware of the gravity of the situa-

[1] The son of Louis XVI. and of Queen Marie Antoinette, born in October 1781, died in January 1789.

[2] Charles Ferdinand, second son of the Comte d'Artois, born in 1778.

[3] Marie Thérèse, the daughter of Louis XVI. and of Marie Antoinette, born 1778.

[4] Louis Antoine, eldest son of the Comte d'Artois, born in 1775.

tion. The opening of the States General was a solemnity conducted with magnificence, which attracted strangers from all parts of Europe to Versailles. My mother, in full court dress, told my father that she was about to start. As she did not see him, she went into his room, and found him in his dressing-gown.

" Do be quick, we shall be late."

" No; I am not going. I cannot go and see that unhappy man abdicate."

In the evening Madame Adélaide was talking of the splendid spectacle which the hall presented. She questioned my father upon some details, of which he professed ignorance.

" Where was your seat, then? "

" I was not there, Madame."

" You were ill, then? "

" No, Madame."

" What! When people have come so far to be present at this ceremony, you could not take the trouble to cross the street! "

" The fact is, Madame, that I am not fond of funerals, and certainly not when a monarch is to be interred."

" For my part, I am not pleased that people at your age should think themselves cleverer than every one else," and with this the Princess turned on her heel.

It must not be concluded from this that my father was opposed to concessions. On the contrary, he was persuaded that the spirit of the time urgently demanded concessions; but he wished them to be made upon a definite plan—to be large and generous, and not exaggerated. It was with mortal fear that he saw the opening of the States General, for, knowing the vagueness of individual wishes, he was aware that no one had settled any point at which concession or demand should cease.

Moreover, he had no confidence in M. Necker. He thought he was inclined to place the King upon a dangerous slope, not with the object of causing a catastrophe, but with the proud idea that he alone could stop the fall, and that thus he was making himself necessary.

The anger of Madame Adélaide was speedily appeased by the course of events.

One day I was playing with the de Guiche children, when I was fetched away much earlier than usual. Instead of the servant who usually carried me, I found my father's own valet waiting. I had an English nurse who spoke French badly; she was given a note from my mother. While she was reading it I went back into the room of my little playmates. Everything was already upside down; they were crying and beginning to pack up. I was wrapped in a cloak, the valet took me in his arms, and instead of taking me back to my parents, he installed me with my nurse in the house of an old English master who had a little room on the fourth storey in a distant part of the town. The next night I was fetched away and taken to the country, where I remained for several days without news of anybody. I was already old enough to feel this exile keenly. The disturbances of the month of June were then beginning, and at that moment the Comte d'Artois, his children, and the Polignac family went away. On my return I found the eldest of the de Guiche children and her sister in hiding with the parents of her nurse. The reason of this fear for the safety of us children was the rumour that the people, as a handful of wretches were styled, were starting out to carry off the children of the nobles and make hostages of them.

I was greatly frightened by this separation, and when the events of October 6 began, my sole preoccupation was the fear that I should be sent away from the house.

My parents lived near the castle, but in the town, as the houses looking upon the castle were inconvenient for people definitely established at Versailles. I do not know who came to warn my father, while he was at table, of the rumours, but too well founded, which were beginning to go about. He went off immediately to the castle; my mother was to meet him there at the time when the princesses began their game. But shortly after his departure the streets of Versailles were filled by a flood of horrible-looking people, uttering wild cries, while gunshots could be heard in the distance. Such part of their language as could be heard was even more frightful than their appearance.

Communications with the castle were cut off. When night came my mother took up her position in a darkened room and attempted, with her face against the closed shutters, to discover the nature of events from what she could hear and see. I was on her knee, and eventually went to sleep. They put me on a sofa to avoid waking me, and she decided to go and reconnoitre for herself, taking with her the same *valet de chambre* of whom I have already spoken. She went to several of the castle gates without being able to get in, till at last she found on sentry duty a member of the National Guard who recognised her, and said, " You had better go home, Marquise; you must not be seen in the street. I cannot let you in, my orders are too strict; and it would be no use if I did, for you would be stopped at every door. You have nothing to fear for your friends, but there will not be a life-guardsman left to-morrow morning."

This was said at nine o'clock in the evening, before the massacre had begun, and the words were those of a reasonable and moderate man, as can be seen from their purport; yet he was privy to this horrible secret, and was

by no means revolted at it, to such an extent had everybody's head been turned.

My mother did not recognise the man at the time, but
afterwards learnt that he was a hosier. She went home
again, frightened, as may be imagined, but less despond-
ent than when she started, for the street rumours declared
that every throat in the castle had been cut.

At midnight my father arrived. I was aroused by the
tumult and by the joy of seeing him, but it was not for
long. He came to say good-bye to us and to get some
money. He ordered his horses to be saddled and to be
led to Saint Cyr by a circuitous route. His brother, the
Abbé d'Osmond, who accompanied him, was to go with
the horses and wait for him at Saint Cyr. These gentlemen proceeded to change their court dresses for travelling
suits. My father loaded his pistols. Meanwhile my
mother was sewing all the money that she could find in
the house into two belts, which she made them put on.
These proceedings occupied half an hour, and they then
started. I wished to embrace my father, but my mother
pulled me away, with a roughness to which I was not
accustomed, and which surprised me.

The door closed, and I then saw her fall on her knees
in an outburst of grief which absorbed my complete attention, and I understood that she had wished to spare
my father the unnecessary pain of seeing our sufferings.
This practical lesson made a great impression upon me,
and thenceforward I never gave way to any demonstrations which might increase the grief or the anxiety of
others.

I have heard my father relate that when he had reached
the meeting-place, the terrace of the orange garden, he
walked about alone for a long time; a man then arrived,
wrapped in a cloak. At first they kept aloof, but then

they recognised one another: it was the Comte de Saint Priest, a minister at that time and a man of sense and courage. They continued their walk for a long time, but no one came, and the hour grew late. Uneasy and astonished, they did not know what to think of this delay in the King's proposed departure, as it was arranged that he should go to Rambouillet that same night. They did not dare to appear in the royal apartments in their travelling dresses; not only would this have been contrary to etiquette, but it would have been a revelation in this situation.

M. de Saint Priest, who had rooms in the castle, decided to go and change his clothes, and made an appointment with my father in a distant spot. My father waited a long time, and at length the Comte appeared. "My dear d'Osmond, go home and reassure your wife; the King is not going to start." And shaking his hand, "My friend, M. Necker, has won the day, and the King and the monarchy are alike ruined."

The King's departure for Rambouillet had been decided, but the orders for the carriages had been given with the full formalities usually in force. The rumour had thus gone abroad. The grooms had hesitated to harness the horses, the coachmen to drive them. The populace had gathered before the stables and refused to let the carriages out. M. Necker, informed of these facts, had gone to discuss them with the King, who was persuaded to stay rather by these obstacles than by the minister's arguments. Though he was accustomed to ride twenty leagues while hunting, to go to Rambouillet on a troop horse would have seemed to him an inconceivable resource. There, as later at Varennes, the chance of safety had been destroyed by those habits of formality which had become second nature to the French royal family. My father was obliged to go home to change his clothes, and as he did not return to the castle that night, he escaped the spectacle of the horrors which were there perpetrated.

As soon as the King's consent to his removal to Paris had opened the castle doors, my mother went to her Princess. She found the two sisters, the Princesses Adélaide and Victoire, in their room on the ground floor, with all shutters closed and one single candle lighted. After the first words she asked them why they were making so sad a day still gloomier. " My dear, it is in order that they may not aim at us, as they did this morning," replied Madame Adélaide, with extreme calm and gentleness. In fact, the mob had fired into their windows in the morning, and not a single pane of glass remained unbroken.

My mother remained with them until the moment of their departure. She wished to accompany them, but the princesses obstinately declined, and accepted this mark of devotion only from their ladies of honour, the Duchesse de Narbonne and Mme. de Chastellux. They followed the sad procession which carried off the King as far as Sèvres ; there they took the road to Bellevue, where my parents went to join them the next day.

However, the uproar did not subside. The excitement at Versailles was intense, and terrible threats were uttered against my mother. It was said that Madame Adélaide had full power over the King, while she in turn was under my mother's influence, who was thus at the head of the aristocrats. This feeling became so violent that at the end of three days the danger was obvious, and we started for England.

My recollections of the journey are but scanty. I can only remember the impression which the sight of the sea made upon me. Child as I was, I conceived a devotion for the sea which has never failed. Its grey and green tints always had a charm for me which Mediterranean blue has never been able to efface.

We disembarked at Brighton. By chance my mother met there Mrs. Fitzherbert, who was walking on the jetty. Some years before she had come to Paris, when avoiding the attentions of the Prince of Wales. My mother, who was her cousin, had seen a great deal of her. Since that time the blessing of a Catholic priest had sanctified, though not legalised, her relations with the Prince; she lived with him in an intimacy which was conducted by both under the forms of ordinary married life. They inhabited a little house at Brighton like ordinary citizens. My parents were received with much effusion, and were induced to spend several days there.

I remember that I was taken one morning to Mrs. Fitzherbert, and that she showed us the Prince's dressing-room, where there was a large table entirely covered with shoe buckles. I expressed my astonishment at the sight, and Mrs. Fitzherbert, with a laugh, opened a large cupboard, which was also full; there were enough for every day of the year. It was a fashion of the time, and the Prince of Wales was the most fashionable of men. This collection of shoe buckles struck my childish imagination, and for a long time I only thought of the Prince of Wales as owner of these buckles.

My parents were made much of in England. French visitors were rare at that time. My mother was a pretty and fashionable woman, and her family overwhelmed her with kindness. We went to spend Christmas with Lord Winchilsea at his beautiful estate of Burleigh. Life was there very magnificent, as far as I can remember, but I was too accustomed to magnificence to be greatly impressed.

Lord Winchilsea's mother, Lady Charlotte Finch, was governess to the English princesses. On several occasions I saw the three youngest at her house. They were much older than I, and I did not like them. The Princess Amelia called me a little thing, which shocked me greatly. I spoke English very well, but did not then understand that this was a term of affection.[1]

[1] See in the Appendix the letters written by Madame Adélaide to the Marquise d'Osmond during this journey.

CHAPTER IV

Return to France—My father's position in 1790—Adventures during a journey in Corsica—Visit to the Tuileries—Touching
meeting with the Queen—Departure of the princesses—Departure from France and arrival at Rome—Flight to Varennes
—The Queen's story—Louis XVI. disapproves of emigration
—Acceptance of the Constitution—My father's opinions—He
resigns—The King's kindness to him—My father rejoins us at
Rome—Murder of the Abbé d'Osmond at St. Domingo—The
Vicomte d'Osmond rejoins the army of the princes.

IN the month of January 1790 my father returned to
France, and three months later we joined him in that
country. I have forgotten to say that he had left the
army in 1788, to take up a diplomatic career. Formerly
he had been colonel of the infantry regiment of Barrois,
in garrison at Corsica.[1] He went there every year.

One of these journeys gave rise to an episode which
was of little importance at the time, but afterwards acquired interest. He was at Toulon, staying with M.
Malouet, the naval commissary and a friend of his, waiting for a change of wind to permit his embarcation,
when he was informed that a Corsican gentleman desired

[1] Appointed colonel of an infantry regiment at Barrois on January 1, 1784, and Chevalier of Saint Louis on April 23, 1786, the
Marquis d'Osmond was Chargé d'Affaires for the Dutch refugees in
France (March 29, 1788). At the request of the Minister of Foreign
Affairs, who assured him from the King that he would reach the
rank of field-marshal just as if he had retained his military position,
he resigned in April 1788. He was appointed the King's minister in
Holland in June 1789. (Manuscript note, found among the papers
of Mme. de Boigne.)

74

to see him. The gentleman was shown in, and after the preliminary courtesies explained that he wished to return as quickly as possible to Ajaccio, and the only felucca in the harbour being chartered by my father, he begged him to allow the captain to accept him as a passenger.

"That is impossible, Sir, as I have chartered the felucca, but I shall be very happy to take you on board."

"But, Marquis, I am not alone; I have my son with me and my cook, whom I am taking home."

"Well, Sir, there will be room enough for all of you."

The Corsican thanked my father profusely, and came to see him frequently for several days, at the end of which the wind changed and they embarked. At dinner, to which my father invited the passengers, who included some officers of his regiment and the two Corsicans, he requested an officer, M. de Belloc, to call the young man who was wearing the uniform of the military school and reading at the end of the boat. The young man refused. M. de Belloc came back irritated, and said to my father, "I should like to throw the unsociable little fellow into the sea. He has an unpleasant face. Will you grant me permission, Colonel?"

"No," said my father, laughing; "and I am not of your opinion. His face shows character, and I am sure that he will be heard of some day."

The unsociable fellow was the future Emperor Napoleon. Belloc has related this scene to me at least ten times, adding with a sigh, "Ah, if the Colonel had only allowed me to throw him into the sea, he would not be turning the world upside down to-day." (It is unnecessary to add that the exile made these remarks long afterwards.)

The day after the arrival at Ajaccio, M. Buonaparte, the father, accompanied with his family, called upon my

father to express his thanks, and from that day his connection with Pozzo di Borgo began. My father called
upon Mme. Buonaparte. She lived at Ajaccio in one of
the best little houses in the town, on the door of which
was picked out in snail shells, *Vive Marbeuf*. M. de
Marbeuf had been the patron of the Buonaparte family,
and history records that Mme. Buonaparte had been very
grateful for his services. At the time of my father's
visit she was still a very beautiful woman; he found her
in the kitchen, without her stockings, in a cotton skirt,
making sweets. Notwithstanding her beauty, the task
seemed appropriate.

After he was ordered to undertake a commission with
respect to the Dutch refugees in 1788, my father was
appointed Minister at The Hague, which position he held
at the time of our stay in England. A quarrel between
the Prince of Orange and the French Ambassador had
decided the court of Versailles to send only a minister to
Holland. The Republic, however, wished to have an
ambassador. This quarrel prevented my father from
taking up his post. He waited with the more patience,
as he hoped thus to secure the rank of ambassador, which
he would not have been able to do forthwith under ordinary conditions.

The town of Versailles had begun to realise the loss
which was caused by the absence of the court. Excitement had subsided, and the sad days of October were
regretted. Upon my mother's return, she was most
kindly received by the very persons who had inveighed
most strongly against her at the time of her departure;
however, we did not stay long. We began by going to
Bellevue for the summer, and we spent the next winter
in rooms in the pavillon de Marsan in the Tuileries.

I can recall in full detail a scene that happened during

that summer. It was many months since I had seen the
Queen. She came to Bellevue under the escort of the
National Guard, a uniform which I had been taught to
detest. The Queen was even then, I think, practically a
prisoner, for the escort never left her. At any rate,
whenever she sent for me I found her on the terrace surrounded by national guards. My little heart was affected
by this sight, and I began to sob. The Queen knelt
down, put her face against mine, and hid both our faces
beneath my long fair hair, begging me to hide my tears.
I felt that hers were falling. I can still hear her words,
" Hush, hush, Adèle! " She remained for a long time
in this position.

All the spectators were affected, but only the carelessness of childhood could have shown emotion at a moment
when there was danger in every action. I do not know
if any report was made of this scene, but the Queen did
not return to Bellevue, and that was the last time I saw
her, except from a distance, during my stay at the
Tuileries. The impressions of that moment, which I
still preserve, are very distinct. I could describe her
dress. She was in a white *picrrot de linon,* with a lilac-
coloured pattern, a full fichu, and a large straw hat, the
broad ribbons of which were tied in a large knot at the
point where the fichu crossed.

Poor princess, poor woman, poor mother! Terrible
was the fate reserved for her! She thought herself very
unhappy at the time, but it was only the beginning of
her troubles. Her son, the second Dauphin,[1] had accompanied her to Bellevue, and used to play in the sand with
my brother. The national guards joined in these games,
and the two children were too young to object to their

[1] Louis XVII., born in 1785, died a martyr's death at the Temple
in 1795.

company. I would not have approached for all the kingdoms of the world. I stayed near the Queen, who held my hand. I have since been told that she thought herself obliged to explain to her attendants that the first Dauphin was very fond of me, that she had not seen me since his death, and that this was the reason of our mutual affection.

Far from subsiding, the Revolution became more and more formidable. The King, who was proposing to leave France, wished to remove his aunts. They applied to the National Assembly, and obtained permission to go to Rome. Before their departure they made some stay at Bellevue.

My father had been appointed Minister at St. Petersburg, to replace M. de Ségur (1790). The Minister's public report explained that this choice had been made because the Empress Catherine would not consent to receive a " patriot " envoy. This circumstance was eventually to make my father's position extremely dangerous. He had, however, no idea of retreat, but wished his wife and his children to leave France. It was arranged that as soon as the princesses should have crossed the frontier, my mother was to follow them.

On the evening before the day arranged for the departure of the princesses, my father, who spent his time among the groups of patriots, heard that there was a feeling against their departure. The demagogues were preaching a crusade against Bellevue, and asserting that the old women ought to be brought back to Paris, that they could not have too many hostages, &c. The docile crowd were already marching on Bellevue.

My father returned at once to the Tuileries, ordered his *valet de chambre,* by name Bermont, of whom I shall speak later, to get ready, took him to the Princesse de

Tarente, who was living in the Faubourg Saint Germain, and with whom he was very intimate, saddled one of her horses, and despatched Bermont, by way of the plain of Grenelle on the Meudon road, to warn the princesses that they must start at that moment.[1]

Orders had been given for the start to be made at four o'clock in the morning, and it was then only ten in the evening. The servants of the princesses began to grumble, and many would have liked the journey to be postponed. Bermont went to the stables, but the horses were not being harnessed. He went back to find Madame Adélaide, told her that there was not a moment to lose, and that he had himself heard the yells of the column which was advancing from the other side of the Seine.

Eventually the princesses consented to enter the carriage of M. de Thiange, which happened to be in the court. Their servants then made up their minds, and the travelling carriages were brought out. Hardly had the last of them passed the gates of Meudon than the gate in the direction of Sèvres was attacked by the mob. It was speedily forced, and the castle was invaded and plundered, but the princesses had escaped danger.[2]

Comte Louis de Narbonne was accused as the cause of their flight, because, as lord of honour to Madame Adélaide, he ought to have accompanied them, but preferred to remain in Paris. My father has always regarded this assertion as one of those absurd slanders which party spirit can raise against those who do not

[1] February 10, 1791. See the letter of Madame Victoire, under date March 21, 1795, in the Appendix.

[2] Reference should be made to the important part played in this, affair by Comte Virieu, narrated in the fine monograph upon him by the Marquis Costa de Beauregarde, of the French Academy, *Le roman d'un royaliste sous la révolution*, third edition, p. 227. (Plon & Co., Paris, 1895.)

share its prejudices. It must be said that my father had a great regard and affection for Comte Louis, which feeling was returned, and that political opinions could not separate them. Comte Louis used to say, " I am the besetting sin of d'Osmond, against which he fights in vain, but I shall never resign myself to seeing him a member of the foolish party." They rarely met, but when they saw one another they were always on terms of perfect friendship.

The princesses were stopped upon the road, but the decree of the Assembly restored their liberty, and they continued their journey. We began ours, which passed off without incident, and rejoined the princesses at Turin.

My mother then spent several months in Rome, in keen anxiety owing to the dangers to which my father was exposed. He rejoined us in the spring of 1792, some months after the flight to Varennes, of which I have heard him give the following account [1] :

The King had resolved to leave Paris and go to a garrison town where the troops were faithful. M. de Bouillé, military commander in the east, was ordered to prepare the halting-places and arrange for the King's journey. My father was in the secret. Under pretext of starting for his Russian post, he was to leave Paris, stop at the frontier, rejoin the King, and take his final orders for the composition of a letter or manifesto, which was to be carried to the Northern courts, explaining the position of the King, who had escaped from the hands of his seditious subjects, and was now able to appeal to every loyal element in France. The King requested particularly that foreign courts would recognise no authority but his own, and would not negotiate with the exiled

[1] See *The Flight of Marie Antoinette*, by G. Lenotre. J. B. Lippincott Co., Philadelphia.

princes. Relations were already highly strained between
the Tuileries and the council of the Comte d'Artois.

My father urged M. de Montmorin to let him start,
but the dilatory habits of this minister, who was not in
the secret, delayed his departure. He dared not start
without his instructions, for fear of raising suspicion.
The day for the flight was approaching, and at length he
was promised that his letters of credit should be ready
the next day.

He was walking in the Champs Elysées, when he saw
the King's carriage pass, returning from St. Cloud. The
Queen leaned out of the window and signalled with her
hand. He did not then understand her signs, but they
were clear to him the next morning, when his *valet de
chambre* came in and told him of the departure of the
royal family. The start had been placed forty-eight
hours earlier, because some changes among the serving-
women of the Dauphin would have brought an untrust-
worthy person to court.

My father had not seen the Queen since this decision,
and could not have received any warning; in any case,
he could not have started without the minister's instructions. He therefore regarded his mission as a failure,
and concerned himself only with the means of rejoining
the King, when he should learn of his arrival at Mont-
médy. This business did not prevent him from walking
about the whole morning. He found the town in a state
of stupefaction. The demagogues were apprehensive,
and the Royalists had not yet manifested their joy. All
was silent, and no one would act. A courier soon arrived bringing the news of the arrest; thereupon the
town was full of the cries and yells of all the rabble who
could be got together. The Jacobins resumed their au-
dacity, and honest people hid their heads.

It was from the window of the pavillon de Marsan that my father saw the dread escort arrive, bringing the illustrious persons back to the castle through the garden. They took an hour and a half to pass from the swing bridge to the palace. At every moment the people stopped the carriage to pour insults upon it, with the intention of dragging out the life-guards, who had been bound to the seat. However, this dreadful procession arrived without bloodshed; had a drop of blood flowed, probably every occupant of that fatal carriage would have been massacred. All were awaiting death, and all were resigned to it.

As soon as it was possible to reach the princes, my father arrived. The Queen related the course of events with gentleness and magnanimity, accusing no one, and blaming only fate for the ill success of the enterprise which might change their destiny.

Those events have been related many times, but the authentic nature of this narrative, gathered from the lips of the Queen herself, induces me to recount such details as have remained in my memory of those which I have heard my father relate.

The travelling carriage had been ordered by Mrs. Sullivan (afterwards Mrs. Crawford; she had been employed by M. de Fersen for that purpose) for the use of one of her friends, the Baroness of Crafft.[1] It was for this same baroness, her family and her attendants, that a complete passport had been obtained and a requisition for post-horses. For some days the carriage had been waiting in the stables of Mrs. Sullivan, and she undertook to place in it such luggage as was necessary for the use of the royal family.

It would have been desirable for the inmates of the

[1] Or Korff. [Translator.]

Tuileries to separate, but this they declined. The danger was so great that they wished, as they said, to perish or escape together. The Prince and Princess, who consented to start separately, went through without difficulty. They, however, were only seeking the nearest frontier, while the King, who was not allowed to leave France, had only one route that he could take. Many precautions had been taken, but one point was overlooked.

The carriage of the Baroness of Crafft was to take the King and Queen, Madame Élisabeth, two children, and the Baron de Viomesnil. Two life-guards in uniform were on the box. Mme. de Tourzel was only informed of the departure at the last moment. She insisted upon the rights of her position, which authorised her never to leave the Dauphin. This argument was imperative upon those to whom it had been addressed, and she was allowed to take the place of the Baron de Viomesnil in the carriage.

The royal party thus had no one with them to act with decision in case of emergency. There were only two ordinary guardsmen to assume this responsibility, however devoted they might be. This decision was learnt too late, and nothing could be done to remedy it.

When the day and the hour arrived, the King and Queen retired as usual and went to bed. They immediately got up again, dressed in clothes which had been sent to them, and left the Tuileries alone. The King gave his arm to the Queen, and as they passed through the wicket-gate his shoe-buckles became entangled and he nearly fell. The sentinel helped him to rise, and asked if he had hurt himself. The Queen thought they were lost, but they were allowed to pass. As they crossed the Carrousel they were met by the carriage of M. de Lafayette; the torches carried by his men lighted up the faces of the royal pair. M. de Lafayette put out his head, and much to their dismay they were recognised, but the carriage went on its way. At length they reached the corner of the Carrousel. M. de Fersen followed them at a distance, and hastened to open the door of a hired carriage in which Mme. de Tourzel and the children had already taken their places. The Dauphin was dressed as a girl, this being the only disguise adopted. They waited for Madame Élisabeth for some moments; she had some difficulty in leaving the palace; a faithful tirewoman accompanied her.

The Marquis de Briges acted as coachman, and the Comte de Fersen got up behind. They passed the barrier without difficulty. The travelling carriage, however, was not outside, as had been arranged. They waited for more than an hour, and eventually realised that they had mistaken the barrier. The point first proposed as a meeting place had been changed, and of this M. de Briges had not been informed.

To avoid re-passing the barrier it was necessary to make a long circuit to reach the spot where the travelling carriage was waiting. The carriage was there, but much time had been lost. The illustrious fugitives immediately got in. It was at that moment that M. de Fersen handed to one of the life-guards who was unarmed his pistols, on which his name was engraved, and which were found at Varennes.

No incident delayed their progress; the postillions had been well paid, and drove rapidly. On seeing Charles de Damas in readiness, the travellers flattered themselves that the delay in their departure would be without serious consequence, and began to entertain hopes of safety. It was extremely hot, and the Dauphin suffered greatly. They lowered the windows, which had been raised, and when they reached the post-house of Sainte Menehould, they forgot to draw the blinds on the side where the King and Queen were sitting opposite to one another.

Their faces, especially that of the King, were well known. The King saw a man leaning against the wheels of the carriage, looking at him attentively. He stooped down under the pretext of playing with his children, and told the Queen to draw the blinds in a few moments, without any show of haste. She obeyed, but when he arose the King saw the same man leaning upon the wheel of the other side of the carriage and examining him closely. The man was holding a crown in his hand, and seemed to be comparing the two profiles, but he said nothing.

The King said, " We are recognised. Shall we be betrayed? It is in God's hands."

However, the horses were put in. The man remained leaning on the wheel in profound silence, and did not leave it until the moment that the carriage started. When they had left the post-house of Sainte Menehould, the poor fugitives thought they had escaped this new danger, and the King said that they would have to try and discover that man and reward him, for he had certainly recognised them, and that he himself would know the man again among a thousand. Unfortunately, he was destined to see him again.

What were the thoughts in the mind of this Drouet, for it was he? Was it pity or hesitation, or did he fear that he could not raise people enough in so small a hamlet as Sainte Menehould? I do not know, but shortly afterwards he got on horseback and took the road to Clermont, where he was post-master, and where he expected to be in front of the travellers.

He had nearly arrived, and was astonished that he had

not yet caught up the carriage, when he met the postillions coming back.

" Is the carriage far ahead? " he cried.

" We have not seen any carriage."

" What! " and he described it.

" It is not on this road, but I saw from the hill a coach on the road to Varennes, which is perhaps the one you mean."

Drouet had no doubt of it. In fact, at the junction of the road to Clermont and the road to Varennes the guardsmen had forced the postillions to follow the latter. They had offered some slight objection, on the ground that the stage was longer, and that they should have given notice at the post-house; but they had proceeded and made such good time that Drouet had had trouble in overtaking them.

We may imagine the alarm of the travellers when they recognised on this foaming horse the man whom they had seen at the wheel. He vigorously reproached the postillions for driving so fast over so long a stage, ordered them to slacken their pace, and threatened to report them to the post-master at Sainte Menehould. It was impossible to urge on the postillions, and besides, the travellers hoped they might still avoid the danger.

A relay prepared by M. de Bouillé was to be in readiness before the entry of Varennes. It was necessary to cross the bridge of the exit from the little town, but only to cross, and as there was an escort with the carriage horses, they did not expect to meet with any obstacle. Day was failing; the relay which was to have been at the bottom of the hill of Varennes was not there. They expected to find it at the top, but there again was no sign of it. The life-guardsman knocked at the window.

" What are we to do? "

" Go on," was the reply.

They reached the post-house. Night had fallen, and they were told that there were no horses in the stable. The postillions refused to start upon another stage until they had rested their horses. While they were arguing, the Queen saw the dragoons walk by, carrying their saddles. She hoped that the detachment and the relay were about to appear, but the carriage horses were placed at one end of the town, the cavalry horses at the other, and the bridge was between them.

The travellers were urged to leave the carriage and rest the children while the postillions were watering their horses. They feared that a repetition of their first refusal might arouse suspicion, and went into the house, but they had already been recognised and denounced. A cart was overturned on the bridge, cutting off communication with the cavalry escort, and the alarm bell was rung; the Duc de Choiseul had lost his way in the cross roads, and trusted to the arrangement proposed at Varennes; when he arrived the only means of saving the King was to place him and his family upon the cavalry horses and to start off along the road to a ford. This manœuvre could only be executed by force and the discharge of several shots. M. de Choiseul urged this procedure, but the King refused, and said that he would never consent to shed a drop of French blood. The Queen did not insist, but her narrative made it clear that she would have adopted the proposal of M. de Choiseul. In any case, she told my father that when the relay was missing she had abandoned hope and had understood that they were lost.

Unfortunately, the Comte de Bouillé had entrusted the important post of Varennes to his son, Comte Louis de Bouillé. His behaviour was marked by an unexampled want of thought and care. Had it not been for the paternal weakness of M. de Bouillé, who entrusted this mission to a youth of twenty, the Revolution would probably have run another course, and would perhaps have ended in nothing more than some useful improvements in the French constitution.

This Drouet, whom the poor King had proposed to reward, now proceeded to domineer over the despairing family, which soon became the object of insult. The only additional detail that I remember is the fact that the Queen praised the behaviour of Barnave during the miseries of the return, especially in contrast to that of M. de Latour Maubourg.

I have said that the King was strongly opposed to the steps which the Comte d'Artois was taking in his name. This opposition did not decrease after the Prince had rejoined his brother, and the princes at the Tuileries were in entire discord with the leaders at Coblentz.

The Queen, with the King's approval, maintained a correspondence, conducted chiefly with the Baron de Breteuil, then at Brussels, its principal object being to prevent foreign governments from joining the intrigues of the princes. This action was concealed from Madame Élisabeth, who inclined to the opinions of her brothers, and consequently confidence was by no means complete, even within this melancholy castle.

My father was the medium through whom the correspondence of the Queen with the Baron was maintained. He carried her letters to the house of M. de Mercy. Sometimes, when they feared to arouse attention by the frequency of these visits, Bermont came to take them from the Queen. My father had certain evidence that a sum of 60,000 francs had been offered him as the price of these papers. If he had handed over one of these letters from the Queen, which he knew he was carrying, he would have been able to sell it at a very high price.

The position of the royal family became more and more intolerable from day to day. At length the King consented to recognise the Constitution and to take the oath of fidelity. Those who accuse him of weakness should put themselves in his position before condemning him. My father never condemned him, but he strongly disapproved of the plan by which the King was to raise every possible obstacle to the Constitution he had just accepted.

"Since you have sworn to it, Sire," he said, "you should follow it frankly and loyally, and carry out its provisions as far as you can."

"It is unworkable."

"Well, then, it will collapse; but this should not occur through any fault of yours."

After this change in the situation, my father strongly objected to the Queen's correspondence with Brussels. She pretended to listen and agree to this advice, but she merely concealed her designs and found another agent; though she showed no annoyance with my father, and did not withdraw her confidence on other points.

These unfortunate rulers did not wish to follow any-one's advice in its entirety, though they received and partially agreed to all the advice that was given them. The result was an inconsistency of conduct which their enemies were easily able to interpret as treachery, and their so-called friends on the banks of the Rhine as cow-ardice, for it must not be forgotten that Coblentz was almost as dangerous and as hostile to Louis XVI. as the Jacobin Club.

The commission which my father would have fulfilled, had the King's flight been successful, was made null and void by the arrest at Varennes. He asked his majesty's permission to resign his St. Petersburg post. In his opinion, as the King had accepted the Constitution, he ought to be served only by those known as patriots, by people who were reputed to be devoted to the Constitution and supported it in reality. My father was a declared aristocrat, notwithstanding the moderation of his opinions; he could be nothing more than an encumbrance, and he announced his intention of rejoining my mother in Rome.

The King gave him permission, and added that when honest men and faithful subjects came back to their own, he would know where to find him again. He thanked him for not proposing to go to Coblentz. The Queen especially insisted upon his departure for Italy.

"You are one of us, M. d'Osmond, and we wish to retain your services."

The King's common sense had realised the dangerous nature of the exiled party organised in Germany, and my father shared these opinions too strongly to feel drawn in that direction. In any case, he would probably have met with a bad reception, for all who had risked their lives in the King's service were regarded with much disapprobation by his brothers the princes, especially by the Comte d'Artois, who was taking the lead at that moment. The more cautious character of the Prince restrained him from action as long as the King was alive.

My father spent some further time in Paris. In his last interview with the King, the monarch awarded him a pension of 12,000 francs from his private purse.

"I am not very rich," he said, "but on the other hand, you are not grasping. We shall perhaps meet again at a time when I can make better use of your zeal, and reward it more worthily."

My mother's health, which was becoming more alarming, eventually decided my father to tear himself from the Tuileries, where he did not wish to stay, and whence he could not easily depart.   He reached Rome in the spring of 1792.

The gloom of these political events was deepened by the loss of his brother, the Abbé d'Osmond, a most promising young man.   He had gone to St. Domingo in 1790, with the idea of securing our estates and preparing a refuge for our family if France became uninhabitable. At the outbreak of the insurrection in St. Domingo he behaved most nobly, but he fell into the hands of the negroes, and was brutally massacred.   My father had retained the Vicomte d'Osmond at the head of the regiment of Neustria, which he was commanding in Strasburg, as long as he remained in France.   But after his departure, the Vicomte, accompanied by all the officers of his regiment, went to rejoin the army of the princes.

CHAPTER V

I SHALL say but little of our stay in Italy. My recollections of it are too vague; I merely remember hearing stories of the quarrels in the little court of the princesses, which even then seemed to me extremely ridiculous. The friction between the ladies of honour had gone so far as to divide the few Frenchmen then in Rome into two parties. The Narbonne party was opposed to the Chastellux party, and the one cordially hated the other.

The attitude of my parents upon this question was settled beforehand by my mother's position with reference to Madame Adélaide: the Chastellux party admitted her rights, and they remained on good terms. The Chastellux children were intimate with myself, as also was Louise de Narbonne, the granddaughter of the Duchess. To avoid jealousy, however, we were all excluded from the presence of the Princess. I did not see Madame Adélaide more than once or twice during my stay at Rome; the fact was that I had passed the age when a child is a plaything. In spite of the domestic quarrels which they were obliged to witness, and under which they suffered, no intrigue was able to dissociate the two old princesses. They died a few days after one another, and the affection which united them had been life-long. Madame Victoire had a great admiration for her sister, which the latter's affection returned.

My mother's feeble health confined her to the house. Every evening a number of people called, the most regular visitors being the prelates Caraffa, Albani, Consalvi, and the Abbé Maury, who was then the coryphæus of the Royalist party. These were all clever and distinguished men, and I learnt to take an interest in their conversation. They spoilt me greatly, especially the Abbé Maury and Consalvi.

The Abbé Maury was exposed to the full force of Roman hatred and intrigue, which aimed at depriving him of the purple to which he was destined by the favour of Pope Pius VI.; his want of tact continually gave openings to his enemies, and his position was correspondingly disagreeable. He used to relate his troubles to my mother, who consoled and encouraged him, while reproaching him at the same time. The Pope appointed him Archbishop of Nicea, and sent him to the coronation of the Emperor Leopold[1] as papal nuncio, thus assuring him of the cardinal's hat.

On his return he confirmed me, and gave me on that occasion a beautiful topaz, which had been presented to him together with several other precious stones by the Emperor. In view of the fabulous and unexampled avarice which he afterwards displayed, I cannot understand how he was able to part with this jewel. Possibly the passion had not reached that pitch at which we afterwards saw it.

[1] Second son of Maria Theresa, Emperor from 1790 to 1792, after the death of his eldest brother, Joseph II.

Monseigneur Consalvi was a man of European reputation, and I shall speak of him later.

The Cardinal of York, the last scion of the unhappy Stuarts, lived in Rome. My mother was the granddaughter of his father's tutor, and he therefore received her with extreme kindness.

He made her promise to visit him at Frascati in the summer, and insisted that she and my father should dine with him frequently during the winter.

He was to be found in a large, ill-furnished palace, with no fire anywhere, a cowl over his head, two greatcoats upon his body, his feet on a foot-warmer, and his hands in a muff. His guests would have been glad to adopt the same costume, for the house was as cold as ice. As a special compliment to my mother, he had a few pieces of wood lighted in the fourth drawing-room, and insisted that he felt stifled in consequence, even at that distance. It must be observed that charcoal was burning beneath his feet. But some royal state must be observed, were it only an eccentricity of this kind. His servants addressed him as your majesty; his guests avoided the use of any title, a custom facilitated by the use of the third person in Italian.

He spoke nothing but Italian and a little English, and the latter so badly that it was difficult to understand him, though if misunderstood he was extremely angry.

His affection was concentrated upon Consalvi, whom he treated as a son; he could not do for a moment without Ercole, as he continually called him, and poor Ercole was often greatly bored in consequence.

He was at that time very angry with his sister-in-law, the Countess of Albani, who had accepted a post at the court of London; he referred to her action in the finest style of offended royal dignity. Here we have another instance of the fact that in the time of revolution it is difficult to foretell to what straits we may be reduced. At this time the Cardinal thought in all good faith that he would rather die than accept an English pension, and yet he afterwards asked to be placed on the list.

I remember an incident which made some stir in Rome. Mr. Wilbraham Bootle, a young Englishman, handsome, clever, of high social position, and immensely rich, fell in love with a Miss Taylor, who could bring her husband nothing but her pretty face. Mr. Wilbraham Bootle, however, aspired to this position, and easily obtained her consent. The marriage day had been fixed. At a great dinner at Lord Camelford's the conversation turned upon an ascent that had been made in the morning to the cross upon the dome of St. Peter's. To reach the cross, it was necessary to pass outside the ball. Mr. Wilbraham Bootle said that he did not possess a steady head, would never be able to reach the cross, and that nothing in the world would induce him to try.

" Nothing in the world ? " said Miss Taylor.

" Nothing, I assure you."

" What, not even if I were to ask you ? "

" You would not ask me to do a thing for which I frankly admit my dislike."

" Excuse me, I do ask you, I beg of you, and if necessary I insist."

Mr. Wilbraham Bootle attempted to laugh the matter off, but Miss Taylor insisted, notwithstanding the interference of Lord Camelford.

The whole company met two days following at St. Peter's, to watch the performance of the task imposed upon the young man.

He performed his trial with great coolness, and when he came down the triumphant beauty came towards him with outstretched hand; he took her hand, kissed it, and said: "Miss Taylor, I have obeyed the whim of a charming girl. Permit me now in return to give you a piece of advice: if you wish to keep your power, never misuse it. I wish you all prosperity, and now good-bye."

His post-chaise was waiting for him in St. Peter's Square; he got in, and left Rome. Miss Taylor had time enough to regret her foolish obstinacy. When I saw her ten years later she was still unmarried, and what has since become of her I cannot say.

I often saw Mme. Lebrun,[1] or rather her daughter, who was one of my playmates. Mme. Lebrun was an excellent person, still pretty, somewhat tactless, at all times of remarkable talent and abounding in all those little affectations which she could claim the right to practise as an artist and a pretty woman. If the term *petite maîtresse* enjoyed a better reputation, it might well be applicable to her.

Cardinal Carandini, the uncle of Consalvi, owned a little house at Albano, which he lent to my mother, and in which we spent two summers. My recollections of this delightful country are but vague, though I very well remember the pleasure with which I used to ride on the gardener's donkey.

Towards the outset of 1792 Sir John Legard arrived at Rome with his wife, who had been a Miss Aston and was a cousin german of my mother. This family relationship led to great intimacy. The money which my parents had brought from France was running low, and only one quarter of the pension granted by the King had been paid. Sir John asked my parents to accompany him to Naples and then to return with him to his Yorkshire estate, where he offered them the most friendly and gen-

Mme. Vigée Lebrun, painter, born in 1755, died in 1842.

erous hospitality. My parents agreed to spend some time with him at Naples, but would not further pledge themselves, and Sir John did not insist.

At Naples we stayed ten months. My mother was very kindly received by the Queen,[1] who enjoyed her society and made her give a full account of the French court and of the beginning of the Revolution, in which she was interested both as Queen and sister.

I was introduced to her daughters, the princesses, and there began my connection, if I may use the term, with Princess Amelia, afterwards Queen of France. We talked French and English, and read together; I used to go and spend the day with her at Portici and at Caserta. She preferred me to all her other playmates. I was less intimate with her sisters, although we were together almost as often. Next to the Princess Amelia, I was especially fond of Antoinette, afterwards Princess of the Asturias. As for Christina, who became Queen of Sardinia, we excluded her from all our games, in which she would have been glad to take a part, although she was older than we.

The two eldest princesses, the Empress and the Grand Duchess of Toscana, were married at this time.

Many foreigners were in Naples at that time, and I believe that society was very lively, though my share in these gaieties was naturally but small. I was sometimes taken to the opera. I was already a good musician, and began to develop a tolerable voice, about which Cimarosa was enthusiastic. He did not give lessons, but he often came to hear me sing, and chose a master for me.

The time for leaving Naples approached. Sir John

[1] Marie Caroline, daughter of the Emperor of Austria, Francis I., and the Empress Maria Theresa, wife of Ferdinand IV., King of Naples; born 1752, died 1814.

Legard again invited my parents to accompany him to England. It was easier to communicate from that country with St. Domingo, from which some help was expected. My father had stored all his ambassadorial furniture in Holland, and of this some use might be made. Finally, and as a last resource, Sir John Legard placed his house at our disposal with all possible tact. During the six months we had spent at Naples he had overwhelmed my parents with marks of friendship. If we stayed in Italy, we should become dependent on the princesses, who were beginning to find their circumstances straitened, while those about them would not welcome a new family to their circle.

These reflections induced my parents to accept the pressing offer of Sir John, after securing the consent of Madame Adélaide. She agreed to their departure, adding that if they were unable to live in England, she was ready to share her last piece of bread with them.[1]

The Queen of Naples attempted to keep my mother there; she even offered her a small salary, but the family resources then held out some hope. The Queen, moreover, was reputed to be capricious, and Lady Hamilton was coming into favour. This Lady Hamilton became so notorious that I think a few words should be devoted to her.

Mr. Greville happened to enter his kitchen one day, and saw a young girl by the fireside with one foot bare, as she was mending the stocking of black wool which had covered it. Her angelic beauty attracted his notice, and he discovered that she was a sister of his groom. He found no difficulty in bringing her upstairs and in-

[1] See the autograph letters of Madame Adélaide to the Marchioness d'Osmond among the documents in the Appendix.

stalling her in his drawing-room. He lived with her for some time, and had her taught to read and write.

The young man's affairs being completely involved, he found himself obliged to leave London very suddenly. At that moment his uncle, Sir William Hamilton, the English Minister at Naples, happened to be at home on leave. His nephew informed him that his chief vexation was the necessity of abandoning a beautiful young girl who was in his house, and who was likely to be turned into the street. Sir William promised to look into the matter.

As a matter of fact, he went to look for her at the moment when the bailiffs were turning her out of Mr. Greville's house, and soon fell desperately in love with her. He took her with him to Italy. What their connection was I cannot say, but at the end of some years he married her. Previously he had treated her with that paternal affection which was natural to his age, and which allowed him to introduce her to Italian society, which is less strict than ours upon these matters.

The girl, who was as beautiful as an angel, though she had never been able to learn to read or write with any fluency, had great artistic talent. She turned to full account the advantages offered by her stay in Italy and by the taste of Sir William Hamilton. She became a good musician, and developed a unique talent which may seem foolish in description, but which enchanted all spectators and drove artists to despair. I refer to what were known as the attitudes of Lady Hamilton.

In conformity with her husband's taste, she was generally dressed in a white tunic, with a belt round her waist, her hair down her back or turned up by a comb, but dressed in no special way. When she consented to give a performance, she would provide herself with two or three cashmere shawls, an urn, a scent-box, a lyre, and a tambourine. With these few properties, and her classical costume, she took up her position in the middle of a room. She threw a shawl over her head which reached the ground and covered her entirely, and thus hidden, draped herself with the other shawls. Then she suddenly raised the covering, either throwing it off entirely or half raising it, and making it form part of the drapery of the model which she represented. But she always appeared as a statue of most admirable design.

I have heard artists say that if a perfect reproduction had been possible, art would have found nothing to change in her. She often varied her attitude and her expression, " from grave to gay, from trivial to severe," before dropping the shawl which concluded that part of the performance.

I have sometimes acted with her as a subordinate figure to form a group. She used to place me in the proper position, and arrange my draperies before raising the shawl, which served as a curtain enveloping us both. My fair hair contrasted with her magnificent black hair, to which many of her effects were due.

One day she placed me on my knees before an urn, with my hands together in the attitude of prayer. Leaning over me, she seemed lost in grief, and both of us had our hair dishevelled. Suddenly rising and moving backward a little, she grasped me by the hair with a movement so sudden that I turned round in surprise and almost in fright, which brought me precisely into the spirit of my part, for she was brandishing a dagger. The passionate applause of the artists who were looking on resounded with exclamations of " Brava, Medea! " Then drawing me to her and clasping me to her breast as though she were fighting to preserve me from the anger of Heaven, she evoked loud cries of "Viva, la Niobe!"

She took her inspiration from the antique statues, and without making any servile copy of them, recalled them to the poetical imagination of the Italians by improvised gesture. Others have tried to imitate Lady Hamilton's talent, but I doubt if any one has succeeded. It is a business in which there is but a step from the sublime to the ridiculous. Moreover, to equal her success, the actor must first be of faultless beauty from head to foot, and such perfection is rare.

Apart from this artistic instinct, Lady Hamilton was entirely vulgar and common. When she exchanged her classical tunic for ordinary dress she lost all distinction. Her conversation showed no interest and little intelligence. Yet she must have had some power of intrigue to reinforce her incomparable beauty, for she completely dominated any one whom she wished to govern. There was first her old husband, whom she overwhelmed with ridicule; then the Queen of Naples, whom she plundered and disgraced; and finally Lord Nelson, who tarnished his glory under the influence of this woman at a time when she had become prodigiously fat and had lost her beauty.

In spite of all that she had extracted from the Queen of Naples and from Sir William Hamilton, she died at length in distress and poverty as well as in disgrace. Upon the whole, she was a bad woman, and had a low mind within a magnificent form.

The Queen of Naples had consented with great reluctance to receive her, and Sir William had used my mother's good offices to secure this favour. But she speedily acquired complete domination over the Queen's mind. There is no doubt that the cruel vengeance executed at Naples in the name of the Queen and of Lord Nelson was instigated, and it may be said commanded, by Lady Hamilton. She persuaded them severally that each of them required this vengeance. My mother was the more grieved, as she was much attached to Queen Caroline, with whom she remained in constant correspondence, and to whom she eventually owed a large debt of obligation.[1]

I have already spoken on several occasions of Bermont, my father's *valet de chambre*. When our departure for England had been decided, my father wished to find him a place in the service of General Acton, at Naples. It would have suited him to perfection, but he declined to hear of it. Some years previously he had married a woman who had been my nurse and became my brothers' nurse, when I had been placed in the care of an Englishwoman. He had several children, who had been left in France. He told my father that he would not leave us.

" But, my poor Bermont, I cannot keep a *valet de chambre*."

" That is true; but you will require a muleteer. You will have to buy mules to travel, and you must have some one to look after them and to drive them, and that some one will be myself."

My father, deeply touched by this devotion, could not but accept it. The mules were bought by Bermont with care and discrimination. He drove them from the box seat, and a young negro, who had been brought as a child from my father's estates, acted as postillion to a coach occupied by my father, my mother, their two children, Bermont's wife, and a young negress in my service, of whom I shall have to speak later.

[1] See the letters from the Queen of Naples to the Marchioness d'Osmond in the Appendix.

My father's resources were not entirely exhausted, and it had been decided that he should travel with Sir John Legard, dividing the expenses; from that moment the latter proceeded to rack his brains upon every occasion to reduce expenses to their lowest point. Hence the idea of buying mules, obstinate and hateful animals, which were a constant source of trouble, while the journey was rendered unbearable and sometimes dangerous by constant cheese-paring.

For instance, Sir John would not have the carriages mounted upon runners, or engage guides and local horses for the passage over the Saint Gothard, in which we were nearly lost. Mounted on a little Neapolitan mule, which had never been ridden, and had never seen the snow, I crossed the mountain, led by my father, who plunged into the snow up to his knees at every step through a dreadful storm. I remember that my tears froze on my face. I said nothing, lest I should increase the anxiety which I saw depicted on my father's face.

" Hold your bridle, child."

" I cannot hold it any longer, papa."

In fact, my skin gloves had been wet and then frozen, and had frozen my fingers, which had to be rubbed with snow. My father wrapped them up in a man's coat which he had, and we continued our route. When we reached the hospice the weather had cleared up a little. Our luggage had been sent on and was at Urseren, so that we could not change our drenched clothes. My father found Sir John at the door talking with a monk, who was urging him to stay.

" What is your opinion, Marquis? "

" Well," said my father, " as the wine is drawn, we shall have to drink it."

" Certainly, gentlemen," replied the monk with frankness; " there are two bottles on the table now, and we have more if that is not enough."

This reply made me laugh and distracted my attention from my sufferings. In early youth there is a certain elasticity which cheerfulness can always restore. Notwithstanding the two bottles, we continued our journey. The storm did not extend to this side of the mountain. My father talked to me, and explained the reason of the avalanches which we saw falling, and the descent seemed to me as pleasant as the ascent had been painful.

We spent some days at Lausanne and then at Constance, where the old Bishop of Cominges had established himself. I caught sight of Mademoiselle in the distance.[1] She had just been taken from Mme. de Genlis. She saw no one, and was regarded with some repulsion by the émigré society established at Constance. We then went down the Rhine by boat, and reached Rotterdam. My father went to The Hague to fetch the boxes which had been stored there. We took ship, reached Harwich, and started directly for Yorkshire.

[1] The Princess Adélaide d'Orléans, born in 1777, daughter of the Duke Philippe Joseph.

CHAPTER VI

IT is time to describe our hosts in greater detail. The
character of Sir John Legard would be an admirable subject for a novel.

He was a combination of the most discordant elements.
Endowed with a brilliant intellect, the most delicate taste,
the most lively imagination, with a supreme desire for intellectual intercourse, he had spent the whole of his youth
in the country society of Yorkshire with associates entirely vulgar. He had there acquired habits of domestic
tyranny, of which his wife was the chief victim, and upon
her he visited his dislike for a mode of life for which she
was anything but to blame.

Mrs. Aston, the mother of two daughters who were
poor, and of a son who was very rich, according to the
custom of the country, was a very lively young widow at
the time when Sir John Legard, an officer in the Guards,
began to pay attention to her eldest daughter. He had
almost forgotten her when he learnt that the younger
daughter was to marry Mr. Hedges, and that the elder
regarded herself as engaged to him.

An explanation took place, in which he pointed out to

her that his means obliged him to live entirely upon his estate, and that he did not wish to ask so great a sacrifice of a girl brought up in the highest London society. My poor cousin did not understand this language, and accepted a hand thus reluctantly offered.

Sir John left the army and settled in Yorkshire. This retirement would perhaps have been less austere if Mrs. Hedges had not forthwith begun a course of action so outrageous as to be a general scandal. Lady Legard was punished for her sister's faults by the increasing severity of her husband. She was a most excellent woman, but absolutely unfitted to share the retirement of a distinguished man; it was not that she was a fool, but she was unable to regard life except in its most material aspects.

Her sole responsibility in the household was confined to ordering the dinner, and this task occupied her a considerable portion of the morning of every day. Once a week for a stated period of time, neither more nor less, she wrote her letters. When her watch marked the hour she would stop in the middle of a page, resume her spinning-wheel, and leave the letter for a week. Another hour was appointed for a walk, consisting of a certain number of turns in the same path. She measured the amount of hemming that she ought to accomplish in a given time, and attached the utmost importance to the completion of her task at the proper moment. Her husband called her Lady Clock, and he was right.

Yet a woman of this character was fond of pleasure, society, and especially of dress. Whenever she found the least opportunity of satisfying these tastes, she made the very most of it. She would never have dared to ask for a horse to go for a ride, much less to pay a call, but if her husband said to her in a solemn voice, " My lady, it would be advisable for you to call at such and such a house," her heart would leap for joy. " Certainly, Sir John, most certainly," and off she went to get out her finery.

If a dinner was in prospect and it was possible for her to wear her three diamond pins, her only jewels, her satisfaction was complete. Her impressions of twenty years before revived, and she forgot the twenty years of marital severity which had extinguished them.

He was always inconsiderate, and often severe. She was invariably submissive, but never seemed to feel his behaviour in the smallest degree. I am sure that if she had felt it or had shown any sensitiveness, her husband would have had too much good feeling to persist in a line of conduct which, even with all the excuse there was for him, was highly reprehensible.

Sir John Legard, having no children, and thus having no object on which to exert his affection or his severity, in view of the fact that his wife was perfectly impassive, surrounded himself with the daughters of his relatives, of whom I formed one, though much younger than they.

We were dreadfully afraid of him, and yet we all adored him. A look less severe than usual was a reward which we appreciated as though it had been a triumph. He usually said good-night to us, and sometimes added my name, and on one or two occasions of high importance he would say, " Good-night, my love," at which I felt inexpressible joy.

We knew perfectly well that nothing escaped him, and that there was not a good thought in our hearts which he did not divine and remember. The fact is, that his continual habit of sitting in judgment on the human race often led him into mistakes, but he was persuaded of his own justice, and this fact we realised and remembered to his credit. Justice is a great means to the acquirement of influence over youth.

I was not one of his favourites; he thought me proud. We have since agreed that it was only reserve; as I was placed in a position in which I considered that his authority over me might be exercised to my parents' dislike, I kept myself well in hand, and gave no opening for reproaches, though I fully appreciated his approval. He took a pinch of snuff every day after dinner. One day some one asked him for a pinch.

" I have forgotten my snuff-box," he said.

One of my playmates offered to fetch it.

·   " Thank you; Adèle has gone."

At that moment I returned, bringing the snuff-box. I had seen him looking for it a moment before.

" Ah, you are right, Sir John," said Lady Legard; " you knew, then, that Adèle had gone? "

" Yes, I knew."

These words, " I knew," remained graven in my memory as one of the most flattering speeches ever addressed to me. What a powerful educational instrument would such influence be if it were not abused. He was a martyr to the gout, especially during the winter, when he was confined to an arm-chair and bore his sufferings with admirable courage. When he was able to move his hands he manœuvred his arm-chair very cleverly all round the house, but he was often reduced to call for help, even to turn the pages of his book, and there was much rivalry among us to perform this service. Sometimes, to show his gratitude, he read aloud to us. He preferred Shakespeare, which he delivered admirably, and accompanied his reading with interesting comments. It is to him that I owe my taste for English literature and such little knowledge of it as I have acquired.

In the summer he recovered his health, and his skill and agility were incredible. In his youth he had been very

handsome, but he had grown very fat, and seemed older
than his years, at any rate to my eyes. He was passionately fond of music. I had a fine voice, but he would
never have asked me to sing for fear of making me self-
conscious. Sometimes he came into the room where I
was practising, on some pretext or other, and would say,
" Go on, child." I was careful to choose the songs which
he preferred, and when I saw that his book remained before him unread, or his paper entirely blank, I felt a
delight altogether free from that vanity with which he
feared to inspire me.

He belonged to the party of Pitt rather than to the Tory
faction, and was a perfect representative of the independent country gentleman. He had no great love for the
nobility, despised the fashionable world, and detested upstarts. He was passionately attached to his country, and
entertained all the prejudices and claims of the English
as to their supremacy over all other nations. He loved the
King because he was the King of England, and the Church
because it realised his rigid morality, not because he had
any special Royalist or religious tendencies.

For two years I drank every day at dessert a half glass
of port wine to this toast, " Old England for ever, the
King and constitution, and our glorious revolution."
This latter phrase probably dated from the moment when
the Legard family had abandoned its Jacobite principles.

Their ancestors had been prominent figures in the Cavalier party; this I was the more inclined to believe, as Sir
John had a very old maiden aunt who would never dine
with him because of this toast. She lived in the little town
of Beverley in the neighbourhood, and thought much of
her nephew as head of the family, although she had two
great grounds of complaint against him, apart from this
toast. One was the fact that he had given up residence

in the manor house, which was too large for his means
and was falling to disrepair, and the other that he did not
retain the guttural " g " in pronouncing her name, which
she insisted was of Norman origin, from Lagarde. She
was always careful to use this pronunciation.

She made much of me, and one fine day we discovered
that this was because of my Norman blood. Sir John inflicted a further vexation upon her; not content with leaving the hall for a smaller house, he left her county.

In spite of their devoted love for their country, the English are by no means rooted to their neighbourhood, if one
may use the term. They show no regret at leaving the
place which their parents or they themselves have inhabited for years, and in moving to a residence more in harmony with their immediate tastes, whether these be devoted to hunting, fishing, horse-racing, boat-racing, agriculture, or any other whim which they call a pursuit, and
which absorbs them as long as it lasts.

I knew a certain Mr. Brandling who left a fine castle
where he had been born and brought up, and a neighbourhood which he liked and where he was esteemed and respected, in order to set up house fifty miles away in the
middle of hideous country, merely because his grooms
could exercise his horses every morning upon a common
which provided a ten-mile stretch of turf, and spared the
horses any walking over the hard high-road. This advantage seemed to him a satisfactory reason for removing
his wife, of whom he was very fond, from the neighbourhood of her family and her life-long friends, while she
never regarded his decision as a hardship, or did any one
consider it eccentric or ill-judged. Unless I am mistaken,
these are characteristics which reveal the true nature of a
people.

During a stay of several months in Switzerland, Sir

John Legard had contracted a love for the Lake of Geneva and for excursions by water, which persuaded him that a lake was necessary to his existence. He bought some acres of ground upon the banks of Lake Windermere in Westmoreland, and resolved to build a house there. Meanwhile he hired a house in the neighbourhood, whither he transported his effects, and we followed him.

I should say that for two years this imperious and domineering character never uttered a word that could have hurt my father's feelings, but lived with him upon the most amiable terms. The truth was that he had a great affection for him, though he was almost as kind to my mother, whom he did not like nearly so well, as she often wounded his prejudices.

The deep generosity of his character outweighed his ill-temper, and his severity towards myself was merely the outcome of his system of education. In any case, up to a certain point he was successful, for when I left his hospitable house after the age of fourteen I did not consider that I entered the world with any special advantages.

During this period of retirement my father was occupied exclusively with my education. I worked regularly eight hours a day at the severest studies. I studied history, and was intensely interested in metaphysics. My father did not allow me to read alone, but only under his supervision. He would have been afraid to see false ideas growing in my young brain, if his wise reflections had not checked their development.

By way of compensation, perhaps, my father, who had a special taste for that study, added some books on political economy to my educational library, and these amused me considerably. I can remember the laughter of M. de Calonne, when he found me in London the next year, reading a volume of Smith's *Wealth of Nations* for pastime, and this was my first intimation that such tastes were not usual in girls of fifteen.

My mother, who was threatened by a weakness of the chest, was obliged to go to London for a consultation, and in consequence it was thought advisable to remain within reach of the doctors. Her family subscribed to meet the expense. Lady Harcourt, her friend, and Lady Clifford, her cousin, undertook this business. The Queen of Naples, with whom she had continued a correspondence, insisted that she should be within reach of medical advice, and sent her 300 louis, telling her that every year the Naples Ambassador would hand her that same amount.[1] Her relatives got together £500, with which it was possible to vegetate in London. My father returned to Westmoreland to fetch my brother and myself, who had remained there.

I cannot refrain from relating a circumstance which impressed me greatly. Sir John Legard was reduced to despair by the prospect of finding himself alone with his wife, and was even more ill-tempered than usual. This made me angry, for she was as kind to me as she could be to any one. One evening we were both in a little waggonette which he was driving. On the other side of the lake was a sunlight effect of such beauty that I was struck by it, and saw that Sir John's attention was also aroused. He was bursting with the desire to speak of it. At length he addressed Lady Legard, and looking at her with animated glance, he said enthusiastically,

" What a glorious sunset! "

" I should not be surprised if it rained to-morrow," she answered.

He turned round without saying a word, as if he had trodden on an electric eel. Child as I was, I understood

[1] See the correspondence of the Queen of Naples in the Appendix.

how ill matched this couple were, and from that moment my sympathy was much keener for the tyrant than for his victim.

My story now brings me to a change of character so extraordinary that I feel bound to relate it. Bermont, whom I last mentioned as an improvised muleteer, had received at Rome, from my father's ecclesiastical friends, a medal inscribed " To the faithful Bermont." Hardly had he reached England when he was seized, he said, with home-sickness. He altered visibly, and at length he warned my father that he could no longer restrain his anxiety for the fate of his children, and that he must go to France to see them. The death of Robespierre made this project possible. My father said to him:

" Go, then, my good fellow. You know how much I have left. Here is a quarter of it. You can come back to us when you have calmed your fears, unless you have found something better to do."

" Thank you, my lord; I do not want any money, I have all I need," and with this he started. Some years before the Revolution Bermont had won a sum of 1,000 crowns in a lottery, and this he had left with my father. He had received the interest up to date, which had been carefully added every quarter day to his wages. The account book dealing with this sum was in his hands. He carried it off, together with a few objects of value which were left to my father, and his action was not discovered for a long time.

When my father came to fetch us, he left my mother alone in London with our young negress. One evening she summoned her servant in vain. Search was made, and at length it was discovered that she had eloped with Bermont, who had come back from France on purpose to fetch her. He had fallen wildly in love with her, and had carried on this intrigue under the eyes of his wife without arousing her suspicion.

A short time afterwards, in London, two men came into the room where I was working by the side of my mother, who was lying on a sofa. My father was reading to us. These two men came to arrest him at the instance of Bermont; he was obliged to enter a cab, and they drove him off to prison. Our despair may be imagined. It was necessary to find bail; my mother, who had not left her long chair for three months, went to look for some one, and succeeded at the end of some hours. My father, however, spent the night in the police station.

Bermont sued for the thousand crowns, plus the interest and his wages, as well as the wages of his wife, from the time of our departure from France. These claims amounted to a considerable sum for poor *émigrés*. The account books which would have demonstrated the punctuality with which he had been paid were in his possession. The lawyers overcame my father's repugnance, and persuaded him to repudiate the debt *in toto*. To establish his claim to the thousand crowns Bermont's only evidence was the regular payment of the interest. This proof he was obliged to produce, and in consequence to abandon a considerable portion of his claim, and to admit his treachery; but for himself and others he had nothing more to lose. He behaved with an insolence and a harshness impossible to describe, and went so far as to appear at an interview with his former master, whose arrest he had procured, without showing the slightest embarrassment; a strange anomaly, impossible to explain.

For twenty-five years he had displayed devotion and fidelity in the most difficult positions. Was he then playing a part in the hope of a later reward, and did his natural character appear when these hopes were falsified? Or

was it that his character had suddenly changed, and that
vice had taken possession of a heart hitherto honourable?
I cannot decide. His poor wife was in despair, for she
had to lament his infidelity as well as his other crimes.

To conclude this affair, I may say that he took the
young negress to Dôle, where he began a series of un-
profitable speculations, and then abandoned her with two
children. She attempted to find work in order to support
them, but was unsuccessful, and one evening she took them
by the hand and left them at the foundling home. For
some days she was not visible. At length her house was
entered, and she was found to be dead of hunger, without
a farthing or a rag of clothing on which she could have
raised money.

She had never complained or asked for help from any
one. Only when leaving her children at the home she had
urged their claims most earnestly, and had cried out as
she went away, " They are not guilty, and God is just! "
This poor girl, who was as handsome as any one of her
colour could be, had a noble heart, and deserved a better
fate.

CHAPTER VII

As I shall constantly appear upon the scenes which I
have to relate, I must devote a few words to my position.
My education had been more thorough and serious than
most young girls of my age had received, my taste was
more developed, and I had a wide knowledge of the literature of three languages, which I spoke with equal facility; at the same time my ignorance of what is known as
the world was profound, and in it I felt myself extremely
ill at ease.

Though I was not beautiful, I had an attractive face.
My eyes were small, but very dark and bright, and contrasted with a complexion remarkable even in England.
My lips were red, my teeth excellent, while I had a great
mass of fair hair. My neck, shoulders, and figure were
correct, and my foot small; but these compensations did
not reassure my anxiety for the redness of my arms and
for hands which never recovered from their freezing during the passage of the St. Gothard, and caused me mortal
embarrassment.

I do not know when I discovered that I was pretty, but
it was not until some time after my arrival in London, and

was then only a vague opinion. The exclamations of the lower classes in the street were the first announcement of the fact.

" You are too pretty to be kept waiting," a carter said to me, pulling up his horses.

" You will never be like that pretty lady if you go on crying," said an apple-woman to her little daughter.

" God bless your pretty face, it's a sight for sore eyes," said a porter as he passed me, &c. In any case, it is precisely true that these compliments, like all others, never struck my attention except when they failed of their purpose. I cannot say if all women feel as I did, but I only noticed the more transitory of them. The first compliments to vanish are those of the passers by, then those heard as one crosses an ante-chamber, then those uttered in public places. As for drawing-room compliments, however inconsiderable one's elegance, one can live long enough on one's reputation.

To return to my youth. I was so excessively shy that I blushed whenever any one spoke to me or looked at me. This failing is not always regarded with due sympathy. It was a real suffering in my case, and reached such a pitch that I was often choked by tears aroused by nothing but an excessive embarrassment which was quite unjustifiable.

Such being my character, I readily resigned myself to remain by my mother's bedside, for she had eventually become almost a complete invalid. I rarely went out for a walk, and was then always accompanied by my father. My amusements were to play chess with an old doctor, or to listen to the conversation of men who came to see my father.

M. de Calonne was one of these; he conceived an affection for our household, and eventually spent his whole time there. I listened eagerly to his stories, which were as interesting as they were gracefully told, until I perceived that the same transaction was related by him in a wholly different manner upon different occasions, and soon discovered that he rarely told the truth. With the exclusiveness of early youth, I forthwith conceived a deep contempt for him, and hardly deigned to listen to him.

No one could have been more affectionate, or better company; more frivolous, or a greater liar. His talent and capacity were infinite, and were only equalled by his mistakes and the foolishness of his actions. Whenever it was possible to go astray, he would listen neither to representations nor advice, but would rush onwards, head foremost. As soon, however, as his errors had been committed, even before he experienced the disagreeable consequences, he foresaw the results, accused and condemned himself, and abandoned the line of conduct he had chosen with a readiness only comparable to his previous obstinacy.

At the time of which I speak, he had quarrelled with everybody, even with the Duc d'Artois, for whom he had ruined himself; he was head over ears in debt, and living under the protection of the Spanish Embassy, to which he had attached himself to avoid arrest; but his gaiety and his spirits were as undiminished as if he had been in the pleasantest situation possible.

At this point I am reminded of a small affair which will give some idea of the greed of English lawyers. A list was posted on the town hall of the people who were immune from arrest for debt, as being attached to different embassies. Spain was then embroiled with England. The Ambassador had taken his departure, and though the list remained in position, it might be removed at any moment. M. de Calonne often went down to the city to make certain that it was there. One day he met a law-

yer, a man of position, whom he had sometimes met in
society.

" What are you doing in this remote district? "

M. de Calonne explained.

" Do not trouble to come again. I am obliged to pass
through this room every day to get to the law courts, and
I will undertake to look, and warn you if any change
should be made."   •

M. de Calonne was profuse in his thanks, and thought
no more of the matter. Months went by, and the question
had ceased to give him any uneasiness. He had some
small legal business, for which he employed his obliging
friend. When he received the lawyer's bill he found:
" Item. To inquiry whether the name of M. de Calonne
was retained on the list of the Spanish Embassy . . . 15s.
Item," &c. The sum amounted to £200. M. de Calonne
was furious, but he had to pay, or rather was obliged to
add that sum to the total of his other debts.

I never entered the society of the *émigrés*, but I saw
something of it, and gathered recollections which are difficult to co-ordinate by reason of their contradictory nature. Actions highly praiseworthy and even moving could
be related of persons whose carelessness, foolishness, and
villainy were revolting.

Women of the highest rank worked for ten hours a day
to get bread for their children ; in the evening they dressed
in their best, met together, sang, danced, and enjoyed
themselves for half the night. This was the fair side of
the picture ; the unfortunate side was the fact that they
slandered one another, told falsehoods about their work,
and complained if one was more successful in her business
than another, in the style of ordinary work-women. This
mixture of ancient society claims and new-born petty malignities was distressing.

I have seen the Duchesse de FitzJames, who lived in a house on the outskirts of London and preserved her ancient state, invite all her acquaintances to dinner. It was understood that each guest should put three shillings under a cup upon the mantelpiece as he left the table. Not only were the shillings counted when the company had gone, but if among the guests any one was thought to be in easy circumstances, he was considered mean if he did not put down half a guinea instead of three shillings, and the Duchesse pronounced her opinion on the matter with considerable acerbity. None the less, a kind of luxury reigned in these houses.

I have seen Mme. de Léon and the whole of this society make up very expensive parties, to which they went in full dress on the top of an omnibus, to the great scandal of the English middle classes, who would not have ridden in that position. These ladies were constant visitors to the pit of the opera, which was chiefly occupied by females, among whom they were not greatly conspicuous by their behaviour.

Morals were even looser than before the Revolution, and those forms which gave a veneer of politeness to immorality were non-existent. The Comte Louis de Bouillé came into a drawing-room intoxicated, sat down near the Duchesse de Montmorency, drew the Duchesse de Châtillon to the other side of him, and observed to a man who advised him to withdraw, " Well, what are you objecting to? I am on my own property," and he laid a hand on each lady.

Nor was M. de Bouillé an isolated instance. There were a large number of dual establishments which had never enjoyed the blessing of the Church. Reduced means, the necessity of joining incomes in order to live, were the motives in some cases and the pretext in others.

Moreover, everything was pardoned, provided that the offender was "well-intentioned." Society was wholly tolerant upon every point but this. These are cases which I have seen, but they are not representative of the main body of the *émigrés*. These, as a whole, led an irreproachable life; such, indeed, their lives must have been, for it was their prolonged stay in England that originally changed English opinion in favour of the French nationality. As for political opinions, they were everywhere as irrational as possible, and those of the *émigrés* who led the most austere lives were the most ridiculous in this respect. Any one who hired rooms for more than a month was regarded with disapprobation; it was better to take them only by the week, for at any moment the tenants might be recalled to France by the counter-revolution.

My father had taken our little house in Brompton on a lease of three years, and this act would have injured his reputation, if he had had anything to lose. But his disapproval of the army of emigration, and in particular his well-known attachment to King Louis XVI. and the Queen, and his fidelity to their memory, were crimes which the *émigrés* could no more pardon than the sagacity with which he judged their immediate extravagances.

I often heard him talk of these things with his brother, the Bishop of Cominges, to whom the former Bishop of Cominges had resigned his see in 1785, and both deplored the blindness of the party to which circumstances forced them to belong.

It would be unjust, in speaking of our life in exile, to pass over in silence the behaviour of the clergy. Their attitude secured the esteem and veneration of the English people, little as they were predisposed to tolerate Popish priests. Every middle-class family eventually had a French *abbé* of its special choice, who taught his language to the children, and often helped the parents in their work.

Living together in societies, some of these good people started small businesses, which helped them to live and to support the oldest and the weakest. In spite of their possible desire to make converts, they were prudent enough to avoid raising any disturbance in this respect, and I cannot remember a single complaint of this nature against any priest, throughout the period of our exile.

This conduct secured for them a veneration, the consequences of which were often touching. Certain of them, for instance, who undertook the marketing for their little colonies, would go to Billingsgate on Fridays, shillings in hand, and there was much rivalry among the fish-vendors to fill their baskets. With good feeling remarkable in people of this class, they would take their shillings and give them ten or twelve shillings' worth of fish. Hence the French priests were astounded at the cheapness of fish. These extravagant commercial transactions continued every Friday for years; the salesmen at Billingsgate had an idea that it brought them good luck.

The unfortunate Quiberon expedition had taken place a long time previously, with deplorable results to all who had joined in it. The sojourn in the island of Yeu will ever be a stain upon the reputation of the *émigré* leaders. M. de Vauban has given an account of it only too faithful.

M. de Frotté, the general's brother, came to London. His mission was to warn the Comte d'Artois that La Vendée was lost unless some prince appeared there. I do not know what brought him to my mother, but he frequently called. Negotiations were protracted, and he was put off with fair speeches; at length he insisted upon a categorical answer, announcing the necessity of his departure. I saw him reach my mother's house like a man in despair. He was bursting with indignation, and this was his story.

The Comte d'Artois had received him, surrounded by what he called his council, the Bishop of Arras,[1] the Comte de Vaudreuil, the Baron de Roll, the Chevalier de Puységur, M. du Theil, and some others, eight or ten in all. It should be noted that the head of M. de Frotté, who was starting the next day, depended upon their secrecy. He reported the state of La Vendée, and the prospects which it afforded. Every one raised objections, to which he replied. It was admitted that the presence of the Comte d'Artois was necessary for success. The difficulties of the journey then came forward, and these he surmounted. The question then arose as to how many *valets de chambre*, how many cooks, physicians, &c., the Count should have (there was no question of almoners at that time). All was discussed, and agreement was secured. The Comte d'Artois took no great part in the discussion, and seemed ready to start. M. de Frotté said in conclusion, " I may inform my brother, then, that my lord will be upon the coast at such and such a date? "

" Excuse me," said the Baron de Roll, with his German accent; " excuse me. I am captain of the bodyguard of the Comte d'Artois, and am consequently responsible to the King for his safety. Can M. de Frotté assure us that the Comte will run no risk? "

" I tell you that a hundred thousand of us would die before a hair should fall from his head, and I can say no more."

" I appeal to you, gentlemen, is that a sufficient security on which to stake the Comte's safety? Can I consent? " the Baron replied.

All answered in the negative, asserting that it was im-

[1] Louis de Conzié (1730–1805). See Taine, vol. i. p. 235.

possible. The Comte d'Artois dismissed the meeting, wishing M. de Frotté a good journey, and regretting the necessity of renouncing an enterprise which he would himself recognise to be impracticable.

M. de Frotté, who was stupefied for the moment, banged the table with his fist, and cried with an oath that they did not deserve that so many brave men should risk their lives for them.

It was directly after this scene that he arrived at our house, and he was still so excited that he could not keep silence. He related these details with a burning eloquence of anger and indignation which impressed me greatly, and which I have never forgotten.

It was probably in consequence of his communications to his brother that the latter wrote his famous letter to Louis XVIII. " The cowardice of your brother has ruined everything." That, however, is an exaggeration. The Comte d'Artois undoubtedly was not one of those desperadoes who go in search of danger, but if those about him had encouraged him instead of checking him, he would have gone with M. de Frotté instead of staying in London.

We must not be too hard upon the princes. Consider what influence power and success can exercise upon men. A minister in power for a few months, a pretty woman, a great artist, a fashionable man, are they not under the yoke of flattery, and do they not honestly think themselves extraordinary beings? If a few moments of flattery can produce this result thus rapidly, can we be astonished that princes, impressed from their cradles with the idea of their privileged importance, should be guilty of those aberrations which proceed from the foolish fact that they think themselves beings apart, whose intercourse is an essential necessity for mankind? I am persuaded that the Comte d'Artois represented to M. de Frotté in all honesty the impossibility of risking his safety, and that these arguments appeared to him final and definite.

When we tell princes that we are but too pleased to die in their service, it is to us but a form of words, as the formula which concludes a letter. But if they take the expression literally and believe that it is a happiness, are they entirely to blame? The fault is much rather attributable to their environment at all times and under every system.

Not one of the councillors in attendance upon the Comte d'Artois had any desire for an adventurous expedition, the prospects of which were wholly uncertain, while the privations and fatigues were guaranteed. The Baron de Roll was in this case the mouthpiece of Mme. de Polastron. Her real and ill-concealed affection for the Comte d'Artois inspired her with fears for his safety, but not for his glory.

The Bishop of Arras was an arrogant and violent character, positive as a prime minister, and wholly occupied with the plots he was hatching against the court of Louis XVIII., for the two brothers were in open hostility, and their agents were continually attempting to outwit each other. The Bishop would have feared more than anything an enterprise which would necessarily have transferred his influence to the military party, the more so as the Prince had no special affection for priests at that time, though the Bishop of Arras could hardly be regarded as a priest.

M. de Vaudreuil, whom we have seen as the despotic lover of the all-powerful Duchesse de Polignac, had become the submissive husband of a young woman, his cousin, whom he had married since their exile, and whose ill-considered conduct would have exhausted his patience if he had noticed it.

I saw a great deal of the Comte de Vaudreuil, but could never discover for what reason his contemporaries regarded him so highly. He had been a leader of that school of exaggeration which prevailed before the Revolution, enthusiastic for trivialities and careless of important matters. With the help of the money which he drew from the royal treasury, he had become the patron of various minor poets who praised him in couplets. At the house of Madame Lebrun he would strike an attitude before a picture, and patronise artists. He lived with them on familiar terms, and kept his fine manners for the drawing-room of Mme. de Polignac and his ingratitude for the Queen, of whom I have heard him speak in the lowest terms. In exile and old, his claims became ridiculous, and he was forced to see his wife's lovers provide for the household expenses by presents which she was supposed to have won in a lottery.

It was not in her own family that Madame de Vaudreuil could have acquired the finer instincts. Her mother, an old Provençal woman, who was not without a certain shrewdness, set her no example in this respect. Here is one instance of a thousand.

During the campaign of the princes, one of her friends, when starting to join the army, handed her a purse containing two hundred louis. " Should I live," he said, " I shall ask for that back again. If I die, I pray you to hand it to my brother."

The friend returned safe and sound. His first care was to run to Madame Vaudreuil. She said not a word of her trust, and the young man was at first too shy to open the subject. At length, after several visits, he resolved to ask for the money.

" Alas! my good friend, if there is any left, it is not much," she said in her Provençal accent. And without the smallest hesitation she handed him the purse, which contained barely a dozen louis.

Such a person was obviously unlikely to bring up her daughters with any strictness, and all profited by her example.

One of them, Mme. de la Tour, had followed her husband to Jersey, where his regiment was in garrison. At that moment the governor of the island was a certain d'Auvergne, a captain in the English navy, who claimed descent from the family of Bouillon, at any rate upon the left side. The Comte d'Auvergne began a very close intimacy with Mme. de la Tour, and she did the honours of the governor's house. The officers jestingly called her among themselves Mme. de la Tour d'Auvergne; but she accepted the title, and, with her husband, children, and brothers-in-law, abandoned the surname of Paulet in favour of d'Auvergne. Thereupon, supporting this claim by means of some papers which Captain d'Auvergne, who died without issue, had left her, she returned to France, and founded a family branch of La Tour d'Auvergne. It had no other claim to exist than that which I have narrated, and yet its existence eventually became undisputed.

In this enterprise she was greatly helped by her brother-in-law, the Abbé de la Tour, a thorough intriguer. At the time of which I shall have to speak, he was the private secretary and fanatical supporter of the Bishop of Arras, and was accustomed to fulminate against every *émigré* who returned to France. One fine morning he disappeared without saying a word, and a fortnight afterwards we learnt that the First Consul had appointed him to the bishopric of Arras. His patron and predecessor was infuriated to the point of madness against this " wretched hedge priest." He never referred to him in any other terms.

I could write pages upon the Vaudreuil family, but they would be neither amusing nor edifying. An exception, however, must be made in the case of Mme. de Serant-Walsh, the eldest daughter, a woman of high character, who was one of the first ladies of the Empress Joséphine. She was remarkably well educated, a clever character, and the Emperor took much pleasure in her conversation in the days when he used to talk. She and Madame de Rémusat were often able to tell him truths useful to himself and to others.

The creditors of the Comte d'Artois became more pressing, and he was obliged to take shelter within the walls of the Palace of Holyrood at Edinburgh, where he was out of their reach. There he remained until an English Act of Parliament decided that arrest was illegal in the case of debts contracted abroad.

The only prince remaining in London was the Duc de Bourbon, who perished so miserably at Saint Leu, an end entirely worthy of his life. His father, having perceived that he had no love for the noise of bullets, expelled him from the army of Condé, where between two heroic generations he did little to maintain the lustre of the great name of Condé. He was not a bad man, and was gentle and amiable in domestic life. His failings probably were due to some natural timidity which made the life of a prince unbearable to him ; he was only at his ease among the lower classes, and there he met with little respect. His amatory disposition, in addition to his dislike for society, tended to drive him into the shadier walks of life. When a conjunction of unavoidable circumstances forced him to appear in good society, he was obviously ill at ease. Yet he had a fine and noble face, and his manners, if cold and embarrassed, were distinguished. An intimate connection with the young Comtesse de Vaudreuil brought him into society for a few months, but he was never at his ease in it.

He went a little more readily into what was known as creole society; this was composed of people whose plantations had not been so devastated as to be hopelessly ruined. London money-lenders advanced little sums to them at exorbitant interest, and eventually lost their money. These creole families were at that time the least unfortunate of the *émigrés*. A certain Mme. de Vigne was one of their richest representatives. She kept up a show of state, spoke of the Duc de Bourbon as neighbour, because he lived in her street, and was sufficiently vulgar to put him at his ease.

It was she who replied to an Englishman who asked her if she were a creole, " Oui, monsieur, et des bonnes, car je roule," of which answer the Englishman was obliged to demand an explanation. Her daughter, a pretty and amiable girl, was the most desired match among the distinguished classes of *émigré* society; she was, however, fastidious. The mills on the plantations ceased to *rouler*, and she was only too happy to marry the English consul at Hamburg. Mlle. de la Touche, a daughter of Mme. Arthur Dillon and Mlle. de Kersaint, who both owned rich estates in Martinique, had been more prudent. The first married the Duc de FitzJames, and the second the Duc de Duras. I was thus brought into close connection with them both, and shall have to speak of them hereafter.

CHAPTER VIII

Morning concerts—General de Boigne—My marriage—Character of
M. de Boigne—The Princes d'Orléans—The Comte de Beaujolais—The Duc de Montpensier—The Duc d'Orléans—Domestic quarrels—Travels in Germany—Hamburg—Munich—Return to London—Story of Lady Mary Kingston.

I DO not propose to relate the romance of my life : every
individual has his own romance, which may be made interesting by truthfulness and talent, but talent I have none.
I shall only say so much of myself as is necessary to explain in what way I became a spectator of the scenes I
shall attempt to describe, and how I reached that point.
For that reason I shall have to give some details concerning my marriage.

My mother's health caused less uneasiness, and she attempted to find some distraction for me. In London she
had met Sappio, formerly music master to the Queen of
France. He had called to see her, had made me sing to
him, and showed much enthusiasm at my powers, which
he cultivated with the more zeal, as he thus increased his
reputation. His wife, a very pleasant little person, was a
good musician. Our voices blended so admirably that
when we sang together in thirds, the windows and glasses
vibrated. The only other instance of this fact I have
known is the case of Mmes. Sontag and Malibran. Its
rarity made this power a valuable acquisition, especially
to artists. Sappio often brought musical friends to see my
mother. They grew into the habit of coming by preference on Sunday morning, on which day a kind of *im-*

promptu concert was eventually held by artists and amateurs. Listeners increased in number, the thing became
fashionable, and at the end of some weeks my mother had
infinite trouble to drive away the crowd.

A certain Mr. Johnson, whom we saw sometimes, asked
leave to bring a friend who had just returned from India.
He knew very few people as yet, and wished to make some
good acquaintances. He came and went without attracting particular attention from us.

Several weeks passed. He came to pay a call, and said
that a sprain had prevented him from appearing sooner,
and pressed my mother so earnestly to dine with him, that
she consented, after raising a crowd of objections. The
only guests were the O'Connell family and mine. Our
host urged Mr. O'Connell to come to him early the next
day, and commissioned him to ask my hand in marriage.

I was sixteen years of age. No one had ever paid me
the smallest attention—at any rate, I had not noticed anything of the kind. The only passion in my heart was filial
love. My mother was overwhelmed with fear that the
feeble resources that supported our existence might fail.
The Queen of Naples had been driven from her estates,
and announced that she did not know if she could continue
my mother's pension. Her lamentations touched my heart
less than my father's silence and his face worn with sleeplessness.

Such were my impressions when Mr. O'Connell arrived,
commissioned to offer me the hand of a husband who had
an income of 20,000 louis, who offered a dowry of 3000
louis, and hinted that as he had no relatives, and not a
being dependent upon him in the world, nothing would
be dearer to him than his young wife and her family.
These proposals were announced to me. I asked for a
day to consider my answer, although my mind was made

up forthwith. I wrote a note to Mrs. O'Connell, to ask her to invite me to lunch as she sometimes did, and to ask General de Boigne to meet me there. He was exactly punctual. I then committed the grave though generous mistake of telling him that I did not care for him in the least, and probably never should, but that if he were willing to secure my parents' future independence, my gratitude would be so great that I could marry him without reluctance. If this feeling was enough for him, I would give my consent; but if he asked for more, I was too frank to promise him anything of the kind, either at the moment or hereafter. He assured me that he did not flatter himself with the possibility of inspiring any deeper feeling.

I insisted that an income of 500 louis should be assured by contract to my parents, the deed to be signed at the same time as my marriage contract. Mr. O'Connell undertook to draft this document. M. de Boigne then said that he could give me no more than 2500 louis as a dowry. I cut short the arguments which Mr. O'Connell was advancing by reminding him of the terms which he had proposed. I concluded all discussion, and went home entirely satisfied.

My mother was somewhat hurt that I had left her at a moment when my future was at stake. I told her what I had done; she and my father, though much touched, begged me to reflect carefully. I assured them that I was entirely content, and this was true at the moment. I was in the full flush of youthful heroism. I had quieted my conscience by telling my suitor that I never expected to love him. I felt certain that I could fulfil the duties of my position, and was in any case entirely absorbed by the happiness of extricating my parents from their difficulties. This was the only point I considered, and I

did not understand that I was making any sacrifice.
Probably at the age of twenty I should have been less
courageous, but at sixteen one does not know that the
rest of one's life is at stake. Twelve days later I was
married.[1]

General de Boigne was forty-nine years of age. From
India he brought back an honourable reputation and an
immense fortune, acquired in the services of the Mahratta princes. His previous life was but little known,
and he deceived me about his past, his name, his family,
and his antecedents.[2] I think that at that time he proposed to preserve the character that he had then assumed.
He had been paying some attention to a pretty girl, the
daughter of a doctor. She had received his advances
somewhat coldly, or had treated him with a fickleness
which he did not understand. On leaving her house, he
suddenly remembered the young girl who had appeared
to him as a vision some weeks before. He wished to
prove to the disdainful beauty that another girl, younger,

---

[1] See the marriage contract in the Appendix.

[2] Benoît Leborgne was born at Chambéry on March 8, 1751; his
father was a furrier. At first he was intended for the law, but after
distinguishing himself at the local college he preferred a military
career. He entered an Irish regiment serving in France, and Clark's
Regiment in 1768. Finding that promotion was slow, he entered a
Greek regiment in the service of Catherine of Russia with the rank
of captain. In 1780 he was taken prisoner and sent to Chios, then
to Constantinople, where he remained in captivity for seven months,
until peace was made. Having reached the rank of major he resigned and went to India. After a period of poverty, during which
he was reduced to giving fencing lessons, Lord Hastings, Governor
of India, sent him on a commission to the Indian princes. In 1783
he was at Delhi. He offered his services to several Hindoo princes,
and after some trouble with the East India Company, he entered
the service of Sindiah. He organised the Mahratta army on European principles, won great victories over the neighbouring princes,
and was appointed general of all the infantry, and then governor
of the conquered provinces with a share of the tribute. This was

prettier, better educated, and of higher birth, would accept him. He offered his hand and I accepted it, unfortunately for both of us.

If a single thought of selfishness had entered my heart at that moment, or if the possibility of happiness had smiled on me for an instant, I doubt if I should have had the courage to support the lot which was mine. But I owe it to myself to say that, child as I was, no such feeling touched my mind, and I saw myself surrounded with luxury, without experiencing the smallest happiness.

M. de Boigne was neither so bad nor so good as his individual actions might lead one to believe. A member of the lower middle class by birth, he had been a soldier for many years. I do not know by what paths he had passed from an Irish legion in the French service to the back of an elephant, from which he commanded an army of 30,000 sepoys which he organised in the service of Sindiah, the chief of the Mahratta princes, who was

the origin of his great fortune. Sindiah died in 1794, and two years afterwards General de Boigne returned to Europe. He married Mlle. d'Osmond in 1798, and had no issue.

The King of Sardinia made him a count, a lieutenant-general, and gave him the Grand Cross of St. Maurice and St. Lazare. He then became the benefactor of his native town. Louis XVIII. appointed him a field-marshal, Knight of St. Louis and of the Legion of Honour. He died at Chambéry on June 21, 1830, where there is a statue to him. His charitable foundations in the town were numerous. He built a theatre, constructed new streets, endowed a fire brigade and scientific establishments, built a Jesuit college, enlarged the hospitals, founded an asylum for decayed gentlewomen, built a lunatic asylum, a home for those without work, left money for teaching trades to poor girls, &c.

"M. de Boigne," writes Mme. Lenormand, "always showed the greatest consideration and deference to his wife, and as long as he was alive Mme. de Boigne went to spend some weeks with him every year either at Buissonrond or at Chambéry. As soon as she arrived to do the honours of his house, he would invite a large number of guests. She herself never spoke of the General but with the respect due to a benefactor."

enabled by this European organisation to become the dominant power in Northern India.

M. de Boigne must have used much skill and cleverness to leave the country with some small portion of the wealth which he possessed, and which none the less amounted to ten millions. The rapidity with which he had passed from the lowest rank to the position of commander-in-chief and from poverty to vast wealth had never permitted him to acquire any social polish, and the habits of polite society were entirely unknown to him. An illness from which he was recovering had forced him to make an immoderate use of opium, which had paralysed his moral and physical powers.

Years of life in India had added the full force of Oriental jealousy to that which would naturally arise in the mind of a man of his age; in addition to this, he was endowed with the most disagreeable character that Providence ever granted to man. He wished to arouse dislike as others wished to please. He was anxious to make every one feel the domination of his great wealth, and he thought that the only mode of making an impression was to hurt the feelings of other people. He insulted his servants, he offended his guests, and his wife was, *a fortiori*, a victim to this grievous fault of character. He was an honourable man, trustworthy in business, and his ill-breeding had even a certain kind of heartiness; but his disagreeable temperament, displayed with all the ostentation of wealth, the most repellent of all forms of outward show, made association with him so unpleasant a business that he was never able to secure the friendship of any individual in any class of society, notwithstanding his numerous benefactions.

At the time of my marriage he was somewhat stingy, but of luxurious tastes, and if I had wished I could have expended more of his fortune than I have done. I think that an older and cleverer woman, with greater powers of dissimulation, and attaching greater value to the pleasures which money gives, with her eye upon that will of which he was always speaking, and which I have seen rewritten five or six times, would have been able to do better both for herself and him in my situation. But a little girl of the utmost honesty and pride could naturally do nothing. I was constantly astounded by the succession of evil passions which I saw displayed before me, while his ridiculous jealousy, expressed in the most brutal manner, aroused my surprise, my anger, and my disdain.

We lived in great state, constantly giving fine dinners and magnificent concerts, at which I sang. M. de Boigne was glad from time to time to exhibit the beautiful and well articulated machine that he had acquired. Then his Eastern jealousy resumed the upper hand; he was furious because I had been seen or heard, and especially if I had been admired or applauded and told me so in the language of the guardroom.

These concerts were then somewhat fashionable, and the most distinguished members of English and foreign society used to be present. The Orléans princes often came and dined at my table, but always as princes. Their manners precluded any familiarity. I was too greatly influenced by Royalist hatred for their father not to be somewhat prejudiced against them; it was impossible, however, not to admire the dignity of their attitude. Of all our princes, they alone received no help from foreign powers.

In a little house at Twickenham, near London, the three of them lived in the most modest but entirely proper style. M. de Montjoie formed the whole of their court, and performed the functions of lord in waiting upon the rare occasions when any form of etiquette was necessary. In spite of my prejudices, I soon perceived that the Duc de Montpensier was as amiable as he was cultivated and distinguished. He was passionately fond of art and music. The Duc d'Orléans endured the music for his brother's sake. Nothing was more touching than the friendship of the two princes and their affection for the Comte de Beaujolais.

He by no means repaid their care. He was unsteady, careless, and idle, and when he could escape to the streets of London he committed all the excesses of a fashionable young man. , In spite of his attractive face and his distinguished figure, the badness of his manners had secured his exclusion from decent society. When he was seen leaving the opera, every one avoided him, for fear of finding him in a state of complete intoxication. His excesses and his drunkenness brought on a pulmonary disease, during which the Duc d'Orléans nursed him like a mother, but was unable to save him. But I am anticipating. At the time of which I speak the Comte de Beaujolais was still under the influence of his brothers, and all that was known of him was an appearance which predisposed people in his favour.

The Duc de Montpensier was ugly, but was entirely graceful and amiable, with manners so distinguished that his face was speedily forgotten. The Duc d'Orléans was comparatively handsome, but neither his bearing nor his manners showed any distinction. He never seemed entirely at his ease. His conversation, interesting as it even then was, seemed somewhat pedantic for a man of his age. In any case, he did not happen to attract me so much as his brother, with whom I should have been very glad to talk more often if I had dared.

After ten months of a very stormy union, M. de Boigne had offered to take me back to my parents. I accepted his offer, and was received with joy. This determination, however, did not please the rest of my family or my society, who wished to use the millionaire for their own purposes, and cared little if I paid for the privilege. It was at that moment that I became the victim and the spectator of the most hateful persecution. I must especially reproach him for the fact that before I was seventeen years of age he had shattered all the illusions with which I had entered the world ten months previously.

M. de Boigne had no sooner abandoned his prey than he regretted his action. Forthwith my relatives and all the most distinguished members of the *émigrés* entered his service. One undertook to spy upon my actions, another to question my servants. This one had interest at Rome, and could procure the annulment of my marriage. That one could find flaws in the contract, &c., &c. Meetings were held at his house, where my character was torn to pieces, and slanders were invented and expressed in prose and verse, which were sold for hard cash. In short, everyone proceeded to persecute a child of seventeen, though they had overwhelmed me with flattery but a moment before.

M. de Boigne himself was very speedily disgusted, and closed both his purse and his house. I afterwards saw in his possession various denunciations of my conduct and base offers of personal service. He had been careful to preserve the names of the individuals concerned, and the amounts which had been asked and paid. These names were sufficiently distinguished to please his plebeian pride, and he discovered a new form of exasperation in showing them to me.

It was impossible to induce M. de Boigne to make any arrangement which would leave me in peace. He promised to reform, while I felt vexed by the injustice of public opinion, which, under the influence of his agents and his money, regarded me as to blame. I therefore decided to rejoin him at the end of three months.

I shall give no detailed description of our married life. It is enough to say that when we were separated he was in despair and thought he adored me; but when we were united he was wearied by my society, and conceived an antipathy to me, and on five or six occasions left me for ever. All these separations were accompanied by scenes which poisoned my youth, a time so ill spent that it had passed before I realised the fact, and I found that it had gone and I had not enjoyed it.

In this year 1800 we travelled to Germany. I spent a month at Hamburg, where *émigré* society was ruled by Mme. de Vaudemont. Ridiculously innocent as I then was, the scandals of this clique were so startling that I could not close my eyes to them, and was correspondingly disgusted. I was no less disgusted by the relaxation of Royalist principles. Altona was a kind of purgatory, where people who proposed to return to France came to prepare themselves for the renunciation of their exclusive principles. Accustomed as I was to another language, all this seemed heresy to me. I often went to Munich, which was occupied by the remnant of the army of Condé, and there I found exaggeration pushed to an extravagance which brought me to the opposite point of confusion. I then became accustomed to accept opinion as such, and invented a golden mean for my personal use.

I remember hearing men argue at Munich that they must never consent to return to France except upon the condition that their castles, including the furniture, should be restored in the condition in which they had left them.   Upon the restoration of property rights and all claims not a doubt was expressed.   Possibly the fulfilment of these desires would have brought some disappointment, for the *émigrés* were so accustomed to say that they had lost incomes of a hundred thousand francs that they had eventually persuaded themselves of the fact.   Any country house, no matter how small, now assumed the dimensions of a castle in their recollections.

I crossed Tyrol, which I thought, in the words of the Prince de Ligne, the finest corridor in Europe.   We then made our way to Verona, to see the sisters of M. de Boigne, whose existence he had hitherto concealed from me, after which we returned to London, where I had the happiness of meeting my father and mother again, from whom I had been separated by this journey.

If I had not promised to avoid these details, I could tell a long story of the different manners in which M. de Boigne annoyed me.   I use the word " manner " of set purpose, for it was rather of the form than of the result of his treatment that I had to complain.   Experience alone can enable any one to realise how these petty malignities, trivial as they separately were, can make life intolerable.   My domestic quarrels did not so utterly absorb my attention as to prevent my grief for the sad fate of my best friend.   In your history, dear Mary, there is no need of skill, but merely of truth, and truthful I will be.

Lady Kingston had become a rich heiress by her brother's death.   The brother had left a son, but had married too late to legitimise the child.   The mother, an interesting person, had died in childbirth with her second infant.   Lady Kingston's father had never been willing to recognise his son's marriage or the child, which he had left to the care of his sister, Lady Kingston. This severity was carried to such a point that during the old man's lifetime Lady Kingston was obliged to hide her interest in the young orphan. She had him carefully educated. As soon as she came into her property she provided for the future of the young FitzGerald, to whom his father had left such little property as he possessed; she sent him into the army, kept an eye upon him, helped him to marry a girl who was an heiress to considerable wealth, and finally, under circumstances very unusual in England, enabled the young couple to begin housekeeping in a house which the Kingston family possessed in London, but did not use. Lord Kingston, a fierce and gloomy character, hardly ever left his Irish estates, where he led the life of a despot.

Lady Kingston had many children, the youngest being daughters. The business of their education brought her to London for several years in succession, and the Fitz-Gerald household formed an agreeable house of call. The wife was gentle and attractive, while the husband was her friend, her son, and her brother. The Kingston girls were brought up almost at his knee.

Lady Mary, the eldest, was one of the most charming girls I have ever met. In her seventeenth year her mother wished to bring her out, but she declined, preferring to continue her studies with her sisters. Her only pleasure was to walk or ride, or sometimes to drive in a dog-cart. Lady Kingston offered no objection to these excursions, provided that Colonel FitzGerald was ready to accompany her. This custom had continued for several years, but Lady Kingston had forgotten to observe that the child had become a charming girl, and that her chaperon was not thirty years of age.

If all the portraits of all the heroes in all the novels

that ever were written were combined to produce ideal perfection, the result would be inadequate as a picture of Colonel FitzGerald. His handsome face, his noble bearing, his mild and expressive features, were merely the outward signs of the admirable qualities of his heart. He was a colonel in the Guards, and adored by his junior officers as well as by his comrades.

Mary often came to spend long mornings, and also evenings, with me. FitzGerald was almost always her chaperon. Her mother was in society,, and her sisters were with their governess. The Colonel was kind enough to bring her, and often came to fetch her in the dog-cart. As soon as we were together, she always had some fresh story to tell of the Colonel's virtues, and would speak of nothing else. I was too young and too innocent to observe the fact, and thought it very natural that she should admire in FitzGerald qualities which were indeed excellent. I was extremely fond of Lady Mary, and was flattered that she should prefer our little house in Brompton Row to the most brilliant society in London, to which her position gave her access. Lady Kingston's half-serious and half-jesting complaints upon this point increased my gratitude and my affection for Mary.

The Colonel, though not a musician, had an excellent voice. We used to make him sing with us, and there was much amusement when he missed an accidental or mispronounced an Italian syllable; he used to say he would force us to sing nothing but Gaelic by way of revenge. Lady Mary gave way with the better grace, as she had great talent in this direction, and they used to sing Irish melodies together with the utmost perfection.

Would that these pleasant evenings, where the only guests were my father and mother, had been as innocent for this poor young couple as for me! I am persuaded

that Mary's passion was anterior to that which inspired
the Colonel. She did not suspect it, and he did not foresee the danger which they were running. Lady Kingston was suddenly recalled to Ireland by the illness of
one of her sons. Not wishing to expose Lady Mary,
whose health was not quite perfect, to the fatigues of
a rapid journey, she started alone, and commissioned the
Colonel to bring Mary to her with greater leisure. It
was during this fatal journey that they both gave way
to the passion which dominated them. I say both, for
I am certain that FitzGerald no more intended to seduce
Mary than she desired this flagrant abuse of confidence.

FitzGerald remained in Ireland while Lady Kingston
was staying there, and accompanied her to London with
her daughter. My marriage had taken place during their
absence. Mary and I used to write to one another, but
her correspondence had ceased. On her return to London
she would not see anybody, and I could not obtain a sight
of her. I was on the Continent when the alarm aroused
by her declining health and her despondency induced her
mother to send her into the country for a change of air,
to the house of her friend, Lady Harcourt.

One morning Lady Mary did not appear at breakfast.
An unsuccessful search was made, and her hat and
shawl were found on the river bank: it was feared that
she had drowned herself, but a workman had seen her
getting into a post-chaise at five o'clock in the morning.
Twelve hours afterwards Lady Harcourt, with true
Methodistical zeal, had advertised her name and her description on every hoarding and in every newspaper. My
mother reproached her for this cruel publicity. " My
dear," she replied, " to every one according to his works;
as she has sinned, morality demands that she should pay
the penalty." Alas, poor Mary, the carelessness of some

and the severity and cruelty of others all conspired to bring about your ruin!

It was supposed that FitzGerald had been called away by regimental business, but this motive was soon found to have been a pretext. Lady Kingston, who was still completely in the dark, had sent for him at the first news of Mary's flight, and he was not to be found. Several days passed; Lord Kingston and his sons, who were all older than Mary, arrived from Ireland and began to search for the fugitives. At length they discovered that a gentleman and his son were embarking in the Thames for America. The clue was followed up, and they discovered FitzGerald and Mary at the moment when the latter had assumed male attire to complete her disguise.

When Lord Kingston entered the room in which they were, both covered their faces with their hands. Mary allowed herself to be taken away, but neither of them offered any answer to the abuse with which they were overwhelmed, except to say, " I am very guilty." Lady Mary was taken back to her mother, but she was not allowed to see her. Her father and her brothers became her inexorable gaolers. She did not attempt to deny the obvious fact that she was *enceinte*. She offered no defence, and admitted her wrong-doing with calm and cold dignity.

She secured an interview with Mme. FitzGerald, and showed much greater contrition in her company, advising her to go to her husband's help. This she was perfectly ready to do, and would have received him with open arms. She announced herself as bringing a message from Mary. While receiving her with affection, he told her that his life could no longer be of any service to any one, and that he would consecrate it to the unfortunate victim whom he had brought to destruction. He

owed her the sad consolation of knowing that the tears
of blood which he was shedding for her fate would never
be dried.

A long time after the catastrophe Mme. FitzGerald
showed me this correspondence, for she did not confine
herself to one effort, and the poor woman's invectives
were all for the persecutors of Mary and FitzGerald.
In the preparations for his departure, he had taken every
precaution to secure his wife's future: when these arrangements were complete, he sent in his resignation to
the general in command, and retired to a little village
in the neighbourhood of London.   Before Mary's departure he sent her, through Mme. FitzGerald, a small un-
sealed note, in which he gave her his address, and told
her that in this retreat he would wait all his life for any
orders she might be able to give him, but would not seek
any communication with her, which might make her position more difficult.   Lady Mary was carried off to an
empty house which her father possessed in Connaught,
on the shores of the Atlantic, in a wildly desolate country, and handed over to the care of two guardians in
Lord Kingston's service.   Her brother challenged Fitz-
Gerald to a duel; he received and returned three shots.
But it was found that he had contrived to extract the bullets from his pistol, and he was obliged to admit the fact.
He said that he did not wish to add to the wrong he had
done Lady Kingston, while to fire in the air would have
been to stop the duel, from which he hoped to meet death.
It was impossible to continue this system of vengeance
before witnesses, and another was prepared.

The time was approaching when Mary was to bring a
child into the world, whose fate was the subject of her
keenest apprehensions.   Unmoved by threats directed
against herself, she trembled for her child.   The woman

in charge of her showed some signs of sympathy. She offered to save the poor innocent, if some one could be found to take charge of it as soon as she had carried it out of the castle. She had no doubt that she could deceive my lord's vigilance thus far. Mary could only turn to FitzGerald, and the woman undertook to send him a letter. Mary wrote to FitzGerald, asking him to send a reliable agent to the neighbouring village to take away the child.

The letter was placed in Lord Kingston's hands. He knew enough of FitzGerald to be sure that he would trust no one but himself to perform the commission. And in fact he arrived alone, on foot and in disguise, at the appointed spot. The next day . . . . .

. . . .

. . . .

. . . .

. . . . . he perished. Mary's letter, which with her miniature was found on him, was brought to the unhappy girl covered with blood . . .; and her brothers boasted of the stratagem by which her hand had enabled them to take vengeance upon Fitz-Gerald.

Lady Mary Kingston was delivered of a still-born child, and went raving mad; it was necessary to place her under forcible restraint. These fits alternated with a kind of apathetic imbecility, but the sight of a member of her family produced an outburst of violence. The public had been angered by the ingratitude of FitzGerald; great indignation was now aroused by the conduct of the Kingston family, even before the occurrence of the final catastrophe.

As for Mrs. FitzGerald, she cried aloud for vengeance, and would have done her best to secure it. But Lord

Kingston's power in Connaught was absolute, and no one could be found to give evidence against him, while this deplorable business had already claimed too many victims. Her anger was appeased. In any case   .   . Lord Kingston and his sons   .   .   .   .   .
.   .   were the objects of general opprobrium in their own country; and I should not be surprised to learn that the prolonged foreign residence of one of them (Colonel Kingston) was due to this cause. Few more tragical situations have appeared in novels than this sad episode of actual life.[1]

[1] Mme. de Boigne has founded upon this story a novel which is unpublished as yet. The stops representing suppressed passages correspond precisely with the number of words omitted.

CHAPTER IX

SHORTLY after my return to London, M. de Boigne
took me to Scotland. He was always glad to separate
me from my family. We stopped in Westmoreland with
Sir John Legard. He was as affectionate and kind to
me as ever, and I was very glad to see him again.

In Scotland I was welcomed to the Duke of Hamilton's house like a member of the family. I spent some
time with him, and went to the Edinburgh races with
his daughters, and to all the consequent festivities. They
professed to discover a resemblance between myself and
the portrait of Queen Mary Stuart preserved in the palace of Holyrood. The observation got into the newspapers, and this resemblance, true or false, made me so
public a character that on the race-course and in public
places I was followed by a crowd, which I must confess
was never impertinent. The observations which I heard
always displayed a keen affection for " our poor Queen
Mary."

We went from house to house, and were shown great
attention everywhere. The Scotch are extremely hos-

pitable; moreover, I had been the fashion in Edinburgh, and no one who has not lived in the serious society of the British islanders can understand the importance of that magical word " fashion." M. de Boigne was less surly than usual. High society, when it was accompanied by wealth and the ceremony of aristocratic life, seemed to overpower him, and he treated me diplomatically, as he saw that society welcomed me. On the whole, this tour was one of the pleasantest experiences of my youth. Returning through Northumberland, we stopped at Alnwick, the beautiful and historical seat of the Dukes of Northumberland. They have had the good taste to preserve it in its original condition, though as a residence it is in consequence not very comfortably arranged, notwithstanding the luxury of the several apartments. Formerly the Dukes of Northumberland used to ring a large bell to give notice that they were at Alnwick, and that their hall was open to any guest who had a claim to sit at their table. This mode of invitation has been replaced by other formalities. The bell, however, is still rung once a year, the day following the Duke's arrival at Alnwick. Such is the respect of the English for ancient custom that the neighbours for ten miles round hasten to accept this form of invitation, though no more direct summons is given. Notwithstanding the equality which the English law professes, England is the one country in the world where feudal customs are most readily maintained and seem to be held in affection. In any case, I cannot say if the bell of Alnwick still rings, for it is thirty years since I last heard it.

We stopped at the magnificent residence of Lord Exeter, built by the Lord Chancellor Burleigh in the reign of Queen Elizabeth, and retaining his name. Lord Exeter had just married for the second time, and the castle was in high festivity. The first Lady Exeter was forgotten, though her life had been strangely romantic.

The last Lord Exeter had one heir, his nephew, Mr. Cecil, who plunged into all the amusements of worldly life, and wearied of them all at the age of thirty. He had a handsome face, excellent talents and capacity, but was bored to desperation. His uncle urged him vainly to get married. He had seen too much of the world, had been played with by too many women, and deceived too many husbands to wish to increase the number of dupes; in short, he had become an eccentric. This was a regular stage in the life of fashionable men when worn out, and was the origin of the dandies.

In this frame of mind he started off one morning alone from Burleigh Hall, with a dog, a pencil, and an album as his sole companions, with the object of making an artistic tour in Wales. His journey was cut short. When he reached a village some thirty miles from Burleigh, he was attracted by the charms of a young peasant girl, the daughter of a small farmer in the neighbourhood. She was pretty and sensible. The wife of the local clergyman had taken a fancy to her, and had given her some education. She was the ornament of the village, which held her in honour, and the praises of Sarah Hoggins were in every mouth. Mr. Cecil's head was turned; his heart was touched by this village beauty, and he did his best to please. He said he was a painter, and added that he had some small capital, but would very gladly start as a farmer if she would consent to become his wife. He bought a farm in the neighbourhood, and married under his true name of Cecil. Ten years elapsed. Mrs. Cecil occupied herself with her domestic duties; on the pretext of selling his sketches and getting orders, Mr. Cecil was constantly from home. He generally came back with some small amount of money, which served to increase the comfort of Mrs. Cecil and secure his prominence in the village, though it did not raise him above the rank of a small farmer. Three children were born, and his wife never suspected their father's real social position.

Eventually Lord Exeter, the proudest of men, who would never have pardoned such a marriage, died, and Mr. Cecil, now Marquis of Exeter, returned to the village and spent some days there. As domestic cares did not demand his wife's presence at that moment, he proposed that they should make a small tour for their amusement, to which she gladly consented, for she would have gone anywhere with Cecil. He hired a stout horse, and provided a saddle and pillion, on which the farmer's wife got up behind her husband, according to the custom then prevailing among this class. Cecil showed his wife several fine houses which she greatly admired. At length they reached Burleigh on the third day, and he went into the park.

"Are we allowed to go through?" she asked.

"Yes, we are. I have a fancy for making you mistress of this park; what do you think of it?"

"I accept most readily."

"Would you care about the castle?"

"Indeed I should."

They crossed the park, talking in this manner, and at length she said to him, "Really, Cecil, this is getting beyond a joke. We shall be sent away."

"Oh, certainly not, my dear; we shall not be sent away."

They stopped at the door of the castle, where a row of footmen were drawn up.

My lord addressed them: "This," he said, "is Lady

Exeter, your mistress. You will consider her orders as mine."

" Yes, my lord."

As they entered the hall, Sarah, who thought she was dreaming, was recalled to herself by the sight of her three children, beautifully dressed, who fell on her neck. She threw herself into her husband's arms.

" My dear Sarah, this is the happiest day of my life."

" It is indeed! " she said.

Here the story ought to end, but truth demands the continuation. The Marquis had thought his wife admirable, so long as she was the chief beauty of her village, but when transported to another environment she lost her confidence and her simple grace; affected and ill at ease, she became awkward and ridiculous, nor did she preserve that fresh beauty which might have condoned her faults. Other beauties, who envied the brilliant position which she had wrested from them, pursued her with their taunts.

Lord Exeter was vexed, and irritation was followed by annoyance, regret, and embarrassment. He no longer wished her to accompany him into society, and neglected her. He was still very glad to find her at home, where she took refuge, but there she was little better off. She could not keep her servants in order, and, deprived of those occupations which had absorbed the greater part of her time, the small amount of reading which had formerly been her recreation was no longer an adequate employment. The writing of the smallest note was a torture to her, from her fear of committing some breach of etiquette. Lord Exeter placed a highly qualified governess in charge of his daughters, that they might not grow up as their mother. This was both natural and reasonable, but the girls and their mother suffered correspondingly.

This change of life first attacked the children; they faded and fell ill. Finally, in less than three years, the happy farmer's wife who had become a great lady, died of a broken heart, to use the English phrase, for which Lord Exeter was not in the least to blame, but which result was due to the force of circumstances. So true it is that one cannot defy the laws and customs which society imposes upon the various classes which compose it without paying the penalty.

A short time after my return to London, M. de Boigne informed me that he had sold our house, and took me to a furnished residence. He announced his intention of leaving England and entrusting me to my parents. Though in my heart I approved of this arrangement, I had no wish to become a topic of public scandal for the third time. The preceding winter he had left me one day when we had invited some five hundred guests to a concert; the story had gone about, both in the newspapers and in every drawing-room. I could no longer venture to believe in the kindness of public feeling, and felt my position very difficult. I therefore offered to follow him at any cost to myself. To this he returned an absolute refusal; but on this occasion we parted without a quarrel, and continued to correspond. He left me in moderate circumstances, though I was able to live respectably in the society which I frequented. He was even good enough to permit me to draw upon his banker to any extent within limits which I was not to exceed, and which I have never passed.

This phase of my life lasted for two years, which are the most peaceful in my memory. I went into society to some extent; I had a pleasant home, where I was adored. My father was in the full vigour of health and strength, and devoted his time to my brother and myself. We had resumed our reading and our studies, and led an intellectual life. My brother had a very fine voice, and we had a great deal of music.

Other amateurs often met at our house, among whom I should not omit to mention the Duc de Berry. He had set up house in London, where he led a life unworthy of his rank and still more unworthy of his misfortunes. His favourite society was that of some creole women, who fully responded to the freedom of his behaviour. These familiarities at any rate were confined to members of the French nationality; but he was also infatuated by an English girl of bad character, whom he took to the races in his own carriage, or to the opera, where she had a seat by his side. Sometimes, when the crowd was excessive, he would be seized with sudden shame, and take refuge in my box or elsewhere. But as we went out we used to hear the girl calling out " Berry! " to summon their carriage. The Duc de Berry's actions were often ill-considered, and he was a victim to fits of passion, in which he lost entire control of himself. This was the bad side, and it is with great pleasure that I can point to the other side of the picture.

The Duc de Berry had much talent, and was cheerful, lively, and companionable. He was an excellent story-teller; his powers in this respect were unusual, and he was aware of them; notwithstanding his rank of prince, he would wait for an opening, and never make it. He had a kindly disposition, was liberal, generous, and yet economical. Though the income which he received from the English Government was very moderate, and his tastes were expensive, he never ran into debt. As long as he had money, his purse was open to the unfortunate as readily as to his own fancies; when his purse was empty he deprived himself of everything until the next payment of his income.

He never shared the political absurdities of the *émigrés*. I have seen him honestly indignant with the people who tried to excuse the attempt made upon the First Consul by means of an infernal machine. I remember a quarrel which he had with M. de Nantouillet, his first equerry, on this occasion.

In this respect he was very different from the other *émigrés*. The Comte de Vioménil, for instance, used to call upon my mother, with whom he had been intimate for a number of years, and because I had said that I thought an infernal machine was a horrible idea, the future marshal told all his friends that he could not run the risk of listening to such language, and his audience shared his indignation.

The Duc de Berry remained an entire Frenchman. One evening we learnt in Lady Harrington's drawing-room, when the Prince of Wales was present, that a little French squadron had been victorious in the Indian Ocean. The Duc de Berry could not hide his joy, and I was obliged to scold him before he would restrain himself within bounds appropriate to our company. The next day he called upon us early, and said, " Well, governesses, I was quite good yesterday evening, but I wish to kiss you this morning as a token of my joy." He kissed my mother and myself, and then began to dance and leap, singing, " They have been defeated, they have been defeated! We beat them on water as on land; they have been defeated! Governesses, now I can say it, as we are alone here."

It cannot be denied that there was some generosity in this joy at a success which was entirely opposed to his personal interests. He was, in fact, the only prince of his dynasty who felt any real patriotism; he was, again, the only prince who had any taste for art, and this he cultivated with some success; in spite of his failings, he was an honourable man. I think he would have made a very dangerous monarch, but he was at any rate the only prince of his family who was in any degree capable of generosity. Sorry as I am to say it, I fear that he was not courageous. I can hardly understand the fact, for this quality seemed entirely suitable to him, but he was continually giving vent to expressions and sentiments which Henry IV. would not have disavowed. If he, then, displayed timidity, and the fact is hardly doubtful, it must be ascribed to the deplorable education of our princes. His brother, however, a less distinguished man in every respect, escaped this fatality.

When the bill concerning debts contracted abroad had been passed, the Comte d'Artois returned to London, as both he and his retinue were growing weary of Edinburgh. There had been many changes in his personal attendants during his last stay in Scotland. For many years he had been closely attached to Mme. de Polastron. She was passionately devoted to him, but not to his reputation, and it is to her influence that we must in some degree attribute the somewhat dishonourable part which this prince played during the course of the Revolution. She was an inmate of his household, and their connection was so openly acknowledged that it had ceased to cause any scandal.

After his arrival at Holyrood, the Comte d'Artois, who was anything but a religious man, was greatly troubled by the zeal with which the Scotch Catholics went to expense in order to procure him Masses and services. At some great festival their forethought obliged him to go twenty miles in order to spend five or six hours in the chapel of a neighbouring nobleman. Tired by this imposition, he wished to have an almoner. Mme. de Polastron wrote to Mme. de Laage, and asked her to find a priest to say Mass, of a social standing sufficiently low to exclude him from the apartments, the Comte's intention being that he should take his meals with his *valets de chambre.* Mme. de Laage applied to M. de Sabran, who said, " I have just what you want, a priest who is the son of my caretaker. He is young, not bad-looking, in no way fastidious, and you will have no trouble with him." The proposal was explained to the Abbé Latil; he accepted joyfully, and was packed off by coach to Edinburgh, where he was installed upon the terms proposed.

The Duchesse de Guiche, after some adventures, had eventually grown very seriously attached to M. de Rivière, one of the King's equerries. The intimacy had begun amid the easy manners of *émigré* life, and he was greatly devoted to her. She left Poland, where she was with her father, the Duc de Polignac, came to London, and was sent to France by the Comte d'Artois to begin an intrigue with the First Consul. In this attempt she failed, and returned to Germany, from whence she came to London, and finally arrived at Holyrood with health greatly shattered. Her malady increased, and M. de Rivière hastened to her side.

The Abbé Latil, however, had not wasted his time; he had secured the confidence of the Duchesse, and domi-nated her entirely. M. de Rivière was only admitted upon condition of sharing the conversion which had been effected in the sentiments of the invalid : he followed all her wishes, abandoned every principle that could displease her, and was the first to adopt the puerile and

narrow pietism which became typical of the little court
of the Comte d'Artois.

Mme. de Guiche, with the help of the Abbé Latil,
made an exemplary end. Mme. de Polastron, who was
present at her cousin's death, was profoundly touched,
and entrusted her heart and her conscience to the Abbé
Latil. This was as yet a secret which was not imparted
to the Comte d'Artois, who while regretting the Duchesse de Guiche, would even mock at the mummeries, as
he called them, which had accompanied her death, and
at the paternosters of Rivière.

Such was the household of the Prince when he reached
London. Mme. de Polastron was suffering from some
pulmonary disease, and her condition grew worse; she
abandoned herself to all the extravagant fancies which
are symptomatic of this disease. As the household income was insufficient, M. du Theil, the major-domo of
the Comte d'Artois, invented a new manner of pro-
curing money. Emissaries were constantly coming from
France. One of the most specious projects was chosen,
and an enterprise was announced for the near future
in Vendée or in Brittany, and by this means some thousands of pounds were obtained from the English Government. Two or three hundred were given to some
poor wretch who went to meet his death on the coast,
and the rest was swallowed up by the caprices of Mme.
de Polastron. I do not know if the Prince was a party
to these swindles. At any rate, he tolerated them, and
must have known of their execution, for when the manœuvre had been repeated thrice within a single month,
Mr. Wyndham found it out, and expressed himself in
energetic terms. It was from Mr. Wyndham himself
that I learnt of it, and in any case it was no secret. The
émigrés in England were accustomed to regard English

money as their legitimate prey, to be secured by any means.

Mme. de Polastron gradually sank. The Comte d'Artois used to spend his days alone with her. Her London house was too small for them to live together, but they lived in the same street. Every day at noon his captain of the Guards would accompany him to Mme. de Polastron's door, would knock, and would leave him when it was opened. The captain came back for him at half-past five for dinner, and brought him afterwards for a stay from seven o'clock to eleven. These long mornings and evenings were passed in conversation. Mme. de Polastron, who could not speak without exhaustion, would listen to the reading of religious books, at first by the Prince, who was afterwards relieved of this task, at her instance, by the Abbé Latil.

Comments were soon added to the reading of texts. The Comte d'Artois was too affected by grief to avoid lending a respectful ear to the words which relieved the sufferings of his friend, and she preached her faith with the fervour of love. He sympathised with her entirely, and she was so far convinced of his feelings that at the moment of her death she took the hand of the Prince, and placing it in that of the Abbé, she said to him: " My dear Abbé, here he is : I give him to you ; take care of him. I recommend him to your care." And then addressing the Prince: " My friend, follow the Abbé's instructions, that you may be as calm as I am in the hour when you will come to meet me again."

There were several people in the room during this scene, among others the Chevalier de Puységur, who told me the story. She bade an affectionate farewell tc everybody, gave advice to her servants, but said not a word of the scandal she had caused. She fell asleep, and the Prince and the Abbé remained alone with her. A short time afterwards she woke up, asked for a spoonful of liquid, and expired.

The Abbé did not lose a moment, but carried off the Comte d'Artois to the church in King Street, where he kept him for several hours, made him confess, and gave him the Communion the next day. From that moment his influence was such that with a mere glance at the Prince he could make him change his conversation. He had ceased to take his meals with the *valets de chambre* after leaving Edinburgh, but only then did he join the Prince's table, where manners were completely changed. The former laxity was replaced by extreme austerity, and M. de Rivière, who was abstemious by principle, returned, and became a leading member of the household. The Comte d'Artois, who was always somewhat embarrassed by this change of front, was infinitely obliged to him for thus preceding him and entering by the same gate upon a path which they followed with the same fervour.

Before the sickness of Mme. de Polastron entirely absorbed the attention of the Comte d'Artois, he often went into society. I used to see him there, especially at Lady Harrington's, where I spent most of my time. There he often met the Prince of Wales, and notwithstanding their different positions, the French prince appeared to greater advantage. His grace, nobility and polish, and his distinguished manner naturally brought him to the front, and the Prince of Wales seemed nothing more than his caricature. In the absence of the Frenchman, the manners of the English prince certainly seemed admirable, but they were manners which in the Comte d'Artois were second nature. Though his face was less handsome than that of the Englishman, he had greater grace and dignity, while his bearing, his dress, and his mode of entering and leaving a room were incomparable.

I remember that on one occasion when the Comte d'Artois had just arrived, and was paying his respects to Lady Harrington, the Duc de Berry, who was standing by me, said: " What an excellent thing it is to be a handsome prince like that; it is half the battle."

This was a jest, but founded upon truth. At that time, indeed, the Comte d'Artois was the ideal of a prince, even more, perhaps, than in his early manhood. At that date he hardly went into French society. He invited men to his house from time to time, and gave some dinners. On New Year's Day, on the festivals of St. Louis and St. Charles, ladies called. He left cards upon every one, and made personal visits to those whom he knew. In this way I have seen him three or four times at my mother's house, though not upon intimate terms. We did not call upon Mme. de Polastron, and this was an unpardonable omission.

I have spoken of the drawing-room of Lady Harrington. This was the only social centre where people could meet, if not without invitation, at any rate with greater intimacy than at an ordinary rout. Lady Harrington would pay thirty calls in a morning, leaving invitations at the door for ladies to go to her house in the evening. As she went she would cross Bond Street several times, and pick up men who were out walking. This manœuvre was repeated three or four times a week, and ended in the formation of a special clique, as is always the case in society. My more sociable French instincts induced me to prefer her parties to the larger gatherings to be found in other houses. Lady Harrington overwhelmed me with kindness, and I enjoyed myself greatly at her house.

It was there that I began a fairly close intimacy with Lady Hester Stanhope, who afterwards played such a strange part in the East. Her celebrity was begun in a highly original manner. Lady Hester was the daughter of Mr. Pitt's sister, who had been driven into her grave by the eccentricities of her husband, Lord Stanhope, whose behaviour had also thrown the eldest daughter into the arms of the village apothecary, near Lord Stanhope's castle. Mr. Pitt, to spare Lady Hester a similar fate, had taken her into his house, and she did the honours of the very insignificant mansion which he was able to maintain upon the scanty fortune with which he had retired from business. During this period of idleness he had appointed himself chaperon of his niece, and remained with infinite kindness until four or five o'clock in the morning at balls which wearied him to distraction. I have often seen him sitting in a corner, waiting with exemplary patience until Lady Hester should be pleased to end his sufferings.

I shall not speak of the influence which induced Lady Hester to go into exile. I have heard that it was the death of General Moore, who was killed at the battle of La Coruña, but this happened after my departure, and I intend to relate nothing that I have not seen, or that I do not know upon positive evidence. At the time of which I speak Lady Hester was a handsome girl of twenty. Tall and well-made, fond of society, of dancing, and of any public function, she was something of a flirt, and a very decided character, with ideas of striking originality. These, however, did not pass the limits of so-called eccentricity. For a Stanhope . . . . [1] she was prudence itself.

At that time I often used to sing with Mme. Grassini.

[1] Some words are suppressed.

She was the first professional singer who had been admitted to London society. To great talent she added extreme beauty, and a sound common sense which enabled her to adapt her behaviour to any company in which she found herself. The Duke of Hamilton allowed her to become intimate with his sisters. The Count of Fonchal, the Portuguese Ambassador, gave delightful parties, which were eagerly awaited. Not only was she invited to concerts, but to all society meetings, even to those of special cliques. She was an excellent actress, and her principles of singing were admirable. She brought contralto voices into fashion, and these almost drove soprano voices from the theatre, though the latter had hitherto been exclusively appreciated. The first great singer in possession of a soprano voice will produce a fresh revolution.

The most extraordinary musician I have ever met was Dragonetti. He then possessed in its perfection that prodigious talent with which he had conquered, subdued, and one may say, tamed the huge and clumsy instrument known as the double bass, which he handled with entrancing results. From the three great strings, which are fingered with the whole hand, he would draw ravishing sounds, and had acquired a degree of skill entirely amazing.

I remember that after a great concert given by the Count of Fonchal, when the crowd had departed, a few of us stayed behind to supper. The conversation turned upon national dances, and upon the tarantella. The daughter of the Ambassador of Naples danced it very well, and I had danced it in past years. The company begged us to try. Viotti offered to play; but he did not know the air, which Dragonetti explained to him. We began our dance; Viotti played and Dragonetti accom-

panied him.   Soon we were out of breath, and sat down.
Viotti ended his task by improvising a charming variation; Dragonetti repeated it on the double bass.   The
violin replied with a more difficult variation, which the
other performed with the same skill.   Viotti cried, " Ah,
you can take it like that?   Well, we shall see."   He
passed on to greater difficulties, which Dragonetti reproduced with the same perfection.   This friendly struggle
continued, to our delight, until Viotti threw his violin
on the table, exclaiming, " What can one do?   He has
the Devil in his body or in his double bass!"

He was transported with admiration.   Dragonetti has
had no predecessor, and as yet no imitator.

CHAPTER X

Quarrels among the bishops—The thirteen—Death of the Comtesse de Rothe—Sorrow of the Archbishop of Narbonne—Reply of the Comte de Damas—Pozzo di Borgo—His rivalry with Bonaparte—Édouard Dillon—Slanders upon the Queen, Marie Antoinette—Duel—A remark of the Comte de Vaudreuil—Pichegru—The Polignac family—Death of the Duc d'Enghien—I leave England.

FRENCH *émigré* society was greatly disturbed by the results of the Concordat. The bishops, who had hitherto lived in harmony, were divided by the questions of the resignations demanded by the Pope. My uncle, the Bishop of Cominges, and Barral, the Bishop of Troyes, were the leaders of the submissive party. The opposition were under the guidance of Dillon, the Archbishop of Narbonne, and of Béthizy, Bishop of Uzès. Hatred and animosity ran high. The party opposed to resignation were in the majority in London; they were thirteen in number, and proudly called themselves the thirteen.

Mme. de Rothe, whose vehemence had not been impaired by old age, never referred to them by any other name. She used to quarrel with my father because he approved of his brother's determination and expressed his opinion aloud. He found but few imitators; some would have gladly joined his side, but did not dare to proclaim themselves. Those *émigrés* who were preparing to return to France were most violent in their protests, with the object of hiding their plans: even while they were packing their effects they continued to denounce the deserters of the day before and to cry out against all that was happening in France.

Such being their frame of mind, any idea or proposal or reasonable suggestion raised a storm forthwith. The bishops who had resigned had originally proposed, after obeying the Pope, to go no further, and not to return to France. But they were so fiercely attacked that they could not hold out; and this situation gave great force to the arguments of a letter in which M. Portalis requested them to come to the help of the Church. After the first uproar occasioned by their departure, the excitement died away and the thirteen became less violent, as they no longer constituted a majority, the minority having retired. The Archbishop of Narbonne and Mme. de Rothe resumed their old intimacy with my father, who was greatly attached to them.

I cannot refrain from relating the story of Mme. de Rothe's death. She had reached the last stages of a long and painful illness, the consequence of which was a complete dissolution of the blood. She had always concealed her sufferings from the Archbishop, to spare him any anxiety, and had continued to do the honours of his drawing-room, that he might not feel any change around him or suffer any uneasiness. On the last day of her life she asked my father to dine with them. Their usual table companions, the bishops, were to go to Wanstead, to the Prince de Condé, and she had not strength to speak loud enough for any length of time to be heard by the Archbishop, who had grown very deaf. Oysters were served, a favourite dish of hers. The Archbishop insisted that she should have some, and she was so good-natured as to try one; then she said in an undertone to my father:

" D'Osmond, do not let him eat too many; I am afraid that his dinner may be disturbed."

Then she turned the conversation upon subjects which would interest the Archbishop, putting in a word from time to time. When dessert, came on the Archbishop was accustomed to go into his room for a moment. As soon as he was gone she cried:

"Ah! I was waiting for this moment. . D'Osmond, shut the door on him and lock it, and then ring the bell."

A servant came.

"William, you must go to the Archbishop and occupy his attention, to prevent him from returning here."

All this was said with great vivacity; she then resumed a quieter tone, and said to my father: "At his age a shock would do him no good, and I feel that my time has come."

"Shall we send for your doctor?"

"My friend, doctors are quite useless, but send at once for a priest; it is more suitable for the Archbishop."

Ten minutes after the door had been shut upon him she had ceased to breathe, and the Archbishop always remained under the impression that she had died quite suddenly when in perfect health. I have often heard him say:

"It is a great consolation to me to think that she felt no pain, and did not foresee her end."

A woman's heart alone could be capable of such devotion.

The Archbishop was fond of Mme. de Rothe; she had grown necessary to him, and now that the habits of fifty years were broken down, he regretted her sincerely. He came to spend the day of the funeral with us. He seemed much affected upon his arrival, but recovered, and ate his lunch with a good appetite. After dinner he found a volume of Voltaire lying about on a table. He began to speak of his connection with Voltaire, of his quarrels and their reconciliation, and then of those works which had made the greatest sensation upon their appearance. He ended by reciting to us an entire canto of " La Pucelle," with which poem he had adorned his episcopal memory. Such is the manner in which men mourn for people who have devoted their entire lives to them, and such behaviour is known as strength of mind or resignation, according to circumstances!

About this time I was one day in the house of Mme. du Dresnay. M. de Damas (known as Damas jeune), who was attached to the Prince de Condé, began a most violent invective against the *émigrés* who were returning to France. Mme. du Dresnay, though she did not return until 1814, was too sensible to approve of this effrontery, and said to him very dryly:

" M. de Damas, when a man is elegantly dressed, like yourself, with a carriage like that waiting for you at my door, when a man is boarded, lodged and cared for as you are at Wanstead, he has not the right to call down destruction upon poor people who are going elsewhere to seek the bread which they cannot find here."

" But, Madame, that is their fault. Do you not know what the King has done for them? "

" No, indeed I do not."

" Well, Madame, he has allowed them to work without losing caste."

This I heard with my own ears.

I have forgotten to say that before my marriage I used to see a good deal of Pozzo at my parents' house. After my marriage the vast jealousy of M. de Boigne, which comprehended the whole universe, including my father and my dog, had entirely withdrawn me from any social intercourse, and I only caught occasional glimpses of the world. Pozzo, moreover, had been making a long stay at Vienna, whither he had accompanied Lord Minto, his patron and friend. This connection had been formed at the time when Lord Minto, then Sir Gilbert Eliot, had been Viceroy of Corsico, where Pozzo was his counsellor and minister. He was afterwards very intimate with my uncle, Édouard Dillon, who commanded an Irish regiment in the English service, which was in occupation at Corsica.

When the British forces evacuated the island, Pozzo was obliged to leave it, as the French party gained the upper hand. I doubt whether Pozzo attached any real preference to the French or English party at this time; he merely wished to espouse the cause which Bonaparte was not supporting. The two cousins had each taken the measure of the other. The intimate association of youth had been succeeded by a hatred based upon ambition. Their sole thought was to be supreme in their island, and they promptly discovered that this was only possible if one of them became the conqueror of the other. I feel quite certain that Pozzo only called in the English because Bonaparte declared himself a revolutionary. It is possible that Pozzo afterwards became a genuine absolutist, but at this time he was very liberal and of a republican tendency. I have heard him improvise pieces upon *la Patria et les Castagnes*, with which I was entirely in sympathy, but which had little resemblance to the principles of the Holy Alliance.

Pozzo was perfectly correct in regarding himself as a rival of Bonaparte at that time. But when this idea was once fixed in his Corsican head, he could never get rid of it, and continued to regard himself as the rival of the conqueror of Italy, of the First Consul, and even of the Emperor Napoleon. He was too sensible to proclaim this idea in set terms, but it was working in his

brain and found expression in the most energetic hatred.
He would have gone to the bottommost pit to find antagonists to Bonaparte, and invariably dogged his steps with
a perseverance to which his distinction of character and
his brilliant talents gave an importance hardly to be foreseen from his social position.

At this time he was continually at our house, passing
alternately from the depths of discouragement and despair to wild extremes of hope and joyfulness; but he was
always witty, interesting, amusing, and even eloquent.
His conversational style was slightly foreign, and this,
added to his constant use of simile, gave it a picturesque
and unexpected colouring which seized upon the imagination, while the originality of his talk was emphasised by
his foreign accent.   He was a most companionable man.
His inadequate knowledge of the world had not yet been
modified by that self-assurance which success afterwards
gave him.   Moreover, it was less startling to see a little
Corsican breaking the rules of polite society at that time
than afterwards, when he displayed his unpolished manner amid the splendour of ambassadorial residences.

Édouard Dillon introduced him to the Comte d'Artois.
Pozzo speedily appreciated the Prince, and while the latter thought he had gained an agent, Pozzo regarded him
merely as an instrument to be used if possible in the
furtherance of his ambition, and especially of his hatred.
The instrument, however, seemed to him entirely blunt,
and he was accustomed to express himself with great
bitterness in referring to the lack of account to which
he had been able to turn it.   Édouard Dillon, of whom
I have just spoken, was my mother's brother, and was
for a long time known as the "handsome Dillon."   A
contemporary chronicler pointed to him as one of the
lovers with whom slander provided the Queen, a story
which was based upon the following foundation.

Édouard Dillon was very handsome, very self-satisfied, and very much in fashion. He was a member of the circle of Mme. de Polignac, and probably offered to the Queen some of those compliments which were her right as a pretty woman. One day he was rehearsing at her house the figures of a quadrille which was to be danced at the next ball. Suddenly he turned pale and fainted away. He was placed upon a sofa, and the Queen was so imprudent as to place her hand upon his heart to feel if it was beating. Édouard recovered consciousness and apologised for his foolishness, admitting that in order not to be late for his appointment with the Queen he had left Paris without breakfasting, and that in consequence of a long-standing wound, which he had received at the capture of Grenade, fainting of this nature occasionally attacked him, especially when he was fasting. The Queen ordered him some soup, and the courtiers, jealous of this small success, insisted that he was intimate with her.

The rumour soon died away at court, but was confirmed in town when he was seen on St. Hubert's Day crossing Paris in the Queen's coach and eight. He had fallen from his horse and broken his arm for the second time while hunting. The Queen's carriage was the only vehicle on the spot, and she ordered it to take my uncle home, returning, as usual, in the King's carriage, as her own was only called out as a matter of etiquette. It is very probable that many stories about the poor Queen have had no more serious foundation than this.

My uncle fought a duel which made some stir. When he was at supper at the minister's house, a man from the provinces, whose name I have forgotten, said to him across the table:

" Monsieur Dillon, I should like to ask you what those little pots are for."

Édouard, who was talking to the lady next to him, answered curtly, " For oats " (*à l'avoine*).

" Then I will send you back some straw," answered the man, who did not know that *pots à l'avoine* were a dish in fashion at that moment.

Édouard did not interrupt his conversation, but after supper a meeting was arranged for the next day at a somewhat late hour, as he did not care to be disturbed in the morning. His antagonist arrived at his house at the time arranged. My uncle had not finished dressing. He apologised for the delay, finished his toilet with all possible care and with the utmost imaginable delicacy. While thus occupied he said to his opponent:

" Sir, if you have no business to call you elsewhere, I should suggest our going to the wood of Vincennes. I am dining at Saint Maur, and I see that I shall have barely time to keep my appointment."

" What, so you intend . . ."

" Certainly, sir; I intend to dine at Saint Maur after I have killed you, for I gave my promise yesterday to Mme. de . . ."

This boundless self-assurance possibly staggered the poor man; at any rate, he received a shrewd thrust, and my uncle went to dinner at Saint Maur, where the duel and the conversation were not discovered until the next day, and then from the talk of a third person. It must be admitted that effrontery of this nature has some attractiveness.

In 1803, at the time of which I am speaking, Édouard had long since laid aside all the airs of a young man, and had become entirely natural and agreeable. When a lady asked him what had become of the person known as the handsome Dillon, he replied with extreme seriousness:

" He has been guillotined."

He had plenty of mother-wit, and an infinite knowledge of the world.   I have never seen any one with better or grander manners.   He had been attached to the Comte d'Artois as lord in waiting when the household was first formed, and remained on intimate terms, though he had no place at the Prince's table.   The regiment of the Irish Brigade, of which he was in command, had occupied his attention for some years.   He had then transferred his responsibilities to his brother, Frank Dillon, his lieutenant-colonel.   In Martinique he had married a creole with a fortune considerable at that time, which allowed him to keep a fairly good house in London.   The Comte d'Artois dined there sometimes, and the other princes very often.

I happened to be there one day in 1804, with a number of people, including the Comte de Vaudreuil.   Bonaparte had just declared himself Emperor, thus destroying the hopes that the *émigrés* had been founding upon his supposed Bourbon policy.   Everybody was discussing the opportunities which he had lost by this piece of effrontery.   Some thought that he might have been Marshal of France, others Chevalier des Ordres, and some went so far as to suggest the post of Constable of France. Finally, M. de Vaudreuil, getting up, turning his back to the fire, and putting his hands beneath his coat-tails, observed in an authoritative tone :

" Do you know what this seems to me to prove?   It proves that this Bonaparte, notwithstanding the reputation which we have built up for him, is in reality a very clumsy scamp."

Commentary is needless.

At the Peace of Amiens, M. de Boigne had returned to France, and urged me to meet him there.   Apart from my own disinclination, I thought I had every reason to keep away from a country destined to further catastrophes.   We knew that an upheaval was in preparation, and that Pichegru was at the head of this intrigue.   He, at any rate, committed no indiscretion, and his conduct was marked by prudence and skill.   He used to live almost entirely alone, often going away for a short time to throw people off the scent : when idlers began to talk of his absence, he would suddenly reappear and show that he had been making a very ordinary journey, and one which was excellent evidence for his want of occupation.

One day he started definitely upon his dangerous expedition; unfortunately for him, he was to be followed by the members of the Polignac family.   They acted very differently.   They paid a round of farewell visits, undertook messages for delivery in Paris, showed a list of persons who were waiting them, and who had probably no idea that their names were thus in use.   It was inconceivable that their journey, after this publicity, should seem to be of no importance; yet they asserted that they were going off in secret.   This was their method of conducting a conspiracy.

The day before their departure I dined with them in the country at the house of Édouard Dillon.   It was necessary to cross a small common on the return journey. The Polignacs were on horseback : they posted themselves on the common, and amused themselves for an hour by stopping the carriages which came up; mine was one of the number.   They demanded my money or my life, and then went off with roars of laughter, saying that it was a kind of foretaste of their future trade.   The next day this whimsicality was the talk and the delight of their entire circle.   This foolishness would not be worth the trouble of narration did it not throw some light upon the character of this Jules de Polignac, which was fatal to the throne and to himself. Though he was then quite young, the discredit of this conduct is entirely his. His brother Armand, who was as stupid as Jules was foolish, was entirely under the influence of the latter.

We soon heard of the arrest of these conspirators, and soon afterwards we learnt the sad fate of the Duc d'Enghien. His father, it must be said, was crushed by the news, which he heard in a dreadful way. The Duc de Bourbon was supposed to inhabit Wanstead, a magnificent castle which the Prince de Condé had rented near London, for during his military career in the army which went under his name, his Highness had not neglected his finances, and was incomparably the richest of the *émigré* princes. His son could not endure the regular life of Wanstead, and was generally to be found in London in a small suite of rooms with one valet, who had attended him from his youth. As his breakfast was late, he rang for Gui three times with no result. He then went down into the little kitchen, and found Gui with his elbows on the table and his head in his hands, shedding tears, with the newspaper before him. At his approach he raised his head and attempted to hide the newspaper. This the Duc de Bourbon did not permit, and he then read the sad news of his son's assassination. Two hours afterwards the Prince of Condé arrived, and found him still in this kitchen, from which Gui had been unable to remove him, and into which he would allow no one else to enter. The Prince de Condé took him back to Wanstead. The care of Mme. de Reuilly, his natural daughter, who was brought up by Mme. de Monaco, afterwards Princesse de Condé, helped to soothe his grief. This excessive grief, accompanied by fits of rage and cries for vengeance, is the best feature in the life of the Duc de Bourbon, and one which I am glad to commemorate.

As for *émigré* society in general, and the princes in particular, the impression made by this event was strangely transitory. Out of respect for the Prince de Condé, the Comte d'Artois decided that mourning, which would have been customary for five days only, should be worn for nine, and thought he had made a great concession. The Prince de Condé thought so too, for he went in person to London to thank the Comte d'Artois. The news arrived on Monday. The Duc de Berry was absent from the opera on Tuesday, but reappeared on Saturday at the next performance.

The Moreau case had been finished, and peace had not been disturbed in France. I therefore decided to accede to the repeated invitations of M. de Boigne. I felt that I was in a false position. The importance of the quarrels which made my life unbearable was now diminished by distance, and I had no sufficient reasons to advance for refusing to obey the orders which M. de Boigne had the right to issue. He had just acquired a charming house, Beauregard, at four leagues from Paris, and wished me to join him there. My parents promised to come and see me if I could secure the erasure of their names,[1] and this eventually decided my action.

[1] From the list of *émigrés*. All the nearer relatives of Mme. de Boigne were even then in France: these included her great-uncle, d'Osmond de Médavy, formerly Bishop of Cominges; and her uncles and aunts, M. and Mme. Argout, *née* d'Osmond, with their son Eugène; Mgr. d'Osmond, a bishop who had resigned the see of Cominges, had returned in February 1802, and had been appointed under the Concordat to the see of Nancy; the Vicomte Joseph d'Osmond and his wife, *née* Gilbert de Voisins, with their son Charles. (See the letter of the Admiral de Bruix in the Appendix.)

At the moment when the Imperial court was organised, the Bishop of Nancy had been appointed almoner to Prince Louis, the Emperor's brother. (*Almanach impérial.*)

CHAPTER XI

In September 1804 I embarked at Gravesend upon a
Dutch vessel with a cargo of whale oil; we ran into a
violent storm, and the sea became very high for so small
a boat. The waves broke over us and the water ran into
my cabin; as it had first washed over the barrels of oil,
it brought a terrible smell, which increased the horrors
of the crossing. The passage was lengthy, as the captain,
who was probably very ignorant of his business, missed
the mouth of the Meuse, and it was not until the fourth
day that we arrived at La Brielle.

Communications had been interrupted by the war, and
I was thus forced to avail myself of the crossing of a
merchantman. Regular steamers were only running to
Husum on the Swedish coast. The crossing was rough
and the land journey a great hardship; the latter would
have been almost impossible for a young woman without escort. Our captain's papers represented him as
coming from Emden; this was an obvious fraud, which
deceived no one. I heard the chief of the customs officials who were on board asking the men who were examining the ship while he was looking over the papers:

" This boat is from Grand Emden? "

" Yes, sir, from Grand Emden."

" All right."

He returned the papers to the captain without further observation; Grand Emden, in their slang, was London. I had no great difficulty at the custom-house; I sent a message to the banker to whom I had been referred, and with whom I ought to have found, together with letters from M. de Boigne, the passports necessary to continue my journey, but he had received nothing. I thus found myself entirely alone in a foreign country, without help or advice. I wrote to Paris to two of my uncles who should have been there with M. de Boigne. Meanwhile I did not know what was to become of me, and my position in Rotterdam had an adventurous appearance which was highly disagreeable. If communications had been easier I should certainly have returned to Grand Emden.

The banker advised me to go to The Hague to see M. de Sémonville, who was all-powerful and could help me on my way. I remember that when I expressed my fears that all communication with England might be interrupted, in which country I had left so many interests, the banker replied:

"Don't distress yourself, Madame, it is impossible. An attempt may be made to stop the Dutch commerce, but this can only last for a few days, and communication will resume its usual course within a week, as water finds its own level."

Notwithstanding his commercial insight, he had not foreseen that a hand would be found strong enough to maintain for years those hydrostatic conditions which he declared impossible for a week, and which, it must be said, ended in an explosion.

As soon as my carriage could be got ready, I went off to The Hague. I wrote to M. de Sémonville to ask for an interview; he immediately sent M. de Canouville to say that he would call upon me. The manners of this latter gentleman caused me some alarm. Under the pretext that he was my cousin, and also, perhaps, because I was young, pretty, and alone, he assumed a humorous and jesting tone which displeased me exceedingly, for the same reasons. I made a note of the fact that all the young men of revolutionary France were familiar, presuming, ridiculous, and impertinent. I had expected as much; I presumed that I should certainly find M. de Sémonville imperious, arrogant, and insolent, and then all my predictions, made with the prudence of twenty years of age, would be realised.

M. de Sémonville arrived; he was in much trouble The sickness of Mme. Macdonald had called Mme. de Sémonville to Paris, and news had reached him the evening before of the young wife's death. M. de Sémonville expressed his regret that he could not hope to offer me any comforts in a house of mourning. Though he was all-powerful in Holland, he had no influence beyond its frontiers, and could only give me passports to Antwerp, where I would have to wait for my papers from Paris. He advised me to remain at The Hague in preference, and placed himself entirely at my disposal. In the course of our conversation he spoke of Monsieur; I thought he meant Louis XVIII., and replied that the King was not in England, thus thinking that I might make a bold avowal of my Royalist principles.

" I am aware of that," said M. de Sémonville gently; " I refer to his brother, Monsieur."

I was overwhelmed, for in England no one had yet been found to refer to the Comte d'Artois as Monsieur, and it was the first time that this title had been given him in my hearing. In the course of our interview M. de Sémonville spoke of the tragical end of the Duc d'En-

ghien with sorrow, in significant contrast with the carelessness which I had left on the other side of the Channel.
I began to feel some misgivings upon the correctness of
my sweeping conclusions made an hour before.   However, I comforted myself with the reflection that M. de
Sémonville was an exception, unlike the rest of his compatriots.   As for myself, I am not quite certain what I
was ; English, I believe, but certainly not French.

At London I had seen a certain M. de Navaro, a Portuguese, who was going to Russia, and had met him again
during the crossing.   He handed to the wife of the
Portuguese Minister a letter of introduction which I had
for her husband, and told her of my forlorn condition.
An hour later the good Mme. de Bezerra came to my
hotel, carried me off, took me to dinner with her, and then
to the theatre in the embassy box.   The next day she
took me about everywhere, and after that I became
the recipient of general kindness from all the society at
The Hague.   Only those who know to what an extent
the diplomatic body can weary of itself will understand
the joy which greeted the appearance of a young lady who
promised some kind of distraction.

Count Stackelberg, a wild musical enthusiast, had
soon discovered that I was a good musician.   There
was a general rivalry to make me sing, and as I was but
a bird of passage, I chirped to their hearts' content.   I
have never had a more brilliant success.   I had the good
sense to see that my popularity was due to the nature
of my environment, rather than to my talents ; however,
I understood that this life could not go on for ever.   I
was therefore sufficiently hard-hearted to tear myself
away from the adoration of the representatives of all
Europe, and to make a tour to Amsterdam and through
the rest of Holland.

Three or four *attachés* announced their intention of escorting me, but to this project I offered strong opposition, and my good friend Mme. Bezerra made them understand that it was entirely against my wishes. During my stay at The Hague I began an acquaintance with Count Nesselrode which eventually became a real friendship.

I stopped at Harlem to buy some hyacinths. It was suggested that I should hear the organ, and, having nothing to do, I agreed. I went into the church, where I was alone, as the organist was out of sight. Most enchanting music began, as the performer was competent and the instrument magnificent; the echo organ answered the main instrument from another point of the church. I was not in the habit of hearing religious music, and wept and prayed with all my heart. I do not know if this was due to my disposition, but I have rarely experienced a deeper impression; with the exception of those hours which grief has graven in my memory, there are few in my lifetime of which I preserve a more vivid recollection than that hour which I spent in the cathedral of Harlem.

I stayed at Amsterdam for three days, and went to pay certain visits that had been arranged, at Brock, Zaandam, &c. M. Labouchère asked me to dinner, where I saw Dutch ladies and gentlemen. I was shown many curious things and heard stories of many more, but at the same time I was glad to leave this town. Notwithstanding its great commercial activity, it seemed dreadfully gloomy. I stopped at Utrecht, took a local carriage to go and see the Moravian institution and the camp which General Marmont commanded in the plain of Zeist. I found that the brethren, who are represented as so happy in the story of Mme. de Genlis, and whom I remembered from my childhood, seemed pale, sad, and wearied. I bought some trifles from them, and a quarrel soon arose, one asserting that his productions were superior, which fact the other denied, and I went away but little edified. I was, however, much impressed by the sight of the French camp. I had recently visited some camps in England, which were far from presenting so brilliant and animated a spectacle, though the French soldiers seemed individually less vigorous, and were not so well dressed.

I saw the carriage of General Marmont pass, with his wife in full dress. The postillions were dressed in gold-braided uniforms, and the carriage was gilded, but was dirty and badly horsed. The whole appearance seemed to me ridiculous, including the General's wife, and I was amused at it, for it was exactly as I had foreseen.

After an absence of ten days I returned to The Hague, where I found letters from my uncles. M. de Boigne had miscalculated the moment of my arrival, and had started for Savoy. I was informed that I should find my passports at Antwerp. I spent an evening with Mme. de Bezerra to take leave of the society of The Hague; M. de Sémonville was there, together with all the Dutch authorities, and the next day I started.

I had been frightened by stories of the strictness of the custom-house officials, and I was more alarmed by the prospect of dealing with the French officials, as my relations with those of the alien office when I left England had been extremely disagreeable. If the English were rude, what might I expect from the French? M. de Sémonville had given me a letter of introduction, but my heart beat when I reached the first French station.

I was very politely requested to enter the office, and was followed by my maids. My carriage was put down as coming from Berlin. An English carriage would have been confiscated, but this as a German carriage might pass on payment of a considerable duty. While I was paying, the young officials of the custom-house admired the carriage, which was a very pretty one.

" It is from Berlin," said the chief inspector.

" Yes, sir, just look; the fact is written on all the springs."

I blushed up to my ears as I followed their looks, and saw printed on the springs " London pattern." They began to smile, and I paid the sum demanded for my German carriage. While the chief inspector was making the entries and handing me the receipts, another was busy with my passport, making out my description in a manner very obliging, but rendering me somewhat ill at ease. The chief noticed this, and half raising his eyes from his paper, said:

" Write down ' Pretty as an angel '; that will be shorter, and will save Madame annoyance."

An inferior official had half opened one door of the boot; I slipped two louis into his hand. One of the clerks came back a moment afterwards and returned them to me, saying with the utmost politeness:

" Madame, here are two louis which you dropped by mistake."

I took them back, feeling somewhat ashamed. Finally, everything seemed to be concluded to my entire satisfaction, when they discovered that my driver's whip was English. They showed me the word " London " printed on the silver butt of the handle; no doubt I had bought it in some shop where English wares were sold, but in France they were prohibited, and it was their duty to allow none to pass. We maintained our serious demeanour throughout this final scene of the charade. They wished me a pleasant journey, and I went off much astonished at finding such kind and witty politeness instead of the rudeness and possible brutality which I had apprehended. I have enlarged upon these details in order to show how *émigrés* who had reason to suppose themselves entirely reasonable were none the less prepossessed with ridiculous ideas about France, and were hostile to France at bottom.

When I reached Antwerp I found at the inn a note from M. d'Herbouville, at that time prefect, saying that he had my passports. I was a near relation of his wife, and he had given orders that he should be told as soon as I reached Antwerp. I was hardly settled in my room at the inn when a great six-foot lout came in, crying his loudest in a shrill falsetto:

"Apollinaire, it is Apollinaire; I am Apollinaire!" and bowing to the ground with elbows out-turned.

It was some moments before I recognised the young d'Argout, whom I had seen some years before in London, where his uncle, who was also mine, as he had married my father's sister, was busy with his education, an occupation which bore due fruit. This was the man who afterwards rose to fame by indisputable merits, though these were accompanied by an awkwardness and clumsiness which he then displayed in full vigour. He gave me a fresh proof of the fact the next morning. He accompanied me to the cathedral of Antwerp, and in spite of my supplications he walked up backwards to the top of the tower that he might give me his hand, a performance no more convenient for me than for him. He then held a small position in the joint custom-house, by means of which he supported his mother. He afterwards became prefect, a peer, and a minister. He was a man of talent, good-hearted and honourable, but his intelligence was almost as clumsy as his manners.

M. d'Herbouville came in afterwards. I found him cold and distant; he had recently been compromised by the inconsiderate gratitude of certain *émigrés* to whom he had been of service, and was therefore adopting an attitude of reserve. He invited me to dinner.

My most interesting visitor was M. Malouet, an old friend of my father, and maritime prefect of Antwerp. M. Malouet had been a Constitutionalist in '89, a term of the greatest reproach among the *émigrés*; none the less, he had continued his friendship with my father, at whose house I constantly used to see him. It was not long since he had left London, and he was not quite sure what kind of welcome I might extend to a prefect of the Republic, or rather of the Consulate. Reassured upon this point by the joy I manifested at beholding a face I knew for the first time in a month, he made a sign for me to be silent, opened all the doors, looked out to see if any one was listening, closed them carefully, pushed a chair into the middle of the room for me, drew up another, and then asked in a whisper for news of my excellent father, adding:

"You see, my dear, I must be careful not to compromise myself."

He gave me a list of rules, recording what I was not to do or say in Paris, in every case to avoid compromising myself, which eventually reduced me to terror, though he had at first inclined me to laugh. My impressions were strengthened by the fact that his rules were supported by examples of the most alarming nature.

"But the country is quite uninhabitable!" I cried involuntarily.

"Hush, hush; that is a fearful piece of imprudence."

He again examined the doors, but would no longer expose himself to another indiscretion. He took leave of me, saying that it would be more prudent of him not to see me again, that d'Herbouville had asked him to dinner, but that he would not run the risk of being tempted to ask me some imprudent question.   There was no great danger, it was rather my words than his that he was afraid of; but the fact remains that he gave me a great fright.   No man can escape his destiny.   Some years later, M. Malouet, who was then a Counsellor of State, was compromised by his action with the Baron Louis, notwithstanding his careful precaution, and was exiled by the Emperor.

At d'Herbouville's house I found his family and some guests.   They were much more congenial than I had expected, in view of the observations of M. Malouet. He had succeeded, however, in disturbing my peace of mind, and I was somewhat afraid for myself and much alarmed for the others, to whom my presence might be a source of danger.   However, I must say that even M. Malouet, and the d'Herbouville family in particular, found an opportunity of speaking with regret, grief, and indignation of the death of the Duc d'Enghien, which the *émigrés* had so entirely forgotten.   Everywhere in all classes, especially among those attached to the Government, I found that this topic was an open sore on my return to France.

I reached the castle of Beauregard without any further adventure, having gone round Paris.   M. de Boigne had not yet returned from Savoy, and I installed myself mistress of this beautiful spot.   I took possession with much sorrow, to which I could give way as I pleased, on November 2, 1804, All Souls' Day, in a cold and penetrating fog, which made it impossible to see three feet before one's eyes.   In the evening I found myself shut in a room without bells and with doors which I could not open, as the locks were different from those to which I was accustomed in England. Bells had been proscribed as aristocratic during the Revolution, and M. de Boigne had not thought of having them put in. I felt a weariness and desolation which froze me to the soul, and I could not have thought myself in a wilder country had I been on the banks of the Columbia. The next day I sent out for a locksmith. He assured me that he could arrange a temporary bell until the wires could be renewed. What a dreadful country it is where locksmiths speak in the style of the Athenæum, and where horses are harnessed with string! My unfortunate brain, twenty years of age, was then for the first time left to its own resources, and was entirely bewildered by the multitude of impressions which I received; I have thus preserved a number of keen recollections of this journey.

CHAPTER XII

I DID not care to be present at the festivities of the coronation, which would have outraged my Royalist leanings. We amused our idle retirement by various quips and cranks. One was somewhat to the point which said that the imperial cloak was allowed to hang loose because the Emperor could not *passer la Manche*. Notwithstanding my prejudices, I was never able to suppress a very sincere admiration for the First Consul. I admired him as the conqueror and the writer of bulletins. No one had explained his vast merits as a legislator and a calmer of passions, and I was incapable of appreciating him by my own judgment. Had I lived in another atmosphere, I should, I believe, have been really enthusiastic about him.

In London my poor mother had often wept with vexation at my political principles, and insisted that I was turning my brother's head in favour of Bonaparte. It is certain that after a near view of our princes, and a distant impression of the First Consul, all my interest was concentrated upon the latter; the death of the Duc d'Enghien had made an impression upon me as transitory as upon those with whom I was then living. Notwithstanding this attraction for the Emperor, I was still bound by a thousand prejudices to what was known as the *ancien régime*. My English education also turned me instinctively in the direction which has since been called Liberal. So far as I can discover, this was the point at which I had arrived when I reached France. M. de Boigne, difficult as I find the fact to understand, was no revolutionary, and upon this one subject of politics we were almost in entire agreement.

At the end of December we set up house in Paris, where I spent the three most wearisome months of my life. Parisian society is so exclusive that there is no place for a new-comer, who is completely isolated until he or she has formed a circle apart. Moreover, my fear of scenes, which M. de Boigne would begin upon any or no occasion, obliged me to a retirement of life which was not conducive to social intercourse. From time to time I found an old woman who remembered seeing me as a baby at Versailles, or another who told me stories of my childhood at Bellevue, but these were not exciting distractions.

I was very kindly received by the Princesse de Guéméné, of whom I have already spoken; she was as useful and serviceable to me as any one could be who was bedridden and saw very few people. The Duchesse de Châtillon, on the other hand, was unendurable : she would keep me for hours, lecturing me upon a multitude of subjects on which her advice was as useless as it was antiquated; she would always begin and end her sermons with these words :

" My little queen, as I have the honour to belong to you," which meant in straightforward language, " Consider yourself highly honoured that I am willing to recognise our relationship," an honour which I did not feel disposed to admit.

In her magnificent residence in the Rue du Bac she lived in a large room, which she called her study, furnished with much old-fashioned luxury, and provided with eight or ten clocks, no two of which kept the same time. A splendid gilded cage hung down like a chandelier, full of birds singing at the top of their voices. This clatter, added to the low and monotonous voice of the Duchesse, got upon my nerves, and made visits to the house a real torture. I never left it without vowing never to return again—a vow I should certainly have kept if my letters from London had not constantly contained messages for Mme. de Châtillon.

This Duchesse de Châtillon was the daughter of the Duchesse de Lavallière, a rival of the wife of the Marshal of Luxembourg, both beautiful and fashionable women. These qualities were thus shared by the daughter. The frame of a looking-glass in this study where she delivered her long homilies to myself was papered with the portraits of her lovers. Not knowing what to do with them, she had added them to the furniture. The number of these portraits was considerable, and they made a very pretty decoration. She had been a free-thinker, but was now a strict supporter of religion. With her became extinct the family of Lavallière, and with her two daughters, the Duchesse de la Trémouille and d'Uzès, the family of Coligny-Châtillon.

The Marquise, who had become the Duchesse de Laval, a former friend of my mother, and my godmother, treated me with motherly kindness. She was as simple as Mme. de Châtillon was pretentious, and never advanced her family claims. I was therefore very glad to visit

her in her cell in the convent of St. Joseph, where she
lived in the practice of a devotion both meticulous and
lax. She gave all that she had to the poor, and her
poverty was so apparent in her dress that one day in
church a man tapped her on the shoulder, wishing to pay
her for his chair.

" You are mistaken, Sir," replied the Duchesse gently.
" It is not I, but that other lady."

The word lady in this situation always struck me as
touching.

The Duc de Laval was by no means pleased with his
wife's position. He tried the experiment of giving her
money, which speedily escaped from her purse; he then
resolved to hire a decent room for her, to pay her moderate expenses and those of her dress, though in this
latter he effected but little improvement. If he had insisted upon dress conformable to her social position, he
would have reduced her to despair; she wished to be able
to walk alone on foot in the mud, and to visit churches
and the poor without being observed. Although she was
not pretty, she had been the most exquisite and magnificent woman at the court of France during her youth; her
uncle, the Bishop of Metz, used to pay all her bills, and
she used to spend forty thousand francs on her dress.
Never had there been a greater change, and perhaps she
would have done better to avoid these two extremes. As
she was, her husband respected her deeply, and her children adored her. Her husband was a really eccentric
character, a phenomenon rare in any country, yet rarer
in France, and rarer still in the class to which he belonged.
Since he entered society, he had always lived splendidly
upon his profits at play without suffering any loss of
reputation. He never seemed to frequent gaming houses
any more than other men of his position. He never went

about looking for pigeons to pluck, but he calculated upon an income of one hundred thousand crowns from cards as he would have calculated upon a revenue from ground-rents. He was the finest and the fairest player that could possibly be met, and a decision of the Duc de Laval on any doubtful point would have been regarded as law throughout Europe.

He had been a good officer, and it was insisted that he had a soldier's eye. He had distinguished himself in the campaign of the princes, where he had been so un-fortunate as to see his second son, Achille, killed before his eyes, the only one of his children for whom he cared. When this army was disbanded, he displayed a paternal generosity to his own regiment, which found no imita-tors and earned him the highest esteem. In the ordinary course of life he professed a selfishness which ran to exaggeration. He met his daughter-in-law walking in the street one day, when it was beginning to rain, pre-tended not to notice her, and said to her in the even-ing:

" Caroline, you must have got horribly wet this morn-ing. I would have taken you into my carriage, but I was afraid of the damp if the door were opened."

A thousand stories of this kind might be quoted, but his children loved him, and every one respected him. He paid a large number of calls, for calling was in his case a rule of conduct; he insisted that it was the best means of preventing scandal about one, as nobody cares to talk about a man who might walk in in the middle of the conversation.

Anecdotes abound of his misuse of words; he had a strange difficulty in realising the true meaning of a word. It was in the expression, not in the idea, that he went wrong. He would speak of some one being whipped into the four corners of an oval court; he had got on horseback in order to arrive *currente calamo*; he had received an anonymous letter signed by all the officers of his regiment. A thousand blunders of this kind are reported everywhere. One of his finest and least known mistakes is the following. A discussion arose as to how far Zeuxis and Apelles [1] were contemporary. The Duc de Laval, who was sitting at supper next to the Duc de Lauzun, said to him:

"Lauzun, what is the meaning of the word contemporary?"

"It means people who live at the same time; you and I are contemporaries."

"Nonsense, you are laughing at me. Am I a painter?"

In the inner circles of society it was supposed that the Duc de Lauzun worked up the stories about the Duc de Laval, with whom he was very intimate. One day he pretended to be vexed with him, and the Duc de Lauzun answered:

"Getting angry, Laval, are you? Well, I will tell no more stories about you, and you will see what you will lose."

He was right, for the sayings of the Duc de Laval had given him a kind of celebrity. His mind has been compared to a dark lantern which illuminates its inside only, a somewhat ingenious comparison, for if he said many dull things, he never said a tactless one.

His eldest son, Adrien, who afterwards became Duc de Laval, was a society man. His name rather than his merit raised him during the restoration to positions

[1] Famous painters in ancient Greece. Zeuxis lived from 464 to 398 B.C., and Apelles in the second half of the fourth century B.C. The latter painted the portrait of Alexander the Great.

in which he did not display adequate capacity,[1] but his achievements were none the less high above the powers of a nonentity, as some people wished to regard him. The desire to prolong his youthful tastes beyond a reasonable age exposed him to some ridicule. He was so unfortunate as to lose his only son, the last member of the branch of Montmorency Laval. His brother Eugène was the most disagreeable character that could possibly be met, and concealed the most barefaced selfishness beneath a puerile and bigoted pietism.

I have heard the Comtesse de Vaudreuil speak of " we pretty women," but it was reserved for Eugène de Montmorency, I believe, to invent the expression " we saints," and I have heard him make use of it. His cousin Mathieu was religious in a very different manner, to which I shall have occasion to refer hereafter.

The Princesse de Guéméné had four children : the Duc de Montbazon, who was married to Mlle. de Conflans; the Prince Louis de Rohan, who had been the first of the numerous husbands of the eldest daughter of the Duc de Courlande (she eventually styled herself Duchesse de Sagan, and ceased to change her name as often as her husbands) ; Prince Victor de Rohan; and Princesse Charles de Rohan Rochefort.

I began a somewhat intimate acquaintance with Princesse Berthe, daughter of the Duc de Montbazon; she had returned to France with her mother to soothe the last moments of the Marquise de Conflans, and though she was already married to her uncle Victor, she was regarded as unmarried for family reasons connected with

---

[1] Adrien de Montmorency, Duc de Laval, the friend of Mme. Récamier and Mme. de Boigne, was successively, under the restoration, Ambassador of the King at Madrid (1814), at Rome (1821), at Vienna (1829), and at London (1829). He refused to serve under the monarchy of July, and died in retirement in June 1837.

inheritance. She was very attractive, lively, good, and companionable, without being pretty; she pleased me greatly, and our acquaintance would probably have become friendship had it not been for her departure to Bohemia, where she settled. Her aunt, Princesse Charles de Rohan Rochefort, had in her youth asserted her intention of giving the world a sight hitherto unprecedented, that of a Princesse de Rohan as an honest woman. It was, however, reserved for the niece to accomplish this ideal, and the poor Princesse Charles was entangled in all imaginable complications. If a husband like hers . . .[1] was any excuse for her, she is acquitted of all guilt, for Prince Charles was no ordinary villain.

I often met Princesse Charles and her daughters at the house of Princesse de Guéméné. The eldest was a horribly ugly, vulgar-looking person, but the best character in the world; she suffered greatly from her mother's indiscretions, which she concealed as far as possible from Princesse de Guéméné. I can remember one trifling circumstance, of which I never think without a kind of shudder.

Some people had been at my house one evening, and the next morning, when I was dressing to go out, the servant said that a woman was asking to speak to me. " Very good, I will see her as I go out," and half an hour went by. As I crossed the ante-chamber to reach my carriage, I saw sitting on a bench, with her thick shoes covered with mud, and a kind of servant with her, Princesse Herminie de Rohan. I staggered with astonishment, drew her into my room, and overwhelmed her with apologies. Unfortunately, she was more confused than myself; she was pale and trembling, and her cold hand clutched mine convulsively. She told me that her

[1] A slight change in the text.

mother had been gambling the evening before at my house, and that, having no money, she had borrowed five louis from my servants; the wish to return that sum immediately had induced her to stake five more, for which she had also to apply to them. In short, she owed them twenty louis, for which she begged me to be responsible, as she would rather owe it to me than be my servants' debtor. As she did not dare to tell me the story, she had commissioned poor Herminie with this business, and she was in a pitiable condition. As may readily be believed, my pity was not withdrawn; I concealed it as well as I could, pretending to think that this little sum would be speedily repaid. Quickly changing the subject, I took her away with me to visit her grandmother, and when I took her home I had the pleasure of leaving her tolerably composed. But her sufferings have always remained in my mind as one of the most painful tortures that a noble heart could undergo, and hers seemed a heart to feel such an experience in all its bitterness. Her plainness and her poor dress had induced my servants to keep her waiting in the ante-chamber.

Her second sister was pretty, and the third, Gasparine, afterwards Princesse de Reuss, and at that time a child, was charming. They had two brothers, who became a credit to the family and settled in Bohemia with their uncles. Their family attempted, with every reason, to separate them from their father and mother. After the death of Mme. de Guéméné, the indiscretions of Princesse Charles became so outrageous that she was forced to withdraw from society.

The first time that I went to a ball in Paris was at the Hôtel de Luynes; I thought I was entering Calypso's Grotto. The ladies all seemed to me like nymphs. The beauty of their costumes and of their figures impressed

me so strongly that only after several evenings of the
kind did I discover that I had actually been accustomed
to see in London a far greater profusion of beauties. I
was much astonished afterwards to find these women,
who were so excellently dressed in society, disgracefully
slovenly at home, with untidy hair, dirty wrappers, and
negligent to the last degree. These bad habits have completely disappeared within the last few years, and French-
women are as careful as English in their domestic life,
and dress in the best possible taste.

I was curious to see Mme. Récamier. I was informed
that she was in the little drawing-room with five or six
other women; I went in, and saw a person whose face
seemed to me highly remarkable, and when she went out
for a few moments afterwards I followed her. Some
one asked me what I thought of Mme. Récamier.

" Charming. I am following her to see her dance."

" That girl? That is Mlle. de La Vauguyon; Mme.
Récamier is sitting in the window there in that grey
dress."

When she was pointed out to me I saw in fact that a
face which had impressed me but little was wholly beautiful. It was the special characteristic of this beauty,
which may be called famous, to appear to greater advantage every time she was seen. She will probably reappear in these memoirs, as our acquaintanceship began
soon afterwards and is still intimate.

My uncle, the Bishop of Cominges, who had become
Bishop of Nancy, was then at Paris. He was anxious
for me to enter the household of the Empress, which
was then being organised, and explained the freedom
which a position at court would provide for me with
reference to M. de Boigne. Apart from the fact that
such a proposal was contrary to my opinions, my tastes

have always been repugnant to servitude of any kind, and I should not care to be attached to a princess at any period or under any government. He returned to the charge several times without success. From his manner of discussing the question as one which merely awaited my consent, I am inclined to think that he was performing a commission, but I never experienced any disagreeable consequences. Whatever may be said, when a refusal was given with proper modesty and without undue emphasis there were never any unpleasant results, nor was constraint ever exercised except upon people who wished to be constrained.

At that time we lost one of our cousins, the Admiral de Bruix, a man whose intellectual talents were greater than his morality. He had played an important part in the Directory, and alone had supported the honour of the navy throughout the Revolution.[1]   .   .   .
.   .   .   . Although he had been one of the foremost on the 18th of Brumaire, he had fallen into disgrace with the Emperor in the course of a stay at Boulogne. The Emperor had wished, against the Admiral's advice, to perform a manœuvre which would cost many lives, and the Admiral had complained in no measured terms. What, however, had ruined him was a remark uttered at a meeting of high dignitaries who wished to raise a statue to the new Emperor.

Though every one was accustomed to his freaks, this remark was passed round and caused great displeasure, and an opportunity for censure was discovered. He was summoned to Paris to account for some expenditure which had been slightly irregular, and was treated with scant consideration; his anger aggravated some pulmo-

[1] Some words are suppressed.

nary disease which had already begun, and he died in poverty so great that he was unable to buy firewood, notwithstanding the luxury with which he was surrounded. But justice to whom justice is due. Ouvrard [1] owed him a great part of his fortune, and on learning of his situation he sent 500 louis in gold to Mme. de Bruix the evening before her husband's death. This was not the hundredth part of the profit which he had made with the Admiral's support, but the Admiral was dying and in disgrace, and the act reflects honour upon Ouvrard.

Admiral de Bruix was a professed atheist, as being an eighteenth century philosopher, and his wife, who shared these principles, did not permit a priest to come near him during the night on which he died. My uncle, the Bishop of Nancy, was requested by the widow to convey the news to the Emperor, and made his way to the morning reception. The Emperor listened to him with apparent grief, and then observed:

" At least, my lord, I suppose we have the consolation that he died in the principles of the Christian faith? Did he receive the comforts of religion? "

My uncle was greatly confused, and could only stammer an embarrassed negative. The Emperor looked at him severely, and turned on his heel. The words of this clever actor did not fall upon barren ground; no great dignitary professed atheism any longer, and every bishop did his best to secure an " edifying end " for the members of his family. However, the Emperor did not wish to disgust my uncle, and treated him very kindly upon the next occasion of their meeting.

[1] Financier and head of the Commissariat under the Republic, the Empire, and the restoration; frequently compromised in bargains which were a heavy expense to the public treasury.

Among the foreigners of distinction who were in Paris at the time of my arrival, the Princess Serge-Gallitzin and the Duchesse de Sagan were the most remarkable.

The Princess Serge, pretty, attractive, and original, seemed to have hardly escaped from her native steppes, and her bearing was that of an unbroken colt. In some old castle she had found an enamel portrait, which had turned her head, and she had rejected a proposed marriage because the husband in question bore no resemblance to the portrait; this cherished work of art she wore round her neck, and was traversing Europe to find the original. I was informed that on the road she was constantly attracted by half resemblances to this imaginary type, finding sometimes the eye, sometimes the mouth, or the nose of her ideal, and was thus obliged to divide her affections among a numerous company. When I knew her she was still characterised by the unstudied gracefulness of her quest. The Duchesse de Sagan bore at that time the name of her first husband, Louis de Rohan; she was handsome, with a very distinguished air and the manners of the best society; she possessed to perfection the talent of Northern women for leading a life of high impropriety beneath an outward show of nobility and decency. All the daughters of the Duchesse de Courlande were fine ladies in the full sense of the term.

At the end of this carnival I was invited, with every one else, to a great ball given by Mme. Récamier, who was then at the height of her beauty and her wealth. The company included a large number of specimens of the new Empire, Murat, Eugène, Beauharnais, the marshals, &c., a great number of the old nobility, of returned *émigrés*, high financial authorities, and many foreigners. I witnessed a somewhat strange event in so mixed a company. The orchestra was playing a waltz, and numerous couples had begun to dance, when M. de Caulaincourt joined in with Mlle. Charlot, the beauty of the hour. At that moment all the other dancers left the room, and they remained alone. Mlle. Charlot felt ill, or pretended to do so, and this ill-omened dance was thus interrupted. M. de Caulaincourt was as pale as death. It can be judged how far the murder of the Duc d'Enghien was still remembered, and how slander against M. de Caulaincourt—and there was slander enough—was generally accepted.

I was told, but it was only gossip, that when the Emperor was organising his household, M. de Caulaincourt, on coming out of the study, announced to his comrades in the ante-room that he had just been appointed chief equerry. All hastened to compliment him, but Lauriston alone was silent.

" Have you nothing to say to me, Lauriston ? "

" No ! "

" Do you think that the post is not sufficiently high ? "

" Not high enough for what it costs."

" What do you mean by those words ? "

" Anything you like."

The bystanders interposed, and the subject was not pursued, but Lauriston, who had hitherto been a kind of favourite, was removed from the Emperor's service, and did not return to Paris until long afterwards. I do not guarantee this anecdote, which was believed among ourselves at the time, but an opposition party is always badly informed. This fact I had every opportunity of learning, when I afterwards lived in intimacy with people engaged in business under the Imperial Government. They proved to me the absurdity of a number of things which I had piously believed for years, and therefore I claim credence only for such stories as I know to be true.

For instance, I was present at a strange scene at the house of one Mme. Dubourg, where the society of the old *régime* used frequently to meet at that time. The Comte d'Aubusson had just been appointed chamberlain to the Emperor. These nominations were highly displeasing to us, and we expressed our objections with more or less acerbity. The Princesse de la Trémouille was pleased to treat M. d'Aubusson with great severity, though they had been intimate friends and although she saw him constantly. He asked her what he had done to deserve this severity.

" I think you know, Sir."

" No, indeed, Madame; it is in vain for me to consult my memory, and yet my recollections go very far back, even to the time when I was obliged to turn you out of the barracks for attempting to seduce the soldiers of my regiment."

The Princesse was petrified for the moment, and her fury then became hysterical. In spite of the partiality of the audience, the laugh was against her. It was asserted that when she was the Princesse de Saint Maurice, and was an energetic patriot at the beginning of the Revolution, she had been turned out of the barracks, whither she had gone to preach insubordination to the soldiers.

Although we were extremely insolent, we were by no means brave. This scene caused some stir; Fouché spoke of it, and Mme. de la Trémouille was obliged to answer for it to the police, after which we were generally most polite to the new chamberlains. Mme. de Chevreuse was almost the only person who ventured upon any indiscretion, but she was so eccentric and her whimsicalities were so universal that action of this kind was merely regarded as an additional caprice. Though red-haired, she was extremely pretty, very attractive, full of wit, and spoiled beyond expression by her mother-in-law, while she had a social position of her own which she turned to advantage with extremely bad taste. The Duc de Laval used to call her the Lady Purveyor of the Faubourg Saint Germain. He was right, for she had all the manners of the upstart, and abused the advantage of her position to extort respect and to display impertinence to any one willing to bear it. At the same time, she could be very gracious when she pleased, and as she found my house very pleasant, I never experienced the smallest of these eccentricities except at Grenoble, in the year of her death. Of this I shall speak later.

CHAPTER XIII

IN the early days of the Empire, opposition society in Paris was very pleasant. As soon as I was initiated and had formed a circle of my own, I found life very delightful.

Every one was beginning to experience some return of peace and comfort, and no one was anxious to risk these advantages, so that political opinion was comparatively peaceful. Two great parties were in existence, the members of the Government and those who were outside the Government. The latter, of whom I was one of the most hostile, confined themselves to epigram and to bad jokes when the doors were closed; for though we did not profess the code of M. Malouet, we were careful to observe due bounds. Some display of severity from time to time in the case of more turbulent spirits kept every one in respect, and increased courtesy of intercourse was the result.

Social distinctions were still somewhat vague; few people possessed establishments of their own, and those who could keep open house in town or country found no difficulty in gathering agreeable society about them. Such was my position during the second winter, and this state of things lasted three or four years. At the end of this time desertions became more numerous; the great majority of the nobility attached themselves to the Empire, and the marriage of the Archduchess carried off the rest. After that, ladies who did not go to the court were few indeed, and if the Emperor's prosperity had continued a few months longer, there would have been none of them.

My uncle had secured the erasure of my father's name from the list of *émigrés* with the less difficulty for the reason that he had no property to claim in France. He came to rejoin me, together with my mother and my brother Rainulphe, towards the middle of 1805. They established themselves in my house in Paris and at Beauregard. I was anxious that my brother, whose livelihood was by no means assured, and who was dependent upon myself, should enter the court service. My mother objected, and my father remained neutral, as he knew that his decision would be adopted by his son, and he did not wish to influence him. He was presented to the Emperor, who showed him much condescension; and was warmly welcomed by the Empress Joséphine, who wished to have him for her equerry or at any rate to attach him to her son-in-law, Prince Louis, in a similar position.

My brother would have preferred to enter the army, but he would have been obliged to enlist. The households of the princes provided an opportunity of securing a commission almost immediately. Young men thus attached first followed the princes to the war without holding any rank, and if they behaved respectably were speedily given a commission. My mother wept, my brother hesitated; some evasion was made, and the post was given elsewhere. In the following winter Rainulphe began a close friendship with the beautiful lady who has since become almost a historical personage by reason of the adventures of Blaye. Madame d'Hautefort and her society were enthusiastic in their opposition to the Emperor. My brother adopted their ideas, and henceforward the project of court service was entirely abandoned.

I cannot refrain from narrating a trivial circumstance which confirms all that has been said about the futility and fickleness of the Empress Joséphine. Mme. Arthur Dillon, the second wife of that Dillon who had married Mlle. de Rothe, and who was killed when acting as general in the army of the Convention, was a creole of Martinique and a cousin of the Empress, who often saw her, and was especially fond of her daughter, Fanny Dillon. We were very intimate with the whole of this family. Mme. FitzJames, daughter of Mme. Dillon by another marriage, was my best friend. When Mme. Dillon was staying with me at Beauregard, she went to pay a visit to Saint Cloud, and the Empress deluded her with the idea that she could enable Fanny to make a fine marriage; on her return she asked me if I would sacrifice a heron's plume to her. M. de Boigne had brought some of these from India and had given them to me.

The costumier Leroi had brought a very poor specimen of a plume to the Empress that morning. Mme. Dillon had said that I had much finer plumes, and her majesty was immediately seized with an extreme desire to secure them. We were still at table when a man on horseback, in the Emperor's livery, came to ask if the plume had been given to Mme. Dillon. It was impossible to refuse. I gave it, and Mme. Dillon sent it off.

The next day came a second message and a note from the Empress. Leroi thought the feather was excellent, but it was mounted in Indian style, and a second would be required to make a handsome plume. I therefore gave the second. The next day Mme. Dillon went to

Saint Cloud, and on her return she explained with some embarrassment that a third was required to complete the aigrette. I gave the third, announcing that I had no more to give. A third note arrived, containing a hymn of joy and gratitude.

Some days afterwards Mme. Dillon told me that the Empress had had an ornament made up of very beautiful cameos, which she wished to present to me. I begged her to spare me the presentation, explaining that the plumes had been given to her, Mme. Dillon, and had not been ·offered to the Empress. After another visit to Saint Cloud she assured me that she had made vain efforts to perform my commission. The Empress had seemed so hurt that it was impossible to resist, and the ornament would be sent to me shortly.

The following Sunday my brother went to pay his respects. The Empress asked after me, spoke with delight of the beauty and rarity of the plumes, and said to him :

" I have nothing so precious to offer her, but I shall ask her to accept some stones which are valuable for their ancient workmanship."

My brother bowed. On returning to Beauregard, the first thing he did was to repeat this conversation, and we held a family council to consider how I should receive this favour. It was impossible to refuse, and in spite of our prejudices we admitted that the choice of the gift had been made in excellent taste. Should I write, or should I request an audience to offer my thanks? And would this latter entail the necessity of a presentation?

I might easily have spared myself all this anxiety and agitation, for from that day to this I have never heard a word of plumes or stones or anything of the kind. Those who knew the Empress well thought that when the case of cameos was sent back to her she found the contents so beautiful that she had not courage to part with them at the first moment of her infatuation. A month afterwards she would have been very glad to give them, but it was then too late.

My great-uncle, the old Bishop of Cominges, had set up house at Saint Germain. His house became a meeting-place for a number of old *émigrés*, whose conversations displayed much the same extravagance as those with which I had been edified during my stay at Munich. However, the influence of Napoleon was felt even within this sanctuary. The two folding-doors in my uncle's drawing-room were opened only for two ladies, and they alone had the right to be announced aloud by his old *valet-de-chambre*. These were the wife of the Marshal of Beauvau and Mme. Campan.

The airs and graces of this latter lady were ridiculous in the extreme. One evening she attempted to overwhelm me with her kindness, to which I made but a feeble response, and I could not refrain from secret laughter at the rebuke which my uncle thought it his duty to address to me upon that point. The idea that Mme. Campan secured from time to time a word of favour from the Emperor had made this boarding-house mistress an important personage even in the eyes of people most hostile to the Government. So great was the prestige of his power at that moment.

At Saint Germain I made the acquaintance of Mme. de Renouard, better known under the name of Buffon. She was a living proof that there is no situation which a noble character cannot dignify. Mistress of the Duc d'Orléans throughout the horrors of the Revolution, she had passed through them all, combining entire devotion to the Prince with a hatred loudly proclaimed for the crimes of which she was a witness and for the authors of them. It is extraordinary that she did not pay the penalty for her frankness, but it seems that she had been able to inspire even these monsters with respect. She remained faithful to the memory of the Duc d'Orléans, and, at the peril of her life, worked for the benefit of his sons, whom she aided to escape from their prison at Marseilles. To them she entrusted her child, who was brought up by them abroad, under the name of the Chevalier d'Orléans, where he died quite young.

A fact but little known is the great desire which M. de Talleyrand felt to marry Mme. de Buffon. Her aunt, the Vicomtesse de Laval, did her best in these negotiations, but was unable to overcome her objection to becoming the wife of a bishop. She became extremely poor. A Swiss, M. Renouard de Bussière, a very agreeable man, paid court to her, and she accepted his suit; but their union was not of long duration, and he died, leaving her a son. When I knew her, she was a widow, living in absolute retirement and occupied solely with the care of this child, whom she was able to recommend, to her. great happiness, to the Duc d'Orléans before her death.

It must be said that this prince showed great gratitude to Mme. de Renouard, and afterwards supported her son. The old connection of my relatives with this family obliged them to break in upon the solitude of Mme. de Renouard. When she was at her ease she was a witty talker, entirely companionable, very interesting when relating her experiences, though she would rarely speak of them, and always unwillingly. She preserved some remnants of her beauty and especially of her charm.

Mme. Récamier came to spend some days with me at Beauregard, where I had many visitors. I returned her visit at Clichy, where she was living in the full security of assured prosperity, when a few days afterwards her husband's bankruptcy was declared.[1] Although she was little more than a social acquaintance, I had no thoughts of dropping her, and hastened to call. Her calmness, nobility, and simplicity in this situation, and the loftiness of her character, stood so high above the habits of her life as to impress me greatly. From that moment dates the keen affection which I bear for her, and which has only been confirmed by the various events through which we afterwards passed.

Many portraits have been drawn of Mme. Récamier, but none, in my opinion, have reproduced the essential features of her character, a failure the more excusable as her variety was infinite. Mme. Récamier was a true type of womanhood as made by the Creator for the happiness of man. She had all the charm, the virtue, the inconsistency, and the weakness of the perfect woman. If she had been a mother her destiny would have been complete; the world would have heard less of her, and she would have been happier. As she had missed this natural vocation, she was obliged to find compensation in society. Mme. Récamier was the incarnation of coquetry; her talent in this respect amounted to genius, and she was the admirable leader of a detestable school. Every woman who attempted to imitate her has become an object of scandal or disgrace, whereas she always emerged unscathed from the furnace into which it was her delight to plunge. The fact is not to be explained by any coldness of heart, for her flirtations were actuated by kindness and not by vanity. She was much more anxious to be loved than to be admired, and this senti-

[1] In February 1806. See *Madame Récamier and Her Friends*, by H. Noel Williams, p. 73 (Charles Scribner's Sons).

ment was so natural to her that she always had some
affection and much sympathy to give her numerous adorers in exchange for the admiration which she strove to
attract; hence her coquetry avoided the usual accompanying selfishness, and was not absolutely barren, if I may
use the term. She thus preserved the affection of almost
all the men who fell in love with her. Nor have I known
any one who could more dexterously combine an attitude
of exclusiveness with a bearing of general friendliness
towards a numerous circle.

Every one has praised her incomparable beauty, her
energetic benevolence, and her gentle courtesy; many
people have praised her lively wit. But very few were
able to discover beneath the easy manners of her social
intercourse the loftiness of her mind and the independence
of her character, the impartiality of her judgment and the
accuracy of her intuition. I have sometimes seen her
dominated; I never knew her to be influenced. In her
early youth Mme. Récamier had adopted a species of
affectation from the society in which she lived, and this
detracted both from her beauty and her wit; she soon
abandoned it when she found another circle in full consonance with her tastes. She became very intimate with
Mme. de Staël, and acquired in her company a taste for
keen intellectual conversations, in which she took the part
which a woman should take, the part of intelligent curiosity, which she could excite about her by her own obvious interest. This mode of amusement, the sole recreation which nothing can replace when once the taste
has been acquired, is only to be found in France and in
Paris. This Mme. de Staël said with perfect truth amid
the bitter experiences of her exile.

The attraction which Mme. Récamier was able to
exert upon famous men caused the beginning of her con-

nection with M. de Chateaubriand.[1]   To him she devoted
herself for fifteen years.   The delicacy of his behaviour
made him worthy of this affection, but I should not like
to assert that he deserved it by his depth of feeling.   The
fact remains that she was both agreeable and useful to
him, and that all her faculties were concentrated upon
the task of softening his violent conceit, calming the
bitterness of his character, ministering to his vanity, and
dissipating his weariness.   I think that he loved her as
much as he could love anything, for she gave him all
she could.

In 1806 I was affected by a malady so strange that I
feel bound to describe it.   Every day a violent headache
preceded a fit of shivering which was followed by a high
temperature, slight perspiration, and finally by a well-
marked attack of fever.   But during the height of the
fever my pulse slowed to a remarkable extent instead of
quickening, and only became normal when the fit had
passed away.   I could eat nothing of any kind, and was
getting visibly thinner.

Sea bathing had done me good in England, and I
wished to try it now, though the doctors did not greatly
encourage the idea.   I was obliged to make the journey
in my carriage.   It lasted five days, and I arrived at
Dieppe in the last stage of exhaustion.   A week afterwards I was walking on the seashore, having recovered
my health with the rapidity of early youth.

For twenty-five years my carriage was the only one of
the kind which had entered Dieppe, and we made a prodigious sensation.   Every time we went out there was a
crowd to see us pass, and the harness in particular was

[1] *Madame Récamier and Her Friends*, p. 179 (Charles Scribner's
Sons).

examined with inconceivable curiosity. The poverty of
the inhabitants was frightful. The Englishman, as they
called him—and for them he was worse than the Devil—
was cruising incessantly before their empty harbour.
With much difficulty a boat was able to escape from time
to time and go fishing, always at the risk of being captured by the foreigner or confiscated upon the return
journey if the telescopes of the watchers had seen it approach a vessel.

As for the comforts arranged for the convenience of
bathers which Dieppe has since organised, they were non-
existent at that time. My brother was able to find a little
covered cart, and with great trouble and great expense,
notwithstanding the universal poverty, a man was hired
to lead the horses down to the sea, and two women to
go into the sea with me. These preparations raised the
public surprise and curiosity to such a pitch that my first
bathes were watched by a crowd on the shore. My servants were asked if I had been bitten by a mad dog. I
aroused extreme pity as I went by, and it was thought
that I was being taken to be drowned. An old gentleman called on my father to point out to him that he was
assuming a great responsibility in permitting so rash an
act.

It can hardly be imagined that the inhabitants of a
seashore should be so afraid of the sea. But at that time
the people of Dieppe were chiefly occupied in keeping out
of sight of it and in protecting themselves from the
disasters which they feared the sea might bring, so that
it was for them nothing more than a means of annoyance
and suffering. It is curious to think that ten years later
bathers were arriving in hundreds, that special arrangements were made for their convenience, and that sea-

bathing of every kind went on without producing any astonishment in the neighbourhood. I have thus attempted to point out that the custom of sea-bathing, which is now so universal, is comparatively recent in France, for Dieppe was the first place where it began.

CHAPTER XIV

General de Boigne sets up house in Savoy—Cardinal Maury—
Mme. de Staël—Stay at Aix—Benjamin Constant—Dinner at
Chambéry—Coppet—M. Rocca.

My life was so monotonous during the ten years of the
Empire, and my participation in great events so scanty,
that I have practically no landmarks by which to guide
my chronology. I shall confine myself to putting down
at random, without reference to dates, such recollections
of this period as deal with personages of some importance, or depict the manners of that society in which I
lived exclusively.

M. de Boigne had begun to build a house in Savoy,
where he had bought an estate.[1] At first he had spent
some weeks every summer there, but these soon became
months. Finally, attracted by the vast importance which
his unequalled wealth gave him in his own country, he
settled there definitely, and became the benefactor of the
place. Beauregard was then too large a house for the
income which he had left me. It was put up for sale,
and bought by the Prince Aldobrandini Borghese, and I
transported my goods and chattels to a little manor in the
village of Châtenay, near Sceaux. The birth of Voltaire
in this house gave it some pretensions to celebrity. This
removal did not take place until 1812.[2]

[1] The estate of Buissonrond, near Chambéry.
[2] See in the Appendix the letter of Mme. de Boigne to her husband,
under date November 24, 1812.

I have mentioned my relations with Cardinal Maury. His return to France was preceded by a very servile letter addressed to the Emperor, which the latter forthwith published. This circumstance provoked a somewhat witty remark from a clever woman who had formerly been the Cardinal's friend. He found his portrait at her house.

" It is very good of you," he said, " to have kept that old engraving."

" I have always been greatly attached to it, your Eminence, and I value it the more to-day, as it preceded the letter."

As soon as we knew that the Cardinal was in Paris, my father called on him, and begged him to come and dine at Beauregard; he accepted eagerly, and the following Sunday we saw an enormous Italian coach discharge seven persons at our door—his brother, his nephew, his nieces, an abbé, and in short his whole household. He told me frankly that as he was going out, he thought he might as well save dinner for everybody. I had preserved a lively recollection of the goodness which he had shown me in my youth, and cannot express my disappointment at this second meeting. His face, his manners, and his language were of a piece, and would have been shocking in an infantry corporal. He told stories in the most frightful taste.

I remember that during this first dinner he related a scene that had happened in his diocese of Montefiascone. The scene took place in a convent, where the nuns, their confessor, and a grand vicar who had been sent to investigate a number of mutual complaints, used such language that the story would have been more fitted for a regimental guard-room than for the mouth of a Cardinal. I was much astonished at these characteristics, and my surprise was shared by my parents. He had been very different when they had known him at Rome, although even then his manners were by no means polished. His brother told us that a severe illness had undermined his moral instincts.

This was soon apparent to everybody. His gluttony and his avarice made him the butt of society, and at Paris he led a life which was the object of general scorn. His sordid meanness was carried to such a point that when he left his hired rooms to enter upon an archbishopric, he spent three hours shivering in his room waiting for the ashes of his only fire to grow cold, so that he might carry them off, not wishing, as he said, to leave them for the landlord's benefit.

One day he was going out of his house with my father. When they were half way down stairs he said to him: " We must go back again. Your visit has distracted my attention, and I have forgotten my usual precaution." They went into his room, and my father saw him take a little saucepan from the fire and shut it up in a cupboard, the key of which he took away.

" You see, my dear friend, when I go out I lock up my stock-pot ; these scoundrels of mine might steal my broth and put in water."

I quote these instances because my father saw them both, but his whole life was a series of similar practices. It was asserted that when he was not dining out he would make his meal on the little cakes that are handed round at evening parties. But when he was at any other table but his own, he would eat with the utmost greediness and vulgarity. It is sad to think that a man who played an important part in the world, and possessed a remarkable intellect, should have been reduced to so miserable a condition by vices so degrading.

At first he often came to my house. He had under-taken to bring my father back to the Government, and sometimes they talked together of the advantages and the disadvantages of the imperial *régime*. The day when the decree upon the state prisons appeared in the *Moniteur*, my father told him that such laws ought to be dis-cussed publicly.

"Oh, indeed," cried the Cardinal, "if he allowed dis-cussion or writing, he would not be there in three months."

"That is what I have thought, but did not venture to say," returned my father.

There were a number of people present, and the Cardi-nal was much embarrassed, and feared he had been com-promised; afterwards he called more rarely, and finally not at all. I had not seen him for some years at the time of the restoration.

I often went to Savoy, and stopped at Lyons during my first journey thither. M. d'Herbouville was prefect of the town, which was one reason for staying there. I was staying at the Hôtel de l'Europe, and arrived late. The next morning the head waiter informed me that Mme. de Staël was in the house, and asked if I would receive her.

"Certainly, I shall be delighted; but I will send her word."

Five minutes afterwards she entered my room escorted by Camille Jordan, Benjamin Constant, Mathieu de Montmorency, Schlegel, Elzéar de Sabran, and Talma. I was very young, and this great celebrity with her ex-traordinary escort overwhelmed me at first. Mme. de Staël soon put me entirely at my ease. I had intended to take some drives in order to see Lyons, but she assured me that I might spare myself the trouble; that Lyons was an exceedingly ugly town between two beautiful rivers, and that if I knew that fact I was as well informed as if I had spent a week in exploration. She spent the whole morning in my room, receiving callers and delighting me with her brilliant conversation. I forgot the prefect and his prefecture. I dined with her, and in the evening I went to see Talma in *Manlius*; he played for her rather than for the public, and was repaid by the delight which she felt and which she communicated to others.

On leaving the theatre she got into her carriage to return to Coppet. She had broken the conditions of her exile and risked any disagreeable results in order to be present at the performance of Talma.

Thus it was that this meteor appeared before my sight, and my head was completely turned. At first she seemed to me ugly and ridiculous. A big red face, a complexion by no means fresh, and her hair arranged in a manner which she called picturesque, in other words, badly done; no fichu, a white muslin blouse, cut very low, arms and shoulders bare, no shawl, scarf, or veil of any kind—such was the strange apparition which appeared in a hotel room at mid-day. She held a small twig, which she was constantly twiddling in her fingers, with the object, I think, of showing off a very beautiful hand, though it was but the finishing touch to the eccentricity of her costume. At the end of an hour I was entirely under her charm, and throughout her intellectual enjoyment of Talma's performance I watched the play of her features, and was surprised to find her almost beautiful. I do not know if she guessed my impressions, but she was always entirely kind, amiable, and charming to me. The next year I met her at Aix, in Savoy, at which watering-place I was staying with Mme. Récamier. It was under pretext of going to see her that Mme. de Staël again broke the conditions of her exile at Coppet, and arrived at Aix. I was almost an eye-witness of many deplorable scenes, when two geniuses used finer intellects than God perhaps has given to any other mortals for the purpose of tormenting one another.

The long-standing relations between Mme. de Staël and Benjamin Constant are perfectly well known. Mme. de Staël retained a keen liking for his intellect, but she had other temporary affections which frequently gained the upper hand. On these occasions Benjamin attempted to begin a quarrel; she then clung to him more completely than ever, and after fearful scenes they made their peace. In the attempt to describe this position, he said that he was tired of being always necessary and never adequate to her needs. For a long time he had cherished hopes of marrying Mme. de Staël. Vanity and interest were motives at least as powerful as his affection for her, but she persistently refused. She desired to keep him in harness to her own chariot, but not herself to submit to the yoke of Benjamin. Moreover, she attached too much importance to social distinctions to exchange the name of Staël-Holstein for that of Constant. There was no greater slave to the most foolish aristocratical ideas than Mme. de Staël, with all her liberalism.

In the course of a journey that Benjamin Constant made in Germany he met one Countess of Magnoz, by birth the Countess of Hardenberg.[1] It was by no means the story of Mlle. Necker over again. She fell violently in love with him, and wished to marry him. I think that the desire of showing Mme. de Staël that an important personage did not disdain his name carried much weight in the eventual consent which he gave.

[1] *Madame Récamier and Her Friends*, p. 138.

Mme. de Staël learnt of this project, and her fury was such that he dared not accomplish it openly. However, he was secretly married, and his wife accompanied him to Lyons. There she took some small quantity of a drug which produced violent vomiting, and declared that she would poison herself once for all if he did not cast off Mme. de Staël by proclaiming his marriage. On the other hand, the latter vowed that she would stab herself if he did anything of the kind.

Such was the state of affairs when Benjamin Constant and Mme. de Staël met at Aix, under the mediation of Mme. Récamier. The mornings were spent in appalling scenes, in reproaches, imprecations, and hysterical attacks. These proceedings were not altogether genuine. We dined together, as usual, at watering-places. By degrees during the meal hostilities were suspended. One witty or brilliant observation would produce another. Their mutual pleasure in this intellectual sword-play became paramount, and the evening passed delightfully, while the morrow saw a renewal of yesterday morning's fury.

At length a treaty was signed under the following conditions: Mme. de Staël would write to Mme. Constant, thus recognising the marriage. But the marriage was not to be published until three months after her departure to America, whither she really intended to go at that time. This concession of affection to vanity never gave me a very agreeable impression. Though Benjamin yielded to outcry, he none the less felt hurt. In any case, Mme. de Staël did not start, and the marriage was recognised, though after a considerable interval. I think that Mme. de Staël was anxious to secure a continuance of that amusement and pleasure which she found in the mind of Benjamin Constant, and wished to take him to

America. Perhaps she thought of the possibility of marrying him when they were once beyond the Atlantic, and his marriage with another woman touched her more keenly at that moment. There was a real bond of sympathy between them, and his treatment of her pretty child, who was so indiscreet as to reproduce his features, was entirely paternal.

I have a keen recollection of one of the days of that period. We all went to dinner with M. de Boigne at Buissonrond, near Chambéry. He had gathered the most distinguished society in the town, including the prefect; there were thirty of us. Mme. de Staël was by the side of the master of the house, and the prefect opposite to her, at my side. She asked him across the table what had become of a man whom she had known as a sub-prefect; he answered that the man was now a prefect, and much respected.

"I am very glad to hear it; he was a good fellow. In any case," she added carelessly, "I have generally found that class of servant very decent."

I saw the prefect turn red and pale, and felt my heart in my mouth. Mme. de Staël did not seem to notice that she had been rude, nor had she intended to be. I quote the fact to point out a strange anomaly in this eminently sociable mind, namely, that she was entirely wanting in tact. Mme. de Staël never considered her audience in the least when she was talking, and, without the smallest intention of causing embarrassment or giving offence, she would often choose subjects of conversation and expressions most disagreeable to the persons to whom she spoke.

I remember that upon one occasion, before a number of people and in the presence of M. de Boigne, she cross-examined me, to know whether I thought it possible for a woman to behave when she had no community of taste or sympathy with her husband, and emphasised her point in such a way as to embarrass me cruelly. Another time I saw her put Mme. de Caumont on trial before twenty persons, and continue before the whole audience a conversation which they had begun with the object of proving that a woman who was not pure and chaste could not be a good mother. Poor Mme. de Caumont was reduced to despair. Mme. de Staël would have been overwhelmed with vexation had she perceived the fact, but she was carried away by her eloquent arguments and her special pleading, nor is any other explanation possible. Did she, then, forget her own manners? The question may be asked, and the answer is that she regarded herself as a privileged person, whose genius justified indiscretions inexcusable in ordinary mortals. This want of consideration for the feelings of other people has made her many more enemies than she deserved.

I return to the dinner at Buissonrond. We had reached the second course, which was proceeding like all wearisome dinners, to the great disgust of the provincial guests, when Elzéar de Sabran, seeing their disappointment, addressed himself to Mme. de Staël from the end of the table, asking whether she thought that the constitutional laws of Romulus would have preserved their influence at Rome as long as they did, had it not been for the religious laws of Numa. She raised her head, understood the appeal, merely replied to the question by a joke, and then became as brilliant and amiable as I have ever seen her. We were all delighted, and no one more so than the prefect, M. Finot, an intellectual man. An urgent letter was handed to him; he read it and put it in his pocket. After dinner he showed it to me. It was an order that Mme. de Staël was to be sent back to Coppet by the police from post to post as soon as he had received the letter. I begged him not to cause a disturbance in my house, and he assured me that he had no intention of doing so, adding with some bitterness, " I should be sorry if she changed her opinion concerning servants of my class! "

I undertook to make her understand that it was time to go back to Coppet, and he confined himself to enjoining the postmaster to issue horses only for the direct route. She had had some thoughts of an expedition to Milan.

In order to return to Aix, we took our places in the coach of Mme. de Staël, which held herself, Mme. Récamier, Benjamin Constant, Adrien de Montmorency, Albertine de Staël, and myself. A terrible storm came on; the night was pitch dark; the postillions lost their way, and we spent five hours on the road instead of one hour and a half. When we arrived we found everybody in a state of great anxiety, as a number of our party who had returned in my carriage had reached Aix three hours before. We were astounded at the time, and at the fright we had caused. No one in the coach had thought of the matter. I remember that the conversation had begun in the avenue of Buissonrond upon the letters of Mlle. de l'Espinasse, which had just been published, and the enchantress, sustained by Benjamin Constant, had held us so completely spell-bound that we had had no thoughts to spare for material affairs.

Two days afterwards she started in the early morning for Coppet, in a state of despair and prostration which would have been quite intelligible in the most ordinary woman.

I have often been since to Coppet, where I enjoyed myself greatly, the more so as I was much spoiled there.

Mme. de Staël was extremely obliged to me for daring the dangers of her exile, and amused herself with my chatter on Parisian society, where she was always glad to be. Her intellectual power was so prodigious that its surplus overflow was ever at the service of other people, but if after a talk with her one left her in admiration, one also left her entirely pleased with oneself. The talker felt that he had been at his best, for there was kindness as well as the wish to be amused in her mode of handling every one. She has said somewhere that superiority is much better shown in approval than in criticism, and she practised her precept. No one was so stupid that she could not get something out of him, at any rate for a moment, provided that he had some experience of the world, for she insisted upon formality. The provincials, and especially the Genevese, were crushed beneath her disdainful indifference; to such she did not trouble to be rude, but ignored their existence.

I was present at a large gathering in Geneva where she was expected, and at which everybody arrived at seven o'clock. She arrived at half-past ten with her usual escort, stopped at the door, speaking only to myself and to those whom she had brought from Coppet, and went away without even entering the room. Thus she was detested by the Genevese, though they were almost as proud of her as of their lake. To be on calling terms with Mme. de Staël was a distinguished honour in Geneva.

Life at Coppet was extraordinary. It seemed idle and irregular in the extreme, and no one knew whether he should be anywhere or do anything at any special time. There was no special place of meeting for any special hour of the day, and every room was always open. Tents were pitched wherever a conversation began, and there they stayed for hours or days, uninterrupted by any of the ordinary affairs of life. Talking seemed everybody's first duty. Yet almost all the persons composing this society were seriously occupied, as is proved by the large number of works from their pens. Mme. de Staël worked a great deal, but when she had nothing better to do, the most trivial social pleasure would absorb her time. She liked amateur theatricals, driving, walks, bringing people together, fetching them to her house, and above all things, talking.

She had no special writing room; a little writing-case of green morocco, which she put on her knees and carried about from room to room contained both her works and her correspondence. Even the writing-case was often enough surrounded by several people, and, in a word, the only thing she feared was solitude, and boredom was the scourge of her life. It is astonishing how many powerful geniuses have been entirely dominated by this impression. Mme. de Staël, Lord Byron, and M. de Chateaubriand are striking examples, and with the object of escaping boredom they have spoiled their lives, and would have been willing to turn the world upside down.

The children of Mme. de Staël were brought up amid this strange life, in which they appeared to take part. Yet they must have had hours to themselves, for it was impossible amid such disturbance that they should have learnt all they knew—drawing, music, and several languages—and have acquired a deep knowledge of the literature of all Europe. In any case, they only did what they wished to do. The tastes of Albertine were very serious: she chiefly studied metaphysics, religion, English and German literature; very little music, and no drawing. As to needlework, I do not think that such an article as a needle was to be found throughout the house of Coppet. Auguste, who was less distinguished than his sister, added an extraordinary talent for music to his literary occupations. Albert, whom Mme. de Staël had herself nicknamed " Lovelace of the Inn," drew very well, but his incapacity marked him out in the society in which he lived. He was killed in a duel in Sweden in 1813.

Mme. de Staël judged her children by their intellectual powers, and her preference was entirely for Albertine. This child preserved much of her frankness and simplicity, notwithstanding the expressions which she employed in her childhood. I remember that when she had been scolded by her mother, a rare occurrence, she was found in tears.

" What is the matter with you, Albertine? "

" Ah, people think I am happy, but my heart is torn in twain." She was only eleven years old, but she spoke what I called the language of Coppet. This was marked by a habit of exaggeration so entirely current that visitors would adopt it. Often when I went away I have attempted to analyse the brilliancy by which I had been attracted for so many hours, and have been forced to admit upon reflection that it was often lacking in common sense. It cannot, however, be denied that Mme. de Staël was, of the whole party, the least inclined to give way to this tendency. When she became unintelligible, it was in moments of inspiration when she carried her audience away with her and was understood instinctively. Usually her conversation was remarkably clear and entirely reasonable, at any rate as regards its expression.

It was at Coppet that the abuse of the word talent began, which has become so constant in doctrinaire cliques. Every member of the society was always full of his talent or thinking of the talent of others. " That does not harmonise with your talent "; " That is in accordance with your talent "; " You ought to devote your talent to it "; " I will try my talent," &c., &c., were phrases which recurred twenty times an hour in their conversation.

The last time that I saw Mme. de Staël at Coppet, she had placed herself in a very false position. After edifying the town of Geneva with the deplorable scenes resulting from a passion which she had conceived for a handsome American, Mr. O'Brien, she had shut herself up at Coppet and mourned his departure.

A young subaltern, the nephew of her doctor, Bouttigny, had returned from Spain severely wounded. Country air was desirable for his health, and Mme. de Staël told Bouttigny to send young Rocca to her house. He had been at school with her sons, and she showed him much kindness. He had an attractive face, and she made him tell her stories of Spain and its horrors, which he did with the frankness of a simple heart. She admired and flattered him; the young man was intoxicated with self-conceit, and became infatuated with her; the fact is certain that the passion was entirely on his side. Mme. de Staël felt nothing more than the gratitude of a woman of forty-five who is adored by a man of twenty-two. M. Rocca began to display his jealousy in public, and his triumph became complete. When I found her at Geneva, M. Rocca was in the full flush of success, and, it must be admitted, a ridiculous figure, and a constant source of embarrassment to Mme. de Staël.

Mme. de Staël, who did nothing by halves, was extremely delighted by my singing; probably she had scolded M. Rocca for his evident disregard of my performances. One evening, I had finished a song, and was standing by the piano talking with some of the guests, when M. Rocca, who still used a crutch, crossed the room and called loudly over the piano in his nasal drawl:

"Mâadame, Mâadame de Boigne, I didn't hear your voice. Mâadame, it goes to the heart."

Thereupon he turned round and went off again upon his crutch. Mme. de Staël, who was sitting near me, sprang up and caught my arm.

"Ah!" she said, "human speech is not his language."

The phrase always struck me as the outcry of a clever woman in love with a fool.

Mme. de Staël was even then complaining of her feeble health, and I think that the consequences of this connection greatly accelerated her death. Her condition caused her great pain, but she kept the secret admirably. Her children honestly and sincerely believed she was suffering from dropsy. Spied upon as she was by a police force of extraordinary energy, it is astonishing that her secret was not discovered. She was at home to visitors as usual, merely saying that she was ill; and immediately after her confinement she fled the spot where she had suffered so much, and which had become intolerable to her, leaving no trace of the event which had taken place.[1]

In view of the Emperor's constant animosity towards Mme. de Staël, he would not have hesitated to announce the secret, had he entertained the smallest suspicion. But it was faithfully kept, and appearances were entirely saved, which proves, by the way, that cleverness can overcome any difficulty.

Doubtless she might have married M. Rocca, but that was the last resource of desperation. She yielded only upon her death-bed at the earnest supplication of the

[1] Louis Alphonse Rocca was born April 17, 1812.

Duchesse de Broglie, after she had revealed to her the existence of the little Rocca.

M. and Mme. de Broglie, as well as Auguste de Staël, made as many efforts to give their mother another legitimate heir as less scrupulous people would have made to avoid this result. I am inclined to think that this incident in her mother's life contributed to direct Mme. de Broglie towards the Methodism which she adopted.

M. Rocca followed Mme. de Staël everywhere, and clung to her in embarrassments which only his passionate devotion could have tolerated, for she was wearied and harassed by his presence, though touched by his affection. He died of grief six months after her death, thus justifying the weakness she had shown by the depth of his devotion.

This, in any case, was the explanation of the intimacy given by Mme. de Staël herself. She was the more delighted to be able to inspire deep devotion at her age, as her lack of beauty had always been a cause of great vexation to her. Her mode of concession to this weakness was unusual: she never said that a woman was ugly or pretty, but merely that she possessed or lacked external advantages. This was her habitual phrase, and one could not say that a person was ugly in her presence without hurting her feelings.

I have related my intimacy with Mme. de Staël at some length. Whether I have added anything to what is known of her, I cannot say, but I have been able to recall recollections which I highly prize. No one who had ever met her could forget the charm of her society. I think her conversation was far more remarkable than her books. It would be an entire mistake to think of her as in the least pedantic or affected. She would talk dress with as much interest as constitutional law, and if, as she said, she had made conversation an art, she had become a perfect artist, for naturalness was the dominant feature of her talk.

She gave enough attention to her pecuniary affairs to avoid any monetary loss. Notwithstanding the apparent carelessness of her habits, she was exact in matters of business, and her circumstances were rather improved than involved. Her exile was terribly harassing to her spirit, and it must be said that under the Emperor Napoleon exile was accompanied by all those petty vexations which can make it intolerable; no one attempted any mitigation of its severity.[1] It was the chief restraint upon that section of society since known as the Faubourg Saint-Germain. I have known several persons thus exiled, of various tastes, habits, fortunes, and positions, and all expressed a despair which became a salutary warning to others. Hence prudence during this period was both scrupulous and general.

[1] Mme. de Staël wrote to Mme. Récamier: "No one can have any idea of what exile is. It is the hundred-headed hydra as regards unhappiness." And again: "One is dead when one is exiled. It is merely a tomb where the post arrives."

CHAPTER XV

Amusements at Coppet—Exile of Mathieu de Montmorency and of Mme. Récamier—Mme. de Chevreuse—Her conduct at the imperial court—Her exile—Her death—Mme. de Balbi—Count Romanzow—Marriage of Fanny Dillon—Ball on the occasion of the marriage of the Grand Duke of Baden—The Emperor's costume—Strange conversation—Formalities of the imperial court—Ball on the occasion of the birth of the King of Rome —The Empress Marie Louise—The Emperor attempts to be gracious.

I HAVE always reproached Mme. de Staël for involving her friends in the misfortunes of the exile which she felt so strongly. During the summer of 1808 Coppet had been a brilliant scene; Prince Augustus of Prussia had made a long stay there. He was deeply in love with Mme. Récamier. Several foreigners and many Frenchmen had joined the brilliant and intellectual opposition led by Mme. de Staël. When this society assumed a separate position, it had proceeded to spread throughout Europe the phrases and the ideas with which it stigmatised the imperial government. These remarks had been carried back to Prussia by Prince Augustus, and there fell upon ready ears. A meeting had been arranged at Coppet for the following summer. The Emperor had been informed of what was going on; his wrath had consequently been irritated afresh, and he had decided that these meetings should not be renewed.

He announced his intentions so loudly that the friends of Mme. de Staël were aware of them, including Mme.

Récamier and Mathieu de Montmorency. Both spoke to me upon the subject, and were agreed that, if only in the interest of Mme. de Staël, it would be advisable to let the storm pass over, to avoid meeting at Coppet, and to let the tranquillity of the opening summer obliterate the memories of the past year. Mathieu and Mme. Récamier wrote a joint letter from this point of view, and entrusted it to Mme. de Châteauvieux, for at that time no one would have dared to send such a letter by post. Mme. de Staël's anger was not characterised by the same prudence, and she entrusted to the next post an answer full of sorrow and reproaches, concluding with this sentence: " Up to the present I have known only the rose-strewn paths of exile, and it has been reserved for those whom I love most of all to show me its thorns, or rather to plunge a dagger into my heart by proving to me that I am nothing more to them than an object of terror and repulsion."

Mme. Récamier and Mathieu de Montmorency no longer hesitated, but started off. Mathieu arrived at Coppet twelve hours before the order of exile which sent him to Valence.[1]

Mme. Récamier had not yet arrived; Auguste de Staël hastened to meet her, found her in the Jura, and advised

[1] The exile of Mme. Récamier and of Mathieu de Montmorency took place in the month of August 1811. There is thus a mistake in the coincidence indicated by Mme. de Boigne. The true chronology seems to be as follows: In 1807 was the brilliant summer gathering at Coppet, at which Prince Augustus of Prussia was present. In 1808 Mme. Récamier does not go to Coppet, as the meetings of the previous year had given offence to those in power. In 1809 Mme. Récamier joins Mme. de Staël at Lyons, and proceeds with her to Coppet. In 1810 Mme. Récamier spends the summer at Aix in Savoy, and then goes to meet Mme. de Staël at the castle of Chaumont-sur-Loire, near Blois. Then the whole colony is transferred to Fossé, at the house of M. de Salaberry, where the summer is concluded. (Cp. *Madame Récamier and Her Friends*.)

her to retreat, in the hope that as the order had not found her at Coppet, it would perhaps be revoked. She took the road to Paris, accompanied by a young cousin whose education she had had in hand for some years, and whose father held a small post at Dijon. When she reached that town she found him at the door of the inn, and he explained to her in a few words that though he was overwhelmed with gratitude for her former kindness, he could not leave his daughter in charge of an exiled person without compromising himself, and he then took the girl away. Mme. Récamier continued her road alone, and reached her own house in Paris by midnight. M. Récamier was horrified to see her.

"Good gracious! What are you doing here? You ought to be at Châlons. Get into your carriage and start at once."

"I can do no more. I have been travelling two nights, and am tired to death."

"Well, have a good sleep; I will order the post-horses for five o'clock in the morning."

Mme. Récamier started off at that time, and went to Mme. de Catelan, who showered all the consolations of friendship upon her, and accompanied her to Châlons with truly heroic devotion, for we have already seen the fear that the epithet "exiled" inspired in ordinary hearts.[1]

The actual terms of this formidable sentence of exile were confined to exclusion from Paris and from a radius of forty leagues round the town. At first special places of exile were assigned, but the regulations were soon relaxed, and outside Paris and its neighbourhood the

[1] See in the Appendix the letter of Adrien de Montmorency. Mme. de Boigne's story is divergent from the accounts hitherto published, though these accounts contain many discrepancies.

whole of the empire was left open. But the prestige of the imperial power was so great that any one who had had the misfortune to displease was everywhere exposed to daily vexations.

The fate of Mme. de Staël became even worse; not only was she exiled to Coppet itself, but those who wished to visit her were obliged to obtain express permission from the prefect. It was in consequence of these new difficulties that she sometimes secured an authorisation to make a short stay at Geneva on the pretext of health, and thus it was that I found her at Geneva, as I have related above. Mme. Récamier was at Châlons, then at Lyons, and eventually went to Italy, where she was still staying at the fall of the Empire.

The subject of exile naturally leads me to speak of one of its victims, the young, pretty, and extravagant Mme. de Chevreuse. I have already said that she held a special position in what was then known as the society of the *ancien régime*. The Emperor would not receive any titled person whose title was not of his own creation, and though the Duc de Luynes was a senator, and most obsequious to the head of the state, the independent attitude of his daughter-in-law was noticed, and aroused displeasure. When she was appointed lady of honour to the Empress, she refused; the Emperor insisted, and sent for her, combating half seriously and half jestingly every excuse she offered. At the same time, he went so far as to threaten to make her family responsible for her caprices. She might go and consult the walls of Dampierre, and they would tell her that they only belonged to the Luynes family by confiscation; it would, therefore, be prudent not to forget this precedent.

Mme. de Chevreuse thus saw herself obliged to accept. It cannot be denied that the Emperor was by no means ungracious to her after thus exerting pressure, and seemed to make the task of winning her over a special caprice of his own. In return she displayed an attitude entirely sulky, both towards him and especially towards the Empress Joséphine and her ladies, whom she overwhelmed with her disdain. It was not that they were inferior in position to herself, but she suspected that they felt less reluctance to accept their positions as court ladies. She would only perform her duties when reduced to extremity, and when she had exhausted all pretexts. She never appeared at the palace if she could escape, and, in one word, was extremely rude.

As long as the Duc de Luynes was alive, he maintained a show of appearances, but after his death Mme. de Chevreuse, who entirely dominated her mother-in-law and her husband, began a series of absurdities. Among other things, I remember that, upon the occasion of a grand party at the residence of the Duc de Luynes, she placed the associates of M. de Talleyrand opposite to a bust of Louis XVI., which was put on a sideboard surrounded with candelabras and a multitude of vases full of lilies arranged like an altar. She took us all to see this contrivance with the delight of a boarding school girl. Although I was almost as outspoken as she was, I considered these tricks as puerile and dangerous, and told her so. She replied:

" What would you have? The little wretch " (this was her invariable title for the great Napoleon) " victimises me, and I must avenge myself as I can."

She succeeded in making herself hated by the whole court, but the Emperor continued to take her part. When the old sovereigns of Spain arrived in France after the events in Madrid, they were provided at first with the usual attendants of honour. Mme. de Chevreuse

was ordered to present herself to Queen Charlotte, and
sent a note of refusal, saying that it was quite enough to
be a slave, and she had no wish to become a gaoler.
The lady of honour, Mme. de la Rochefoucault, to whom
this reply was addressed, carried it to the Emperor, and
the order of exile was the result.

As she had done all in her power to provoke this sentence, one would have thought Mme. de Chevreuse would
have borne it courageously. The real state of affairs
was very different, and when the first excitement was
over she was crushed. There was no step, no protesta-
tion, no supplication which she did not make in the hope
of securing pardon. As her hopes diminished her health
declined, and she eventually died of vexation in the third
year of her exile. She lived successively in Luynes,
Lyons, and Grenoble, bringing to every locality that capricious temper which ruined her life. Although I was
not her friend, my relations with her were fairly intimate. When she learnt that I was in Savoy during her
stay in Grenoble, she wrote to me saying how much she
regretted that the difficulties which hampered the move-
ments of an exile would prevent her from coming to see
me. I replied that I would go to Grenoble, a determination which obliged me to travel an additional
forty leagues on leaving Chambéry. I informed Mme.
de Chevreuse of the day of my arrival, and the old
Duchesse de Luynes was waiting for me at my inn.
Mme. de Chevreuse was so ill that it was impossible for
her to come and see me or to receive me at her house,
but she would be delighted to have a visit from me the
next morning.

An hour later, standing at the window, I saw pass by
in a carriage, covered with red and I think with white,
an apparition in full dress, which seemed to me to be

that of Mme. de Chevreuse.   I asked the servant at the
inn who it was, and he said :

"It is Mme. de Chevreuse, going to the theatre.   She
goes there every day."

I thought this treatment somewhat strange ; however,
she was so unhappy that I did not wish to show her any
displeasure.   The next day poor Mme. de Luynes came
to tell me that Mme. de Chevreuse had not slept, that
she was resting at that moment, but would certainly see
me in the evening.   I expressed my regret that I could
no longer prolong my stay, ordered my horses, and went
away.   The fact was Mme. de Chevreuse shrank from
displaying the terrible change in her fortunes to one who
had not seen her since the days of her highest prosperity.

Apart from her exile, Mme. de Chevreuse had another
vexation which poisoned her life.   Her hair was extremely red.   She was persuaded that no one suspected
it, and was constantly preoccupied with this care : two
hours before her death, as her hair had grown somewhat
during her last illness, she ordered it to be cut and thrown
into the fire before her eyes, that no trace might be left.[1]

As her children had been so indiscreet as to have hair
of a fiery red, she had conceived a horror of them, and had
declined to see them.   With all these eccentricities, which
were due to some hereditary taint and were accentuated
by the indulgence of Mme. de Luynes, Mme. de Chevreuse had fine qualities : her heart was in the right place,
and, without any pretentiousness, she had an original
manner of discussing the most ordinary affairs of life
which always made her attractive, and she could be very
pleasant when she wished.   She was the only person who
was forced to enter the imperial court.   Those, therefore,

[1] The Duchesse de Chevreuse, *née* Narbonne-Pelet, died at Lyons
in July 1813.

who were not anxious to be summoned did not fail to quote her case as a proof that this fate was inevitable. Yet nothing was so easy to avoid by means of an attitude of reserve. The sentence of exile, except in two or three cases occasioned by private vengeance, only fell upon persons whose hostility was noisy and truculent, and they became forthwith repentant and compliant.

Mme. de Balbi was an exception to this rule. Exiled from Paris by an obvious mistake, she would never allow the smallest step to be taken to explain the error or to secure her pardon. She established herself quietly at Montauban, and lived there upon the best possible terms with the authorities, thus avoiding the persecution with which they might have afflicted her. There she remained until the restoration, in dignified calm, and suffered less from her exile than those who exerted themselves to bring it to a close. I have often been asked at that time:

" How is it that you are not exiled? "

" It is because I do not go out of my way to seek exile," I used to reply, " and am not afraid of it."

My house, in fact, was one of those where opinion was most outspoken. I saw many members of every party, and was agreeable to them all. My opinions were known, but were not expressed with bitterness. Moreover, we did not intrigue with inferior conspirators, the paid agents of disturbance and disorder, for whom my father entertained a scorn which he had communicated to me. I saw a great deal of the diplomatic body: Count Tolstoi and Count Nesselrode were constant visitors, as also were the Semffts and Count Metternich. When they were replaced by the Prince of Schwarzenberg, de Kourakan, &c., the new diplomatic body separated in a marked degree from the opposition and devoted itself to the imperial court.

The obsequious respect of foreigners for the new greatness often excited our laughter. I can remember that old Count Romanzow, Chancellor of Russia, excused himself one evening for reaching my house late by saying that he had been detained because Monseigneur the Arch-Chancellor had done him the honour of requesting him to make up a game. Those of us who had never dreamt of calling this man anything but plain Cambacérès were not a little astonished by this language. By degrees, however, these formalities became established; and if the Empire had lasted a few years longer, we should have adopted them in our turn, as we had already done in the case of the imperial family.

I was brought most directly into connection with the court through Fanny Dillon. The Emperor had undertaken to get her married, and she did not allow him to forget his promise, while her innocent manner of reminding him amused him greatly. However, he kept her waiting a terribly long time. The marriages of Mlles. de Beauharnais and de Tascher with the Grand Duke of Baden and the reigning Prince d'Arenberg had greatly raised her claims. She had however, condescended to consent to marry Prince Alphonse Pignatelli, the younger son of the house of Egmont. I do not know if the marriage would have taken place, but death carried off the bridegroom. After that, the Empress Joséphine successively mentioned Prince Aldobrandini, who would be made King of Portugal, and the Duke of Medina Sidonia, while she had a moment's anxiety upon the subject of the Prince of Neuchâtel. Eventually, during the spring of 1808, she spoke to me of her fear that she might be forced to marry Prince Bernard of Saxe-Coburg, whom she thought somewhat too German.

In the middle of the summer her sister, Mme. de Fitz-

James, expired in my arms after a long illness caused
by her husband's annoyances. He had begun to regret
her bitterly, I believe, when it was too late to save her.
Her last words were to recommend her mother to my
care, and I carried her off to Beauregard with Fanny.
The same day the Empress arrived from Marsac, and,
in spite of her mourning, Fanny went off to Saint Cloud
two days afterwards. She came back in despair: the
Empress had told her that General Bertrand was the husband whom the Emperor destined for her. The disappointment was great, and she felt it deeply. She
was in tears when the Emperor came into the apartments of the Empress. She ventured to reproach him
for deceiving her hopes, and grew so excited that she
actually said, " What, Sire! Bertrand? Bertrand?
Why not the Pope's monkey? "

This remark sealed her fate, and the Emperor said
dryly, " That will do, Fanny," and left the room.

The Empress undertook to persuade him otherwise,
thinking herself that Bertrand was not sufficiently important to marry a relative who was under her special
care. She promised to send an answer by the end of the
week. Poor Fanny spent the interval in tears. She
went back to Saint Cloud, saying that she had decided
to refuse Bertrand at whatever cost, and her mother
greatly encouraged her. She came back having accepted him, and entirely reconciled to her fate. The
Empress had shown her a prospect of high position, and
the name of Bertrand hidden beneath a dukedom. She
spent the evening in choosing the title which would
sound best, but which she never secured. I have always thought that this was a piece of spite on the Emperor's part in return for the remark about the Pope's
monkey.

The interview took place at Beauregard: Mme. Dillon declined to be present, and I was left in charge. Never had a sulkier or more slovenly *fiancée* appeared before a future husband. The General, however, was not repelled, and precisely one month after the death of Mme. Fitz-James, Mme. Dillon accompanied her other daughter to the altar, with a repugnance which she did not attempt to hide. The civil marriage took place at my house in Paris, and the wedding at Saint Leu, at the house of the Queen of Holland. I had been invited, but found a pretext for refusal.

To do justice to Bertrand, for a man of limited ideas he was entirely upright. He was a good husband and son-in-law, and we have always been on the best of terms. He was said to possess much capacity in his own profession. The Emperor was a good judge, and marked him out, but I think that his true merit was blind and unlimited devotion.

Fanny Dillon used to go driving at Saint Cloud with my horses and servants. One day when a household official was putting them in their place, my coachman said to him:

" Of course, I will go where you like. We never come here for our own pleasure, so I do not care."

This piece of effrontery delighted our foolish partisanship. It recalls to me the remark of a sentinel uttered some years later at a moment when the imperial court was full of sovereigns. This functionary addressed a cabman who had stopped in the court of the Tuileries, and called out to him:

" You, there! be off. Unless your master is a king you cannot stand there."

The Emperor was much amused at this story, for there were real kings among those thus treated.

I have often seen the Emperor Napoleon at the theatre, or driving in a carriage, but only twice in a room. The town of Paris gave a ball on the occasion of the marriage of the Princess of Baden. The Emperor wished to return it, and tickets were sent out for a ball at the Tuileries to many persons who had not been presented at court. Some of us young women received tickets, though we had not been present at the municipal ball, and after discussing the matter, we agreed that it was our duty to go. Dancing went on in the Galerie de Diane and in the Salle des Maréchaux. The public were confined to these rooms according to the colour of their tickets, and mine took me to the Galerie de Diane. There was no communication between one room and the other, and the court passed into the rooms successively. The Empress, the princesses, their ladies, and their chamberlains, all in full dress, entered in the train of the Emperor, and took up their position upon a platform prepared beforehand. After watching the performance of a kind of ballet, the Emperor came down alone and went round the room, speaking exclusively to the ladies. He wore his imperial dress (which he almost immediately afterwards abandoned) : the waistcoat and white satin knee breeches, the white shoes with gold rosettes, a coat of red velvet cut straight in the style of Francis I., with gold embroidery upon all the seams, the sword sparkling with diamonds above the coat, orders and stars also of diamonds, and a cap with the feathers held up by a diamond buckle. The costume was well designed, but was utterly unsuited for him on account of his small size, his corpulence, and clumsiness of movement. Perhaps it was prejudice on my part, but the Emperor seemed to me frightful, and looked like a mock king. I was standing between two women unknown to me. He asked the first her name, and she replied that she was the daughter of Foacier.

" Ah ! " he said, and passed on.

According to his custom, he also asked my name, which I told him.

" You live at Beauregard ? "

" Yes, Sire."

" It is a beautiful spot, and your husband employs much labour there; I am grateful to him for the service he does to the country, as I am to all who employ work-men. He has been in the English army ? "

I thought it shorter to answer " Yes," but he con-tinued :

" That is to say, not entirely. He is a Savoyard, is he not ? "

" Yes, Sire."

" But you are French, entirely French, and we there-fore claim you, for you are not one of those rights easily surrendered."

I bowed.

" How old are you ? "

I told him.

" And frank into the bargain. You look much younger."

I bowed again. He stepped back half a pace, and then came up to me, speaking lower in a confidential tone :

" You have no children ? I know that is not your fault, but you should make better arrangements. Believe me, I am giving you good advice."

I remained stupefied; he looked at me for a moment with a gracious smile, and went on to my neighbour.

" Your name ? "

" A daughter of Foacier."

" Another daughter of Foacier!" and he continued his promenade.

I cannot express the deep aristocratic disdain with which the phrase " another daughter of Foacier " left the imperial lips. Neither the name nor the persons have ever come before me since that time, but it has remained in my memory with the inflection of that voice which I then heard for the first and last time. After he had made his round, the Emperor returned to the Empress, and all the gilded troop went off without commingling in any way with the plebeian horde. At nine o'clock in the evening all was over: the guests might remain and dance, but the court had retired. I followed the example of the court, being strangely impressed by imperial manners. I had seen other monarchs, but none who treated the public in so cavalier a fashion.

Some years afterwards I was present as an onlooker at a ball given upon the occasion of the baptism of the King of Rome. I think it was the last imperial festivity. It took place in the Tuileries, in the theatre room: the court alone was present, and persons who had not been presented were given tickets for the boxes. A dozen of us ladies who belonged to the opposition went there, and we were forced to admit that the spectacle was magnificent. Uniforms were prohibited, and our old soldiers seemed ill at ease, but the young ones, especially M. de Flahaut, rivalled the grace of Archambault de Périgord. The women were elegantly and magnificently dressed. The Emperor, followed by his escort, crossed the room as he arrived to reach the platform which occupied the back. He walked first with such speed that almost everybody, not excepting the Empress, was almost obliged to run to keep up with him. Dignity and grace were thus out of the question, but this rustling of skirts and rapid pace seemed to symbolise a dominant power which suited him. It was magnificent, though not in our way.

He seemed, indeed, the master of all this magnificence. He was no longer in his imperial costume, and the simple uniform which he alone wore in the midst of all this full dress made him a yet more striking figure, and spoke more loudly to the imagination than all the gold lace in the world. He was anxious to be gracious and kind, and made a far better impression upon me than at the other ball. The Empress Marie Louise was a fine woman, fresh in appearance, but somewhat too red. Notwithstanding her dress and her precious stones, she seemed very vulgar and entirely without distinction. A quadrille was performed, danced by the princesses and the court ladies, several of whom were our friends. I saw there the Princess Borghese, who seemed to me the most ravishing beauty that I had ever looked upon : to all her perfections was added the air of candid maidenhood as complete as any young girl could have, though if history is to be believed, no one ever had less right to it.

The Emperor was anxious that the women he had wished to attract to his court should have an opportunity of seeing its splendours. He cast obliging glances upon the boxes, and remained for a long time beneath ours, evidently of set purpose. In any case, there were already too many of our party at court, and there was no need for him to trouble about those who were left outside.

CHAPTER XVI

DURING the years which passed between these festivals of which I have just spoken, the two societies of
the old and the new *régime* were habitually separated;
they met, however, at ambassadorial receptions and at
the houses of foreigners. I remember seeing the whole
of the imperial court at a very magnificent ball given by
the Duchesse de Courlande. She had set up house in
Paris on the occasion of the marriage of her youngest
daughter with Comte Edmond de Périgord. I do not
know whether the passion of the Duchesse de Courlande
for the Prince de Talleyrand was previous or subsequent
to this marriage.

Mme. Edmond, who has become almost an historical
personage under the name of the Duchesse de Dino, was
little more than a child, exceedingly pretty, attractive,
and gracious; her intellectual power was already obvious.
She possessed every attraction except that of naturalness, and pleased me greatly, notwithstanding this want
of the greatest charm of youth. Her mother, who was
entirely occupied by her own intrigues, had left the care
of her education to an old Jesuit teacher, who had turned
out a very accomplished and well-instructed pupil.

Providence had made her a pretty and lively woman, but the moral part of her education, that of precept and practice, had been neglected, or rather those sights which her precocious intelligence had seen about her were not calculated to give her the best ideas upon the duties which a woman is called upon to fulfil. Possibly she would have escaped these early dangers if her husband had been her equal in power, and if she had been able to love and honour him. This, however, was impossible, for the distance between them was too great.

I insist upon these reflections because I am convinced that, whatever be the advantages with which a woman is born, her conduct in the world is nearly always the result of her environment. Many a woman has been an object of scandal who, under other conditions, might have been a pure wife and mother. I am a believer in fireside education. If youth has been spent in the principles of healthy morality, simply professed and continually practised, a young woman is surrounded, as it were, by barriers of adamantine strength, the weight and power of which she does not feel, but which become second nature. To break such bonds, perversity must rise to an extraordinary height. Let us therefore be charitable to those who have been exposed to the seductions of the world, unprotected by this defence.

I have just mentioned the name of M. de Talleyrand, but I shall not venture to speak of him, or to give any sketch of a character which rather belongs to the graving tool of the historian: it is the latter who must weigh the wrongs of his private life against his services as a statesman, and draw the balance between them.

In these scattered notes, in which I am amusing myself by reviving, like a series of shadows, without order or connection, the different recollections which recur to memory, I am more inclined to enlarge upon minor circumstances which are striking enough to remain in my memory, but are not of sufficient importance to be mentioned elsewhere. Historical personages do not come within my view except as personally connected with myself, or when I have collected detailed information concerning them upon the accuracy of which I can depend. At this moment I find myself precisely in the position of the public—an ill-disposed public, be it said —with reference to the Prince of Benevento; later, perhaps, I shall have an opportunity of speaking of Prince Talleyrand. We shall see, when I reach that period.

The cardinals, who were scattered about France, were permitted, or rather ordered, to meet in Paris at the time of the Emperor's marriage with the Archduchess. Consalvi was one of their number; he came to be put up at our house, and hardly left us during his short stay. I was much struck by the lucidity and clarity of his intellect as he explained to us the position, which theology and politics had made so complex. In the interest of religion he was sincerely anxious to please the Emperor's wishes, and yet the canons of the Church opposed his wish so directly as to prevent its accomplishment.

Unless I am mistaken difficulties were raised, not merely by the form in which Joséphine's marriage had been annulled, but to a greater extent by the personal position of the Emperor. He was excommunicated *vitando*. This did not prevent him from receiving the sacraments, or incapacitate any priest who should administer the sacrament to him in case of necessity, but the other ecclesiastics could not be present. Thus, the cardinals were ready to appear at a ball or any festivity, but the bench reserved for them during the administration of the sacrament of marriage remained empty. I think that had it depended solely upon Cardinal Consalvi, he would have found some means of compromise. Several of his colleagues were more violent and less reasonable than he, and the position of any one who withholds the patrimony of St. Peter is so positively specified as ex-communicate *vitando* by the laws of the Church, that it was impossible to evade these laws, as soon as they had been invoked.

On his side, the Emperor wished to carry the matter with a high hand, and his fury at the sight of the empty cardinals' bench was extreme. Some were sent into for-tresses, while others, of whom Consalvi was one, were obliged to return to towns arranged for their exile. I do not remember if it was at this moment, or previously, that they had been forbidden to wear their red stockings and cap; it was from this prohibition that they gained the name of " Black Cardinals," which distinguished them throughout the course of these ecclesiastical po-litical quarrels.

The short stay which Cardinal Consalvi made at Paris revived the friendship existing between us, and though my childish remembrances had been outraged when meet-ing Cardinal Maury, I was, on the other hand, delighted with his colleague. My opposition to the imperial gov-ernment was strongly inspired by party spirit, but at the same time I have always been amenable to arguments which bore a character of impartiality. I was touched and edified to see Cardinal Consalvi, in his position as a persecuted man, speak with such gentleness when he la-mented the extremes to which he had been brought, and find means to avoid them with such evident good faith.

He had several conferences with the Minister of Pub-lic Worship, and proposed compromises, the details of which I have forgotten, and which he related to us hour by hour; but the Emperor would listen to no one. The public remained persuaded that the absence of the cardinals was simply due to the fact that they would not admit the divorce, and this I believe to be a mistake. I was absent from the marriage festivities, as from those of the coronation. I credited my political repugnance with this want of curiosity, but I have since discovered that my idleness was the leading motive. I thought that the trouble involved was far worse than the pleasure which would have been gained, and was entirely satisfied by a second-hand account of the festivities, of which I read the next day in my armchair, congratulating myself that I had escaped the fatigue of them.

I only saw the illuminations, which were incomparably more beautiful than any I can remember. The Emperor, who had no lack of magnificent ideas, conceived the notion of a canvas model of the great Arc de l'Etoile as it exists at the present day, and this improvised monument made a surprising effect. I think that this is the first example of that wise idea now adopted of trying the effect of buildings before definitely erecting them. The Arc de l'Etoile obtained all the approval which it deserved.

My uncle, the Bishop of Nancy, was present at the council of French bishops who met at Paris with the object of coming to some agreement upon existing differences with the Pope; no result was obtained. My uncle's attitude was entirely episcopal, but sufficiently governmental to secure the Emperor's favour. He gave him a disastrous mark of his satisfaction by appointing him Archbishop of Florence some time afterwards. He had done much good at Nancy, where he enjoyed the highest respect and was very comfortable. To leave such a residence, where he was regularly and canonically established, in order to take violent possession of an Italian diocese against the wishes of the clergy and the Pope, was a grievous calamity, and brought down upon his head that clerical hatred which never forgives.

He reached Paris in despair. My father, who had a deep affection for him, fully sympathised with his position. They discussed the matter at length, and after weighing respectively the dangers of displeasing the Emperor or breaking with fellow ecclesiastics, they concluded that it was not advisable to assume this responsibility alone. The Bishop of Nantes, du Voisin, and the Archbishop of Tours, Barral, had been promised important sees in Italy which were under the same disadvantageous conditions as that of Florence. My uncle decided that acceptance by the Archbishop of Tours was not enough, but that if the Bishop of Nantes accepted, he would be forced to follow suit. Mgr. du Voisin was regarded as a clever theologian, and was the most highly respected prelate in the Gallican Church. My father approved this view, and after my uncle had announced it to the Minister of Public Worship, he went to pay his respects to the Emperor, who received him very kindly. The three bishops who had thus been nominated met several times. My uncle was then staying with us. He told us one morning that the Bishop of Nantes had just set off for Nantes after a formal refusal, and that consequently he was about to betake himself to Saint Cloud with the Minister of Public Worship, to give in his own refusal. Mgr. de Barral had not yet come to a decision.

The Bishop ordered that his travelling carriage should be packed, that he might return to Nancy the next day. He remained talking for a long time with my father and myself, going over the numerous excellent reasons which made his decision irrevocable. It was late when he returned. At dinner we were talking of straw hats, and the Bishop said to me with a forced smile:

"My dear, I hope you will let me get you what hats you want, for I think the most beautiful are made in Tuscany."

My father and I exchanged a look of surprise. The next morning the Bishop took the high-road to Nancy, but only to pack up, and continued his journey to Florence. We were careful to avoid any explanation. When an intellectual and conscientious man thus acts against his own judgment and has decided his attitude, there is nothing more to be said. I never learnt anything further of the matter. I do not know whether the Emperor had intimidated him or persuaded him, but neither process could have been easy in the case of a man whose morality was in no way inferior to his intellect. The fact took place precisely as I have related it.

On his return from Florence in 1814, the decision he had taken had proved too unsuccessful to admit of any discussion of the past. It was eventually the cause of my uncle's death, for the hatred of the *émigré* and clerical parties united in full acerbity to embitter the rest of his life. Notwithstanding the high reputation which he enjoyed at Nancy, whither he returned, these forces drew sufficient venom from his unfortunate stay at Florence to torment him so far as to shatter his health. If he had remained at Nancy, none of these tribulations would have happened to him, and he would have found that the Popes were his protectors instead of bitter antagonists desiring revenge;[1] but to resist the Emperor's

[1] Mme. de Boigne, brought up in the ideas of the eighteenth century, and imbued with the Jansenist and Gallican spirit, was in-

will, no matter how excellent the motives, seemed at that time to be a species of insanity, and he himself attempted to establish this idea.

Alexis de Noailles received a sub-lieutenant's commission, and was ordered to join the army. He declared that he did not wish to serve, and resisted all representations. He was arrested and carried off to prison, but still held out. The Emperor was minded to send him to Charenton. With great trouble, permission was obtained for him to stay at Vincennes. At length, unable to overcome his opposition, and possibly fearing that this madness might become contagious, the Emperor released him, ordering him to leave the empire, where he would have no vestry conspirators. Satisfied with giving him this ironical nickname, he opened the doors of his prison while closing those of his country. He is the only person, to my knowledge, who ever resisted the Emperor, as Mme. de Chevreuse was the only woman who was ever forced to accept a position at the imperial court.

Alexis de Noailles was not the only man to be thus nominated; a dozen similar commissions were sent out at the same time to the younger members of those families whose opposition was most loudly proclaimed. They were issued after a fancy-dress ball given by Mme. du Cayla, where so much magnificence was displayed that rumours of it reached the Emperor's ears. He was quite willing that people outside the Government should vegetate in peace and quiet; as soon as any one attracted

different to the practices of religion, though not hostile to religion as such. At the close of her life her sentiments changed, and she died with the consolations of religion, which she asked and received in full consciousness. Here she is speaking and judging from a worldly point of view, which is by no means that of the Head of the Church.

notice by any means, it was necessary to attach him to the Government, and he would recognise no marks of distinction which did not come from himself. In any case, his judgment in this instance was well founded, for, with the exception of Alexis, all these sub-lieutenants, thus hastily improvised by force, became zealous supporters of the imperial crown. I cannot say if at this time Mme. du Cayla had begun that intimacy with the Duc de Rovigo which was evidenced by her son's likeness to him.

After she had attracted public notice by her relations with Louis XVIII., a thousand scandalous stories were spread abroad concerning her. Of these I had never heard anything; she was as agreeable as any one could be, with a complexion utterly ruined, was lively and extremely anxious to please. She lived on bad terms with her husband, who was something more than eccentric, but was full of tender care for her mother-in-law, who adored her. If I had been asked for information about her at that time, I should have represented her as a young lady entirely well conducted, even somewhat prudish and of ostentatious piety. I remember that upon one occasion, when she had danced a quadrille on Shrove Tuesday, she found some one else to take her place in it the next Saturday, although the other seven partners offered no objection to a second performance.

Mme. du Cayla showed the utmost attention to the old ladies who formed her mother-in-law's society, and to the bishops or clergy of the "little Church." We thought that she was following her taste, but she has since proved that a spirit of intrigue and desire to improve her reputation were her primary motives. She never failed to fast at the appointed times with ostentation, a practice much more remarkable under the Empire than under the restoration. Few people at that time made much show of outward practice, and balls went on without scruple during the first two weeks of Lent, though not after mid-Lent. I remember that the Comte de Palfy was so ill advised as to give a ball on Good Friday, which was attended by only two ladies even from the imperial court.

This recalls to my mind the conversion of Jules de Polignac. I have never been able to believe in the sincerity of his devotion, and my incredulity is based upon these facts. There was in Lyons a rich heiress, whose mother was under the influence of the priests of the " little Church," as those opposed to the Concordat were called. The marriage of this girl with Alexis de Noailles, at that time leader of the sect, was arranged by them. He went to Lyons to conclude arrangements, and in one week succeeded in displeasing both daughter and mother so entirely that the marriage was broken off. Jules de Polignac, who had been allowed to stay at Vincennes by the special favour of the Emperor, for he had only been condemned to three years' imprisonment, a term long since completed, now flattered himself that the imperial clemency would grow weary of thus arbitrarily aggravating his troubles, and cherished hopes that he might leave his imprisonment. Adrien de Montmorency, showed much friendliness to the prisoners of Vincennes.

The rupture of the marriage of Alexis de Noailles was discussed one evening at my house.

" Dear me," said Adrien, " I have just been telling the story to Jules. I told him that if he was as good a Catholic as he is a Royalist, it would be quite easy to arrange this marriage for him. His position, as coming from Vincennes, would immediately turn the scale in his favour."

A week had not elapsed when we learnt that Jules had begun to practise piety in the most edifying manner. The very unorthodox amusements which he had hitherto followed were now cast aside, and his friendships were changed. He eventually established a revolution so entirely complete in his thoughts and habits that his director, whom he had chosen from the best known priests of the little Church, was able to inform his co-religionists at Lyons that M. Jules de Polignac was a man after their own heart. Negotiations for the marriage were begun, and were carried far enough to seem likely of accomplishment as soon as he should leave Vincennes. But the Emperor cut the matter short, and ordered a marriage between the rich heiress and M. de Marbœuf. It was at this period that he began his caprice of ordering marriages as he pleased for all girls who had more than fifty thousand francs income. This infringement of private rights largely contributed to the unpopularity which he eventually acquired. Resistance was, however, possible. The d'Aligre family is a case in point.

M. d'Aligre was chamberlain, and the Emperor asked the hand of his daughter for M. de Caulaincourt, a proposal which he pretended to accept with joy. A few days afterwards, however, he came with a downcast air to say that Mlle. d'Aligre had an invincible dislike to the person of the Duc de Vicence. The Emperor did not insist, and M. d'Aligre thought he was saved; a short time afterwards he learnt that M. de Faudoas, the brother of the Duchesse de Rovigo, was to be proposed as his son-in-law. He therefore patched up a marriage between his daughter and M. de Pommereu in a week, under pretext that she preferred him to all her suitors. The Emperor was somewhat distant with M. d'Aligre, but as he had nothing to fear, he felt himself more independent than many others.

As for Jules, he continued his sanctimonious behaviour, by which he could not profit until the restoration, for he remained a prisoner until 1814.

CHAPTER XVII

I CAN never remember without shame the unpatriotic wishes which we cherished, and the guilty joy with which our partisanship received the news of our military reverses. Since that date I have read the portrait drawn by Machiavelli of the *fuori inciti,* and I blush to think that I must admit a resemblance. The *émigrés* of all times and all countries should use it as their manual; it is a mirror which should make them shudder at the sight of their own faces. Doubtless our sentiments were not shared by the majority of the country, but I believe that the masses had become profoundly indifferent to military successes. When the cannon announced that some brilliant victory had been gained, a small number of persons grieved, a somewhat larger number rejoiced, but the general population remained almost unmoved. The people were sated with glory, and knew that fresh success implied fresh efforts. A victory was the forerunner of a conscription, and the capture of Vienna was merely the prelude to a march upon Warsaw or Pressburg. Besides, the accuracy of the bulletins was doubted, and their appearance excited but little enthusiasm. The Emperor was always more coldly received in Paris than in any other town.

In strict truth I must, however, say that upon the day when the twenty-sixth cannon shot announced that the Empress had been confined of a boy, a long shout of joy went throughout the town, which resounded as though evoked by an electric shock. Everybody was at the windows or the doors. The silence was intense while the first twenty-five shots were counted, and the twenty-sixth produced an uproar. This event completed the Emperor's happiness, and completion is always admirable. I should not like to assert that even the fiercest antagonists did not feel some slight emotion at that moment.

We invented a story about this child, to the effect that the birth was fictitious. ·This was sheer nonsense. The Emperor was passionately fond of the child, and as soon as the little king could distinguish anybody, he showed a special preference for his father. Possibly paternal love might have induced the Emperor to be more careful of the lives of men. I have heard M. de Fontanes say that, one day when he was at lunch with the Emperor, the King of Rome was playing about the table, and his father followed him with tender glances, when the child fell and hurt himself slightly, and there was a great uproar. Peace was restored, and the Emperor fell into a gloomy reverie, and then said aloud, addressing no one in particular:

"I have seen the same cannon ball carry off twenty from one file."

He then resumed the business discussion with M. de Fontanes from which he had been distracted by reflections the course of which can easily be followed. In any case, his misgivings were beginning, and possibly contributed to his philanthropic tendencies.

Were I to try and relate all the stories of the Emperor,

I should never end, but as these reached me only from opposition sources, I am inclined to doubt them. If the glasses of the opposition showed objects in false colours, they certainly magnified them. I have been astonished to find how men who must, we thought, be as great as the purpose for which Napoleon employed them, became small and inconsiderable when his support was removed. One of his special talents was to discover with his eagle glance each man's special powers, to turn those powers to account, and thus to make the utmost possible use of them.

The only people for whom he had an invincible repugnance were the true liberals, those whom he called idealists. When once he had given this title to a man, there was nothing more to be said: he would willingly have sent his victim to Charenton, and regarded him as a social scourge. It seems, alas! that we shall be forced to admit that Bonaparte's genius for government inspired him correctly, and that these dreamers of the happiness of nations, estimable as they doubtless are, are of no special service, and serve only to excite the passions of the mob by flattering them, and thus to disorganise society. I did not think so at that time, and the Emperor's hatred for idealists whom I would willingly have made my oracles seemed to me a great error.

Among these idealists he classed M. de Chateaubriand. This was a mistake. M. de Chateaubriand cared nothing about the human race; he was entirely occupied with his own personality, and with the task of erecting a pedestal from which he could look down upon his age. This was a difficult place to assume, side by side with Napoleon, but he worked incessantly, and his memoirs will show the world with what toil, with what perseverance, and with what hopes of success. He succeeded so far that he always made for himself a little atmosphere of his own, of which he was the sun. As soon as he left this environment the outer air affected him so painfully that he became unbearably morose. But while he was in his own atmosphere no one could be kinder or more amiable, or send forth his beams with more grace. For the Chateaubriand of this latter position I had much liking, but the other side of his character is hateful.

If he had confined himself to his work as an author, to which his eminently artistic character impelled him, he would have been known solely for his goodness and kindness, apart from some bitterness due to criticisms of his works. But he had an ambition to be a statesman, and this brought him into regions where his claims were ill received; this failure produced a number of evil passions within him, and poured floods of bitterness into his style which will make most of his writings unreadable when time has brought forth impartial readers. M. de Chateaubriand had an instinct for the feeling of the moment. He could guess the public taste, and flatter it so admirably that though he was a partisan writer, he none the less became popular. For this purpose he was ready to change his views entirely; to praise that which he had scorned, and to scorn that which he had praised. He had two or three principles dressed up according to circumstance, so that they were not always recognisable, but enabled him to avoid every difficulty and to claim complete consistency. This was all the easier for him as his intellect, which was little short of genius, was never troubled by any consideration of morality which might have stopped him. He believed in nothing in the world except in his own talent, and before this altar he was continually prostrate. In speaking of the restoration and of the Revolution of 1830, if these notes should be continued to that point, I shall often have an opportunity of meeting him on my road.

Under the Empire I thought him merely a conscientious man of genius, who was persecuted because he refused to blow the trumpet of despotism, and because he had given in his resignation as the minister of Valais upon the occasion of the death of the Duc d'Enghien.

Le Génie du Christianisme, L'Itinéraire à Jérusalem, and the poem of the *Martyrs,* recently published, justify our admiration. I thought indeed that the enthusiasm of some ladies was a trifle exaggerated, but I joined in it up to a certain point. I can remember a reading of the *Abencérages,* given at the house of Mme. de Ségur. He read with the most touching and emotional voice, with that faith which he possessed for every production of his own. He threw himself into the sentiments of his characters so far that his tears fell upon the paper. We shared this keen impression, and I was completely spellbound. When the reading was over, tea was brought in.

" M. de Chateaubriand, will you have some tea? "

" I will ask you for a cup."

Immediately an echo went throughout the *salon.*

" My dear, he would like some tea."

" He is going to have some tea."

" Give him some tea."

" He wants some tea."

And ten ladies started up to serve the idol with tea. It was the first time that I had been present at such a spectacle, which seemed to me so ridiculous that I resolved never to take part in it. Hence, though my relations with M. de Chateaubriand have been somewhat continuous, I have never been enrolled in the company of his *Madames,* as Mme. de Chateaubriand used to call them, and I have never reached the point of intimacy to which he only admitted real adorers.

When we left Beauregard in 1812 to set up house at Châtenay, M. and Mme. de Chateaubriand were living at the Vallée aux Loups, ten minutes' walk from my house. He had made a charming home, and was extremely fond of it. We were friendly neighbours, and often found him writing on a corner of the drawing-room table with a worn-out pen which would hardly pass through the mouth of the wretched bottle which contained his ink. He would utter a cry of joy when he saw us pass his window, thrust his papers under the cushion of an old easy-chair which served him as a portfolio and a desk, and rush out to join us with the gaiety of a schoolboy let out from his class. At that time he was entirely agreeable. I cannot say as much of Mme. de Chateaubriand. She had plenty of talent, but used it to extract the bitter and disagreeable elements from every object. She did her husband much harm by continually irritating him and making his home unbearable, and though always most considerate towards her, he could never secure domestic peace.[1]

I have said that she had some talent, and the fact is indisputable. At the same time (and only the sight of her would persuade one of the fact), her middle-class pride was wounded by the literary reputation of M. de Chateaubriand, which she considered derogatory. Under the restoration she most passionately desired titles and positions at court, to compensate for this vulgar suc-

[1] "Chateaubriand had married on March 19, 1792, at the age of twenty-four, a young orphan girl, very pretty and fairly wealthy, Mlle. Céleste Buisson de la Vigne. . . . She was the victim, faithful notwithstanding and always devoted, of a hopeless egoism and a perpetual inconstancy."—*Madame Récamier*, (American Edition), vol. ii. pp. 33 and 36.

cess. She loudly advertised the fact that she had never read a single line of her husband's publications. As, however, she continually told him that a country which had the glory of possessing him, and was not governed by him, was in a wretched state, and proved the fact by certain passages from the Apocalypse, of which she had made a profound study, he pardoned her scorn of his merits by reason of her devotion to his claims. The amount of money swallowed up by this household, though their life was far from ceremonious, is another proof, among thousands, of the inevitable results of want of system. In any case, M. de Chateaubriand admitted himself that nothing seemed to him so insipid as to live upon a regular income, from whatever source derived. He wanted to realise his capital, squander it, feel the pinch of poverty, get into debt, be appointed an ambassador, expend upon caprice the salary intended to defray his household expenses, resign his post, and become more embarrassed and more deeply in debt than ever; he wished to abandon a position where he had twenty-five horses in his stables, and have the pleasure of refusing an invitation to dinner under the pretext that he could not afford a cab; in short, he wished to experience every variety of sensation in order to avoid boredom, for that upon the whole was the great object and secret of his life.

Notwithstanding this chaotic existence, in which M. de Chateaubriand associated without the smallest scruple those who were devoted to him, he was an agreeable and companionable acquaintance. If he could refrain from revolutionising one's life, he was inclined to make existence very pleasant. From time to time he even showed a desire to make some sacrifice to those who loved him, but this was a custom too contrary to his nature to be persistent. Thus, although wearied by her presence, he permitted Mme. de Beaumont to follow him to Rome, where he abandoned her, and she died in almost complete isolation. So again, after having changed his mode of life and entered society to attract Mme. de Z., he saw her go mad without a single sigh of grief. Thus, again, he hardly consented to write a very cold newspaper article in honour of the memory of Mme. de Duras, who lived only for his sake for twelve years.[1]

I might add many names to this list, as M. de Chateaubriand always had the greatest facility in attracting attention, without considering the trouble that he might cause. Of his many intimacies, the one which held the largest place in his heart was, I think, that with Mme. C. de X., who became the Duchesse de Z. The story of this poor woman is in consonance with that morality which existed before the Revolution, and which we have been asked but recently to regret.

Mme. Z. de Y., as charming and accomplished a young lady as can be imagined, married in 1790, thanks to the immense fortune to which she was heiress, C. de X., the eldest son of the Prince of ———. Though he did not possess his wife's distinguished talents, he was by no means devoid of capacity, was very handsome, and entirely in fashion. The young couple made quite a sensation when presented at the Tuileries, in spite of the serious nature of events at that period.

Soon the storms of the Revolution separated them. M. de X. emigrated; his wife remained with her family, whose misfortunes she shared. She accompanied them

[1] Mme. Récamier said: "M. de Chateaubriand has a great deal of nobility of character, immense self-respect, very great delicacy. He is ready to make the greatest sacrifices for persons he loves, but he has not a shade of veritable sensibility. He has caused me great suffering more than once."—*Madame Récamier*, vol. ii. p. 314.

to prison, where she was the guardian angel of her relatives, and among others the old wife of Marshal Z., her husband's grandmother. She served his grandmother as a daughter or as a servant, until the day when the scaffold cut short these cares. She saw her own father perish, and consoled her mother; in short, she attracted the admiration and veneration of all who were imprisoned with her. As soon as the prisons were opened her first desire was to rejoin her young husband, for whom she felt the tenderest affection. To leave France was not an easy matter; however, by dint of courage and skill she succeeded in securing a landing upon the shores of England. Her daughter, whom she had entrusted to an American captain, had preceded her by some hours, and with this child in her arms she hastened to her husband's door. C. de X. was then attached by fashion to the train of Mrs. Fitzherbert. She was at least forty-five years of age, but the pleasure of being a rival of the Prince of Wales, who did not disguise his jealousy, made her seem charming in the eyes of M. de X., and he was somewhat annoyed by the arrival of his pretty wife. Under pretext of economy, he hastened to take her to a little cottage in the north of England. She did not complain as long as he stayed with her. But business soon called him to London, where his visits became more frequent, until he set up house there.

He was extremely intimate with M. du L. de V., a young man far less handsome but much more amiable than M. de X. The latter showed him the sad letters of his young wife, complaining of the trouble that they caused him. M. du L. reproached him for abandoning her, and added that he deserved misfortune.

" You call that misfortune. The happiest day of my life will be that which relieves me of her lamentations."

M. du L. eventually proposed to C. de X. that he should try to alienate the affection of his wife. This friendly offer was eagerly accepted. The two friends went down together to the cottage. A few days afterwards C. de X. went away, leaving M. du L. to spend the long winter days with a woman twenty years of age, who was weary and depressed. She was as attractive as she was pretty, full of talent and wit. M. du L.'s head was already turned by her letters; he fell passionately in love with her, and found no difficulty in playing the part which he had undertaken. To the husband he regularly reported his progress, and announced his success at the end of several months. The latter then announced that he proposed to visit the lonely couple. Mme. de X. was awakened from the pleasant dreams which she had cherished by the impending arrival of the husband she had injured, and gave way to unbounded despair. M. du L. made vain attempts to soothe her, and at length decided to reveal the immoral compact by means of which he had succeeded, and showed her the correspondence to confirm his statements.

Mme. de X. was a pure and noble woman: she was revolted by such hateful treachery, and remained crushed by this horrible revelation. The next day she set off to Yarmouth with her child, announcing her intention of finding refuge with her mother. Her husband was delighted to be rid of her. M. du L. hastened after her, caught her up before she had embarked, made his peace, accompanied her, and was pardoned. But for her the illusion of love was destroyed. M. du L. was punished for his guilt by the passion and depth of his feeling for her, which afterwards wrecked his life.

Mme. de X., her mind sullied and her affections blunted by the conduct of two men whom she had loved, reached

Paris amid the saturnalia of the Directory, in which she
took but too energetic a share.   She has herself summed
up the consequences in these few words:

"I am very unhappy: as soon as I love one, another
appears who pleases me more."

.   .   .   .
.   .   .   .
.   .   .   .   her attachment
to M. de Chateaubriand was almost a rehabilitation.

This intimacy was at its height when M. de Chateaubriand started for the Holy Land: the lovers arranged
to meet at the fountain of lions in the Alhambra.   Mme.
de X. had every intention of keeping so romantic an appointment, and was at the spot on the day arranged.
During the absence of M. de Chateaubriand she had permitted Colonel L. to distract her uneasiness with his
assiduous attentions.   While she was at Granada, awaiting the return of the pilgrim from Jerusalem, she learned
of the Colonel's death.   Thus, when M. de Chateaubriand arrived, full of excuses for his delay and of
panegyrics upon the punctuality of his beloved, he found
a woman in deepest mourning, bewailing with extreme
despair the death of a rival who had been successful
in his absence.   The whole of their tour in Spain was
spent in this manner, M. de Chateaubriand combining
the functions of consoler and adorer.   He dates the cool-
ing of his affection for Mme. de X. from this period,
though their intimacy lasted for a considerable time.

The publication of the *Itinéraire* added new lustre to
the popularity of M. de Chateaubriand, and increased the
desire of several people to see him.   He made use of this
fact to improve the position of Mme. de X., arranging
that his acquaintance should only be made through her,
and putting a period to his exclusiveness.   This must

be counted to his credit, as he acted solely in the interest of Mme. de X. People paid her attention in order to attract M. de Chateaubriand. As she was a charming woman, she pleased by her own merits as soon as she was known.

For a short time she formed part of a *coterie* composed of Mmes. de Duras, de Bérenger, de Lévis, and others. But she soon wearied of them and withdrew to her own room, where her first-rate talent was employed upon serious occupations. Thus she lived until the restoration. She then plunged into the vortex of society, and was seen dancing at a great ball, decked in rose-coloured finery. Her husband, who had never lost sight of her, arranged a reconciliation. She assumed the title of Duchesse de Z. She was offered rooms at the residence of X.; there was talk of a possible brother for the sister who had been married for some years. Every one noticed the strange manners of Mme. de Z. The Hundred Days arrived; terror seized her, and her strangeness of manner increased. For some months attempts were made to hide the fact, but at length it was necessary to place her under restraint. She has now been confined for twenty years, and has never recovered her reason. Such was the fate of a person endowed by nature with the highest gifts. I cannot but think that she deserved a better fate than the life which she led. Had it not been for that fatal journey from England, which brought her, wounded and disillusioned, to the disturbances in Paris under the Directory, she would probably have followed a better line of conduct. I have reason to believe that her husband regretted his behaviour more than once, together with the sacrifice which he had made to the false god of gallantry, which was paramount at the time when he entered society. He cannot have failed to recognise that he was primarily responsible for his wife's wrongdoing. M. de Chateaubriand had certainly intended to rehabilitate her in her own esteem and in the eyes of the world. But he was incapable of any sustained attention to the affairs of another person, and was too entirely absorbed by consideration for himself.

It was at the time that Mme. de X. began her retirement that the society of the *Madames* was definitely formed. The chief members were the Duchesses de Duras, de Lévis, and Mme. de Bérenger; the other members are too unimportant to mention. These three ladies had each of them their special hour: M. de Chateaubriand was received, and they were at home to no one else; and goodness only knows what he had to suffer if he gave one of them some minutes that belonged to another. They were so proud of their success that their porters had orders to inform visitors that they were not at home because it was M. de Chateaubriand's hour, and it is said that the announcement was often prolonged beyond the due time, to make the greater impression. The scenes which these ladies made by their mutual reproaches became a source of general amusement. But every evening all recovered their good temper, and went off to pay the most assiduous attention to Mme. de Chateaubriand, whom they overwhelmed with care and kindness. One day, when she had caught a slight cold, she asserted that she had received five possets in one morning, accompanied by the most charming notes, which she displayed with amusing sarcasms upon these ladies. At bottom, however, she was by no means displeased by this homage from the great.

It is said that the success of Mme. de Lévis was tolerably complete; Mme. de Duras was consumed with jealousy, while Mme. de Bérenger resigned herself to other modes of displaying her power. The *Madames* of the second rank did not raise such high claims. Those who had been admitted to the friendship of Mme. de Lévis thought her both pleasant and pretty. She seemed ugly and surly, when seen at a distance which I never felt tempted to cross.

Mme. de Duras was a daughter of M. de Kersaint, of the Convention. She and her mother had spent the years of revolutionary uproar on their plantations at Martinique. When Mme. de Kersaint brought to London her stalwart daughter of twenty-two, who was by no means pretty, she found that her daughter's marriage with the Duc de Duras had been arranged almost beforehand; he was reduced to a state of poverty which made him dependent to an irksome degree upon the Prince de Poix, his uncle. Though the fortune of Mlle. de Kersaint was not very considerable, it was quite satisfactory to M. de Duras. She had hardly disembarked when he married her, and for a long time she adored him.

M. de Duras was first gentleman of the King's chamber; these officials came on duty for successive years, and when the *émigration* began, those entitled to serve did not fail to appear. M. de Duras had already performed his year of service upon one occasion, in waiting upon Louis XVIII., and his turn came round once more a short time after his marriage. He left London with his wife, to go to Mitau. When he reached Hamburg he received an official communication, stating that the King would consent to receive M. de Duras in view of his position, notwithstanding his marriage, but that the daughter of a Conventionist could not expect to be received by the Duchesse d'Angoulême. Mme. de Duras was formally excluded from Mitau. M. de Duras was a man of honour, notwithstanding certain ridiculous points: he did not hesitate to take his wife back to London and to stay there with her. Mme. de Duras felt extremely hurt, and I have always imagined that this insult was the origin of that independent feeling which eventually proved an honour to her character. After a stay of some years in England, the Duras household returned to France with two little girls, the only children that they had.

Mme. de Duras soon perceived her superiority over her husband, and made him realise the fact with a frankness which led to discord. At the time of her infatuation for M. de Chateaubriand, which was as innocent as it was extravagant, she was looking for some distraction from her domestic annoyances. In her youth Mme. de Duras had no very attractive qualities, but she had a lively spirit, a lofty heart, and true distinction of character. The higher the scene in which she was called to play a part, the more obvious her true worth became; this fact I had long before discovered.

Mme. de Bérenger, when she was Mlle. de Lannois, had married the Duc de Châtillon-Montmorency, who was brought to a miserable end by this fine name. He was at Yarmouth, ready to embark on a packet, when a change of wind obliged him to wait. The captain of the frigate *La Blanche*, learning that the Duc de Montmorency was at the inn, offered him a passage on his frigate, which was to take the subsidy money to Hamburg. The *Blanche* was utterly lost at the mouth of the Elbe, and the Duc de Châtillon was drowned. His widow enjoyed her liberty for some time, and eventually married the least attractive of her adorers, Raymond de Bérenger. Her mind was serious and distinguished, but not sufficiently superior to reach the level of ordinary mortals. I was greatly afraid of her.

Among the women who adored M. de Chateaubriand

was Mme. Octave de Ségur, though she could not claim his affection. Her story is so romantic that I propose to relate it, though I may be anticipating in some degree.

Mlle. d'Aguesseau married for love her cousin german, Octave de Ségur. Under the Directory the young couple enjoyed complete happiness. They lived with their parents, and provided for their personal expenses by translating English novels. They had three sons, whose education was becoming a care, when Octave was appointed a sub-prefect by the First Consul. His wife followed him to Soissons. The Comte de Ségur, their father, joined the Government, which had become imperial, and was appointed Grand Master of the Ceremonies, while Mme. Octave was made lady-in-waiting to the Empress Joséphine. Domestic happiness was forthwith disturbed; the long absence necessitated by the duties of Mme. de Ségur developed a jealousy in Octave, which his passionate heart cherished unknown to himself. Etienne de Choiseul became the object of his anxieties, it is said without the smallest reason. He was like Orosmane, " cruelly wounded, but too proud to complain."

Mme. Octave accompanied the Empress to Plombières, and her husband obtained leave to spend some days with her. He arrived upon a magnificent moonlight evening. Mme. Octave was not expecting him : she had gone out, and her husband followed her; she was walking with Etienne de Choiseul. Octave did not reveal himself, left Plombières without a word to anyone, and did not return to Soissons. Search was made in every direction in vain; nothing could be heard of him. At the end of a year Mme. Octave received by post a note which bore the Boulogne postmark and these words: " I am, dear Félicité, about to brave an element less agitated than this heart, which will never beat except for you." This note was closed by a seal which she had given him, and which bore the words: " Friendship, esteem, and eternal love."

Philippe de Ségur started immediately for Boulogne, but could find no trace of his brother. He was, however, on board of one of the pinnaces where Philippe looked for him, but he played his part of soldier so perfectly that none of his comrades suspected his disguise. He followed the grand army to Germany. Several years elapsed, and a second note was handed to Mme. de Ségur which bore merely the words engraven on the seal, in the handwriting of Octave. This was the only sign of his existence, and after a period of despair Mme. Octave eventually . . . consoled herself. . .
. . . . Her three sons, . . . were . . . her first interest, and she watched over them with most thoughtful care. Octave had been made a prisoner, and had been taken to a little town in the depths of Hungary; it was not until long afterwards that he learnt of the death of Etienne de Choiseul, who was killed at the battle of Wagram. He then desired to see his country once more. The steps which he took to obtain his liberty were unsuccessful, and were outstripped by events. Peace at length liberated him, and he returned to France in 1814.

His wife was reduced to despair by his return. .
. . . .
. . . . Whether it was that Octave had been warned of the fact upon his arrival, or could not trust himself, he wished to remain upon a footing of simple friendship with his wife, reserving his first affection for his sons. He treated her with a grave politeness which never changed. Mme. Octave, piqued by this attitude, felt reviving within her that passion

which her husband experienced in secret, and employed all her powers to attract him.

" Take care, Félicité! " he would say to her sometimes; " it is with my life that you are playing."

At length he gave way and indulged in those feelings which had always reigned exclusively in his heart. Some months of happiness recompensed him for long years of suffering. Mme. Octave followed her husband and her eldest son to the garrison, where both were serving in the same regiment   .   .   .   .   .

.   .   .   .

.   .   .   .

.   .   .   .

.   .   .   .   Octave secured an exchange, and wished his wife to leave the garrison. Under pretext that her son was remaining, she wished to spend the winter there; Octave objected, and an angry scene took place. For the first and last time he reproached her with arguments based upon the trouble which she had taken to bring him back to her side.

He went back to Paris alone, hired a lodging of the kind which would best suit him, and spent his time arranging it in full conformity with his taste. He requested her several times to join him, but she persistently refused. At length he wrote that if she were not in Paris before six o'clock upon a certain day, she would repent it all her life. She did not come, and at nine o'clock Octave jumped into the Seine. He was discovered with his hands firmly clasped. He was an excellent swimmer, but having resolved to perish, his will had overpowered the instincts of self-preservation.

Mme. Octave was overwhelmed with grief and remorse, and retired to a convent. I have seen her in her cell, a very touching spectacle. The arguments of her sons, who were devoted to her, notwithstanding their deep affection for their father, brought her back to the world, where she leads a somewhat retired life—a life, however, less striking to the imagination than that of her convent cell.

At an age when disinterested affection was so rare, the passion of Octave is certainly remarkable. He was a handsome man, and very companionable when he could overcome the timidity and embarrassment which the strange character of his first adventure always caused him. Though his wife was not entirely pretty, she was extremely attractive, and was able to win affection, for, notwithstanding the cruel events of her sad life, she preserved devoted friends among women whose conduct was above reproach.[1]

[1] Several omissions, very short and of little importance, in no way modifying the general sense of the text, have been made in this chapter. The names written in full by Mme. de Boigne have been replaced by X, Y, Z. The dots indicate the length of the suppressed passages, but in other respects the text is in conformity with the manuscript.

CHAPTER XVIII

I HAVE no more to say of the disastrous retreat from
Moscow than of the glorious campaigns which preceded
it. Upon all of these events my information is only
general. I am not writing history, but merely putting
down my knowledge of certain details. When public
affairs come under my special cognisance, I shall treat
of them with the same exactitude as I have used in dealing with social anecdotes.

The fall of the Empire was approaching, and we were
foolish enough not to be afraid: the truth is that the
strong and clever hand of the great man had, so to speak,
stifled anarchical passion. Who, in any case, could have
foreseen the calamities which were to accompany the fall
of this Colossus? Every man of common sense must
have trembled, but we rejoiced with the carelessness of
partisans. At the same time, it is only right that excuse
should be made for us. The yoke of Bonaparte was becoming intolerable, and his head had been finally turned
by his alliance with the house of Austria. He listened
only to flatterers, and would not bear any contradiction.
He had reached the point when he could no longer endure the truth, not even the truth of figures.

The arbitrary nature of his despotism was felt even

278

in private homes. I have already spoken of his whim for finding husbands for the daughters of private citizens, and his measures for forming guards of honour attacked in turn the sons of families in easy circumstances. Those affected were young men of twenty-five or thirty years of age, who might have considered themselves free, as they had escaped or satisfied the conscription. Obviously they had no taste for a military career, as they had not followed it at a time when everything summoned them. Most of them were married and possessed households, and enlistment was an unforeseen calamity which turned their lives upside down. The prefects had orders to enforce the measure, particularly upon those families which were regarded as ill-disposed towards the Government. It became fairly obvious that the Emperor wished to have in his hands a certain number of hostages against any ill-feeling.

This was in the first instance a revival of an old Greek idea : the Emperor was said to have remembered that Alexander had thus acted towards his Macedonians before beginning his Asiatic campaign. This legion was formed in the midst of tears, imprecations, and hatred conceived by every element in the population which could rouse disaffection against the imperial power. The legion joined the army for the first time in Saxony in 1813, was present at the disastrous battle of Leipsic, endured the painful retreat of Hanau, and was destroyed by hospital sickness at Mayence. It was disbanded, but obliged to re-form again immediately.

The guards of honour served during the campaign of France in 1814, and were crushed at the battle of Reims. If ever a troop underwent suffering, they surely did. They were not even able to cheer their memories with the recollection of victory. And yet this legion was faithful to Napoleon for a longer time than any other body. It was only with difficulty and delay that it assumed the white cockade, while it greeted the Hundred Days with joy, and those who composed it remained imperialists as long as possible. In view of these facts, we need not talk of establishing principles and drawing conclusions. It is none the less true that, notwithstanding the military ardour so rapidly developed in these young recalcitrants, the enlistment of the guards of honour contributed more than any other measure to swell the tide of hatred against Bonaparte which was everywhere rising, and began to find expression in bold words.

I remember that M. de Châteauvieux (the author of the *Letters of St. James*), who was absent from Paris for two years, arrived at the beginning of 1814. His first visit when he reached the town was to my house. There he heard speeches of such hostility that, as he has since told me, his chief desire was to get away. Throughout the night he dreamt of nothing but dungeons and Vincennes, although he had made a firm resolve never again to visit so imprudent a society. The next day he continued his round of visits, and was astonished to find the same attitude and the same freedom of speech everywhere, even among the middle classes and in the shops. We were not struck by the fact, because the change had been gradual and general. It was apparent even at the table of the Minister of Police, where the Abbé de Pradt said that there was one *émigré* whom it was time to recall to France, and that was common sense. M. de Châteauvieux was petrified by our conversation; yet he was a constant visitor at Coppet, and accustomed to violent opposition language.

The Government officials were completely disorganised. I went sometimes to the house of Mme. Bertrand; her husband was Grand Marshal of the Palace. One morning I saw an officer arrive, coming from the Emperor's army, then another sent by Marshal Soult, then an envoy from Marshal Suchet, all bringing news of most disastrous events. Poor Fanny was on thorns. At length, by way of culmination, an Illyrian official appeared. He proceeded to tell us how he had been tracked throughout Italy, and with what difficulty he had reached the French frontier. She could no longer hold out, and said to them, with extreme vivacity:

" Gentlemen, you are all wrong. Last night excellent news came in from every quarter, and the Emperor is entirely pleased with all that is going on."

Each man looked at his fellow in astonishment, and it was clear to me that this remark was intended for myself. I smiled, and left the field entirely free for their lamentations, which were probably deep and loud as soon as they were alone.

If their side were under illusions, ours were no less absurd. We imagined that the foreign powers were working in the interests of our passions, and any one who should have attempted to enlighten us in this respect would certainly have been regarded as a traitor. We had concluded that the Prince of Sweden, Bernadotte, was the most active agent in forwarding the Bourbon restoration.[1] We had assumed that he was in Brussels, surrounded by French princes, and we would not abandon the idea.

One evening M. de Saint Chamans came to tell us that Colonel de Saint Chamans, his brother, had just arrived

---

[1] For the arrangements of Bernadotte, see the curious story of the mission to Sweden and Russia entrusted to the Comte de La Ferronays by Louis XVIII. *Souvenirs tirés des papiers du Comte A. de La Ferronays*, by the Marquis Costa de Beauregard, p. 327 ff. Also *Mémoires du Chancelier Pasquier*, vol. ii. pp. 213-4.

from Brussels, and assured him that neither Bernaaotte,
nor our princes, nor a single foreign soldier was in
Belgium, and that the Swedes were somewhere or other
behind the Rhine. Not only did we refuse to believe
him, not only did we suspect the veracity of the Colonel,
but we were so angry with M. de Saint Chamans that
we almost looked upon him as a traitor. He was treated
with marked coldness as a suspicious character.

Such is the honesty and justice of parties. There is
no doubt of our good faith, and when I remember that
I shared these unreasonable impressions, I am entirely
indulgent towards the illusions and the unreason of party
members. I am only astonished that the sight of these
faults in themselves or in others does not induce them
to amend their ways, and I can hardly understand intolerance in the case of those who have passed through
a series of revolutions as we had done. It must, however, be recognised by way of excuse for our foolishness
that we were obliged to guess the truth from the official accounts, which almost always disguised it.

The Emperor had grown to think that the country
had no right to inquire into the affairs of the empire;
that these were his personal business, and that he owed
no account to any one. The battle of Trafalgar, for
instance, was never officially reported in France, so that
no newspaper mentioned it, and we only learnt of it by
secret intelligence. When such pieces of news are passed
over, malcontents have every right to invent fables such
as that of the Swedish and Bourbon army which we had
imagined as ready in Belgium.

Events were proceeding, and the enemy feared to
march on Paris; they were frightened by the very
thought. We, who should have feared this intention,
welcomed it with our prayers. The disorganisation of

the Government became obvious. Unfortunate con-
scripts filled the streets, and no preparation had been
made for their reception. They were perishing with
hunger on the kerb-stones, and we used to take them into
our houses and give them rest and food. Before disorganisation made arrangements impossible, they were
cared for, clothed, and sent off to the army within
twenty-four hours. The poor boys reached the army
to perish, having no powers of self-defence.

I have heard Marshal Marmont relate that at Montmirail, in the hottest of the fire, he saw a conscript standing calmly at ease.

" What are you doing there? Why are you not
firing? "

" I would fire as well as anybody," replied the young
man, " if I knew how to load my gun."

The Marshal had tears in his eyes as he repeated
these words of the brave young man who thus remained
exposed to bullets which he could not return.

As the tide of war approached, it became more difficult to conceal the truth concerning the futility of the
enormous efforts made by Napoleon and his admirable
army; the result was inevitable. I must ask pardon of
that generation that has since grown up in admiration
of the Emperor's liberal principles; but at that moment
friends and enemies alike were suffocating beneath his
iron hand, and felt a desire to rise against him with
equal force. To speak frankly, he was detested; every
one regarded him as the obstacle to peace, and peace
was the first necessity for every one.

Abbiamo la pancia piena di libertà, said to me one day
a postillion at Verona, refusing a crown struck with the
effigy of liberty. France in 1814 would gladly have said
in its turn, *Abbiamo la pancia piena di gloria*, and of

glory she wished no more. The allies were not mistaken upon this point, and were quite able to regard this weariness as the mainspring of their success, but they feared that it was not yet sufficiently complete for their own security. In order to revive the public spirits, a courier was sent with orders to hand over, in the middle of a parade at which the Empress was present, the flags and swords of the Russian generals who had been made prisoners at the battle of Montmirail. ˌThe time for these pretences had gone by, and the courier was not sufficiently dust-stained to reassure the Parisians.

On Sunday, March 25, we saw, after the parade, a magnificent regiment of cuirassiers starting off; they had arrived from the Spanish army and were about to join the Emperor's army, for which purpose they were proceeding along the boulevard about three o'clock. I have seen few troops by whose appearance I have been more greatly impressed. On the morning of the next day scattered members of them appeared at the barriers of Paris making their way to the hospitals; they and their horses were more or less wounded, and their long white cloaks were stained and covered with blood. It was evident that fighting was proceeding quite close to us. I met several of them when I went for a walk in the Jardin des Plantes, and the contrast with their appearance the evening before went to my heart. After two hours, my mother and I again passed along the boulevards. Even in this short time their aspect had been entirely changed; they were now thronged with the population of the outskirts of Paris, walking onwards, mixed up with cows, sheep, and their poor little possessions. The people wept and lamented, relating their losses and their terrors, and naturally venting their anger upon any one who seemed more fortunate. It was impossible to proceed except at a walk: our carriage came in for its share of abuse, though that was not necessary to make me understand the ugliness of war when seen at close quarters.

We reached home without difficulty, but somewhat frightened and deeply moved. The distant boom of cannon was soon heard, and we learnt that in the ministerial offices and in the households of the princes of the imperial family preparations were made for departure. At nightfall the courts of the Tuileries were filled with waggons, and it was said that the Empress was leaving the city, though no one would believe it. We spent the whole of that Monday in the greatest anxiety and in the midst of the most contradictory rumours; every one had a certain piece of news, which entirely overthrew a no less certain piece of information brought by some one else. The next day, at five o'clock in the morning, everybody was instantly and loudly informed by musketry fire and a cannonade that Paris was vigorously attacked on three sides. At the same time we learnt that the Empress, the court, and the Imperial Government had departed.

We were living in a house in the street Neuve des Mathurins. Our highest windows gave a full view of Montmartre, and towards the end of the morning we watched the capture of this position. Shells passed over our heads. Some fell upon the boulevards and put to flight the fine ladies in feathers and furbelows who were walking about among the wounded brought back from the barriers and the reinforcements of arms, men, and supplies, which were being sent thither. Many people left Paris. I had no wish to go away, and as my father considered that the roads in such confusion would be more dangerous than the town, he authorised us to stay.

Eugène d'Argout, my cousin, who was wounded at the battle of Leipsic, and had not been able to take part in the French campaign, undertook to provide for our safety. He began by getting in provisions and buying supplies of flour, rice, several hams, and in fact everything that was necessary for spending a few days in confinement. He then put out all the fires, closed all the shutters, and made the house look as deserted as possible. He also dragged a large hay-cart which had come in from the country that morning under the archway, intending to fix it against the large door if the town was captured. He then told everybody that any one who was outside would not come in until peace was restored.

Eugène had taken part in all the wars for the last ten years, and had seen the capture of many towns. He said that the smallest obstacles were enough to stop a soldier, who was always in a hurry, fearing that he might be forbidden to plunder by his officers.

People came from time to time to tell what news could be learnt in the suburbs. When the cannonade was silent on one side it began upon another. Sometimes the noise approached and sometimes became distant, as positions were captured or fresh attacks were made. What we chiefly feared was the arrival of the Emperor, as we did not know where he was.

Alexandre de la Touche, the son of Mme. Dillon, was living in the Tuileries with his sister, Mme. Bertrand. He came in the morning to beg me to leave Paris, and I refused absolutely. Soon afterwards we learnt that hostilities had been suspended and negotiations for a capitulation begun. He came back, and positively went down upon his knees before my mother and myself to induce us to depart, beseeching us to let him put in our horses. We told him that it was hardly the right time for departing, as the danger had passed.

" It has not, it has not! If I could only tell you what I know! But I have given my word. Start, I beg of you, start!"

We refused, and he went away, weeping, to rejoin his mother and sister, who were waiting for him with the carriage. This persistence on the part of M. de la Touche returned to my mind when I was told some days later that the Emperor had given orders to blow up the powder magazines. He certainly believed that he was in possession of a secret which would be revealed with disastrous effect.

I shall never forget the night which followed this exciting day. The weather was magnificent, the moonlight splendid, the town entirely calm, and my mother and myself stood at the window. Our attention was attracted by the noise made by a very small dog gnawing a bone at some distance. From time to time the silence was only broken by the challenges of the sentinels of the allied army, who answered one another as they went their rounds upon the heights which overlooked us. It was these foreign accents which first made me feel that my heart was French. They impressed me very painfully. But we were too afraid of the Emperor's return for this impression to last.

The square and streets were full of the French army, bivouacing on the pavement in sadness and silence. Its attitude was most admirable; it neither exacted, demanded, nor even expected anything. It seemed as if these poor soldiers felt that they had no claim upon the inhabitants whom they had not been able to defend. However, eight thousand men under the command of the Duc de Raguse had been engaged for ten hours against forty-five thousand foreigners, and had left them thirteen thousand dead to collect. Thus the allies could not believe how few were the troops that defended Paris on the following days. History will do justice to the foolish malignity which has accused Marshal Marmont of betraying the town, and will restore the brilliant action of Belleville to the place which it should occupy in our military annals.

I am about to begin my story of the restoration. As my position brought me into the intimacy of most influential people, I have seen events close at hand from this time. I cannot say if I shall be able to relate them with impartiality; this is a quality of which everybody boasts, and which no one really possesses. People are more or less influenced, entirely unconsciously, by position and environment. At any rate, I shall speak independently, and will tell the truth as I believe it. More than this I cannot promise.

CHAPTER XIX

My personal opinions in 1814 are doubtless of little interest to any one but myself. It is, however, a task which amuses me, thus to take stock of myself at different periods of my life, and to observe the variations which have marked them.

My Anglomania had for the most part disappeared, and I had become once more entirely French, socially, if not politically. As I have already said, the challenge of the hostile sentinels affected me more than the noise of the enemy's cannon. I had experienced a sensation of patriotism, transitory as it was. By position, by tradition, by recollections, by environment, and by conviction I was a Royalist and a Legitimist. But I was rather anti-Bonapartist than a partisan of the Bourbons; I detested the tyranny of the Emperor when I saw it in operation. I had no great opinion of those of our princes whom I had seen face to face. I was assured that Louis XVIII. held different principles. The extreme animosity which existed between his little court and that of the Comte d'Artois gave reason to hope for the truth of this statement. I had left England before the vicissitudes of exile had brought the King to that country, and I lent a ready ear to my mother's praises of him, which were given in spite of the fact that in her eyes he laboured under the disadvantage of being a Constitutional of 1789. It was upon this same disadvantage that my hopes were founded, for upon careful consideration I found that I was invariably as liberal as my aristocratic prejudices would allow, prejudices which I fear will accompany me to the grave.

The organisation of the political life in England has always seemed to me the most perfect in the world. On the one hand is the complete and real equality in the eyes of the law, which assures individual independence and therefore inspires the individual with self-respect ; on the other hand are the great social distinctions, which create defenders for the public liberties, and make these patricians the natural leaders of the people, who return in homage what they receive by way of protection. This is what I have wished for my own country, for I can only conceive of liberty, apart from licence, as based upon a strong aristocracy. This is a fact which nobody in France understood—neither people, nor middle classes, nor the nobility, nor the King himself. Equality among us is a disease engendered by vanity. Under pretext of this equality, every one claims the right to superiority and domination, and fails to recognise that if any one is to be inferior, the existence of superiors must be readily admitted.

On Wednesday, March 31, to resume the thread of my story, at seven o'clock in the morning M. de Glandevèse was at our house. He came to consult my father upon the advisability of assuming the white cockade, and said that an enormous number of people were inclined in that direction. My father undertook to calm their zeal for a few hours; it would not do for such an attempt to end in failure. It was prudent, therefore, to await the moment when the allies would make their entry—that is to say, at mid-day.

M. de Glandevèse went to transmit these views to the different meetings. My father, on his side, soon learnt that Marshal Moncey, commander of the National Guard of Paris, had gone away in the night, after summoning his second in command, the Duc de Montmorency, and entrusting him with full powers. My father went to the Duc de Laval, in the hope that he might be able to induce his cousin to declare in favour of the cause which we wished to see triumphant.

It was nearly ten o'clock. My mother and myself were at a window on the first floor, when we saw in the distance a Russian officer followed by several Cossacks. When he had nearly reached our house he asked where Mme. de Boigne was living; at the same time he raised his head, and I recognised Prince Nikita Wolkonski, an old acquaintance. He saw me at the same moment, dismounted, and came into the house; his escort took up a position in the courtyard, and two Cossacks stood as sentinels before the archway door, which remained open. I have always considered that the terror with which people were inspired by the Imperial Government was shown by the fact that their fears overcame the Parisian love of sightseeing under these circumstances. Notwithstanding the curiosity which these Cossacks must have aroused, being as they were the first that had appeared in Paris, during the hour that Prince Wolkonski continued his visit there was no crowd before the door, and the passers by did not even stop for a moment. Had they been more religious, they would readily have crossed themselves to avert the danger of merely beholding a spectacle which seemed to them to be compromising.

Prince Wolkonski,[1] as may be believed, was effusively welcomed. He told me at once that Count Nesselrode [2] had ordered him to come to us, to assure us of entire safety and protection, and then to ask my father what were the reasonable and possible hopes of our party, as the Emperor Alexander was arriving before any decision had been taken. We sent to fetch my father from the house of the Duc de Laval. Prince Nikita was repeating his questions to him, when my cousin, Charles d'Osmond, who was then little more than a child, rushed into the room, out of breath, shouting and weeping with enthusiasm.

" Here it is, here it is! " he said; " it has been adopted without opposition," and he showed us his hat decorated with the white cockade. He came from the boulevard, and was about to return thither. My father, addressing Wolkonski, said to him:

" I could not possibly give you a better answer, Prince. You see that these colours arouse love, zeal, and passion."

" You are right, Marquis. I will make my report upon what I have seen, and I hope to receive confirmation of this news everywhere as I go."

Prince Wolkonski afterwards told me that, having passed through the streets to the barrier, he had met on his road nothing but demonstrations of grief and anxiety, and not a sign of joy and hope. I think that he gave a

---

[1] Prince Wolkonski, aide-de-camp to the Emperor Alexander, had been ordered to accompany to Paris M. Pasquier, the Prefect of Police, who had come to the headquarters of the Russian Emperor at Bondy, together with M. de Chabrol, Prefect of the Seine, and the municipal authorities of the capital. The Prince was at the same time to prepare apartments for the Emperor. Cp. *Mémoires du Chancelier Pasquier*, vol. ii. p. 249.

[2] He was at this time Minister of Foreign Affairs.

full report, for the Emperor Alexander entered Paris no less undecided than he had been in the morning.

My mother and myself went to take our places in the rooms of Mme. Récamier. She was then at Naples, but M. Récamier retained her house in the Rue Basse du Rempart. We found ourselves in a first floor apartment, on a level with the boulevard, in the narrowest part of the street. My father, on thus installing us, made us promise to give no signs which might be interpreted as an expression of opinion, and to receive no visitors who might arouse attention. He thought that so much consideration was due to the hospitality and the very moderate sentiments of M. Récamier.

We soon saw on the pavement of the boulevard a number of young men walking past, wearing the white cockade, waving their handkerchiefs, and shouting " Vive le Roi! " but there were very few of them. I recognised my brother among them. My mother and myself exchanged mournful and anxious glances; we still hoped that the band would increase. They dared not advance beyond the Rue Napoléon, which is now the Rue de la Paix; thence proceeding to the Madeleine, they retraced their steps. We saw the band pass five times, but were unable to cheat ourselves with the hope that it had grown larger. Our anxiety became greater and greater.

It was certain that if this demonstration remained ineffectual, all who had joined in it would be lost, and this idea was fundamentally correct. It was a feeling clearly to be seen in the eyes of all who observed these poor young men with their white cockades going by. They inspired neither anger nor hatred, and still less enthusiasm. They were regarded with a kind of pity as madmen and devoted victims. Several passers by displayed their astonishment, but no one opposed their action or molested them in any way.

Eventually at twelve o'clock the allied army began to march past our window. The apprehensions which I had been experiencing throughout the morning were too real for my patriotism to become prominent, and I admit that I felt nothing but relief. As the head of the column approached some white cockades were bashfully brought out of pockets and displayed on the side-walks. But they were by no means numerous, though the white handkerchief which the foreigners all wore upon their arms as a sign of alliance had been immediately interpreted by the population as a demonstration in favour of the Bourbons. Our faithful escort of young men surrounded the sovereigns, shouting at the top of their voices and making themselves appear as numerous as possible by dint of zeal and activity. The women did not spare themselves; white handkerchiefs were waved, and cheers were given from windows also. As the sovereigns had found Paris gloomy, silent, and almost deserted until they reached the head of the Place Vendôme, so they found it animated and excited from that point to the Champs Elysées.

Must I admit that the anti-national faction had concentrated in this spot to welcome the foreigner, and that this faction was chiefly composed of the nobility? Was it right or was it wrong? I cannot now decide, but at that moment our conduct seemed to me sublime. For the most part it was entirely disinterested, if party spirit can ever be considered so, and it was ennobled in every case by personal danger. None the less, in the midst of our hatred and our momentary infatuation I considered as entirely foolish and unnecessary the conduct of Sosthène de la Rochefoucauld, who went with the authorisation of the Emperor Alexander, to put a rope round the neck of the statue of the Emperor Napoleon, in order to drag it down from the column. We must do no justice to the young men who joined in that bold display of the morning, and say that they refused to lend themselves to this foolish enterprise, and that Sosthène found no one to accompany him except Maubreuil, Sémallé, and other adventurers of the kind.[1]

I have forgotten to say that Count Nesselrode had informed me through Prince Nikita that he was going to ask me to give him dinner that day. I had asked the Prince to come also. I saw on the boulevard several persons whom I was very glad to invite to meet these gentlemen, but, faithful to the promise exacted by my father, I went myself into the street to invite them. The only names I can remember are those of M. de Chateaubriand, Alexandre de Boisgellin, and Charles de Noailles. We were all assembled when Prince Wolkonski and one of his comrades, Michel Orloff, arrived, bringing a note from Count Nesselrode. He sent his excuses for his inability to come, and with them a paper which he said would easily secure his pardon until he could come and fetch it in person in the evening. It was the declaration which was to be posted, and which announced the intention of the allies not to treat with the Emperor or with any member of his family. It was the result of a conference held at the house of M. de Talleyrand, at the moment of the Emperor Alexander's arrival. He had begun the discussion with these words:

" Well, here we are at last in the famous Paris. It is you that brought us, M. de Talleyrand. Now, there are three things that we can do: we can treat with the Em-

[1] In the *Mémoires du Chancelier Pasquier*, who was then Prefect of Police, and consequently possessed exact information, full details of these different events will be found. See vol. ii. chap. xi. ff.

peror Napoleon, we can establish a regency, or recall the Bourbons."

" The Emperor is wrong," replied M. de Talleyrand. " There are not three things we can do; there is only one, and that is the last that he has mentioned. All-powerful as he is, he is not powerful enough to choose. If he were to hesitate, France, which expects this reward for the grief and humiliation which consumes it at this moment, will rise in a body against the invasion. And your Imperial Majesty knows full well that the finest armies melt away before the anger of a nation."

" Very well," replied the Emperor. " Now, what is to be done to attain your object? Remember that I do not wish to impose commands, but merely to yield to the wishes expressed by the country."

" No doubt, Sire; we have but to give the country a chance of making its wishes heard."

This dialogue was reported to me the very next day by one who was present at the council.

In the evening Count Nesselrode came, and the warmth of his reception I can leave to be imagined. We had so often talked anti-Bonapartism, I will not say with him, for he was too great a diplomatist, but before him, that he had no need to inquire into our feelings at that moment.[1]

I cannot refrain from quoting a piece of irony which amused me afterwards, especially since 1830, when M. de Vérac appeared a confirmed Legitimist. He had reached that solid position by beginning as a chamberlain to Napoleon, and was one of his most zealous officers. Having learnt that the Russian officers were dining at my house, he came in the evening to ask for a pass with the object

---

[1] Count Nesselrode had been for a long time First Secretary of the Russian Embassy in Paris.

of going to the allied camp to see M. de Langeron, his relative and friend. While the gentlemen were talking he came up to me, and said in a low tone and with much emotion:

"And the Emperor, is there any news of him? What is he doing? Is it known where he is?"

I understood him perfectly, but pretended to mistake him, and replied, likewise in a whisper:

"He is staying with M. de Talleyrand."

M. de Vérac was entirely disconcerted. The amusing part was that he never attempted to inform me of my mistake or to explain for which emperor he was asking. This was the only piece of vengeance that I took upon the imperial chamberlains.

Count Nesselrode talked a long time with my father concerning affairs and people. Among other things, he asked him if he thought it advisable to leave M. Pasquier in charge of the police. My father answered that the office could not be in cleverer or more honest hands, and that, if he consented to retain his post, his help might be regarded as a piece of good fortune, and that his word could be trusted entirely.

I cannot remember if it was this evening or the next day that a Royalist meeting took place at the house of M. de Mortefontaine. The meeting sent a deputation to the Emperor Alexander expressing its wishes. I can only remember that my father came back wearied, disgusted, and despairing: all the folly of the *émigré* party and the most foolish opposition had appeared in triumph. The discussion turned only upon victory, persecution, and vengeance on fellow-countrymen, at a moment when the country was at the feet of a foreign monarch. Sosthène de la Rochefoucauld was already one of the ringleaders of these ridiculous absurdities.

My drawing-room remained as full as ever; all the young men who had joined my brother in the procession through the boulevard appeared there. And though they were but a feeble army to procure a change of dynasty, they sufficed to crowd my small apartments, the more so as my usual social circle came, together with foreigners. I cannot sufficiently praise the perfect politeness of the Russian officers in these conditions; their sole desire was to overwhelm us with kindness and favours, and in order to reconcile us to our situation, they had nothing but praise and admiration for our brave armies. Not a single remark escaped them which could have wounded or offended a Frenchman, whatever his party. Such were their master's wishes, and they were scrupulously followed apparently without the smallest difficulty. It was always with a tone of respect that they spoke of France. Possibly this was the best way to magnify their own successes, but there was a certain grandeur in the idea which was only possible to a generous soul. The heart of the Emperor Alexander was generous indeed at this time.[1]

.   .   .   .

.   .   .   .

.   .   .   .

.   .   .   .

At the beginning of the spring of 1814 the weather was magnificent, and all Paris was out of doors. No event in this town, no battle, foreign occupation, revolt or disturbance of any kind, could influence or restrain the toilet of the women. On Tuesday they were walking in all their finery upon the boulevards in the midst of the wounded, daring the shells. On Wednesday they came to see the allied army march past. On Thursday they wore

[1] A passage has been suppressed.

their elegant costumes to visit the bivouac of the Cossacks in the Champs Elysées.

Strange both to sight and thought was the spectacle of these inhabitants of the Don peacefully pursuing their habits and customs in the midst of Paris. They had no tents or shelter of any kind: three or four horses were tied up to each tree, and the riders, sitting near them on the ground, talked together in quiet and harmonious accents. Most of them were sewing, mending their clothes, cutting out and preparing new garments, repairing their shoes or the harness of their horses, or altering for their own use their share in the pillage of the preceding days. These, however, were the regular Cossacks of the Guard, and as they rarely went on scouting duty, their plundering was less successful than that of their brethren, the irregular Cossacks.

Their uniforms were very handsome. Wide blue trousers, a long tunic also of blue, standing out across the chest and fastened tightly round the waist by a large belt of black varnished leather, with buckles and harness of shining copper, to which their weapons were slung. This half Oriental costume and their strange horsemanship—as the elevation of their saddles puts them in a standing position and prevents any bending of the knee—made them an object of great curiosity to the Parisian lounger. They readily allowed people to approach them, especially women and children, and the latter were positively upon their shoulders.

I have seen women take their work in their hands to examine more closely their mode of sewing. From time to time they amused themselves by uttering a kind of growl, when the curious women recoiled in fright. They uttered cries of joy and burst into roars of laughter, which were shared by those whom they had alarmed.

They did not allow men to approach so close, but sent them away merely by a calm, quiet gesture and a word which probably answers to the " stand back " of our sentinels. It is obvious that no one ventured to disregard this order. It was not entirely exclusive, for if a man came up with women and children they paid no attention to him.

They had every reason for remaining by their horses, for never under any pretext would they take a step. When they were not sitting on the ground they were on horseback. To go round the bivouac from one group to another they would mount their horses. They were also to be seen holding their lances in one hand and a jug, or plate, or even a glass in the other as they went about the business of their little households. I say a glass, because I have seen one of them quietly get up, mount his horse, take his lance, bend to the ground to take up a gourd, then ride thirty paces away to get water from a tub which was surrounded by a guard, drink the water, return to his position with his empty bottle, get off his horse, replace his lance in the general bundle, and resume his work.

These nomadic customs seemed to us so strange that they keenly excited our curiosity, which we satisfied the more readily as we were persuaded that our affairs were proceeding excellently. Partisan success hid from us the bitterness of a foreign bivouac in the Champs Elysées. I will do my father the justice to say that he did not share this impression, and that I could never induce him to go and see this spectacle, which he always insisted was rather sad than curious.

CHAPTER XX

It was during that Thursday evening that Count Nesselrode said to me:

" Should you like to see the document on the strength of which we risked the march on Paris? "

" Most certainly," I replied.

" Well, here it is."

He drew from his pocket-book a very small piece of paper, all torn and crumpled, upon which the following words were written in sympathetic ink: " You are groping about like children, when you ought to be walking on stilts. You can do all that you want to; please do all that you can. You know the sign. Have confidence in the one who gives it you."

I do not think I am mistaken in a word. This note, written by M. de Talleyrand after the retreat of the allies from Montereau, reached them near Troyes, and the instructions given to the bearer of these strange credentials had a great deal of influence on the decision which brought the allies back to Paris. In any case, they were decided by the fact that it was much more easy to leave France by retreating through Flanders than through

Champagne, which was already exhausted, wretched, exasperated, and quite ready to rise against them.

The foreigners were very much more uneasy and very much more astonished with regard to their stay in Paris than we were. They were neither blinded by party spirit nor disillusioned with regard to the prestige which the name of the Emperor Napoleon inspired. The marvels of the French campaign prevented them from believing in such complete and real destruction of the army, and they expected to see it rise up from underground. This sentiment was evident from all that they said, and they had the good sense not to be greatly reassured by us, for they could judge of our futility on many points.

At all events, we were right when we assured them that the country was so disgusted, so wearied, so eager for tranquillity, and so surfeited with glory, that it had completely seceded from the Emperor, and asked for nothing but security. There had never been a time when the patriotic sentiment had less force in France; the Emperor had perhaps weakened it by his immense conquests, whilst thinking to increase it. We scarcely recognised a compatriot in a Frenchman of Rome or of Hamburg. Perhaps, too, and to this idea I am more inclined, the system of deception which he had adopted had disgusted the greater part of the country. The bulletins never spoke of anything but our triumphs; the French army was always victorious, the enemy's army was always beaten; and yet successive defeats had brought it from the banks of the Moskowa to those of the Seine.

No one believed in official news. People exhausted themselves in trying to discover the key to the enigma, and the masses ceased to take much interest in events on which they could only speculate. Affairs were no longer public, when no exact information could be obtained, and when inquiries were forbidden. The Emperor had worked so hard to establish the fact that it was his business and not ours, that finally we took him at his word. And whatever may have been thought and said of late years, certain it is that in 1814 every one, including his army and the public functionaries, was so tired that the only desire was to be relieved of duties no longer dictated by a wise and reasonable will. Absolute power had intoxicated and blinded him; it is not perhaps given to a man to be able to bear the weight of it.

The Duc de Raguse once explained to me the nature of his connection with the Emperor in a phrase which is more or less applicable to the whole nation:

" When he said: *All for France,* I served with enthusiasm; when he said: *France and I,* I served with zeal; when he said: *I and France,* I served with obedience; but when he said: *I, without France,* I felt the necessity of separating from him."

Well, France had reached this latter point: she considered that he no longer represented her interests; and as nations, even more than individuals, are ungrateful, she forgot the immense benefits that she owed to him, and overwhelmed him with her reproaches. Posterity in its turn will forget the aberrations of this sublime genius and his weaknesses. It will see the poetic side of his stay at Fontainebleau; it will avoid all mention of the obstinate haggling by which he strove, after his heroic farewells to the eagles of his old battalions, to get a little more furniture to take with him into exile; and in this posterity will be right. When a figure like Bonaparte appears amid the ages, we ought not to remember the few shadows which might darken some of its splendour. But we must explain how it was that contemporaries, who had all been dazzled by him, found his splendour no longer a source of life, but rather of pain and grief.

Early on the Friday Count Nesselrode sent us word that the sovereigns were going to the Opéra. Our domestics went off at once on a campaign to get boxes for us, so that we might be there in full force. The florists were in demand, and requested to supply us with lilies, which we wore in our hair, in bouquets, and in garlands. The men wore the white cockade in their hats. So far all was as it should be, but as a Frenchwoman I blush to tell of our behaviour at this performance.

In the first place, we began by applauding the Emperor Alexander and the King of Prussia with enthusiasm. Next, the doors of our boxes were left open, and the greater the throng of foreign officers who entered, the more delighted we were. There was not a single Russian or Prussian subaltern who had not the right and also some desire to join the crowd. Two or three foreign generals who were in my box considered this familiarity less charming than I did, and turned them out, to my great disappointment. I was somewhat consoled, however, by the presence of the generals, and by the visit of the Russian ministers and of Prince Augustus of Prussia, whom I had known for a long time.

Just before the arrival of the sovereigns in the imperial box, some young Frenchmen of our party went in and covered the eagle which surmounted the draperies of this box with a white handkerchief. At the end of the performance these same young men shattered the eagle with hammers, amidst our enthusiastic applause. I took part in all this, with the rest of my party. I cannot say that it was in accordance with my conscience, for I felt some misgivings which I could not entirely define. These demonstrations, no doubt, had an implied meaning—the fall of Bonaparte and the presumed return of our princes. It was that which we were really inaugurating, but our purpose was not sufficiently plain.

I did not experience any feeling of restraint, two days later, at the Comédie Française, when a man, coming from the stage with a large paper in his hand, fastened this to the curtain with pins, and then, standing back, let us see the *fleurs de lis* in the place of the eagle. This was plain, and the enthusiasm knew no bounds. The Emperor Alexander rose in his box and pledged himself definitely by his applause.

Some bad verse was sung in his honour to the tune of *Henri IV.*, the last line of which was, " He is giving us back a Bourbon." Fresh enthusiasm; every one burst into tears. That evening does not weigh on my conscience, but it seems to me that the Opéra performance at least was a great mistake.

Parties are too easily persuaded of their universality. We might have been convinced only a short time previously that we were merely a very trifling fraction of the nation, and yet we gaily proceeded to affront the honourable sentiments of the country while cruelly wounding the feelings of the army. That eagle which it had borne victoriously in all the capitals of Europe we seemed to be offering up as a holocaust to the inhabitants of those same capitals, who perhaps scarcely respected us for this display of anti-national feeling.

Undoubtedly this was not our object, any more than it was our idea; but it certainly did not require a great amount of malevolence to explain it in this way. The fallen party may honestly have believed this, and it is not surprising that such conduct should engender those long hatreds which die out with such difficulty. It is with great regret that I own it, but the Royalist party is that which least loves its country for the country's sake; the quarrel which sprang up between the various classes has made the nobility hostile to the land where its privileges are not recognised. And I fear that the nobility is therefore more in sympathy with high-born foreigners than with French *bourgeois*. Common interests attacked have established affinities between classes and broken up nationalities.[1]

On this Friday, the day of the Opéra, we were at dinner, when the door of the dining-room opened noisily and a Russian general suddenly burst in. He waltzed round the table, singing, " Oh, my friends, my dear, dear friends! " Our first idea was that he was mad, and then my brother exclaimed, " Why, it's Pozzo! "

And it was he. Communication was so difficult under the Imperial Government, that, in spite of the intimacy between us, we did not even know that he was in the Russian service. He had not known where to find us until a few minutes before his arrival in such delight. He went with us to the Opéra, and from that time I was scarcely a day without seeing him at least once. It was through him, partly, that I was initiated into current events. It was not that I interfered; but he found me dependable, always interested and discreet, and he liked to *sfoggursi,* as he used to say with me. I

---

[1] This passage applies only to a narrow clique, whose folly and exaggerated language none the less inflicted much harm upon France, and still more upon the legitimate monarchy, as every one acknowledges. It was this clique which made the Hundred Days possible. But these errors and this ridiculous behaviour were far from acceptable to the entire Royalist party or to all the nobility. Mme. de Boigne, her father, and many others besides, are typical examples.

was all the more ready for this, as I have always liked taking part in politics as an amateur.

It seems to me that when one's disposition is so unfortunate as to prevent exclusive and religious attention to our future lot, which is to be eternal, the subject most worthy of interest for a serious mind is the present state of the nations on earth.

My Russian friends had let me know that on leaving the Théâtre Français on the 4th, after the inauguration of the *fleur de lis*, the Emperor Alexander was to drive to the headquarters of the army. General Pozzo was recognised by the Provisional Government, and it was therefore for him to communicate to it Alexander's orders. The precautions taken by the Allies, under these conditions, for securing their retreat without passing through Paris again, prove the terror inspired by the phantom army before them, and prove, too, the influence which the great name of Napoleon could still exert upon them.

In France that name was powerless and aroused no sympathy. It was in vain that Napoleon had called the Normans and the Bretons to the help of the Burgundians and the inhabitants of Champagne, thus reviving the old names of the provinces. These phantasmagorias, in which he had been as lucky as he was skilful, had now lost their prestige, with that of victory. The Breton felt himself no more electrified than the inhabitant of Finisterre. Either the Allies were ignorant of this, or they feared the awakening, but certain it is that it was not without continual apprehension, and summoning of reinforcements, that the foreigners remained in the capital of France.

The news that negotiations had been opened between

Prince Schwarzenberg and Marshal Marmont postponed the departure of the Emperor of Russia. It cannot be denied that the wise, moderate, and generous behaviour of this sovereign justified our enthusiasm for him. He was at that time thirty-seven years of age, but he looked much younger. A handsome face and a still better figure, an expression that was both gentle and imposing, predisposed every one in his favour. The confidence which he had in the Parisians, going about as he did without any escort and almost alone, won all hearts.

He was simply adored by his subjects. I remember, a few weeks later, arriving one night at the theatre just as he was entering his box. The door of it was guarded by two great giants of his army, who observed so strictly military an attitude that they did not dare move to wipe their faces, which were bathed in tears. I asked a Russian officer what had happened for them to be in such a state.

" Oh," he answered carelessly, " the Emperor has just passed by, and probably they have managed to touch him."

Such a piece of good fortune was so highly valued that they could only express their happiness by tears. I had often seen the Emperor, I had even had the honour of dancing the polonaise with him, without weeping for joy like his guards. But I was sufficiently struck by his superiority to regret keenly that our princes resembled him so little. It was not until some years later that mysticism developed in him a suspicious tendency which eventually became madness. All contemporary memoirs agree in recognising in him two totally different men, according to the epoch of which they speak, and the year 1814 was the zenith of his glory.

M. de Chateaubriand's pamphlet, *Bonaparte and the Bourbons,* printed at a rate that was not quick enough for us in our impatience, made its appearance. I remember reading it in a perfect transport of admiration and with torrents of tears, and was much ashamed of my emotion when it came into my hands again some few years later. The author then displayed the true nature of this party action by the incense he burned on the Saint Helena altar, and has thus judged it more severely than anyone else. As I am compelled to own how completely I shared in his mistake, it would be very ungracious for me to call it a crime in him.

Foreigners, less blinded than we were, realised all that the pamphlet meant, and the Emperor Alexander took offence at it. He had not forgotten that he had lived in deference of the man so violently attacked. M. de Chateaubriand already fancied himself a statesman, but no one else had yet thought of such a thing. He took a great deal of trouble in order to obtain a private audience with Alexander.

I was deputed to speak to Count Nesselrode about it, and it was granted. The Emperor only knew M. de Chateaubriand as an author, and he was left waiting in a room with M. Étienne, the author of a play which the Emperor had seen the previous evening. In passing through this room, on his way out, the Emperor found the two men waiting there. He first spoke to Étienne about his play, and then said a few words to M. de Chateaubriand with regard to the pamphlet, which he professed not to have had time yet to read. He preached to the two authors of peace between literary men, and assured them that they ought to make it their business to amuse the public, and not to interfere with politics.

He then moved on, without giving M. de Chateaubriand a chance of uttering a word. The latter threw a very bellicose glance at Étienne, and went away furious.

Count Nesselrode, although annoyed at the incident, could not help laughing when he gave us the details of this interview. I have never been able to make out whether the association of M. de Chateaubriand with Étienne was the Emperor's cleverness or his mistake. M. de Chateaubriand, though, had taken precautions in order to avoid any such mistake. From the very day following the arrival of the Allies he had arrayed himself in a fancy uniform; over this he wore a thick cord of red silk as a shoulder-belt, to which was attached an immense Turkish sword, which he dragged across every floor with a fearful clatter. He certainly looked much more like a pirate captain than a peaceable writer. The costume seemed a trifle ridiculous even to his most devoted admirers.

I do not remember which day of that eventful week one of my relatives assured me that he knew an officer who said that, on the day of the battle of Paris, he had received an order, brought to him by M. de Girardin, to blow up the powder stores of the Invalides. This was repeated in my drawing-room, and it reached the ears of Count Nesselrode. He asked me whether I could get to know the name of this officer, and obtain further details of the adventure. I sent for the person who had mentioned it, and he told us that M. de Lescour, an artillery officer in command at the Invalides, had been fetched to the gate on Tuesday evening in the dusk, and that he had found Comte Alexandre de Girardin there on horseback, all covered with dust; that the latter had given him a formal order from the Emperor to blow up the powder stores. M. de Lescour had not been able to refrain from a gesture of horror, and M. de Girardin had then said :

" Do you hesitate, Monsieur ? "

Lescour, fearing that another man would be entrusted with the fatal commission, recovered himself, and replied :

" No, General; I never hesitate to obey my chiefs."

Upon this reply, M. de Girardin started off again at a gallop. The person who told me this offered to bring M. de Lescour the following morning to see me. Count Nesselrode begged me to consent. The Duc de Maillé, who was present at the interview, remembered having seen M. de Girardin on the Louis XVI. bridge on the day in question, at the time stated. He was riding very quickly, and the Duc was surprised to see him turn to the right, which would be in the direction of the Invalides. M. de Lescour called on me the next day, and in the meantime I had received a note from Count Nesselrode asking me to send him on. He went, was introduced to the Emperor Alexander, received many compliments and the St. Anne Cross. He returned to me in a transport of delight and gratitude. He appeared to me to be a very simple, straightforward man.

A few days later the Princesse de Vaudémont, his protectress, lectured him severely for publishing this affair. He was taken to luncheon at the house of Mme. de Vintimille. Mme. de Girardin and Mme. de Greffulhe, her nieces, were there, and they cried a great deal. General Clarke, whom Lescour was accustomed to obey as Minister of War, reproached him with having sold himself to the enemy. He was surrounded, and every one tried to induce him to deny the story. He did not entirely consent, but he was persuaded to sign a declaration in which he affirmed that, although he did receive the verbal order from a superior officer, it was so dark that he was not sure that he recognised him, and he was perhaps mistaken in the name he had given.

On. leaving the house he came to me and told me what he had done.

"Monsieur de Lescour," I said, "you have ruined yourself. When you make statements of such gravity you ought to be very certain that not the slightest detail of any circumstance should vary, and it is a very important detail that you have now retracted. I am sure that this will cause grave doubts about your veracity, and that the persons who have extorted this disavowal from you in your weakness will be the first to profit by it in order to inculpate you."

The poor man agreed that I was right, and he was in despair. The result that I prophesied to him was not long delayed. It was speedily settled that M. de Lescour was a wretched adventurer, who had invented the whole of this fable in order to make a position for himself. He was quickly sent away to a post at Cette. M. de Girardin soon secured the favour of our princes, and poor Lescour was persecuted by him. I never saw him again, and I do not know what became of him.

It is generally agreed that this story should be rejected as untrue. And yet when I think the story over, and then remember the hurried departure of Mme. Bertrand upon an order from her husband; when I think of the passionate entreaties of M. de la Touche, so desirous that we should start that very day; of M. de Girardin's quick, silent visit to the staff, and of how he confined himself to hearing the news of the capitulation before returning to Juvisy, where the Emperor was awaiting him; of M. de Maillé's meeting him on the bridge, and of the direction in which he was riding, which certainly was not the way a man would go if he were in a hurry to reach Fontainebleau; then I must own that I am rather inclined to believe in the veracity of M. de Lescour, and to consider him as a victim sacrificed by his own weakness to the interest of others.[1]

[1] Chancellor Pasquier writes in his Memoirs: "When everything had been carefully and thoroughly examined, it was proved that the supposed order had never been given, and that the account was invented by a man who was trying to push his way. . . ." The Chancellor adds that "no one would have consented either to carry or receive such an order verbally."—Vol. ii. p. 236.

CHAPTER XXI

I NOW arrive, with repugnance, at what history can
only call Marshal Marmont's defection. No doubt history will later on clear this of all the calumnies that
have been added to it, but the sincere attachment that I
have for him makes me regret infinitely that an action
which was quite defensible in itself should have been
conceived by a man in whom the very thought of it
was wrong. It is quite true that the Marshal was only
guilty of opening negotiations with Prince Schwarzenberg without the Emperor's knowledge. But he was
greatly attached to Napoleon personally, he had been
highly favoured and very kindly treated by him, so that
his proper attitude, and perhaps his duty, was to cast
in his lot exclusively with Napoleon's fortunes. He
himself felt this so thoroughly that this incident in his
life exerted the most grievous influence over his actions,
and made him very unhappy when once the first moment
of excitement was over.

I had a reason for studying the details of this affair: I was asked to draw up an account of it, and I endeavoured to get at the truth with all the more care because I wished to exclude the possibility that any of the facts reported could be contradicted. The papers concerning it were all collected and handed over to M. Arago in 1831, as he said he wished to publish them. But, as sometimes happens, courage failed him when he had to deal with a friend who was outlawed by popular passions. In any case, the following details of this event appear to me to be exactly true.

The Emperor Napoleon paid a visit to Marmont's army in camp at Essonnes. He praised him highly for his conduct in the Paris affair, where he had held the enemy in check for four hours after receiving King Joseph's order to capitulate. Napoleon promised rewards to the division and the promotions requested by the Marshal. He then went into the details of his plans with him as to what was to be done later. He ordered him to march in the night with his ten thousand men, in order to take up his post again on the heights of Belleville.

" Sire, I have not four thousand men in a condition for the march."

The Emperor turned the subject, and a minute later again referred to the ten thousand men. The Marshal repeated that he had not four thousand under his orders, but this did not prevent the Emperor from arranging for five thousand to be on one road, three thousand on another, and two thousand with the artillery, as though the ten thousand men really existed elsewhere than in his will and his desire.

This was not mere aberration: he had adopted this method throughout the whole French campaign, and it had succeeded. He would not have dared to ask regiments which were in reality so weak for the miracles he expected from them, but by appearing to count thoroughly on what he wanted he obtained it. When he had finished developing his plans to Marmont, the latter asked him where and how he should cross the Marne. The Emperor struck his forehead: " You are right," he said: " that is impossible. We must think of another way to surround Paris. Consider the matter yourself, and let me know everything you hear. Wait for fresh orders."

The Emperor returned to Fontainebleau. Marshal Marmont was stupefied at the idea of surrounding Paris, which was then guarded by two hundred thousand foreigners, who were daily expecting two hundred thousand more, whilst the Emperor could at the most only dispose of thirty thousand men. He foresaw the destruction of what was left of the poor army, and perhaps the destruction of the capital, if, as the Emperor hoped, he should succeed in evoking demonstrations hostile to the allied army.

It was not the first time that the Emperor's projects had appeared to him wildly out of proportion to his remaining forces.

On the night of the battle of Champaubert the chiefs of the regiments engaged went to supper at the Emperor's, each having something to eat as he arrived. There were still four or five at table, among whom were Marmont (Duc de Raguse) and General Drouot.

The Emperor was walking up and down in the room, drawing a picture of the situation, and trying to show that he was nearer to the banks of the Elbe than the Allies were to those of the Seine. He noticed that his words produced no response, and that the marshals gazed at their plates without looking up.

He approached General Drouot, and, laying his hand on his shoulder, said to him:

" Ah, Drouot, I want ten men like you! "

" No, Sire, you want a hundred thousand," answered the General, and this noble reply cut short the plan of campaign.

The Duc de Raguse had given himself up to his memories, and was overwhelmed by painful thoughts when M. de Montessuis arrived to see him. The latter had been his *aide-de-camp*, and had remained on familiar terms with him, though now a very ardent Royalist. He had brought him the documents and proclamations that had been published in Paris: the fall of the Emperor decreed by the Senate, the orders of the Provisional Government, and letters from several persons who were supporting this Government, persuading the Marshal to follow their example. General Dessolles, his intimate friend, M. Pasquier, of whose honour and probity he was sure, were among the number. The importance was pointed out to him of giving an armed force immediately to the Provisional Government, so that it might take a more dignified part in the council of the foreigners. Further on it was insinuated that this very force would allow it to make conditions with the family whom fate seemed to be calling back to the throne of its ancestors.

Montessuis loudly emphasised the precedent of Monk and the *rôle* of saviour of the country. He pictured the Marshal as the recipient of the general gratitude for the institutions which France would owe to him, and of his recognition by the army as its protector. The Marshal, on the other hand, recalled the extravagant words of the Emperor, conceived the fatal idea of saving him in spite of himself, and was weak enough to be seduced by this project.

However, he called together the chiefs of the regiments (and there were more of them than the strength of the army justified), and submitted to them the proposals that had been made to him and the position in which they then were. All of them, with the exception of General Lucotte, voted for submission to the new Government. M. de Montessuis was entrusted with the task of establishing communication with Prince Schwarzenberg's staff. Plans were proposed on both sides, but nothing passed in writing.

Such' was the state of affairs when the marshals sent from Fontainebleau to demand the regency arrived at Essonnes. The remaining details I had from Marshal Macdonald, who, after telling me them, took the trouble to dictate them, when I was trying to get exact information for the article which M. Arago had undertaken.

The marshals had no orders from the Emperor to take Marshal Macdonald into their plans, whatever may be said to the contrary. They stopped with him whilst awaiting the passport for which they had asked the staff of the Allies, then stationed at Chilly, just above Longjumeau. They told him the motive of their journey to Paris. Marmont confided to them all the details of his position in relation to Prince Schwarzenberg. He might at any moment receive the acceptance of the demands he had made. But he told his colleagues that he should refrain from taking any personal step until the fate of their own attempt should be decided. They arranged that he should go and visit his posts, and that he should contrive not to be found until their return; that then, according to their success, they would decide amongst each other what was the best thing to do and how to act in common.

Marshal Ney remarked that perhaps this commencement of negotiations with one of the marshals would raise hopes that the chiefs of the different corps might be set at variance, and thus would prevent the acceptance of the regency for which they were about to ask, and that it would be better for Marshal Marmont to accompany them, in order to prove that they were of one mind. The others adopted this opinion, and the Duc de Raguse made no objection to accompany them.

Before leaving, and in their presence, he thrice repeated his orders to the chiefs of the different corps which he was leaving at Essonnes, to the effect that they were not to stir until his return. He promised to be back the following morning. The passport did not arrive from Chilly, and the marshals, impatient at this delay, presented themselves at the outposts, and were conducted to the headquarters of the vanguard at Petit Bourg, where they hoped to get an escort given to them. They entered the castle, and the Duc de Raguse, who had no authority from the Emperor, remained in the carriage. Prince Schwarzenberg, however, was at the outposts, and on learning from the subalterns that the Duc was there, he sent to ask him to come in. He had a few minutes conversation with him, and told him that his proposals had been sent to Paris, and that they had been accepted.

The Marshal replied that his position was now changed; that his comrades were entrusted with a communication with which he fully agreed, and that all that had passed between them must now be considered as nil. Prince Schwarzenberg assured him that he understood his scruples perfectly well, and they entered the drawing-room together, to the astonishment of the other marshals. The Duc de Raguse told them what had just taken place between him and Prince Schwarzenberg, and how relieved he felt by this explanation. He accompanied them to the Emperor Alexander's, and it was he who spoke most eagerly in favour of the King of Rome and the regency. There was no great merit in this, for it certainly was their own cause that the marshals were now pleading.

After this imperialist conference the Emperor Alexander had a meeting with the members of the Provisional Government and with those who were most deeply involved in the Royalist movement. He argued against the Bonapartes in the first conference, and against the Bourbons in the second one, persuading himself that he was acting with the greatest impartiality. After the council, which was prolonged until the break of day, he dismissed the Fontainebleau envoys, telling them that he must consult the Allies, and that they must wait until nine in the morning for the reply. It has been said that he already knew about the Essonnes movement, but that seems impossible. It is very certain that he gave them no news of it, and all the fine speeches reported as having been made by him and by the marshals to Marmont are completely false.

The marshals went to Marshal Ney's to await the hour fixed by the Emperor. They were all breakfasting there when some one came to tell Marshal Marmont that he was wanted. He went out of the room, and very soon came back, looking as pale as death. Marshal Macdonald asked him what was the matter.

" My *aide-de-camp* has come to tell me that the generals wish to begin a movement with my division, but they promised to wait for me, and I must rush away to stop everything."

During this rapid speech he was fastening on his sword, and he now took his hat. The *aide-de-camp* was Fabvier, and he told us that the marshals had scarcely left Essonnes when Napoleon had sent for Marmont. A second and then a third message arrived for him to go to Fontainebleau, and the third time there was an order for the general in command to go to the Emperor in case the Marshal should still be absent.

The generals, uneasy about their position, were convinced that the Emperor had heard of their interviews with the enemy. They were seized with fear, and sought their own safety in the execution of the movement which Marmont had distinctly forbidden on starting for Paris. The Marshal sprang into a carriage that was standing in Marshal Ney's courtyard. At the barrier he was not allowed to pass, and he had to return to the staff major of the place, who sent him to the governor of the city. In short, he lost so much time in getting a passport that a second *aide-de-camp*, Colonel Denis, arrived. He announced that, in spite of his orders to Fabvier that they should wait for him, the chiefs had begun the march as soon as he had started; that he, Denis, had accompanied them as far as Belle-Épine; from there they had taken the Versailles route, and that by that time they must have nearly arrived, so that the harm done was irreparable.

Marshal Marmont remained in Paris, where he learnt of the fury of his division on discovering for what reason it was at Versailles. He started immediately for Versailles, but the troops had already left and were on the way back to Fontainebleau in full mutiny. He hurried after them, harangued and persuaded them, and finally brought them back to Versailles. On this occasion he certainly accomplished one of the most energetic, difficult, and boldest enterprises that any one could have attempted.

This then is the exact truth, which I was able to gather on verifying all the facts, with reference to Marmont's defection. It will be seen that his action was merely confined to opening negotiations unknown to the Emperor.

In order to be thoroughly impartial, I must admit that he was to blame in other respects. Marshal Marmont was a typical French soldier. He was kind, generous, brave, and candid, but he was changeable, vain, easily led away by enthusiasm, and the most inconsistent of men. He always acted on the impulse of the moment, without reflecting on the past and without thinking of the future. He found himself placed in a position where every one about him applauded the action of which he was supposed to be the author, and emphasised the importance of it. He was saluted everywhere by the name of Monk. He was told, too, that a resolution had been made from the very first day not to come to terms on any conditions with the Empire, that the proclamation of the 30th confirmed this, that the steps taken by the marshals could not therefore have any success.

He, on his side, said to himself that his generals had only executed what he had proposed to them in circumstances which were unchanged, since the regency had been refused, and that it would scarcely be generous to disavow them, &c. Anyhow, as the result of good or bad reasoning he finally persuaded himself that he ought to assume the responsibility.

The agreement with Prince Schwarzenberg was drawn

up the following morning, signed, ante-dated, and sent to the *Moniteur*. Not content with that, the Marshal received a deputation from the City of Paris, which came to thank him for the service he had rendered. Their address, and his reply to it, were published in the *Moniteur*. In short, he went to a great deal of trouble to give his action all the appearance of a perfidy that he had not committed, but to which his presence among the marshals gave a treasonable colouring.

There would be no existing proof of the truth of the account I have just given, but for the following circumstance. His *aide-de-camp*, M. de Guise, the same man who in 1814 drew up the ante-dated agreement with Prince Schwarzenberg, was searching among his papers after the Revolution of 1830, when he found by chance, at the back of a drawer in a writing-table, an old crumpled letter. It was from General Bordesoulle, announcing the departure of the troops from Essonnes, apologising for acting against his orders, and explaining that the request of the Emperor thrice repeated had induced him to this decision.

Although Marshal Marmont suffered cruelly from the slanders circulated about him, when once the excitement in which he was kept was over, he never thought of this letter, and indeed had completely forgotten its existence. That alone suffices to paint the man. This document will probably be published; I have read it several times.

The marshals entrusted with the proposals from Fontainebleau presented themselves at nine o'clock before the Emperor Alexander. The latter refused to treat with them on any further terms than Napoleon's abdication pure and simple. As a peremptory argument, he made the most of the defection which had begun to manifest itself in the French army. The marshals, still relying on the first news brought by Fabvier, protested the fidelity of the army. The Emperor smiled, and told them that Marmont's corps was then on the way to Versailles. The marshals started away without seeing their comrade Marmont again. They found no trace of his division on the Fontainebleau road.

I have gone into detail with this story, in the first place because the facts have been distorted by party spirit, and in the second place because I do not think any one knows them better than I do. For the purpose I have already stated, I collected all the proofs and all documents possible; and I went to the trouble of examining how far they coincided with each other, in order not to advance anything that could be disputed with the least shade of foundation. I have perhaps a clearer and plainer knowledge of this affair than the Marshal had himself, for he began by believing that it really was a subject for commendation, and he did not discover his error until he was assailed by atrocious slanders. He was again to blame for his excessive scorn of these.

The chiefs who acted with violence against Napoleon at Fontainebleau, on seeing the torrent of popular opinion turning again in favour of the great man whose misfortunes recalled his genius, endeavoured to conceal their action behind that of the Duc de Raguse. National pride preferred an outcry of treason to an acknowledgment of defeats. Hence the theory was speedily established in the minds of the people that the Duc de Raguse had sold and delivered up, one after the other, Paris and the Emperor. The one imputation was just as false as the other.

The marshals, on their return to Fontainebleau, dragged the Emperor's abdication from him by violence. Marshal Ney hastened to inform the Allies of this fact on the return of the envoys from Fontainebleau to Paris. Marshal Macdonald told me that the others were very much astonished to hear Count Nesselrode thank Ney for his important communication.

It is now time to return to events as seen from our position. On Monday I did not see any one who knew how events stood, but on Tuesday morning people came to tell me of the victory. Pozzo informed me that the day before had been a very critical time. The Emperor was surrounded by men who were beginning to be alarmed at the situation of an army in a city like Paris. The reports about the occupied provinces were not reassuring. The people, oppressed by the miseries consequent on war, were ready to rise. Every one Austrian had no ears for anything but these tales, and no tongue for anything but to repeat them.

Prince Schwarzenberg began to reproach himself for the proclamation to which Pozzo had obtained his signature, as he naturally did not want to take on himself the responsibility of the prolonged stay in Paris. The question at issue, in the absence of the Emperor of Austria, was the future fate of his daughter and of the sceptre of his grandson. The King of Prussia, as every one knew, was completely dominated by the will of Alexander; it was thus on that alone that such great resolutions depended. One cannot be surprised that he was agitated, nor can one blame his hesitation. This was such that Pozzo believed the game was lost during the close of the day and half of the night.

The Duc de Vicence, who had hitherto solicited an audience without success, now succeeded in securing a long interview. The marshals had an audience of no smaller length, but the impression which they made on the Emperor Alexander was victoriously combated by the persons who composed the Provisional Government and his council. It was explained to the Emperor that none of them would have compromised themselves so far except for the engagement signed with his name. If he went back now on the promise he had given not to treat with Napoleon, nor with his family, the fate of all those who had trusted to his word was exile or the scaffold. This question of individual generosity had great influence with him.

He had already decided, as he has since said, when he sent the marshals away at nine o'clock, in order to give a reply. He gave a hint to Pozzo, to Count Nesselrode, and perhaps even to M. de Talleyrand. But he would not pronounce definitely without appearing to consult the King of Prussia and Prince Schwarzenberg.

On Tuesday morning all hesitation had disappeared, and with this news we learnt what risks we had run. These were very real and very individual, for by the way in which we had compromised ourselves there would have been nothing else for us to do than to follow the rear of the Russian baggage-train if the Allies had given the government back into the hands of the Bonapartists. The regency in reality would have been nothing but a transition for returning promptly to the imperial *régime*.

My Châtenay people came to me in the greatest distress, saying that they did not know what was to become of them. The mayor of the place had taken flight, and the deputy mayor was hiding upon my premises. My house had first been occupied by a military staff, who, on finding the wine-cellar good, had taken away all the wine there was not time to drink, and had left it absolutely empty. The fresh arrivals were not very pleased at this. Detachments of all kinds and of every nationality had followed each other, exciting the terror of the inhabitants of the village, who had learned at their own expense that the Bavarian and Wurtemberg armies were most to be feared.

Thanks to my intercourse with the Russians, I very easily obtained protection. Prince Wolkonski let me have two Cossacks, belonging to the Guard, to stay at Châtenay, and a subaltern to install them there. I went myself with them; my carriage was therefore escorted by these inhabitants of the steppes, and I must confess that this rather amused me. I admired the way in which they helped their little horses to mount the hills. They let their lance touch the ground, and then, placing it under their arm-pits, or holding it with both hands like an oar, they leaned on it, throwing the point forward as they advanced, very much in the same way as one uses a pole in a boat.

I found all my people in great consternation. They had adopted the white cockade, so that they might work more peaceably in the garden, which skirted the road leading from Choisy to Versailles. Although I do not pretend to know much about strategy, I could not understand how it was that there were some of the Allied troops in the lines. This seemed strange to me, and was not explained until my return to Paris.

My Cossacks were provided with a card covered with seals and signatures, with the aid of which they exorcised all the demons which, in fifty different uniforms, presented themselves at our doors. One of them spoke a little German, the others supported him in Russian, and this they lavished with a degree of loquacity which appeared to astonish the German soldiers as much as it did me. But the card always settled the argument in their favour. I saw them at work several times during my few hours' stay at Châtenay.

I was informed that, besides the wine, my guests had carried off all the bed-clothes, a fair number of mattresses for their wounded men, and all the feather-beds, or rather, they had emptied the feathers out; and in this way, finding themselves in possession of the bed-cases, they had gone in numbers into the lake, caught the fish it contained with their hands, and carried them off in these said bed-cases. This strange mode of fishing seemed to me funny enough to be noted. It is fair to say that they only pillaged the houses that were deserted by the inhabitants, and that they only burned down those where a feeble resistance was attempted.

I lodged my Cossacks at my gardener's house. His wife was very much afraid of them, for the most alarming stories had been told about them to the people. The first evening, while she was preparing their supper, her child, which was in the cradle, woke up and began to cry. The Cossacks said a few words to each other, and then one of them went across to the child. The poor mother trembled with fear; but the Russian took the child out of bed, and, sitting down with it on his knees before the fire, warmed its feet in his hands. His comrades talked to it and made grimaces; the child smiled at them, and from that time forth they were its nurses. When I returned the following week they said to me:

" Madame Maria, nice woman!" whilst she, on her side, put her child into their arms when she wanted to attend to her housework.

Besides their liking for children, they were very fond of flowers. They used to walk for hours up and down in front of the conservatories, looking in through the glass, and when the gardener presented them with a bouquet they thanked him as though very much delighted, but they did not touch anything. Their protective powers included the whole village, and when a detachment approached, the cry of " Cossacks! " passed from mouth to mouth. Day and night they were always ready to answer the call, and consequently there were no depredations committed in Châtenay from the time they were installed there. I may as well mention that for this service rendered to the parish one of my neighbours denounced me during the Hundred Days.

My father, I must confess, did not perhaps suffer as he should have done on seeing the tricoloured cockade humiliated, but when it was a question of the white flag, all his patriotism was wildly aroused once more. The thought of seeing the Comte d'Artois make his entry into Paris, surrounded solely by foreigners, made him rebellious. He conceived the idea of forming a kind of National Guard on horseback composed of our young men. He mentioned this to Count Nesselrode, who obtained the consent of his imperial master. The Provisional Government adopted it when it was being arranged.

My brother was the first to go and inscribe his name at the house of Charles de Noailles. My father had mentioned him to my brother and his friends as the most suitable man for their captain. Charles de Noailles was delighted at the idea, and could not be grateful enough. He and his daughter came to thank my father with effusion. But from the very next day there was war in the camp. We were not yet emancipated, but ambitions for place and power were already rife, and the intrigues of courtiers were already agitating their minds.

Charles de Damas and his set gave the signal. Although they were in close intercourse with the Noailles family, they strongly opposed the choice that had been made of Charles de Noailles, were zealous in their efforts to find out all the misdeeds of his father, the Prince de

Poix, at the beginning of the Revolution, and did their utmost to prevent any one from giving his signature. This somewhat checked enthusiasm, but in the end a hundred and fifty young men were found, who equipped and armed themselves and supplied themselves with all that was necessary within four days, and were quite ready before the arrival of Monsieur.

From this time forth the nobles of the former court considered nothing but their own interests, both with regard to money and advancement; their one object was to establish their claims and pretensions over those of the others. Consequently they were one of the greatest obstacles to the dynasty which they wanted to perpetuate.

We do not mean by this to assert that these sentiments are peculiar to this class; they probably belong to all men who have anything to do with power. I saw a second Revolution, brought about by the *bourgeoisie*, and, as in the one which I am now describing, after the fifth day all generous and patriotic sentiments were absorbed by ambition and private interests. If only we knew exactly what it cost the powerful will of the Emperor to constrain the military pretensions after the 18th of Brumaire, it is probable that we should find there the same spirit of intrigue and egoism.

CHAPTER XXII

ON the tenth day of their entry the foreigners assembled
at the Place Louis XV. to sing a *Te Deum*. I witnessed
this sight from the window of Prince Wolkonski's apartment, as he was quartered at the Naval Ministry. I
felt no emotion at the mere sight of troops and people in
the square. It is evident that sounds exercise more influence than sights over my mind, for when a most solemn
silence had been established and the religious chanting of
the Greek priests was heard, blessing these foreigners
who had come from all parts to triumph over us, the patriotic chord, touched a few days previously by the challenges of the sentinels, vibrated once more in my heart
more powerfully and continuously. I felt ashamed to be
there, taking part in this national humiliation, and from
that time forth I ceased to make common cause with the
foreigners.

I might have taken comfort, however, on looking at the
society assembled in the gallery of the house of the Naval
Ministry. It was filled with the wives of generals and
chamberlains of the Empire, and their hats were more
covered with *fleurs de lis* than ours were.

That same day M. de Talleyrand begged my father

urgently to go to Hartwell [1] and to take a message from the Provisional Government. He refused peremptorily, and his action seemed to me quite natural. I was so thoroughly imbued with the idea that he would not accept anything, I had heard him say so often that when one has been out of public affairs for twenty-five years one is no longer fit to attend to them, that I had no doubt in my mind that he would continue to stand aloof. When, therefore, during the first weeks, it was suggested that he ought to be the King's minister, I smiled, and felt very sure that he would refuse every effort of any kind whatever.

Upon my father's refusal to go to Hartwell, Charles de Noailles was sent. I do not know whether he fancied that he had thereby won a victory over my father, and that, quite groundlessly, he felt guilty of indelicacy, but ever after that time he was never at his ease nor on familiar terms with us. On his return from England he took the title of Duc de Mouchy. When, later on, my father did consent to return to public life, I regretted that he had not accepted this mission. A wise, moderate, reasonable man and a good citizen would have been a more suitable envoy than a mere courtier like Charles de Noailles. Then, too, my father was not of the stuff of which favourites are made. His influence, if he had had any, would not have lasted long. He could have done nothing better at that moment than to inspire the Declaration of Saint-Ouen, a measure very necessary when it appeared in order to repair the harm done by Monsieur. That poor prince was ever the scourge of his family and of his country.

I have not attempted to dissemble the small amount of esteem I had for Monsieur's character from all that I saw

[1] Residence of King Louis XVIII. in England.

and knew of him, but enthusiasm is so contagious that upon the day of his entrance into Paris I was quite under the influence of it. My heart beat fast, my tears flowed, and I felt the keenest joy and the most profound emotion.

Monsieur possessed to perfection the outward forms and the language capable of inspiring enthusiasm. He was gracious, courtly, *débonnaire,* obliging, anxious to please and good-natured, but at the same time dignified. I have never. known any one who acquired in such perfection the attitude, the forms, the bearing, and the court language desirable in a prince. Add to this a great courtesy of manner which made him charming at home and beloved by all who came in contact with him. He was more capable of familiarity than of affection, and had very many intimate friends, about whom he did not care the least in the world.

An exception should perhaps be made of M. de Rivière. Even when he had openly shown his devotion and had not to unbosom himself exclusively to him, their friendship ceased to be as affectionate until it was revived by the nomination of M. de Rivière as tutor to the Duc de Bordeaux. Then they were again united by an object to which they were both devoted, the attempt to consolidate the power of the congregation to which both of them belonged. This, however, belongs to another period.

The evening before his entrance into Livry, Monsieur had slept at a little house belonging to the Comte de Damas. It was there that the newly improvised mounted National Guard awaited him. He exerted all his attraction to fascinate his new Guard, no very difficult task, considering the mental attitude of these young men. He distributed several pieces of white ribbon, which the members of the Guard then wore in their button-holes. This is the origin of the Order of the Lys, which was promptly rendered ridiculous by the prodigality with which it was bestowed. But at first, and accompanied by all Monsieur's cajoleries, the young men were charmed with it. They brought back their prince in the midst of their squadron, and were beside themselves with joy, royalism, and love for him.

Monsieur, on his side, was so visibly delighted, appeared so full of the present moment and so completely oblivious of any hostile or painful memories, that his appearance must have inspired confidence in the pretty speech made for him by M. Beugnot [1] in the account given in the *Moniteur*:

" Nothing is changed; there is merely one Frenchman the more."

For several days there had been a lively discussion as to whether the army should keep the tricolour cockade or whether it should officially take the white cockade. The Duc de Raguse asked with warmth to be allowed to speak. Permission was granted, and he urged vehemently that the flag consecrated by the victories of twenty years should be retained. The Emperor Alexander, ever ready to defend all generous ideas, supported the demand. It was actively combated by all those who, through interest or passion, desired a counter-revolution. The choice of the cockade would determine the restoration of former privileges or the continuance of interests created by the Revolution.

M. de Talleyrand, too much of a statesman not to appreciate the importance of such a question, would certainly have decided in favour of the new colours if he had been free to judge. But he knew our princes and those

---

[1] Jacques Claude Beugnot, State Councillor, Count under the Empire and Minister under the Restoration. (1761-1835.)

who were with them, and was aware of the value which they attached to externals. He was too shrewd a court-ier to wish to offend them; he attached the greatest value to winning their good-will, and, remembering former ex-periences, he once more became the man of the ante-chamber. He beguiled the Duc de Raguse with pleasant words and false hopes. During this time he persuaded old Marshal Jourdan to get the white cockade adopted at Rouen, on the ground that Marmont's soldiers were wear-ing it. When once it was adopted by one corps of the army the question was settled.

The Duc de Raguse, nevertheless, was one of the few officers who went to meet Monsieur wearing the tri-coloured cockade, and for this he was never forgiven. This demonstration failed to win back the Bonapartists to him, and alienated the new court from him. It was a proof of his good faith, and shows how, in all his actions, he was led by what struck his fickle fancy as the duty of the moment. A few officers had no cockade, but the majority wore the white one.

At the beginning of the morning almost all the National Guard, which lined the road, wore the tricolour. Gradually this disappeared, and when Monsieur passed by, if there were only a few white cockades, there were scarcely any tricolours.

Before dismissing this subject of cockades I must men-tion that from Mme. Ferrey's terrace, whither I had gone to see the procession pass, we caught sight of M. Alex-andre de Girardin on his way to the barrier with a white cockade as large as a plate. M. Ferrey started on seeing it, and told us that he had met him that very morning on the Essonnes road. Both of them were riding, and M. de Girardin was coming from Fontainebleau. He be-gan a violent diatribe against the cowardice of the Pa-

risians and the treachery of the officers. His fury with
the Allies and his hatred of the Bourbons were expressed
in so loud a voice and in such offensive terms that on
arriving at the posts where the foreigners were stationed
M. Ferrey drew rein and signified to him his intention of
leaving him, which, as a matter of fact, he had been trying
to do all the time by changing his speed. M. Ferrey could
not believe his eyes on seeing him three hours later decked
out with this enormous white cockade.

History will relate, but too accurately, all the mistakes
committed by Monsieur during the time when, as Lieutenant-General of the kingdom, he exasperated all hatreds,
stirred up every kind of discontent, and more especially
showed a lack of patriotism which scandalised even the
foreigners.

Count Nesselrode gave me an idea of it upon the day
when he showed such liberality in giving up our strong-
holds that the Emperor Alexander was obliged to check
his anti-French generosity. Pozzo groaned and exclaimed every now and then:

" If things go on like this, the work that we have done
with such difficulty will last no time."

The Emperor Alexander was very anxious to bring
about a reconciliation between the Duc de Vicence, whom
he liked very much, and the royal family. The share
which public opinion, wrongly, as I believe, attributed to
him in the murder of the Duc d'Enghien made him odious
to the princes. Monsieur refused to receive him at his
house. The Emperor, vexed at this resistance, determined
to arrange a meeting. He invited Monsieur to dinner,
and not only was the Duc de Vicence present, but the
Emperor took a great deal of notice of him, and made a
point of trying to bring him nearer Monsieur.

The dinner party was cold and stiff. Monsieur felt hurt, and went away directly afterwards, leaving the Emperor furious. He walked up and down in the room, among his more familiar friends, inveighing against the ingratitude of people for whom others had conquered a kingdom at the risk of their lives, whilst certain people had not cared to risk theirs, and would not now yield on a simple question of etiquette. When he had calmed down it was pointed out to him that Monsieur was perhaps the more susceptible precisely because he felt that he was under such great obligations; that it was not a question of etiquette, but of sentiment, for he believed that the Duc de Vicence was guilty with regard to the Ettenheim affair.

"I have told him that he was not," said the Emperor.

No doubt this assertion ought to have had great weight with Monsieur, but the public was not then enlightened about the matter, and it was very easy to understand his repugnance on remembering that the Duc d'Enghien was a near relative of his.

The Emperor continued walking up and down.

"A relative, a relative," he muttered; "his repugnance!" and then, suddenly stopping short and facing his interlocutors, he added:

"I dine constantly with Ouvaroff!"

If a bomb had fallen in the middle of the room it could not have produced a greater shock. The Emperor continued his promenade; there was a moment of bewilderment, and then he spoke of other things. He had just revealed the motive of his anger. Every one then understood his persistence during the last five days in wishing Monsieur to admit M. de Caulaincourt.

It was said that General Ouvaroff had strangled the

Emperor Paul [1] with his enormous thumbs, which certainly were of a remarkable size. Alexander was shocked to see our princes refuse to sacrifice their private susceptibilities for the sake of politics, when he himself sacrificed so much more.

It will easily be understood that all argument on this subject ceased, and Pozzo went to Monsieur and told him that he must receive the Duc de Vicence. The latter did not abuse the situation; he went once to the house of the Lieutenant-General, and never presented himself there again.

This discussion, which bitter memories served to make extremely personal for the Emperor Alexander, separated him from the Tuileries and brought him nearer to the Bonapartist grandees. With an assiduity prompted by a generous mind and wrong reasoning, he had already hurried off to Malmaison [2] with affectionate rather than helpful words. After this scene at dinner he went to Saint-Leu,[3] and the welcome that he received from those that he was dethroning touched him the more deeply when he compared it with what he called the ingratitude of the others.

The visit to Compiègne completed this impression, but we shall come to that subject presently.

Monsieur received women. Any one who liked appeared at his house, even Mlle. Montansier, an old theatre lessee, for whom the Prince had had a fancy when a young man. The sincere joy of most of us, however, covered this lack of etiquette.

[1] The Emperor Paul I., the father of Alexander I., reigned from 1796 to 1801. He was assassinated in the Michel Palace, St. Petersburg, during the night of March 23 (March 12, old style) by a plot of the courtiers.

[2] Where the Empress Joséphine was living.

[3] Residence of Queen Hortense.

In the *salons* of the Tuileries persons hitherto separated by the most opposite opinions now met. We showed
great affability to the ladies of the Empire. They were
hurt at our advances in a place where they were accustomed to reign exclusively, and they considered us impertinent. As soon as they felt themselves no more
alone, they considered themselves paramount, an excusable impression. We meant very well; we were too well
satisfied not to feel sincerely kind. But there is a certain ease, a certain freedom in the manner of women of
good society, which gives them the appearance of being
at home everywhere and of doing the honours wherever
they may be. Women of the other class are often
shocked at this, consequently the pettinesses and the
little jealousies of the *bourgeoises* were stirred beneath
the jewels which adorned their breasts.

Monsieur succeeded better than we did. He was
charming to every one, said the right thing to each person, managed this heterogeneous court with wonderful
tact, appeared dignified but good-natured, and enchanted
every one by his graceful manners. There was a gala
performance at the Opéra, at which all the Allied Sovereigns were present. All three of them, for the Emperor Francis arrived before Monsieur, went into a large
box at the back of the house. Monsieur occupied the
King's box, over which the French arms now replaced
the eagle that had been so roughly torn down. He went
to pay a visit to the foreign sovereigns during the first
interval; they returned it during the second.

There was nothing very remarkable that evening except the admirable behaviour of the public, the tact with
which it comprehended all the allusions on the stage and
took part in all that went on in the house. For instance,
when Monsieur went to see the sovereigns, every one

arose and was perfectly silent. But when they returned his visit, there was wild applause, as though to thank them for this homage to our Prince. Parisians in a body are singularly impressionable.

As public affairs advanced the King was the more impatiently awaited. Every day those who surrounded the Lieutenant-General steadily urged him to adopt the attitude of a party chief; and if the Emperor Alexander had not been there to moderate this tendency, we should have seen all the talk of Coblentz put into action.

The old officers of the army of Condé, those who had escaped from La Vendée, came out of their retirement, fully persuaded that they were conquerors, and wishing to adopt a triumphant attitude. This claim was quite natural. Accustomed for the last twenty-five years to consider their cause as associated with that of the Bourbons, on seeing their throne restored they persuaded themselves that they had triumphed. On the other side, the servitors of the Empire, accustomed to domination, could not easily accommodate themselves to these untimely claims.

A man who had won his epaulettes by helping to gain a hundred battles was rebellious on seeing another man, who had come from a tobacco bureau or a lottery, wearing the same epaulettes, wishing to domineer over him, entering by preference the Tuileries which had formerly belonged to him and his people, and in his turn addressed as *Mon vieux brave* by those in authority there.

It required great skill and impartiality to be able to respect these transitions, and Monsieur had neither the one nor the other. Besides, it was almost impossible to satisfy such natural and incongruous requirements.

CHAPTER XXIII

FINALLY the King's gout allowed him to leave Hartwell. His journey through England was accompanied
by all imaginable rejoicing. The Prince Regent received him in London with extreme magnificence. Pozzo
was sent by the Emperor Alexander to compliment him.
He found him on board the English yacht. Here the
King received him as a man to whom he owed the greatest obligations. He accompanied him to Compiègne,
and, continuing his way, went to report his mission to
the Emperor.

The latter started at once to pay a visit to Louis
XVIII., intending to spend twenty-four hours at Compiègne. He was received there with the coldest formality. The King had ransacked his vast memory for
details of all that had taken place in interviews between
foreign sovereigns and the Kings of France, and intended to be faithful to tradition.

The Emperor, finding neither informality nor cordiality, instead of remaining to talk familiarly, as he had
intended to do, asked, after a few minutes, to retire to
his apartments. He was conducted through three or
four magnificently furnished suites on the same floor of

the château. He was told that these were destined for Monsieur, the Duc d'Angoulême, and the Duc de Berry, all of whom were absent. Then, after a portentous journey through corridors and up hidden staircases, he arrived at a small door which led into a very modest suite of rooms. It was that of the governor of the château,. and was quite outside the grand apartments. This was the suite destined for him.

Pozzo, who accompanied his imperial master, was suffering tortures, for at every turn in the corridors he saw that the Emperor's very reasonable annoyance was increasing. The latter, however, made no observation about the matter; he merely said very briefly:

" I shall return to Paris this evening. Let my carriages be ready after dinner."

Pozzo managed to bring the conversation round to this extraordinary lodging, and to attribute it to the helplessness of the King.

The Emperor answered that the Duchesse d'Angoulême was sufficiently like a housekeeper to have been able to attend to it. This little spice of malice, of which Pozzo made the most, relieved his mind, and he returned to the drawing-room rather less vexed. But the dinner did not repair the harm done by the lodging.

When the King was told that dinner was served, he asked the Emperor to take his niece in, and then passed before him with the slow waddle to which the gout had reduced him. On arriving in the dining-room only one armchair was placed at the table, and this was for the King. He was served first, all the honours were rendered to him with affectation, and he only distinguished the Emperor by treating him with a kind of familiarity and paternal kindliness. The Emperor Alexander said himself afterwards that the King adopted the attitude with which Louis XIV. would have received Philip V. at Versailles had he been expelled from Spain.

Almost as soon as dinner was over the Emperor went to his carriage. He was then alone with Pozzo. For a long time he remained perfectly silent, after which he spoke of other things, and then finally with bitterness about this strange reception. There had been no question whatever of business, and not a word of thanks or of confidence had been uttered either by the King or by Madame. He had not even heard one pleasant sentence. From that time, therefore, the friendly intercourse for which he had been prepared was impossible.

The Emperor paid and returned visits of etiquette, and gave orders through his ministers; but all marks of friendship, all forms of intimacy, were exclusively reserved for the Bonaparte family.

This conduct of the Emperor Alexander contributed more than a little to facilitate the return of the Emperor Napoleon in the following year. Many people believe, and appearances authorise the opinion, that Alexander regretted his work, and was attached to the new dynasty. He delighted in saying, over and over again, that all the royal families in Europe had lavished their blood in helping the Bourbons to recover three thrones, while none of them had risked a single scratch.

This visit to Compiègne, upon the details of which I can have no doubt, proved to what a degree the truth may sometimes appear improbable. Certainly King Louis XVIII. was intelligent; he had common sense, and was not swayed by passion or timidity; he delighted in talking, and had a gift for saying happy things. How is it that he did not realise all that he might have obtained from these advantages, in his position, when with the Emperor? I will not attempt to explain the diffi-

culty.   As to Madame, she lacked the good breeding
which would have shown her that in this circumstance
the most friendly reception would have been most
suitable.

Nearly all those about the King's person found themselves observing etiquette for the first time.   They had
the zeal of neophytes, and, in spite of their feudal names,
all the pride and insolence of upstarts.[1]

The Emperor Alexander was not the only person who
returned dissatisfied by his visit to Compiègne.   M. de
Talleyrand, to whom the King owed the throne, was
received coldly by him and very badly by Madame.   And
the King avoided any mention of business with such affectation that after a stay of a few hours he started back,
like a courtier who had paid his respects at Versailles,
very much embarrassed in his position as Minister and
party chief at having no message to take back to his
colleagues and his associates.

The marshals of the Empire were better received.
The King was able to say a few appropriate words, to
the effect that he was aware of the occasions on which
they had especially distinguished themselves.   He indicated, too, that he did not separate his interests from
those of France.   This was very wise and clever.

All the favours were reserved for a few old women
of the former court who had hastened to Compiègne.
In spite of their age, they were somewhat scared at
Madame's costume, for she was dressed in English style.

The long separation between the British Isles and the
Continent had produced great differences of dress.   With

[1] Perhaps, too, they remembered the conduct of the Russian
Government towards the political *émigrés* and Condé's army.   See
Souvenirs tirés des papiers du Comte A. de la Ferronays (1777–1814),
by the Marquis Costa de Beauregard, of the Académie française.
1 vol. in 8vo, 2nd edition, 1901.   (Plon & Co.)

much difficulty they persuaded Madame to give up this
foreign costume for the day of her entry into Paris.
She persisted in wearing it until then, and indeed for a
long time afterwards when she was not on ceremony.
This was again her pride, and was misunderstood.   The
poor Princess had so much dignity in misfortune that
she ought to be forgiven a few mistakes in her prosperity.   My mother and I were called in to the feminine
council as to the toilette that should be sent to her at
Saint-Ouen.

The King stayed there two days, and received all the
notabilities.   My father was among the number, and he
was well received by the King.   Madame, in spite of the
familiar kindliness with which she had seen him treated
by her mother, the Queen, did not appear to recognise
him.

My father came back very well satisfied with his visit
personally, but vexed to see the bevy of intriguers hover-
ing around this new court.   Some of them based their
claims on the fact that they had done everything, and
the others on the fact that they had done nothing, for the
last twenty years.

I have no definite idea how the Declaration was elab-
orated which is known as the Declaration of Saint-Ouen,
so different from that of Hartwell, the authenticity of
which we always denied, but which was only too real.
All that I know is that M. de Vitrolle drew it up, and it
filled me with satisfaction.   I saw that my dream was
about to be realised.   My country was to enjoy a representative and truly liberal government, and legitimacy
would give it the seal of permanence and security.   As
I have said, I was rather a liberal than a Bourbonist.   I
had a proof of this then, for, in spite of the fits of contagious enthusiasm to which I had for some time aban-

doned myself, the Declaration of Saint-Ouen caused me joy of quite another character.

Many people began to agitate immediately for a modification of that Declaration. I will not venture to say of all of them that this was retrogression as far as ideas were concerned, and there was perhaps wisdom in treating the Declaration as too advanced at that time. Perhaps the concessions of power were really beyond the actual needs of the country. It was not yet educated for a Constitution, and was accustomed to feel constantly the hand of the administrative government. Undue relaxation involved the risk that this unbroken steed might bolt. Experience has since taught me to appreciate fears of this kind; but at the time of the Declaration of Saint-Ouen I was too young to conceive such ideas, and my satisfaction was full of confidence.

We went to see the entry of the King from a house in the Rue Saint-Denis. The crowd was very great, and most of the windows were decorated with festoons, mottoes, *fleurs de lys,* and white flags.

The foreigners had had the good grace to confine their troops to barracks, as they had done for the entrance of Monsieur. The city was given over to the National Guard, which from that day began the honourable career of patriotic service which it has since well continued. It had already won the esteem of the Allies and the confidence of its fellow-citizens.

The absence of foreign uniforms was a restful sight. General Sacken, the Russian Governor of Paris, was the only officer to be seen in the city. He was very well liked, and we felt that he was watching to see that the orders given to his own troops were kept.

The procession was escorted by the old Imperial Guard. Others will tell of the mistaken treatment of

the Guard both before and after that day; all that I have
to say is that its aspect was imposing, but that it froze
us. It marched quickly, silent and gloomy, full of remembrances of the past. It stopped, by a look, our outbursts of affection for those who were arriving. The
shouts of "Long live the King!" died on our lips as
it rode by. Here and there were heard shouts of "Long
live the Guard! Long live the Old Guard!" but it did
not welcome these, and appeared to accept them in deri-
sion. As it passed by the silence became general, and
soon nothing could be heard but the monotonous tramp
of the quick step striking our very hearts. The consternation increased, and the contagious sadness of these
old warriors gave to the whole ceremony the appearance
of the Emperor's funeral rather than that of the King's
accession.

It was time for this to end. The group of princes
appeared. We had been ill prepared for their arrival,
but they were greeted warmly, although without the enthusiasm which had accompanied Monsieur's entrance
into Paris. Were our impressions already somewhat
exhausted? Were people dissatisfied with the Lieutenant-General's brief administration, or had the sight of
the Imperial Guard chilled enthusiasm? I cannot tell,
but certain it is that the gloom was very noticeable.

Monsieur was on horseback, escorted by the marshals,
the officers-general of the Empire, those of the King's
household, and of the line. The King was in an open
carriage, with Madame at his side. In front were the
Prince de Condé and his son, the Duc de Bourbon.

Madame wore the feather toque and the dress with
the silver thread that had been sent to her to Saint-Ouen,
but she had managed to give a foreign touch to this Parisian costume. The King wore a plain blue coat with

very large epaulettes, and the blue order and badge of the Saint-Esprit. He had a handsome face, which was expressionless when he meant to be gracious. He presented Madame to the people with an affected and theatrical gesture. She took no part in these demonstrations, but remained impassive, and in her way was the counterpart of the Imperial Guard. Her red eyes, though, gave the impression that she was crying. Her silent sorrow was respected, and every one sympathised with her in it, so that if her coldness had only lasted that day no one would have dreamed of reproaching her for it.

Prince de Condé, already almost in his dotage, and his son did not seem to take any part in the proceedings. They only figured there as images in the ceremony. Monsieur alone appeared there to advantage. He had a frank, contented expression on his face, identified himself with the populace, bowed in a friendly and familiar way, like a man who finds himself at home and among his own people. The procession ended with another battalion of the Guard, which reproduced the impression of the first detachment.

I must own that, as far as I was concerned, the morning had been very painful in every way. The people in the open carriage did not correspond to the hopes I had formulated. I was told that Madame, on arriving at Notre-Dame, sank down on her *prie-Dieu* in a way that was most graceful, noble, and touching. There was such resignation, and at the same time such gratitude, in this action that tears of sympathy had flowed from all eyes. I was also told that on arriving at the Tuileries she was as cold, awkward, and sullen as she had been beautiful and noble in the church.

At that time, the Duchesse d'Angoulême was the only

person of the royal family whom people remembered in
France. The young generation knew nothing of our
princes. I remember one of my cousins asking me just
then, whether the Duc d'Angoulême were a son of Louis
XVIII., and how many children he had. But every one
knew that Louis XVI., the Queen, and Madame Elisabeth had perished on the scaffold. For every one Madame was the orphan of the Temple, and all the interest
aroused by such frightful catastrophes was felt for her.
The blood that had been shed baptized her as the
country's child.

Much, indeed, was owing to her, but she should have
accepted these regrets with greater readiness. Madame
did not rise to the delicate situation; she expected these
regrets haughtily, and accepted them stiffly. In reality
she was full of virtues and kindness, a French princess
at heart, but she managed to make people think that she
was disagreeable, cruel, and hostile to her country. The
French believed that she detested them, and in the end
they detested her.

She did not deserve this, and certainly people were not
thus inclined at first. It was the effect of a fatal mis-
understanding and of false pride. With a little grain
of intelligence added to her noble nature, Madame would
have been the idol of her country and the palladium of
her race.

A few days after his entry into Paris the King went
to the Opéra. Œdipe was being given, and he once
more began his pantomime with regard to the Duchesse
d'Angoulême, not only on arriving, but again at the illusions to which the part of Antigone lent itself. All
this was comedy, but although the public was more inclined to watch the play in the box than that on the stage,
the King's demonstrations had no success, for they ap-

peared too affected. The Princess lent herself as little
as possible to this behaviour. She was better dressed
that night, and was wearing some beautiful diamonds.
She bowed with great nobility and very graciously, and
appeared at her ease during this function as though she
had always been accustomed to everything by right of
birth. Without being either beautiful or pretty, she was
very distinguished, and she was a princess whom France
could very well present to Europe. Monsieur shared
her ease of manner, and to this added an appearance
of gaiety and good humour. He was at first the most
popular of these princes among the public. The initiated, however, saw him under another aspect.

CHAPTER XXIV

THE King first received the ladies who had formerly been presented, and then, the next day, he received us. He treated me with special kindness, called me his little Adèle, talked to me of Bellevue, and said all kinds of nice things. He always took special notice of me whenever I went to court, although I went very little to the Tuileries.

On arriving at Madame's, her maid of honour, Mme. de Serent, asked me my name. As she was very deaf, she asked me to repeat it, but Madame said in her quick, dry way:

" Why, it is Adèle! "

I was much flattered at this sort of recognition, but it went no further. She then asked me one of those idle questions, after the manner of royalties, which did not give one to suppose that there had ever been anything between us before. My intercourse with Madame was never on any other footing.

It was that same day, I believe, that, when Marshal Ney's wife came to pay her court, Madame called her Aglaé. She was very much horrified at this. She saw in it a reminiscence of the time when she was admitted to

Madame's presence, as her mother was chambermaid to the Queen. I am convinced that Madame meant, on the contrary, to show her great politeness, just as she did to me when she referred to me by the name of Adèle. Her tone, though, was so unpleasant, her speech so curt, her gestures so brusque, and her expression so cold, that it did not ever seem as though her words could be kindly meant. People have told me that, when one knew her intimately, these surly ways disappeared, but I never had the honour of being admitted into her intimacy.

After these first receptions attention was given to the regulation of court dress and etiquette.

Madame made a very serious business of this. Such strict attention given, at such a time, to the length of lappets and the size of mantillas appeared to me to be a triviality unworthy of the situation.

A court costume had to be chosen, and Madame would have liked to return to hoops, as at Versailles, but the rebellion against this was so general that she gave way. But to the imperial costume all the "paraphernalia" of the former style of dress was added, and this was singularly incongruous. To our Grecian style of hairdressing, for instance, these ridiculous lappets were added, and the elegant *chérusque*, which completed a garb copied from Van Dyck, was replaced by a heavy mantilla and a kind of pleated plastron. At first Madame was very particular that all this should be strictly observed. The model given to her tradespeople had to be copied exactly, and she was very much displeased with any one who attempted any modification. Later on the Duchesse de Berry having emancipated herself from this servitude, others followed her example. The lappets were then worn very wide, and as they looked like a veil, they were not without a certain grace. The mantilla, on the other hand, was so scanty that it no longer crushed the dress.

When all this was settled, the next thing was to determine the etiquette of precedents, and this matter was the King's affair. It was chiefly with the help of the Duc de Duras that this task was accomplished, and the honours of the throne room were established in the place of the honours of the Louvre. M. de Duras, who was more *duke* than the late M. de Saint-Simon, was extremely anxious that the distinctions attached to this title should be marked as definitely as possible, and he invented the procedure adopted. Monsieur and Madame disapproved strongly of it, and the separation between the ladies was never enforced at their receptions.

The new etiquette delighted the duchesses and roused the anger of the others, particularly of the elderly ladies of the former court. It must be admitted that precautions had been taken to make the distinction as offensive as it could be to those who attached any importance to it. The arrival was through the Marshals' Hall, which then served as the guards' room and led to the staircase. The blue drawing-room, which was only dimly lighted, had then to be crossed. We all stayed in the Salon de la Paix, which was almost as dark. The duchesses continued their way and entered the throne room, which alone was brilliantly lighted. One of the folding doors leading into it remained closed, and an official stood there to refuse admittance to any one who had not the right to enter. The faces of the former court ladies were worth seeing each time that one of the fortunate women of the new *régime* crossed the Salon de la Paix, as it were over their bodies. Indignation was constantly renewed, and the subject was the every-day text of outbursts which frequently entertained me.

The poor duchesses were exposed to sarcasm of all kinds, and all that was said of those of the Empire can easily be imagined.

The closing of the door announced the entrance of the King in the throne room. He went the round, saying a few words to the duchesses or to the titled persons, as they alone were called. After this he placed himself in front of the chimney-piece, with his attendants around him, and either remained standing or sat down, according to the state of his gout. The door was then opened once more and we entered in procession, turning short to the right, passing by the throne and arriving in front of him, where we stopped to make a deep curtsey.

When he did not speak to us, and this was the case for nine women out of ten, we continued to file along, and went out by the door that led into the drawing-room just before the Diana Gallery, which was styled the council room. When the King spoke to us, and the most highly favoured were granted no more than two or three phrases, he closed his audience by a slight inclination of the head. We replied by another deep curtsey, and then followed those who had preceded us out of the room.

We crossed the Diana Gallery, and on descending the staircase arrived at Madame's reception room. As she said much more than the King, and spoke to every one, there was always a block at her door. With a little diplomacy, however, and a great deal of pushing, we contrived to get inside the room. She was standing not far from the door, her maid of honour by her, and the rest of her suite at the end of the room.

She alone, although elaborately dressed, wore no court mantle. After a very short time she recognised every one, without any help from her maid of honour. We stopped in front of her, and she said the right thing to every one. Her manner alone was defective, for with her words and a little more affability she would have held her court very well. When her little bow signified to us that the conversation, which was of a much more uncertain length than the King's, was over, we again made our curtsey and went on to the Duc d'Angoulême.

He was always taken unawares, for with his awkward fussiness he could not stay long in one place. His words were as awkward as he was himself, and he was a great trial to those who were interested in the family. It is none the less probable that if this prince had succeeded his uncle immediately, the Restoration would have lasted and there would have been tranquillity. I shall frequently have to speak of him.

On leaving the Duc d'Angoulême we were in the vestibule of the Pavillon de Flore—that is, in the street, for in those days it was paved and had neither doors nor windows, so that it was entirely exposed to the inclemencies of the weather. We were not allowed to go back through the rooms of the palace, so that the only alternative was to go down into the basement, along the open passage where the kitchens were; or to cross to the Pavillon de Marsan in our carriages. In the first case we had to go our way with neither shawl nor cloak, as etiquette did not permit either within the Château. In the second case we had to go as far as the square for our domestics, as they were not allowed to approach any nearer. The courtiers who had been entrusted to regulate all these forms and ceremonies had shown no consideration for the comfort of the persons for whom they were intended.

On arriving at the Pavillon de Marsan we went upstairs and found Monsieur there, always perfectly gracious and obliging. He possessed the art of appearing to hold his court for his own enjoyment and diversion. We then went down again to the ground floor, where the Duc de Berry, with neither grace nor dignity, received us with perfect ease of manner and with witty good humour. I cannot really judge his attitude as a prince, for he had always treated me familiarly. His father and he had brought with them from England the custom of shaking hands. The Duc de Berry kept it up for his old acquaintances, and I fancy that Monsieur too never quite relinquished it until he mounted the throne. After the first few days, though, he did not honour me any more with this distinction, which became unusual.

The reception was certainly very badly organised, for we never came away from it without feeling bored, tired, and discontented. I was among those who were well treated, and yet I never went willingly, and as rarely as possible. It was a real infliction, for we had to change our dinner hour, array ourselves in a most uncomfortable costume which we could never wear elsewhere, be at the Tuileries at seven o'clock, wait there an hour for the sake of seeing the duchesses go by, as we used to say, struggle before Madame's door, catch cold in the outer corridors, in spite of our precaution of wrapping the trains of our dresses around our head and shoulders, thus making ourselves look impossible objects, and then have difficulty again at the Pavillon de Marsan in finding our domestics. Unless they were very intelligent, we were apt to lose them frequently in these peregrinations. As no man was admitted to these receptions, the poor women in full dress were to be seen running after their carriages to the middle of the square. To all these annoyances must be added that of our being on our legs for three hours. It was at this price that we obtained

the honour of being ten seconds before the King, a minute before Madame, and about the same time with the
princes. It was out of all proportion.

The persons entrusted with court ceremonies ought to
have some care to make them convenient. The Restoration and its servitors never took any trouble upon that
point. They wanted to re-establish the old conditions,
and they never considered that the place and the customs
had changed. For instance, a lady at Versailles was always followed by two lackeys, often by three, and by a
sedan chair which took her directly to the ante-chambers.
These customs removed her difficulties of communication.
Our mothers never failed to remind us of this fact, after
a diatribe about the way in which the duchesses trampled
upon them, as they expressed it. They could not reconcile themselves to this, and they told us that at Versailles one never noticed the privileges allowed to titled
women. Duchesses had then no other prerogatives than
that of being seated at the King's dinner and this rarely
happened, because it would have been necessary to be
present at the whole meal, and it was more convenient
for them only to put in an appearance and go away.

They certainly were seated when there was a state
dinner, but as untitled ladies were not then present, the
difference of treatment was never marked. These ladies
forgot, in their annoyance, that the carriages of the duchesses used to enter a reserved court, that their sedan
chairs, followed by three lackeys instead of two, and covered with red velvet, used to enter the second ante-
chamber, and that there were other prerogatives attaching to their position which nearly resembled the custom of awaiting the arrival of the King in the reception
room, but which the force of habit made less disagreeable
to our mothers.

The only reason for which I envied the ladies of the throne room was the advantage they had in being able to get through the tiresome drudgery of these receptions more quickly than we could. The King's reception was every week, but the Princes only received once a month.

I will now return to 1814. Sir Charles Stewart, the brother of Lord Castlereagh [1] and English Commissioner to the Army of the Allies, gave a magnificent ball. The sovereigns were present, and the Emperor and the King of Prussia danced several polonaises, if the polonaise can be called a dance.

The man takes a lady by the hand, and walks a few seconds along with her to a measured step. There is then a change of partners, and it is usually, I believe, the women who leave the men; but here the princes took the initiative, in order to be polite to every one. During this promenade they talked all the time to their partners. As the Emperor Alexander was very tall and very deaf, when his partner was short he had to bend down to her, an attitude more obliging than graceful.

It was in the midst of this ball that the Duke of Wellington appeared for the first time in Paris. I can see him now entering the room with his two nieces, Lady Burgers and Miss Pole, hanging on his arm. There were no eyes for any one else, and at this ball, where grandeur abounded, everything gave way to military glory. That of the Duke of Wellington was brilliant and unalloyed, and a lustre was added to it by the interest that had long been felt in the cause of the Spanish nation.

It was at this same ball that the Grand Duke Con-

[1] Minister of Foreign Affairs. Much will be heard of him hereafter during the ambassadorship of the Marquis d'Osmond in London.

stantin,[1] after the departure of the Emperor Alexander, asked for a waltz. He was just beginning to dance it when Sir Charles Stewart stopped the orchestra and asked for a quadrille, which Lady Burgers wanted. He was devoted to her.

The conductor hesitated, looked at the Grand Duke, and continued the waltz.

" Who has dared to insist on having this waltz played? " asked Sir Charles.

" I," answered the Grand Duke.

" I alone give orders in my house, Monseigneur," said Sir Charles. " Play the quadrille," he continued, turning to the conductor.

The Grand Duke went away very angry, and was accompanied by all the Russians.

This made a great stir, and the powers that be were compelled to interfere in order to arrange matters. That, I fancy, was the first of the impertinences which Sir Charles scattered throughout a progress which he began as Lord Stewart and continued as the Marquis of Londonderry.

The two princes, nephews of the King, had arrived successively in Paris in the midst of these numerous events, and their advent produced no great impression. The Duc de Berry then evinced a desire for society. He paid a few visits, and came to my house. I arranged to have some *soirées* for him, with music. He enjoyed them with great readiness, and showed very naïvely and intelligently his delight at the situation in which he found himself once more.

The rudeness inherent in his nature was very evident

---

[1] The Emperor Alexander's brother. He resigned his rights to the throne in favour of his younger brother Nicolas, and died in 1831.

from time to time. I remember speaking to him once on behalf of Arthur de la Bourdonnais, a fine young officer who had served under the Empire, and who wished to be under him. He listened to me with interest and good nature, and then, suddenly raising his voice, asked:

" Is he a nobleman? "

" Certainly, Monseigneur."

" In that case I do not want him; I detest noblemen."

It must be owned that this was a strange assertion in the midst of a drawing-room filled with the nobility of France, and besides, it was not true. He had told himself, with excellent good sense, that he must not be exclusive, and that he was called to be the popular prince of his family. And with his usual want of thought he had thus chosen the place for making a profession of faith in terms unsuitable anywhere. I knew him well enough not to reply, as he would have enlarged upon the subject if I had answered.

The Prince de Condé opened his house, and every one went there eagerly. This old warrior appealed to all imaginations. He had lost his memory, and made mistakes in consequence which were sometimes amusing, and of which the malice of those present made the most. It was said later that he did this intentionally, but I do not believe it. The Duc de Bourbon would have done the honours of the palace if he had known how to set about it, but he had brought with him all the shy awkwardness of his exile. He presented Mme. de Rully as his daughter, and asked all the women he knew to be kind to her. That was his usual commonplace phrase, and I have heard him repeat it to twenty persons during the same evening. Every one was quite willing to do as he asked, for Mme. de Rully was perfectly amiable, and she had the bearing, the behaviour, and the manners of a woman of the best society.

We very quickly saw that the great services rendered by M. de Talleyrand offended M. de Blacas. He alone governed the King, and he did not care to admit any one to share his predominance. The prejudices of the royal family, justified perhaps by the earlier behaviour of the Prince de Talleyrand, but which recent events ought to have effaced, served the plans of the favourites only too well. Every one saw very soon what M. de Talleyrand had himself recognised from the very time of his visit to Compiègne. Obligations too public to be denied annoyed the King, and M. de Talleyrand had no influence and no strength to hope for except outside the Tuileries. He did not attempt to make himself the man of France, for he was too unpopular with the country, but he did try to make himself indispensably necessary through his influence with the foreigners.

In his desire to free himself from the control of M. de Talleyrand, M. de Blacas would have liked to make friends for himself of people who were distinguished in the country. More moderate, less exclusive than the other political *émigrés* who had returned with the King, far from blaming my father for his refusal to adopt the prejudices of the *émigrés*, he realised all the value of a Royalist who was devoted, wise, and who knew and judged with sanity the state of mind in France, to which country he had returned ten years ago. He would have liked to attach him to his fortunes, but my father, incapable of entering into any cabals, had thrown in his lot with M. de Talleyrand ever since his conduct during the entrance of the Allies, and he received M. de Blacas's advances very coldly.

It was during the time of these ostensible flatteries from

the favourite that the nomination of my father to some ministry was announced to me every day. I did not feel greatly disturbed, as I was persuaded that for no position would he consent to lose his liberty. I cannot describe the astonishment I felt when he told us one day that the Embassy of Vienna had been offered to him, and when he pointed out many reasons for accepting it. He found my mother and myself so reluctant about it that he eventually conceded that the only ambassadorship he would not refuse was that of London.

From the moment that it was clear to me that there was a position he would not refuse, I understood that he would accept any post, and that he would finally perhaps solicit one. I said to my mother that we ought no longer to try to exercise an influence which would only embarrass my father, and she was all the more easy to persuade as she herself had no dislike to an important embassy.

Cardinal Consalvi did not fail to exercise a certain influence on my father's decision. He had great esteem for his talents, his probity, his wisdom, and he was very anxious to see him become influential. They were about the same age, and the Cardinal did not admit that ambition ought to cease at their time of life. He was himself a proof of the usefulness of a sane and judicious man, for at the very beginning he put a stop to all extravagances long meditated by the clergy who had remained abroad. He came frequently to my house, without staying there as he had done before, for business now claimed him.

I have nothing to change as regards the opinion I had formed of his capacity and his wisdom. Shortly after he went to London, during the stay that the Allied Sovereigns made in that capital, and, thanks to the spirit of propriety which ruled his actions, he succeeded in maintaining all the dignity of his position and of his character without shocking the customs of the country, where the prejudices of the people were still extremely hostile to Popery.

CHAPTER XXV

AFTER the public had received the Declaration of Saint-Ouen, the next thing was to formulate a Charter; but either because the period of reflection had begun, or because people were ready to adopt the concessions suggested, an opinion arose that these concessions were too extensive.

M. de Talleyrand, in his speech to the King, had very neatly observed that barriers were supports; the court feared that they were obstacles. Whilst supposing that it was wise not to flood with excessive liberty a country which for a long time had been under severe constraint, it was a great mistake to nominate three men to draw up the Charter who professed most energetically their dislike for representative government, namely, Chancelier Dambray, M. Ferrand, and the Abbé de Montesquieu.[1]

[1] Vicomte Dambray, formerly Advocate-General to the Parliament of Paris, President of the Chamber of Peers at the Restoration. (1760–1829.)

Comte Ferrand, former Councillor of the Parliament of Paris, an *émigré* who had returned in 1800; appointed by Louis XVIII. Postmaster-General; peer of France; member of the French Academy. (1751–1825.)

The Abbé de Montesquieu-Fezensac; the clergy's deputy to the

They then boasted, and have since owned, that the Charter was only, in their eyes, a transition to the *ancien régime*, or rather to absolute monarchy. Institutions which had been created by time, manners, and customs, and which formed insurmountable obstacles to arbitrary power, had been swept away by the revolutionary torrent. Whatever may have been their intentions, France took their work seriously, as she has since proved.

In spite of my dislike for ceremonies, I wished to be present at the royal session where the Charter was to be promulgated. My Liberalism was shocked at the way in which the Saint-Ouen conditions had been modified. The Charter seemed to me to be a mystification. This impression was by no means general; every one was busy trying to find the article in it which he could utilise for his own benefit. I was little edified by my compatriots on this occasion. The King was wonderfully well received. The ceremony was very fine, but it lacked that seriousness and that religious feeling with which a great nation should receive the tables of the law. Attention was chiefly directed to the new costumes, the new faces, and to old customs which had become new again from long disuse.

When the King ended his speech, which was well composed, and delivered in an imposing voice, with the words, " My Chancellor will tell you the rest," an almost audible smile went round the house. After the reading of the Charter, M. Dambray read the list of peers. He commenced with the dukes and peers of the *ancien régime,* and then went on to those of the new one. On

States General 1789; emigrated after August 10; after the Restoration Home Secretary and French peer; member of the French Academy; Louis XVIII. created him duke; he left the Chamber of Peers at the time of the Revolution of 1830. (1756–1832.)

arriving at the senatorial peers he read among others
the names of Comte Cornet and Comte Cornudet in so
perfectly impertinent and disdainful a tone that I was
scandalised, and could not help saying to my neighbours:

" A strange way certainly to make partisans! These
people, to whom a considerable favour has been granted,
are by that very tone of voice relieved of all obligation."

Only six new peers were made, among whom was
Comte Charles de Damas, who has already been mentioned as commanding one of the red regiments of the
King's household. Consequently, a few days later, Comtesse Charles de Damas, who since then has belonged to
the extreme Opposition, said to me:

" I meet people who blame these proceedings. For
my part, as I am convinced that the King has much more
intelligence and judgment than I have, and that he is in
a better position for knowing what is wise, as soon as he
utters a wish I fall in with it without a moment's
hesitation."

I remember this phrase, because I was delighted to
repeat it to her word for word in 1815, when she was so
furious that all the Bonapartists should not be put to
death on mere hue and cry.

When the Charter was promulgated the foreign sovereigns went away.

Before the King's arrival Monsieur, as Lieutenant-
General of the kingdom, had sent commissioners entrusted with very important powers to the provinces.
They were to take the evidence of the authorities, examine the condition of the country, judge its state of
mind, and indicate measures likely to tranquillise it.
This commission might have been very useful, and my
father was nominated to take part in it. By a misprint
the name of his brother, the Vicomte d'Osmond, was put

on the list in the *Moniteur,* and my father was all the
more zealous to let it stand as the other nominations,
belonging for the most part to the immediate friends of
Monsieur, informed him that the task would be super-
ficially and badly carried out. Modest though he was,
he was rather hurt to think that there had been an idea
of placing his name on such a list.

Monsieur de Talleyrand explained to him that when
his name had been proposed he had thought that the
commission would have been quite differently composed;
that there would have been men in it whom it would be
possible to trust with ample and real power. After the
nominations made by Monsieur the sole object had been
to limit these powers.

On all occasions M. de Talleyrand was as considerate
as possible to my father. Their acquaintance dated from
their early youth; and, although they had followed very
different lines, and their intercourse had been interrupted
for twenty-five years, he always made much of the capacity and loyalty of my excellent father.

My previsions about the change that had come over
my father's inclinations were very soon justified, for,
after refusing to go to Vienna, he accepted the Turin
ambassadorship. In spite of his superior reason and
judgment, in the midst of this general place-hunting he
could not avoid some touch of ambition.

M. de Talleyrand spoke to him of Turin as leading
promptly to London, considering that M. de la Châtre
was incapable of holding out there; even more influential
was his observation that Turin, being regarded as a family ambassadorship, ensured the right to the Cordon
Bleu.[1] Now my father had always wished for this decora-

---

[1] Knight of the Order of the Holy Ghost. This was an order of
knighthood created by Henry III., suppressed in 1791, and re-

tion above everything else, so true is it that the ideas of early life leave strong traces in the most elevated minds! To be a knight of this order seemed to him the finest thing in the world. If M. de Talleyrand had been Minister, my father would have been included in the first promotion.

I must here relate an episode which confirms how strongly youthful impressions remain engraved on the mind. My father had been appointed French delimitation commissioner after the treaty of peace. This task was not at all pleasant, as he keenly felt. The attitude of his colleagues, the Rosamowski princes and Count Wittenstein, was charming; Baron Humboldt and Sir Charles Stewart disguised their demands under polite phrases. But the basis of these transactions depended on the rights of the strongest, a subject always very painful for the weaker side.

My father came through it as well as circumstances would allow. The King saw him several times, and expressed his satisfaction.

When the question of the ambassadorship of Turin came up, things did not go quite smoothly. My mother was furious, I was grieved, my brother annoyed, and finally my father decided to yield to our wishes. He went to the King and represented to him that, having refused the ambassadorship of Vienna, he would be too inconsistent in accepting that of Turin.

The King answered that the cases were quite different; that he understood his refusal of Vienna, but that the King of Sardinia was his brother-in-law. And this strange argument appeared conclusive to my father.

established by Louis XVIII. It was the first and the highest of the decorations of the old monarchy. There has been no promotion to it since 1830.

The King, who was anxious to persuade him, told him that he was inclined to grant him anything that might be agreeable as a favour and a mark of content and satisfaction. My father invented a request for the right of entry to the *cabinet*, which meant permission to pay his court on days of reception in one room rather than another.

It was after obtaining these two results, at the end of a long conversation, that my father returned home very much delighted, informing us that he had not been able to resist the King's orders any longer. It was not until later, and after he had accepted, that M. de Talleyrand promised London and the Cordon Bleu.

I cannot sufficiently repeat that my father was the most straightforward of men and the least capable of any pettiness I have ever met, and yet he yielded then to seductions which would not have exerted any influence upon him twenty-five years previously. As for me, I passed from one amazement to another without making any progress in the courtier's arts.

This appointment brought us back from the country, where we had gone to rest after so agitating a winter and a spring. My mother had had a fall which prevented her from moving, so that all the worries of the preparations for the departure fell upon me. These cares, together with the sorrow that I felt at leaving my friends and changing my habits and customs, absorbed me so entirely that I had little time for the consideration of public affairs; consequently these are now less clear to my mind. But I can still remember a few special facts.

Mme. de Staël arrived very soon after the King. Her happiness at returning to Paris was increased by the joy she felt in showing off the young beauty of her charming daughter.

In spite of her hair of somewhat daring colour and a few freckles, Albertine de Staël was one of the most delightful persons I have ever met, and her face had an ideal and angelic purity such as I have never seen in any one else. Her mother was very happy and very proud of her. She was thinking of marrying her, and suitors soon came forward.

Mme. de Staël was accustomed ever since her daughter's childhood to say that she would be able to oblige her to make a love match; and I certainly think that she used her authority to lead her daughter's choice to a duke and peer, a wealthy *grand seigneur*. It was by more personal gifts that the Duc de Broglie justified the preference accorded him. Again I am anticipating events, for this marriage did not take place until the following year.

The hatred that she had for Bonaparte had made Mme. de Staël a great Royalist. She was amazed herself that she was not one of the Opposition. The superiority of her mind, though, did not allow her to fall into our absurd intolerance. I frequently saw her. At my house she expressed my own sentiments, but at her own house I was often scandalised by the conversation of her set. She admitted all opinions and all ways of expressing them, and would fight to the death for the cause that she upheld. But she always finished these bouts with a courteous parade, for she did not care to deprive her *salon* of any adept at this kind of fencing who could bring into it any variety.

She liked all kinds of notabilities, whether of intellect or of rank, and even those whose fame was due to the violence of their opinions. To people who, like myself, lived in the narrow ideas of party spirit all this appeared very shocking, and I often left her *salon* indignant at the language there in use. I used to say, according to the expression of our coterie, that it was really too strong.

We went to say good bye to her a few days before leaving for Turin. A young man leaning on her arm-chair was declaiming in so hostile a way against the royal government and showing that he was so passionately devoted to the Bonapartists, that Mme. de Staël, after vainly attempting to bring his vindictive eloquence to a playful tone, was compelled, in spite of her habitual tolerance, to silence him. It was the unfortunate Labédoyère. If he had continued to act upon the lines of his conversation, there would have been no reproach against him. But only a few weeks later, won over by the solicitations of his wife's family, he consented to allow himself to be appointed colonel in the service of Louis XVIII., and before the end of a year he was called upon to pay for his guilty treason with the price of blood on the plain of Grenelle.

Monsieur fell dangerously ill, and his condition caused the keenest anxiety to all those who called themselves Royalists. I shared this anxiety very sincerely. Our prayers for his recovery were answered, but alas! neither for his happiness nor for ours! He spent the time of his convalescence at Saint-Cloud. We went there from Châtenay to pay our court to him, and he was very gracious and very talkative. He showed us all the splendours of Saint-Cloud with great satisfaction. He said laughingly that no one could accuse Bonaparte of having spoilt the furniture. Long deprivation of these royal magnificences made him appreciate them all the more.

At Saint-Cloud I met the Chevalier de Puységur. I had left him a few years before in London the most amiable, agreeable, and sociable of men. We were great friends, and I was delighted to see him. I found a

cold, affected, disobliging, silent personage; such a meta-
morphosis I could not understand. I went away in embarrassment because my own advances had not been
reciprocated.

I heard a few days later that, besides the Anglomania
which had made him dislike everything French, he was
annoyed by his aged appearance. He had lost all his
teeth, and had hitherto failed in his attempts to replace
them. A more skilful operator afterwards helped him
to be rather more sociable, but he never recovered his former graciousness, and remained surly and morose. He
did not come to my house, but I frequently saw him
at my uncle Édouard Dillon's.

One day when Lord Westmeath, who was interested
in agriculture, had been to Saint-Germain in the morning,
he asked us how cattle were fed in the suburbs of Paris.
He thought there was only a small proportion of pastur-
age. We felt it our duty to explain to him that he would
find more on other routes, but the Chevalier cut us short.

"You are right, my lord," he said; "there is no pastur-
age; the horrible cows eat thistles in the ditches: and
besides, you would never be able to discover our meadows
in France, as the grass is not green."

"What do you mean? The grass is not green?
What colour is it, then?"

"It is brown."

"When it is scorched by the sun."

"No, always."

I could not help laughing and saying:

"What strange information for a Frenchman to give
to a foreigner!"

The Chevalier replied sharply:

"I am not a Frenchman, Madame; I am of the Pavillon de Marsan."

Alas! he spoke truly, and in this sarcastic outburst may be found the text of the whole conduct of the Restoration, of all its faults and of all its misfortunes.

The Chevalier de Puységur is the one man I have seen most deeply affected by the loss of a very handsome face. Women are generally accused of such pettiness, but I do not know any woman who ever carried it to such a degree. He had become perfectly unbearable, and young men who had heard people speak of his good manners, his intelligence, and his grace looked in vain for any trace of these qualities. His greed had become extreme; he would have liked to monopolise every favour, and Monsieur must be congratulated upon the patience with which he bore his demands, in memory of his former devotion, which I believe was very sincere.

Many years later, and beyond the point where I intend to close these memoirs,[1] in April 1832, during the worst of the disastrous epidemic of cholera, I called one morning upon the Duchesse de Laval: the Duc de Luxembourg, her brother, and the Duc de Duras were there. I had just heard from Baron Pasquier, who had witnessed it, the account of the death of M. Cuvier, who had fallen a victim to the scourge which was ravaging the capital. He had given proof at that supreme instant of all the sublimity of his immense intellectual distinction, and a strength of mind which continued up to his very last breath, while he retained all his tender-heartedness. M. Pasquier had been deeply touched by this, and had made me share his impression.

I arrived at the house of the Duchesse full of my subject, and I repeated the details that I had just heard.

[1] After ending her diary at the Revolution of 1830, the Comtesse de Boigne began it again and continued in a fragmentary way until after the fall of the July Monarchy.

The two dukes listened in an indifferent way. M. de Luxembourg then turned towards M. de Duras and asked him in a low voice:

" Who is this M. Cuvier? "

" He is one of the gentlemen of the King's garden," answered the other.

The illustrious Cuvier one of the gentlemen of the King's garden! I was stupefied. Alas! Alas! I said to myself, such words from the lips of the captains, the guards, the gentlemen of the chamber, the confidants of the King of France, explain sadly enough the Cherbourg journey! Europe was envying us the glory of possessing Cuvier, and the court of the Tuileries was ignorant even of his existence. The two dukes were of the Pavillon de Flore, just as M. de Puységur was of the Pavillon de Marsan.

We had seen a considerable number of English women arrive one after the other. I have already mentioned how strange their costume appeared to us, but I was still more astonished at their behaviour. The ten years that had just passed without any communication with the Continent had made them borrow their fashions from their own colonies. They brought into our climates the easy-going manners and customs of the tropics; among others, those great square divans on which they reclined rather than sat, men and women indiscriminately. The great ladies had preserved a certain tradition of the suavity of manner of French women, and were convinced that this was accompanied by free and easy customs. Now all this is very easy to imitate, but as they had not the original before them, they had reproduced an imaginary model which vastly astonished us.

Nothing is farther from the truth than this idea adopted for the most part by English writers about

French women. They can generally converse with ease, but in no country is behaviour more calm and more severe. And even before the Revolution, when morals were much less strict, outward forms were much more rigorously observed.

It is usual with us for women of doubtful reputation to behave perfectly in society. I do not know whether morality gains anything, but society is certainly more agreeable. The English women, on the contrary, appeared to have thrown propriety to the winds. In M. de Talleyrand's drawing-room, all the women, according to the custom of the ministerial *salons* of those times, were seated on armchairs placed at regular intervals round the room. I remember that a certain little Mrs. Arbuthnot, a young and pretty woman who had set up a claim to the affections of the Duke of Wellington, left the ladies' circle, joined the group formed exclusively of men, leaned against a little side-table, put her two thumbs on it, sprang lightly on to it, and remained seated there with her legs swinging, her very short skirts scarcely coming lower than her knees. An entire colony of English ladies soon came, and proved to us that Mrs. Arbuthnot's customs were not exclusively reserved to herself.

I often saw Lady Nesselrode, but without caring much for her. She was certainly cold and stiff enough. She was very intelligent, and was then commencing the exclusive domination which she afterwards exercised over her husband. She was jealous of everything which she feared might have any influence upon his mind, and on this account she favoured me with a considerable dose of her ill-will.

Princess Zénéide Wolkonski was subject to another kind of jealousy of an entirely Oriental sort; she would not allow her husband even to look at a woman. From the time that she arrived in Paris she kept him in seclusion. A few months before, in a fit of jealous frenzy, she had bitten a fairly large piece out of her lip. The scar was still red, and interfered with her beauty, which was nevertheless great. I do not know why I found grace with her, but she allowed poor Nikita to come to my house. Europe has since then rung with the quarrels and follies of this extravagant couple.

My brother began to feel the want of a career, and regretted keenly that he had yielded to the instigations of his coterie. My mother was all the more distressed by this, because she felt guilty of having influenced his decisions. She determined to ask the Duchesse d'Angoulême for an audience. This princess was extremely good and kind to her. She spoke to her about her father, and it was rare for her to begin such a conversation; and what was even more unusual, she spoke to her of her husband. She regretted that his extreme timidity gave him a certain awkwardness which prevented people from appreciating his real merit, though according to her it could not fail to be recognised eventually. She gave proof of an extreme affection for him.

She promised to interest herself in the fortunes of my brother, and a few days later he received his nomination as major. This was an abuse of privilege, and one of those which chiefly alienated the army and irritated the country. But it had become so general among the people with whom we were intimate, that it would have been impossible to appear without those epaulettes for which nevertheless one had no reasonable right to ask.

My father was much hurt by this folly, which he would not have solicited for his son. My mother did not appreciate this political idea. My brother was delighted to obtain a commission, and I to see him with it.

The repugnance of Madame to speaking of her parents reminds me of a strange circumstance. The Comtesse de Châtenay was often taken by her mother, the Comtesse de la Guiche, to see Madame when both of them were still children. Madame remembered this, and treated her with kindly familiarity; she received her several times privately. One day she said to her:

" Your father died young, did he not? "

" Yes, Madame."

" Where did he die? "

Madame de Châtenay hesitated a moment, and then answered:

" Alas! Madame, he perished on the scaffold during the Terror."

Madame recoiled as though she had trodden on an asp; a moment later she dismissed Mme. de Châtenay. And from that day not only did she cease her former kindness, but she treated her worse than any one else, and avoided speaking to her whenever she could. I do not attempt to explain the feeling which dictated this conduct, for I cannot imagine what it was. I only tell the story faithfully.

CHAPTER XXVI

IMMEDIATELY after the Restoration the Dowager Duchesse d'Orléans [1] left Barcelona and established herself in Paris. She welcomed my parents with her old familiarity and kindness.

We went there frequently. Thanks to her age, any scandal to which her surroundings might have given rise was out of the question.

She was completely subjugated by a man named Rozet, formerly a member of the National Convention, to whom she believed she owed her life, and who had accompanied her in Spain. He took advantage of her gratitude in every way, and, under the name of Follemont, which he had adopted, he was so entirely the master in her house that every one said he was her husband. Afterwards, however, a little Mme. de Follemont appeared on the scene, who had been married to him for thirty years. In any case, the Princess was completely under his guardianship. She had no will but his, and she overwhelmed him with the most ridiculous, exaggerated, and puerile

[1] Louise Marie Adélaide de Bourbon, born in 1753, daughter of the Duc de Penthièvre. In 1769 she married Louis Philippe Joseph d'Orléans, then Duc de Chartres. She died in 1821.

attentions. He was excessively fond of good living,
and she would take the trouble to send him a carp's
tongue or a pike's tail from her end of the table. She
saw to his coffee herself, arranged his game at cards,
and was careful that he should sit where there was no
draught. " That is M. de Follemont's place," she would
say, and so make any one get up who had taken his
seat. She took advantage, in fact, of her rights as a
princess to display attentions which she carried to foolishness. She would relate ten times a day the services
that M. de Follemont had rendered her, at the risk of
his life. The circumstances were disputed by persons
then in France, but the good Duchesse believed in them
herself sincerely.

All those who made up the honorary household were
compelled to bow to the supremacy of M. de Follemont.
This they did, though at the same time they inveighed
against him, and the more so because, though spending a
great deal of money, he kept up the establishment in a
style that was utterly *bourgeois* and disagreeable for the
inmates. I do not think, however, that he robbed the
Duchesse d'Orléans. He managed things badly, because
he had no idea of handling such a revenue, and did not
know how to keep up what should have been a great
position. But he had no children; he looked upon the
riches of the Duchesse d'Orléans as his own patrimony,
and would not have dreamed of taking anything from
it. He did not leave any fortune. His widow needed
the small pension which the Duc d'Orléans continued to
allow her after the death of his mother.

It will easily be understood that the Duchesse d'Orléans's mode of living did not attract many people. It
was painful for those who were attached to the Princess
and her family. My parents were among the number.

My father long remained a frequent visitor, but gradually
the available space was entirely occupied by M. de Follemont's courtiers. This latter was in an impossible position, whatever his affection for the Princess.

I was introduced to the Duchesse de Bourbon.[1]   I cannot tell how it chanced that I never returned after the
first visit. It is the more inexplicable as she received
every day, and her house was very pleasant.

The Duc d'Orléans paid a visit to Paris, and secured
an ostensible reconciliation with his mother. M. de
Follemont's presence had caused a complete rupture between the mother and children. He paid his court to
the King, gave orders for the Palais Royal, at that time
quite uninhabitable, to be put in order, took possession
of his property once more, and then returned to Sicily
to fetch his family, consisting of the Duchesse d'Orléans,
Mademoiselle,[2] and three children, the Duc de Chartres,
Princesse Louise, and Princesse Marie. The Duchesse
d'Orléans was then *enceinte,* and the child born was the
Duc de Nemours.

Ten years previously I had left three Princes d'Orléans
in England, and only one now remained. The eldest son
had robust health; he had been born before the more
than free life led by his father had vitiated his blood.
The Comte de Beaujolais added the profligacy of his own
youth to his father's excesses, and he was the first to
succumb. His two brothers tended him with the deepest affection, and accompanied him to Malta, but they

[1] Louise Marie Thérèse Bathilde d'Orléans (1750–1822), sister of
Philippe Joseph, wife of the last Prince de Condé, who died at Saint-
Leu in 1830, and mother of the Duc d'Enghien, who was shot at
Vincennes in 1804.

[2] Adélaide Eugénie Louise d'Orléans (1777–1848), known by the
name of Madame Adélaide, which she adopted after the Revolution
of 1830.

could not save him. The Duc d'Orléans was destined
to suffer a loss which affected him yet more deeply.
His favourite brother, his veritable second self, the Duc
de Montpensier, as kind, amiable, and gracious as he
was distinguished, died of a strange illness, which seemed
to be due to a taint in the blood.

M. de Montjoie, too, the faithful friend of these
princes, their companion in all the vicissitudes of their
adventurous life, was killed at the battle of Friedland.
It was said that the cannon ball which carried him off
came from a battery commanded by his brother, an artillery officer in the corps of the Bavarian army. Events
of this kind do not inspire the same horror in German
and Swiss families as in ours. They are accustomed
to see brothers serving under different Powers and exposed to the risk of meeting on opposite sides.

Mademoiselle had left France with Mme. de Genlis [1];
they had taken refuge in a convent.

After the catastrophe of her father's death, her mother
being in prison, the family claimed the young princess.
She was torn away from Mme. de Genlis and entrusted
to the care of her great-aunt, the Princesse de Conti.
The latter, who was very intelligent, appreciated and
loved her, but had not the courage to protect her sufficiently and shelter her from the persecutions to which
all the *émigré* party subjected her. There was a plan
formed to get from her, under the form of a letter to
the King, a profession of faith in which she should dis-
own her father and her brothers. In this struggle, which

---

[1] *Née* Du Crest de Saint Aubin (1746–1830). She was the niece of
Mme. de Montesson, morganatic wife of the Duc d'Orléans, father of
Philippe Joseph. The secret marriage took place in 1773. This
prince was the widower of Louise Henriette de Bourbon Conti, who
died in 1759. His son, the Duc de Chartres, confided the education
of his children, princes and a princess, to Mme. de Genlis.

continued during three years of Mademoiselle's early youth, may be found the explanation of her character, of her virtues, which were peculiar to herself, and of that shade of bitterness sometimes visible. She went with her aunt to Hungary, where they stayed for some time.

The Duchesse d'Orléans, on escaping from the Paris prisons, settled in Barcelona. She did not take any steps to approach her daughter, but after the Princesse de Conti's death she was obliged to offer her a refuge. Mademoiselle suffered so much from the unseemly behaviour of M. de Follemont that she was obliged to complain to her brothers. They went to fetch her from Barcelona; the Comtesse Mélanie de Montjoie was placed with her, and remained with her always.

The marriage was then being arranged between the Duc d'Orléans and the Princesse Amélie of Naples. She had first been destined for the Duc de Berry. This alliance was about to be concluded at Vienna, during the Queen of Naples's visit to that city with her two daughters. The Duc de Berry, who was then in love with one of the de Montboissier girls, made some unseemly joke in public about the few charms he found in the young princess. His remarks came to the ears of the Queen. She wrote him a dignified, noble, and yet kindly letter, in which she took 'back her word and broke off all engagements as far as her daughter was concerned. She sent a copy of this letter to my mother, and I read it several times.

I have no certain details of events in Sicily after the marriage of the Duc d'Orléans. I only know that his mother was present, that M. de Follemont succeeded in embroiling her with all her family, and that she returned with him to Barcelona.

There were quarrels between the English and the

court, and the Sicilians took part in them. The Queen was displeased with her son-in-law, so that he was obliged to leave the palace and retire to the country with his family. Shortly afterwards the English had reason to believe that the Queen was negotiating with Napoleon to exterminate them in the island and repeat the Sicilian Vespers. I do not know what confidence can be attached to this accusation, but it served as a pretext for expelling the Queen from Sicily. She intended to go to Vienna through Constantinople, and died on the journey before arriving there. The news arrived just as the Duc d'Orléans was installing his family in the Palais Royal.

The Duchesse d'Orléans was good enough to remember our intercourse as children, and she welcomed me with a kindliness which revived my affection for her, an affection which increased each day when I saw her exercising all the virtues, in addition to all the graces which can accompany them.

The Duchesse d'Orléans was not pretty. She was even ugly; tall and thin, with a red complexion, small eyes, and irregular teeth. But she had a long neck, her head was well set, and she had a very distinguished air. She was admirable in full dress, was very gracious, and at the same time extremely dignified. Then, too, in her little eyes there was such expression, an emanation from her pure, great, noble soul, and her glance was so changeable, so full of feeling, so kindly, so encouraging, so stimulating, so grateful, that it formed full compensation for any sacrifice on my part. I am convinced that the Duchesse d'Orléans owed part of the fascination she exercised over the most hostile people to the influence of that look.

She was very well received at the court of the Tuileries, the Duc d'Orléans less so, and Mademoiselle with great coldness. I do not think there was ever a reconciliation with her, not even by letter, and the Duchesse d'Angoulême could not dissimulate the repugnance she felt for the brother and sister.

I heard my uncle, Édouard Dillon, say that he was at Hartwell when the Duc d'Orléans paid his first visit there. The visit had been under discussion for a long time, and Madame had only consented with difficulty.

The Duc arrived earlier than he was expected one Sunday, as every one was returning from Mass. Madame met him as she was crossing the hall, followed by all who lived in the castle. On seeing the Prince she turned extremely pale, her legs trembled, and words died away on her lips. He advanced to support her, but she repulsed him. She was obliged to sit down, as she was very faint. Every one gathered round her, and she was led away to her apartments.

The Duc d'Orléans was deeply hurt, grieved, and annoyed. He was left alone with my uncle, and, as it was impossible to keep up any pretence, he spoke to him bitterly of this scene, and expressed a wish to go away at once. Édouard proved to him how desirable it was to avoid a scandal, and offered to go to the King for him and take his orders. The King was with his niece, and he sent word to the Prince that Madame was subject to this kind of indisposition, that she was better again, and that by dinner time there would be no further sign of it.

A few minutes later he received the Duc d'Orléans in his study. I do not know what passed between them. Madame made the best of it at dinner, and even spoke to the Duc d'Orléans of this palpitation to which she was subject. There was no truth, however, in this, and the

Prince was very glad, as can be imagined, to get into his carriage and drive away directly after the meal.

Scenes of this kind leave traces which are not forgotten by either side.

Madame's ostensible repugnance to the Duc d'Orléans decreased as time went on, but she could neither conquer nor dissimulate that with which Mademoiselle inspired her. On the other hand, a sincere and mutual friendship sprang up between her and the Duchesse d'Orléans. Madame usually called her " my real cousin." [1]

My father would have liked my brother to be attached to the house of Orléans, as his name gave him old family rights there. The kindness of the Duchesse d'Orléans to me allowed me to speak of this to her. Although she was in deep mourning for her mother, she used to receive me often, and she promised to attend to this matter. A few days later she told me that the Duc d'Orléans had made so many promises already that he was not likely to have any posts that he could dispose of. That was not exactly the truth, which was as follows:

The Duc d'Orléans was already surrounded by a few persons belonging to what was still called the *ancien régime*. Instead of wishing to increase the number, he wanted to complete his household with those of another order, who belonged to the revolutionary interest. He was keen-sighted enough to realise that it was greatly to his interest to deal cautiously with them, and his policy was always directed to secure this amalgamation. It would have been a very clever idea for the princes of the royal family, but I should be sorry to assert that it was entirely simple for a prince of the blood thus to dissociate himself from their policy.

[1] They were first cousins by their mothers, who were daughters of the Empress Maria Theresa of Austria.

It is certain that from the very first day the Duc d'Orléans, though I am sure that he did not conspire against them, avoided any association with their proceedings, and his whole attitude was that of a man very glad to be thought in the opposition.

M. de Talleyrand very nearly followed the same line of conduct.

If he had been as respected in the country as he was important, he would not have hesitated; but the Restoration was too much his work for him to venture to separate himself from it on account of private animosities. Disgusted with all the rebuffs which were showered upon him at the Château,[1] he wanted to go away, and he proposed himself for the Vienna Congress, the importance of the negotiations and the presence of the sovereigns justifying that of the Minister of Foreign Affairs.

His *salon* was very amusing. The doors did not open till after midnight, but all Europe crowded there, and in spite of the strict etiquette of the reception and the impossibility of moving one of the heavy seats occupied by the women, one could always find a way of spending a few moments there which were amusing, or interesting at any rate, for a spectator.

Mme. de Talleyrand, seated at the end of the two rows of armchairs, tranquilly did the honours. The remains of her great beauty adorned her stupidity with a fair amount of dignity.

I cannot refrain from telling a somewhat indecorous story characteristic of this courtesan, then such a *grande dame*.

My uncle, Édouard Dillon, who in his youth was known as " Handsome Dillon," had had all the successes

---

[1] The Tuileries were called the Château during the whole time of the Restoration.

that such a nickname suggests. Mme. de Talleyrand, then Mme. Grant, had been attracted by him, but as his time was occupied elsewhere, he did not pay much attention to her. The rupture of a *liaison*, which greatly affected him, made him decide to leave Paris and undertake a journey to the East. This was an event in those days, and the mere idea of it added an interest of curiosity to his other fascinations.

Mme. Grant redoubled her attentions, and finally, the evening before his departure, Édouard consented to return home with her to supper after the opera. He found a very charming flat, the table laid for two persons, and all the studied refinements which belonged to Mme. Grant's profession. She had the most beautiful hair imaginable, and Édouard admired it. She told him that he did not yet know what it was like, and, after retiring into her dressing-room, she came back with her hair loose and covering her like a veil. She was a second Eve, before any dress material had been invented, and, with less innocence than her ancestress, *naked and not ashamed*. The supper was finished in this primitive costume.

Édouard started for Egypt the following day. This took place in 1787.

In 1814 this same Édouard, on his return from exile, was driving with me to call on the Princesse de Talleyrand, to whom I was to introduce him.

" The contrast," he said to me, " is so amusing between this visit and the one I paid formerly to Mme. de Talleyrand, that I cannot resist telling you of my last and only interview with her."

He then related me the preceding story. We were both much amused, and curious as to what her attitude would be towards him. She received him wonderfully well, and in a very simple way. But after a few minutes she spoke of my head-gear, admired my hair, wondered how long it was, and then, suddenly turning to my uncle, who was just behind my chair, she said:

"Monsieur Dillon, you like nice hair, do you not?"

Fortunately our eyes did not meet, as it would have been impossible for us to have kept serious.

Mme. de Talleyrand did not keep her naïve remarks solely for her own use; she had some to spare for M. de Talleyrand. She never failed to remember that such and such a person (another of my uncles, for instance, Arthur Dillon) was one of his fellow-students at the Seminary. She would address him from the other side of the drawing-room, and call upon him to affirm that the ornament he liked best was a pastoral cross of diamonds which she was wearing.

When someone advised her to have larger pendants to her pearl ear-rings she answered:

"Do you imagine I have married the Pope?"

There are too many of these absurdities to quote. M. de Talleyrand met them all with his imperturbable calm, but I am convinced that he must often have wondered how he could have married this woman.

I was at Mme. de Talleyrand's on the day of M. de Talleyrand's departure, and I saw her when she was told that Mme. de Dino, then Comtesse Edmond de Périgord, was accompanying her uncle to Vienna. The meeting place had been arranged at a country house near Paris. An indiscreet person told her this in a very innocent way.

Mme. de Talleyrand made no mistake about the importance of this meeting, which had been arranged so secretly. She could not conceal her anxiety nor yet recover from it. She was not mistaken in her previsions, for from that day forth she never saw M. de Talleyrand again, and she was soon after banished from his house.

M. de Blacas was more gracious and attentive to my father after M. de Talleyrand's departure, but it did not suit him at all to join the cabal that was in formation beneath his eyes.

For some years we had frequently seen the Princesse de Carignan, niece of the King of Saxony.[1] She had married the Prince de Carignan,[2] at the commencement of the Revolution. He was then far removed from the crown, but recognised as a prince of the blood. She had adopted revolutionary ideas, and had won her husband over to them. He was absolutely devoid of the most ordinary intelligence. She was at this time a widow with two children, and quite ruined. She had urged her claims successively in the ante-chambers of the Directory, the Consulate, and the Empire.

It suited the Emperor to listen to them. She took back her title of princesse, and he divided all the property of the house of Carignan that was not sold between her son and the son of the Comte de Villefranche,[3] uncle of the late Prince de Carignan. This son was the issue of a marriage contracted in France with a Mlle. Magon, the daughter of a shipowner of Saint-Malo. His sister, the Princesse de Lamballe, had been greatly angered and distressed by this union, which the Sardinian court never recognised.

---

[1] Charlotte Albertine de Saxe Courlande, daughter of Charles Christian Joseph, Prince of Saxony and of Courlande (1779–1861).

[2] Charles Emmanuel Ferdinand (1770–1800).

[3] Eugène Marie Louis de Carignan (Villefranche), 1753–1785. The son in question here was Joseph, Chevalier de Savoie (1783–1825), married to Mlle. de La Vauguyon. Of this marriage a son was born, who was recognised as Prince de Savoie Carignan in 1834, and a daughter, married to the Comte de Syracuse.

The Princesse de Carignan, who was a Saxon, had, on her side, married a M. de Montléard secretly. She had had several children by him, whom she had carefully concealed from the time of their birth. She only owned to the two Carignans. The elder of the two in 1814[1] was a tall, beautiful girl[2] of fifteen years of age, very simple, very natural, and a very agreeable child.

The boy, whose childhood had been neglected almost absolutely, so that he had run about Paris with all the small boys of the neighbourhood, had been in a pension at Geneva for a few months at this time; the King of Sardinia sent for him, and established him at Turin. He now became an important personage. As the King had daughters only, and his brother no children, the Prince de Carignan was heir presumptive to the crown.[3]

The Duc de Modène, brother of the Queen of Sardinia,[4] and married to her eldest daughter, would have considered it simpler to change the order of succession. Austria supported his claims. The revolutionary opinions of the parents, and the conduct that the Princesse de Carignan continued, militated against the young Prince de Carignan; but he was of the house of Savoy, and that was a great point in his favour in the King's eyes. To secure his recognition and the public proclama-

[1] Mme. de Boigne is mistaken here. The elder of the children was Charles Albert (1798–1849), King of Piedmont in 1831, on the extinction of the elder branch of the house of Savoy. With him commences the dynasty of Savoy-Carignan. He died at Oporto in Portugal (July 1849), after abdicating in favour of his son Victor Emmanuel II. on the preceding March 23.

[2] Elisabeth Françoise, married to the Archduke Rénier of Austria in 1820.

[3] On this question consult *La Jeunesse du Roi Charles-Albert*, by the Marquis Costa de Beauregard, of the French Academy, 1 vol. in 8. (Plon & Co., publishers, Paris, 1892, 2nd edition.)

[4] Marie Thérèse Joséphine of Austria, wife of Victor Emmanuel I., King from 1802 to 1821.

tion of his rights was one of the most important features of the mission confided to my father. It was of great interest to France that Austria should not add Piedmont to the states that it governed in Italy.

The Princesse de Carignan wanted to obtain permission to go to Turin with her daughter. The young Princess would have been received and even retained, but all gates were barred to her mother.

From the time that she heard of my father's nomination she scarcely left our house, as she had some fresh motive to urge every hour for obtaining the mediation of the Ambassador, who was quite inclined to attend to the Prince's affairs in a very active way, but not at all inclined to obtain the return of the Princess. Her presence would have been a continual difficulty for her son and for France, which declared in his favour.

The other Carignan (Villefranche) had married Mlle. de La Vauguyon, and this family, too, was agitating to get his legitimacy admitted by the Turin court. The argument was that the late King at the point of death had recognised the Comte de Villefranche's unsuitable marriage.

My father was not always free to listen to these minute explanations. I had to take my share, and this was a foretaste of the worries that awaited me at Turin.

We started at the beginning of October.

APPENDIX[1]

I

Letter from the Queen Marie Amélie *to* Madame la Comtesse de Boigne.

Brussels, *April* 21, 1835.

My sister has informed me of the cruel misfortune that you have experienced, my dear friend, and I will not delay a moment to express to you all the sympathy that I feel. To lose the object of such great care and affection, and to lose it in such a terrible manner, is agonising for a heart like yours; and mine, which is so attached to you, is with you in grief. I will not say more to you. I pity you with all the sympathy of the most sincere friendship.

Your very affectionate,

Marie Amélie.

Letter from General Pozzo, *at the time Russian Ambassador in England, to* Madame la Comtesse de Boigne.

Hashbeynham [Ashburnham?] House,
April 29, 1835.

My niece has just given me the news of the misfortune which has fallen on you. My first thought is to tell you of my grief when I realise all the sorrow this sad event must have caused you. Nothing is more bitter in life than to see interests disappear that

[1] In the French, the orthography and punctuation of the original documents are scrupulously reproduced. They are all autographs.

393

we have formed for ourselves; we feel our loss the more because we have counted on them with the partiality with which each regards his own handiwork. In spite of all these reasons for regret, I hope that you will find in your own strength of mind and in the attentions of your friends the means of bearing your loss without being prostrated by it. I should like to be near you to contribute my share in this. . . . Charles and his wife tell me that they have called twice without being able to see you. I do not like your persistence in your isolation. You have more need than ever of the society of the small number of your intimate friends. . . . You know my feelings so well that I have no need to express them. Call your customary good sense to your aid: I expect much more from it than from all that I can say to you, except that I am your very sincerely devoted

Pozzo.

NOTE ON THE OSMOND FAMILY.

Letter bearing no signature.
Address: Monsieur le Mᴵˢ d'Osmond, *Rue de*
Bourbon, n. 61, Paris.

Osmond, a Norman family, comes into notice with Rollon and is always attached to its dukes. The history of France (during the reign of Louis D'outre mer) shows us the Chevalier Osmond appointed tutor to Richard II. when, after the assassination of his father, slain by the Duke of Brittany, the Norman States felt obliged, in order to save the life of their young Duke, to put him under the protection of Louis. History tells us, too, how Osmond managed to withdraw his pupil from the treachery of the King of France.

A branch of this house accompanied William to England and occupied high offices there. William, in speaking of Osmond, said that he was his right arm. St. Osmond was Bishop of Salisbury after having enjoyed the title of Duke Dorzét [Dorset?], which has since passed to the house of Sackville. This branch is no longer in existence, or at least it is unknown.

It supplied the first adventurers who occupied Apulia; it ruled there, founded Avers, and after a long period found itself constrained by the Norman Hautevilles, whom it had attracted to that place, to renounce the sovereignty.

Of this house, which formerly had great possessions, was of high consideration in Normandy, claimed as its ancestors the Comtes de Sées, and lastly supplied canonesses to Remiremont and Counts of Lyons, there are no more left than . . . (See genealogical table).

Consult: de Normanorum—the Chronicles of Monte Cassino; those of Mont St. Michel; the History of France; Revolution of Naples (Gianoni); Gaillard (*Rivalités*); the discourse which was awarded the Academy prize at Ste-Marie at Rouen; investigations about Norman families; Morrery.

This, my dear, is all that I can tell you about a race which once filled very high offices and whose posterity is almost forgotten.

Adieu.   Friendly greetings.

September 12.

GENEALOGICAL TABLE OF THE FAMILY D'OSMOND IN THE NINETEENTH CENTURY

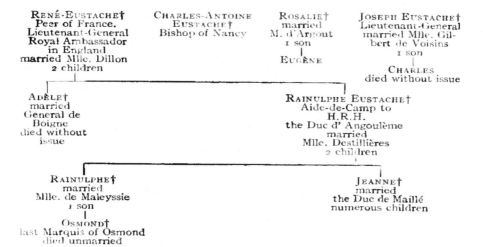

RENÉ-EUSTACHE† Peer of France. Lieutenant-General Royal Ambassador in England married Mlle. Dillon 2 children

CHARLES-ANTOINE EUSTACHE† Bishop of Nancy

ROSALIE† married M. d'Argout 1 son EUGÈNE

JOSEPH EUSTACHE† Lieutenant-General married Mlle. Gilbert de Voisins 1 son CHARLES died without issue

ADÈLE† married General de Boigne died without issue

RAINULPHE EUSTACHE† Aide-de-Camp to H.R.H. the Duc d' Angoulème married Mlle. Destillières 2 children

RAINULPHE† married Mlle. de Maleyssie 1 son OSMOND† last Marquis of Osmond died unmarried

JEANNE† married the Duc de Maillé numerous children

III

Letters from MADAME ADÉLAIDE, *daughter of Louis XV., to the* MARQUISE D'OSMOND.

November 29, 1789.

I have received the two locks you sent me, Madame. They are very well made, and I thank you very much for them. I have, however, a reproach to make you, which diminishes the pleasure they have caused me: that is, that they were accompanied by no letter from you. Write to me, then, and as often as you can. Send me news, but especially of yourself, your husband, and your children.

Paris is tranquil; there is bread in abundance, provisions for at least eight months, no more riots at the bakers' shops, because a firm hand is kept there. I hope it will last, and that, seeing that the efforts made in this direction were useless, people will keep quiet. Minds appear to be much less agitated, and publications are beginning to have a sale. There are very good ones among them, and some very absurd. It is to be hoped, too, that our regeneration will soon be accomplished, and that at Easter we shall be able to return to Paris. I am not there yet because my lodging is not ready. I go on living here in solitude, seeing nobody but our own people. I should be very happy if I could get them all together with all their belongings. Tell me, too, what sort of life you are leading and whom you see. Do you see M. the Duc d'O., the Duchesse de Laval, M. de Calonne? Do the two men see anything of each other?

Adieu, Madame. Be assured of all the friendship that I have for you. Embrace M. d'Osmond and Adèle.

PARIS, *December* 31, 1789.

I take advantage of the departure of l'Epine to write to you, Madame. I suppose you have not received my last letter, in which I scolded you for not having written to me when you sent your locks and thanked you at the same time. They are charming. I asked you also many questions about the life you are leading and that of the French who are in England, whether they see many people and what society is like.

I have been here since Monday, and am very uncomfortable. My apartments are small: except the antechambers and the large library, my own room and everything else is very small. All is very calm here and the supply of provisions is assured. That is all the tranquillising news I can give you. We are all very well: I look upon this as a miracle after the assaults we have endured. I send many messages for M. d'Osmond. I hope that both of you have no doubt of my tender friendship.

MARIE-ADÉLAIDE.

TURIN, *March* 15, 1791.

I have not been able, Madame, to keep the promise that I gave to write to you on arriving at Chambéry. I asked Count Louis [1] to send to you immediately on his arrival in Paris. He promised he would: I hope that he has done so. We arrived in very good health, in spite of all the unfavourable winds and the terrible storms that we experienced almost through the whole of France. It has all been well made up to us here, not only by the whole family, which overwhelms us with kindness and attentions, but by everybody. I cannot tell you what I felt at the bridge of Beau-voisin. On the French side there were hootings and most horrible looks: when once we had passed the barrier we heard cries of "Vivent Mesdames!" and clapping of hands. This difference is very striking for any one who has travelled the last five years in the provinces. To fancy yourself in an enemy's country when you are in your own, and in your own land when you are among

---

[1] De Narbonne. He had accompanied "Mesdames."

strangers, makes an impression on you which it is impossible to describe or to express. Adieu, Madame! Be assured of all the friendship I have for you and for M. d'Osmond. Embrace Adèle and Rainulfe.

When shall we see each other again? Send your answer to Rome, where I shall certainly be in three weeks.

ROME, *May* 21, 1793.

I must seem to you, Madame, greatly to blame for having let two posts go by without thanking you for sending me news: but truly, truly, I have always found the post gone; for I did not know the days, and thought it was necessary to write on Wednesdays and Saturdays.

I am glad to hear that you are better; but I cannot be quite glad that the air of Naples does you good: you can guess why. I wish it were the air of Rome; but your health will always weigh with me more than my satisfaction and the pleasure I should have to see you. You will console me for your absence by telling me your news.

M. d'Osmond must have suffered great pain, and poor Bermond, in his attachment to his master, must have bitterly regretted his awkwardness. It is very fortunate that nothing was broken, though perhaps it is all the more painful.

It is not easy to get news from France. Of the four couriers who were overdue, three arrived on one day, but with stale news. The fourth is not here yet. I know, however, that they are well at the Temple. It seems that nothing new has been decided about their liberty.

It is true it was said (but that is some time ago) that M. de Malsherbe had permission to enter, but I have not heard anything of this since. You doubtless know that the Bretons are always advancing and gaining in numbers, and it is asserted positively that Nantes is taken.

The Comte d'Artois has not yet returned to Hanover. The Regent told me that he awaited him with great impatience, that he had received very good news of him, but that he did not yet speak of the date of his return. If ever I have good authentic news from Paris, you may rely upon my sending it to you.

Friday's courier from Germany brought us no news. Things are always in the same position. The Emperor publicly expressed his disapproval of all the Prince of Cobourg's declarations, as having been made without his knowledge and participation.

Adieu, Madame! Be assured of all the friendship I have for you. Keep in good health: you could not give me greater pleasure.

I send all kinds of messages by you to your husband. I hope that his finger is cured. Embrace Adèle and Rainulphe, and even Rainulphe's little dog.

P.S.—I did very well not to hurry in sending off my letter. This morning we have received excellent news from Germany: that of a fresh battle, of which I send you the account that I have written out for you. Further, M. de Chastellux, whom I prevented writing to you, because I wished to be the first to tell you the news, asks me to send you this letter and to tell you that the Duchesse de Fitzjames assures us that we need have no anxiety as to the personal views of the Emperor, who does not like the Constitution any better than the Republic. There is no object in my telling you this, because Consalvi would surely not allow you to remain in ignorance.

I embrace you again with all my heart.

I unseal my letter once more to tell you that I have just received a letter from the Princess of Piedmont,[1] who informs me that the Duc de Chablais had just sent a courier with the news that the patriot general named Casabianchi, a Corsican by nationality, had been taken by the militia and conducted as prisoner to Démont. (It is he who has replaced Biron at Nice.) The next in command to him (Casabianchi) has written to General Vins to demand the surrender of the prisoner, if, as he said, he had not already been assassinated. General Vins answered that it was not customary to massacre those who acted in self-defence; further,

---

[1] Madame Clotilde of France, sister of King Louis XVI., married to Charles Emmanuel IV., King from 1796 to 1802. The Church gave her the title of "venerable." She died at Naples in 1802, before the abdication of her husband.

that the Piedmontese had no general who was anxious to be captured in order to be exchanged, and that so it was for him to indicate on what conditions he claimed his surrender. They have found many important papers on him and schemes of attack that may be very useful.

My letter is rather piecemeal and cut up. I beg you to overlook this: I fancy that will not displease you. But this is the end of it, for we have no more couriers to expect, except the one which is perhaps the most interesting for us, and the one which will surely not arrive—the courier from France. I believe I have no common sense; but no matter. I always chatter.

Address:
    To MADAME LA MARQUISE D'OSMOND, *Naples.*

HEADQUARTERS OF QUIÉVRAIN,
May 1, 8 P.M.[1]

The army of the French Jacobins, foreseeing that it was going to be attacked, and not wishing to labour under the disadvantage of acting on the defensive, in which it has never succeeded, arranged for a general attack to-day. If it was a May-posy that it wanted to offer the nation, its offering was most baneful. The battle was general and bloody, and the defeat of the Nationalists complete. In the morning before daybreak all their forces were in movement. They marched against our centre, passed St. Sauve, and advanced to Esneu. Our outposts, not being able to resist a whole army, retired. They were reinforced, and then the innumerable artillery of the Nationalists came into action with the greatest violence. Our centre, which held out till ten o'clock, was overwhelmed by numbers, gave way, and fell back for half an hour towards the rear. But our left did marvels; it turned the right wing of the French and drove it in. The balance was quickly restored at the centre, and the patriots were driven back with the greatest vigour beyond their camp. The rout was so complete that a part of the Jacobin army fled into Valenciennes. The carnage was very great. Bar-

[1] In the Princess's handwriting.

co's regiment in particular displayed extraordinary and invincible courage, fully avenging the barbarity of the patriots who gouged out the eyes of one of the regiment who had fallen by hazard into their hands. Twenty-one cannons were captured from the Nationalists, twenty-two cases of powder and provisions of war, together with the horses that drew them. Their loss in killed and wounded cannot be exactly calculated; it must be considerable. Ours does not amount to two hundred men, but there are three officers dangerously wounded.

Our right wing, which was specially charged to cover Condé's blockade, had no chance of doing very much in the morning, but at two o'clock in the afternoon it was heard cannonading briskly between Condé and Valenciennes. This ceased before nightfall, and everything seems to show that we have had a decided advantage on this side as well, but we have not yet received any details.

Extract from a letter from MONSIEUR of May 1.

The Austrian army under the orders of H.S.H. the Prince of Saxe-Cobourg has displayed to-day its customary valour, and won a considerable advantage over the army of the patriots. The right wing, under the orders of General Comte de Clairfaït, forced the trenches of the mountain of Ansin, a quarter of a league from Valenciennes, and established itself there, after taking several pieces of artillery, killing a considerable number, and capturing some prisoners.

Extract from a letter from TOURNAY of May 2.

All preparations are being made to commence the siege of Condé to-morrow or the day after. The gunners are all busy filling bombs. The bastion and the earthworks are almost finished.

The patriots have lost 2400 to 2500 killed, 1400 prisoners, 21 cannons, 17 waggons.

The 19th.

I am delighted, Madame, with the good news which M. de Narbonne has brought me of your health, and, from what you tell me, I am sure the good air that one breathes at Albano has greatly contributed to it. You wish, then, to increase my regret at seeing myself detained in Rome without the power of leaving it. If I attempted anything of the kind I should certainly be reprimanded by M. d'Arlincourt. I must be prudent to the end, and consent to deprive myself of what might be agreeable to me in order to be able to do what is necessary. The letter from the Duchesse de Laval is very touching. I will do what I can for her Abbé, but you know well that my means are unfortunately limited.

Adieu, Madame! Get well quickly. I cannot bring myself to say, come back quickly into this bad air; but I shall be very glad to see the season arrive when one can live here with impunity and fearlessly. Be assured of all the friendship I have for you. Kiss Adèle and Rainulfe for me.

ROME, *September* 7, 1793.

I have long been wishing to write to you, Madame, but I have had neither the courage nor the strength to do so, prostrated as I have been by a heat of which you never had an idea during the two years you lived here. Perhaps you have had the same heat, but at least at Naples you can breathe in the evening, I am told.

Ah! what news from Paris? Why are our happiness, and the hopeful news from home and abroad, clouded by the brutality that is employed towards the unfortunate Queen? What courage and firmness she has shown! How she has spoken to all that rabble! How great she is in her misfortune! It is not the first time that we have seen such things, and if only everything had depended on her! They say that her firmness has made such an impression that they have not yet dared to question her and to commence her trial. May God bring her through it! She well deserves thus much.

I have had news of you from M. de Chastellux, to whom M.

d'Osmond often writes. I hope Naples may cure all your troubles, and that I may see you again in good health.

Adieu, Madame! I love you and embrace you with all my heart. Kiss the children for me. Rainulphe must certainly talk like the lazzaroni. He must be very comical.

Address:
To MADAME LA MARQUISE D'OSMOND, *Naples.*

ROME, *September* 6, 1793.

You are very kind, Madame, and you compensate very agreeably for the time that has elapsed since I had news from you. I dare not yet give myself up entirely to joy, particularly for the deliverance of my unhappy niece. I hope, however, that nothing will happen to her. Her courage has made a deep impression, and will always do so. It is not the first occasion on which she has shown it: and so she is still alive.

The news from Toulon, that you must know by now, is excellent. I hope that all the southern provinces will follow the good example. Lyons will have no difficulty: it is distinguishing itself. That is a part of the kingdom where Louis XVII. is entirely recognised.

They say that Signor M—— is somewhat embarrassed: he does not know where to go; he is not wanted anywhere. I hope that all these scoundrels will find themselves without houses, and will suffer the pain that they have assuredly well deserved. God will do justice to them, since men would not.

Adieu, Madame! keep in good health, and never doubt my entire friendship! My warmest remembrance to M. d'Osmond. What a man that Mr. Pitt is! If you learn any details about what has passed at Toulon, you would give me great pleasure in acquainting me with them, for we only know the fact. That is always a very good thing to know, but history would do well to complete our joy.

Address:
To MADAME LA MARQUISE D'OSMOND, *Naples.*

ROME, *September* 29, 1792.
(It should be 1793.)

You are very kind, Madame, to give me news and such good news. We knew of the capture of Toulon, but we had no confirmation of the details, which we are delighted to learn. The departure of the ships and the troops of the King of Naples causes me great pleasure. These forces establishing themselves at Toulon announce that the whole province will soon move. Marseilles displays great weakness, and is always changing its sentiments. Even the loyal are not what they ought to be: perhaps they are waiting to be stronger before declaring themselves.

I understood quite well the account you sent me, with the exception of some words which I could not read. With a magnifying glass, I shall perhaps understand them.

Unfortunately, alas! the Queen of Naples puts too much confidence in the news from her daughter.[1] I am very much afraid that as regards the Queen the information is false. All the gazettes and even some letters declare that she is still at the Conciergerie, but her trial has not yet begun. Her courage has made a great impression: I hope it will save her. Alas! if everybody had had as much! Gaston [2] continues to do marvels, but he is not yet at Paris. I think entirely as you do: I desire the moment of his arrival, but I fear it. Such is the situation in which we have been for four years. Gustine is at last dead: he died like a coward, which was inevitable. What a difference between the deaths of those of the right cause and of these monsters!

Your story gave me great pleasure, and I see kindness in it. What happiness for you to have found relations as pleasant as the Chevalier Legard and his wife! I must be allowed my share of gratitude. This fact may perhaps reassure you about Adèle's growth: I reached womanhood at the same age, and I grew a great deal that very year, so you can entertain hopes that she will not always remain as little as you fear. I am quite persuaded that she will enjoy much better health. I am very glad that M.

[1] The Empress, wife of Francis II., Emperor of Germany since March 1, 1792, when he succeeded his father, Leopold II.
[2] A Vendean chief, who died in 1793 after some successes.

d'Osmond is well. I have done his commissions, and also those with which you charged me for Victoire, who asks me to thank you and to remember her to you.

Adieu, Madame! I love you and embrace you with all my heart, as I do all your family, great and small. Give my compliments to Adèle. It seems to me that she had no reasonable grounds for intellectual growth, she was already so astonishing. As for Rainulphe, he is a strange little creature.

When you have news, I shall always be ready to hear it, for here we have very little sure information.

ROME, *September* 5, 1793.

In return for the message you sent me, Madame, I forward you the copy of an account, printed and sent to the Secretary of State, of what happened at Toulon. I think it will give you pleasure. If there is any error you must pardon the copyist, who was in a great hurry in order not to miss the post. The reading of this account will awaken in you sentiments very different from all those which we have experienced up to the present. You will recognise in it the true sons of France, and I sincerely hope they are not reserved alone for the town of Toulon, and that we shall see them henceforward everywhere.

I hope you will tell me the result of your blood-letting. They say that the doctors are better fortunately at Naples than at Rome. I hope, too, that the indisposition of my little friend is caused only by his teeth, as they are very forward. I really hope that he will be better afterwards.

I am extremely hurried, so I finish by embracing you, you and yours, with all my heart.

ROME, *September* 22, 1793.

So you desire, Madame, that I should be doubly pleased to receive your letters, as you want to wait for good news before writing to me. Your own affairs, however, are so interesting to me that I like to hear of them sometimes.

I was quite right not to trust the news of the Empress on the subject of the unhappy Queen. To-day it is said that she has been taken back to the Temple on the pretext that she was not in safety, and that a party of the aristocracy might carry her off. Well, whatever the reason, I would that the news were true, because there she would at least be with her family, and that would give me some gleam of hope for her. Otherwise all the news from every quarter is excellent. God grant that all may go well with us!

I am in despair about the poor Duchesse de Laval's misfortune, all the more as it seems to me that she loved him the most. He promised to be a most exemplary person, marvellously right-minded, and he conducted himself admirably. I have had no news of the poor Duchesse. I wrote to her and asked her to let me hear of her, but I do not know if the letter will reach her, because I addressed it to Dusseldorf, not knowing where to find her.

I send you a sample of snuff to see if it is what you like. Neither Mme. de Narbonne nor I can remember. If you like it, tell me, and I will keep you supplied; if not, I will send you another kind. Poor little Louise [1] has the smallpox, but very mildly up to the present. She is at the second day of the rash, and has only the normal amount of fever.

I am very much troubled by your anxiety about my friend Rainulphe, but I hope that the liveliness of your imagination exaggerates. Hooping-cough in childhood is alarming but not dangerous. Anyhow, I hope and desire sincerely that he will relieve you from all your anxiety. It is not surprising that Adèle's indisposition has had no consequences. It almost always happens like that. Her fatness of which you tell me proves me that she is well. Has she grown a little? The Princess of Piedmont has just sent word to Victoire that the brave town of Lyons has fallen, but that fortunately the troops had retired with their artillery. Whither? I do not know at all. Things go very slowly in Piedmont. This morning's courier brought us the grievous news that Lyons was taken, but that the garrison, to the number of 10,000, had cut their way out, had killed many of the patriots,

[1] Louise de Narbonne, granddaughter of the Duchesse.

and had retired to Provence or to Vivarais, and were going to make an effort to gain Toulon. God grant they may! As to the fate of our unfortunate niece, the news from Paris and in the gazettes is horrible. The extreme party are more furious against her than ever, and she has not left the Conciergerie, as we had been led to flatter ourselves. In Flanders and Germany all goes well, and also in La Vendée. They are fighting all the time.

Adieu, Madame! I love you and embrace you with all my heart.

ROME, *December* 6, 1793.

You saw, Madame, from my last letter that I had not been informed of the crowning-point of horror and of our misfortunes.[1] I asked M. de Chastellux to tell you that I had not the strength to unseal my letter. I know only too well your attachment to these unhappy victims, and I very much fear that your health may suffer again. We are in dread for the three victims who are not yet sacrificed, but from these monsters what good can we expect?

I imagine that you were very much edified by the death of the first of all. He retained his character right to the end, and died like a coward, crying, shrieking, demanding mercy of the people, who only answered by throwing mud at him. At last we are rid of him, too late, though, it is true.[2]

I do not know why my letter was such a long time on the road. I hope that this one will arrive more quickly. Yours was at least one post behindhand.

I am charmed to hear that Rainulphe goes on well. You have no more cause for anxiety. I love you with all my heart, and I embrace you and M. d'Osmond too.

ROME, *January* 31, 1794.

The reason for which you employed this in-folio to write to me, Madame (and you did very well), prevented me from writing

[1] Death of Queen Marie Antoinette, who mounted the scaffold October 16, 1793.

[2] Louis Philippe Joseph d'Orléans, "Philippe Egalité," guillotined at Paris, November 6, 1793.

myself until I had received a letter from you. I assure you that this has been a privation for me, but as I know how dear the post is in other countries, I did not wish to put you to the expense, being sure, besides, that you had news of us through M. de Chastellux. I was very much grieved at the death of the Chevalier de Bernis. Independently of the friendship that I had for him, and of his trustworthiness and the help that he has so often been, I think he is a great loss to France at the present moment. The Regent had put his confidence in him, so he felt his loss deeply. Poor M. de Marange followed him in about fifteen days, so that I cannot discharge your commissions for him.

The campaign has been most disastrous, but if France comes to herself again, if opinion changes, as all letters assert that it will, if La Vendée and the Chouans continue their successes, would that not be much better than to see each one drawing a few provinces into his train? A great number of the priests are recalled to the south; many have gone there, and these report to their fellow priests that the position of things there is very satisfactory. The Toulon fleet, with which they tried to frighten us so much here, continues in harbour, and cannot leave because it has neither vessels in seaworthy condition nor crews. In the river at Genoa and at Nice the patriots are dying of a kind of plague, and their number is very much smaller. If they are not reinforced in the spring, it will be impossible for them to do anything, and in spite of the *terroristes*, as Monsignor Caraffa calls them, I believe we are in perfect safety here.

Your relations are charming. I love them with all my heart, and I am more grateful to them than if it were for myself that they did all they do. I can quite understand your being always a little sad, but you let your gloomy ideas go too far. We must hope that they will never be realised. Have more confidence, more courage; have mercy on yourself, and banish all the fancies with which you love to torture yourself. There are plenty of real cares, without going out of the way to look for more.

What you tell me about Adèle causes me great pleasure, but does not astonish me. She has always been very precocious in intellect and wit. As for her face, I do not believe a word of what you tell me. It is your fear that makes you talk so, for she has always been pretty, she is pretty, and she will be pretty. Arthur needs no recommendation. He has every recommendation of person and conduct, but what tells most with me is that he is your brother. I shall have great pleasure in seeing him. I thank you in advance for the present which you announce. I shall be delighted with it, especially as it is your own work, always provided that it costs you nothing, for otherwise it would have a very cold welcome.

We have had almost a French winter: a very long frost and a great amount of snow. Yesterday it began to be milder, and I hope that the fine weather is coming. Tell me whether I should do better to employ this paper, whether it is cheaper, and write to me always in the same way, without any envelope, for I assure you that I hardly look at the exterior: it is only what is inside that causes me pleasure.

Adieu, Madame! Be sure that nothing can change the friendship I have for you. I embrace you with 'all my heart. Adèle too, and Rainulphe, whom you do not mention. That is very wrong of you. My compliments to M. d'Osmond.

Address:

Madame la Marquise d'Osmond, *Etton, near Beverley, Yorkshire, England.*

Rome, *April* 19, 1794.

I am very much afraid, Madame, that I made a mistake in my calculations when I wrote to you at Lausanne, and that I did so too late, but I only received your letter yesterday.

It was high time that the conspiracy at Naples was discovered. It was awful, but fortunately it has been effectually crushed, at least I hope so, and it seems that it was not possible to have acted more admirably. These hateful extremists, who have sprung from hell, have frightfully long arms, which they stretch out over all Europe, as their plots were discovered and disconcerted simultaneously in Naples, Piedmont, Genoa, and Poland.

The news from France is very good, but I am far from daring

to flatter myself that it is true. It is to the effect that the whole family has been saved, and is at Condé, in the hands of the Emperor. Caraffa assured us that he had some very good news, and very reliable, about which we might rejoice, but that he had given his word of honour not to say anything of it till he had received information of the arrival of the Emperor in the Low Countries. Yesterday evening he repeated this to me, and said, "A little patience and you will see!"

Do you know why I went to see you? It was originally for myself, to please myself: there you have my first reason. Well-ordered charity begins at home. And then I flattered myself that I should not displease you.

The Infante [1] appears to be more charming the more I know her. I hope that your journey will continue to be pleasant. I am afraid you will not find merely bad roads, but you are no coward. I congratulate you on that. You will tell me to what place I must address my letters, otherwise I could not write during your journey. Calculate carefully when you will be in London.

Victoire has had rheumatism in the knee and leg, and so has been unable to get out this very trying week, but she is well now. To-morrow is Easter Day, the advent of which I see with very great pleasure, out of greediness, or, worse than that, out of my desire to eat meat. Adieu, Madame! I love you, and embrace you with all my heart.

A thousand messages to M. d'Osmond and Adèle. Embrace Rainulphe. My compliments to the Chevalier and to My Lady, whose name I cannot possibly pronounce or spell.

Address:

Madame la Marquise d'Osmond, *Lausanne, Switzerland, Poste Restante.*

---

[1] Marie-Amélie of Austria, daughter of the Empress Maria Theresa, married to Ferdinand, Duc de Parme, grandson of Philippe V. of Anjou, King of Spain.

ROME, *August 23,* 1794.

I am prostrate at your feet, Madame, asking you a thousand million billion pardons for being so late in answering your letter. If I liked, I could perhaps find some excuses, but I prefer loyally pleading guilty and throwing myself on your indulgence, on which I count. All I ask of you is, to be assured that my heart has no share at all in my fault: it is and always will be the same for you.

What did you say at the death of Robespierre? Paris is all ablaze. So much the better: I have long been desiring this condition of things, for we can only get out of our difficulties in that way. If we had had a really good civil war, every man would be now by his own hearth. In spite of the incredible things that are occurring in Brabant and in Germany, I am far from being discouraged. Providence will have no one meddle in her designs: she has punished us; she will pardon us. I would that a piece of news which was told us yesterday were true. Although it is affirmed, I dare not yet flatter myself that it is correct. It is to the effect that at Marseilles they had a procession in which the image of the Virgin was carried, and that there were cries of "Long live the King!" and "Long live religion!" This town, like all Provence and Low Languedoc, is in insurrection. If it is sincerely in earnest the rest will soon follow suit, especially if Monsieur is recognised as Regent by the Powers. They flatter our hopes, but what a long business it is! The patriots are retiring from Piedmont and from Nice. We are told that they have left all their sick, baggage, and supplies there. Though this news is guaranteed and has every appearance of probability, we have been deceived so long and so often that I have become a little like St. Thomas. Under God, our salvation will come (it is a very extraordinary thing) from a nation that is our natural enemy. It is true that evil . . . but we must confess that we have thoroughly deserved it.

We have had a passable summer. The great heat has not been so extreme, except for five or six days, nor of nearly so long duration as last year. All our colony is very well, thank God: and, thank God, too, we have discovered a treasure: a doctor, an *émigré,* who was at Pisa, an excellent man, and the best aristocrat

I know. Providence sent him to us, for we intended to have another, but I have learnt since that he is not very good, and, as we did not know his name and had described him imperfectly, this one was sent to us. How are you? How did you stand the sea? Although I deserve to be punished, I hope you will not push matters so far as to deprive me of your news. That would be too severe. I should like you also to tell me how I could manage to get my letters to you, so as to put you to the least possible expense. Thank Adèle and kiss her for me: Rainulphe too, and M. d'Osmond. My compliments to your good Chevalier and his wife. I love you and embrace you with all my heart.

IV

Letters from Madame Victoire, *daughter of Louis XV., to the* Marquis *and* Marquise d'Osmond.

Rome, *May* 3, 1792.
(It should be '93.)

I cannot let M. d'Osmond go away, Madame, without telling you again how sorry I am that your household has departed, but I hope that the air of Naples will not suit you, and that, circumstances becoming favourable, you will return to Rome. It is a great comfort in misfortunes to have about us persons so attached to our family. Be assured of this my feeling for you, Madame, and also of my friendship. I embrace you with all my heart.

Victoire.

Address:
Madame la Marquise d'Osmond.

Rome, *October* 25, 1792.
(It should be '93.)

I thank you, Madame, for the plan of Toulon which you sent me. I will simply ask you, when you have any news that you wish me to know, write to me direct, for Adélaide did not tell me anything about you. We certainly had some plans of Toulon, but not so exact and so minute. I am always in great anxiety about our unhappy and heroic Queen. The King and Queen of Naples ought to be very well satisfied with the experiment of their troops. It is an excellent beginning. I have done your commissions with regard to the Chastellux. They are writing to you, so I will say nothing for them, except that they are good and excellent friends whom one is very happy to possess, and friends on whom one can count. Could you give me news of that honest and excellent man, d'Arlincourt? With all the horrors that are committed in Paris, I am anxious about him. I should like to know that you are in good health, also M. d'Osmond, to whom I pray you to give a thousand messages for me. I hope that your son is well now. I am convinced that he is, and that his little troubles come from his teeth. Good-bye, Madame! I love you and embrace you with all my heart.

VICTOIRE.

ROME, October 6, 1793.

I have not had courage, Madame, to write to you since our last and abominable misfortune. I could quite imagine all that must have passed in your heart, but your friendship for your husband and for your children must support you. Ah, never, Madame, shall I forget the tender attachment and the zeal which M. d'Osmond has shown for our blessed martyrs; and those who most know it will not forget it. Be assured of this! You and your children will see this some day. I have sent M. d'Osmond a portrait of the King and of the Queen; that of the King seems to me good; no one is more worthy than M. d'Osmond to possess it, and I am glad to give him this mark of my friendship for him. I am having one done of Elisabeth from a portrait I have of her; it will be in plaster of Paris. If you think that it would please the Queen of Naples, you could give it to her, and I would send you another. It will be finished very soon. Adieu, Madame! I love you and embrace you with all my heart.

VICTOIRE.

Address:
MADAME D'OSMOND, *Naples.*

October 29, 1793.

Monsieur, the news from Toulon astonished me almost as much as it grieved me. We must indeed submit to the will of God and not reason about it, for everything that is happening is far beyond all human reason. Let us hope firmly and hold our peace. I cannot express the pleasure that your letter caused me. Oh, how happy one is to know an honest man like you! But I had no doubts on that subject.

Our honest man, d'Arlincourt, can give us no more of the money he had destined for us. He wants the rest for his son. I am very anxious about him, and really more distressed for him than for myself. I shall never forget the service he rendered us nor the manner in which he rendered it. You will certainly be very pleased to see the Englishman who will give you my letter. I was delighted to see him, and glad to hear him speak, though he is no orator. Do not forget, Monsieur, to tell Mme. d'Osmond that I will answer her soon. Be assured, both of you, of my friendship. I embrace you both with all my heart.

VICTOIRE.

Undated. (Commencement of 1794).

Monsieur, I received your letter with great pleasure. The wishes that you form for my happiness at this reopening of the year I believe to be very sincere, and rest assured that I reckon on your attachment with pleasure. Mme. d'Osmond's condition appears to me terrible, but her patience and her great courage give me the hope that she will recover, and that we shall have the satisfaction of seeing her again. Courage assists remedies to act beneficially. Give her, I beg you, a thousand messages for me, and assure her of my loving friendship. You do not speak of your children; I hope that they are well. Rainulphe must be very big now. England is displaying very great energy; she deserves to be rewarded, and I hope she will be, in spite of all the unimaginable things we see just now. My friends the Chastellux will doubtless have told you how kind the King and Queen of Naples are to us, and what excellent relatives they are. In every way they deserve to be adored by their subjects, and it appears that they are so infinitely. I hope that our peace will not be disturbed.

Adieu, Monsieur! Be assured of my friendly sentiments for you. I embrace you with all my heart.

VICTOIRE.

Address:

MONSIEUR LE MARQUIS D'OSMOND.

August 2, 1794. ROME.

Compliments apart, Madame, I am very sorry that you have left us, and if I had not the hope, the certainty even, that you would return to our country, I should be much more grieved. You may be convinced that I shall never forget your family, and my desire is to be in a position to render it service. I do not speak of the news, which is unintelligible, as my confidence is unchangeable. I hope that you will give me news of yourself. The heat here is horrible at this moment. I am very much inconvenienced by it, but not ill. M. de Chastellux will be sure to give you the news. I finish my letter by assuring you of my friendship and by embracing you, Madame, with all my heart. I embrace your husband and your children.

VICTOIRE.

Lines written at the end of a long letter from the family of CHASTELLUX, *dated from Rome, March* 21, 1795.

I conclude, Madame, this letter from all your friends and mine. I hope that the English post is re-established, and that we shall have news of you more often. As I count upon you and M. d'Osmond, upon the attachment, the zeal and the intelligence which procured us the happiness of being here, and out of sight of all the horrors, I have recourse again to your family to try to procure for us in England a loan of 60,000 to 80,000 francs, repayable two years after our return to France, and bearing interest every year until repayment. I am not ashamed to confess that we are in great straits, and have scarcely enough to live on. That is exactly our position. In spite of everything, I am very well.

Your brother has not yet arrived.   Be assured, Madame, that you can always count upon my loving friendship.   I embrace Monsieur and Madame, Rainulphe and Adèle, with all my heart.

VICTOIRE.

I am very much pleased, Monsieur, at the success of your demand in Spain.   It is a small beginning of good fortune for you, and for me in having contributed to it.   I embrace the husband and wife and the children with all my heart.

ROME, *April* 25, 1795.

Address:

MONSIEUR THE MARQUIS D'OSMOND (*to Etton, near Beverley, Yorkshire*),[1] *Trout Beck, near Rydal, Kendal, Westmoreland, England.*

[1] Words struck out.   Address altered by the postal authorities.

V

Letters from QUEEN CHARLOTTE OF NAPLES, *daughter
of the Empress Maria Theresa, and sister of the
Queen Marie Antoinette, to the* MARQUISE
D'OSMOND.

Undated (after *October* 16, 1793).

I have received the very worthy and interesting letter of Mme.
FitzJames, my dear, and I have also read all that you tell me. If
my poor health and unfavourable circumstances allowed me, I
should take the opportunity of seeing you. I deserve to be excused if I have a horror of a great nation that has so cruelly sacrificed its masters, that has practised all barbarities, ignominies,
and atrocities upon my unhappy sister. I see and hear everywhere all the horrors, abominations, and cruelties that it will yet
commit . . . It has lost its interest for me, but human nature
shudders at it.

I pity you and the few honest folk there are, for belonging to
these cannibals,[1] and beg you to believe me your constant friend.

---

[1] Cannibals. The following lines, taken from *Les Origines de la
France contemporaine*, of Taine, prove that the word employed by
the sister of Queen Marie Antoinette is unhappily only too correct:
"The people of Caen did worse. Major de Belsunce, who was
no less innocent and had solemn pledges for his safety, was torn to
pieces like Lapérouse in the Fijian Islands, and a woman ate his
heart." (Vol. iii. p. 107.)
"M. Guillin was living at his château of Poleymieux, near Lyons.
He was hacked to pieces alive, his head was cut off and carried about
on the end of a pike, his body dismembered and a morsel of it sent
to each parish. People dipped their hands in his blood and smeared
their faces with it. . . . Some people at Chasselay had the forearm

My dear friend, I send you the two letters for the two princesses at Rome, and I send you another which you will give in due course to the interesting Princesse de Tarente. Her attachment to my unfortunate sister renders her dear to me. I send you back her touching letter. It is with much regret that I see you leaving me and going far away, but I am left with a little ray of hope, that of seeing you again in happier times. I shall be charmed when this happens, for you have won my entire esteem and friendship; and, in spite of my position, which keeps true friends at a distance, I understand the value of your friendship, and I esteem highly the noble frankness which made you own it to me. I wish you a happy journey, and I hope that your health may not suffer from all these distressing memories. May God grant a happy issue, and save the three interesting and dear victims and the remains of their unfortunate parents! How happy should I be if I could contribute to this! It would make me love life again. Be so friendly as to give me news of yourself and of everything that concerns you: it will always be so interesting for me. A thousand compliments to the worthy M. d'Osmond and to your charming children. Give a thought sometimes to one who, although far removed from you, will never forget you, and who, though having seen so little of you, knows by her feelings how unbounded her friendship would have been if she had more often enjoyed your fascinating company. Adieu! Keep happy and well. Do not forget me, and may I see you again some day and prove that friendly sentiments for you are invariable in the heart of

Your sincere friend
CHARLOTTE.

February 19, 1794.

of the dead man roasted, and then devoured it at table." (Vol. iv. pp. 197–8.)

"At the Abbaye, an old soldier named Damiens buried his sword in the side of the Adjutant-General de la Leu, plunged his hand into the wound, tore out the heart, and put it to his mouth as if to devour it. The blood, says an eye-witness, dripped down from his mouth and gave him a sort of moustache. At the Force they dismembered Mme. de Lamballe. . . . In the Rue Saint-Antoine her heart was carried about and bitten!" (Vol. vi. pp. 52–3.) Edition in 18mo.

'My dear Friend,—

am very much afraid that you will have been unjust towards me, accusing me of forgetfulness, but, if so, you will have done me a wrong of which I am incapable. I have had so much writing to do, and my head has been so painful and so feeble that I have not been able to do it. The discovery of our Jacobins and of the plot that they were weaving, with all the attendant pain, alarm, and vexation; the loss of the virtuous Mme. Elisabeth and the solitary state of those dear, unhappy orphans, a thing that rends my maternal heart; then the continually changing events of the war; the delivery of my daughter, a bad harvest, continual false alarms which have menaced us with a revolution and in a few hours armed all the provinces; then earthquakes and an awful eruption of Vesuvius which in a few hours swallowed up all the Torre del Greco as far back as eighty handbreadths in the sea; the darkening of the sun for six days by an incessant shower of dust, the lava being so terrible that whole countries were devastated, more than 30,000 men ruined, and damage done to the extent of nearly nine millions of ducats; one squadron taking the sea and blocking the Marguerite Islands, another ready to leave Toulon, without speaking of that of Brest—you will agree, my dear friend, that with all this I have had a prodigious number of things to occupy and torment me. My health and my nerves have suffered greatly. Now the Emperor has returned. There are always ups and downs in the defensive campaign; one dare not think what will come of it; in truth it is enough to make one despair. A fourth campaign appears to be neither to the taste nor within the means or power of any one; and with whom are we to make peace? What will be its results, its guarantees? As for its results, they make one shudder. I only suffer for my dear children; as for myself, I feel that I am at the end of my career, which will not be long now, for one cannot resist so many shocks. What an abominable plot they have discovered at Turin! The same circumstances as in our case, the same means and methods, and, on the very day even that it was to break out at Turin, we had a false alarm at Naples. In England they have also distorted two discourses of St. Just. They are printing another under the veil of secrecy; in this their infernal systems are explained and worked out; their maxims and awful immorality make one shudder. Your letter, my dear friend, speaks just as if it read my soul. I cannot deny that I should like to be able to flee into a desert or into a convent, to cut myself off from the world. It is impossible to do good, so many difficulties and impediments hinder one; and having this responsibility, without the power of doing good, with the melancholy experience of mankind that the present times have brought us, I should like to hide myself in the utmost depths of solitude. But nine children, seven not yet established, bind me to the world in spite of myself. . . . I dare not speak to you of the France of yore, of all the murders, impiety, thefts, wickednesses of every kind that are now committed there. They have armies on land and sea, completely supplied, that can hold their own and make head against the best troops and squadrons. I own that all this humiliates me; I begin to lose courage and to relinquish all hope of tranquillity and order. This is very sad. I would like, my dear friend, to be able to console you. I would like to be good for something, and not to give you my gloom. Give me in full detail news of all that concerns you. Count upon the sincere and eternal friendship of your very attached friend,

CHARLOTTE.

July 8, 1794.

MY VERY DEAR FRIEND,—

I am answering a very charming letter received from you on August 15. If I did not already love you infinitely, this letter, all the tender, noble, virtuous, generous, and sincere sentiments that it contains, would attach me to you for the rest of my life. . . . I respect, and am humiliated by, what you tell me of the conditions that you lay down for the continuation of your dear friendship, and while suffering from your delicacy in not wishing to permit me to act as a friend, I respect and admire, but my heart suffers. You wish to have news of us. You are very friendly and kind to interest yourself in it, and I give it to you such as I have it. It is gloomy, but so am I also. I am now at Caserta, where I saw you for the first time, where hours passed and seemed to me only minutes—where in fact you made, at our very first meeting, such a profound impression on my heart. I am living here in close retirement with my children. I am far from the town, and hope it will be long before I put my foot in it again. I see nobody but those whom absolute necessity compels me to receive. My children, reading, writing, drawing, sad reflections . . . all that is more than enough to fill the day. My children are all the dearer to me since I have seen such a cruel future being prepared for them. My daughter Mimi is of a marriageable age, enjoys marvellous health, is as tall as I am, and is always charming. My son is taller than I am by two inches. All the little ones are well. Harmony reigns among them, and in that I find my consolation. So much for my family. My eldest daughter is recovering, though a little slowly, from her miscarriage. My second daughter is to be confined in the month of November, and is very well. The marriage of my son is postponed on account of the misfortunes of the times, which do not allow us to think of it.

As for Italy, it is always threatened. The regicides are trying at this moment to penetrate into the country from two sides, Genoa and Piedmont; but I am like you, and although everybody is terribly alarmed and fearful of an invasion, I have no apprehension of such by land. That requires time, and leaves one the leisure to take precautions. As long as the English keep the sea I am tranquil, but if they diminish their forces or display less activity, there is everything to fear. I ought out of delicacy, my dear and sensitive friend, to conceal from you my ideas on this subject, but my sincerity opens my heart to speak to you just as I think. If the Tricolour arrives before Naples, if bombs fall, frightful terror will numb the faculties and the intellect. When women see their husbands and sons killed or wounded and their houses burned, they cannot stand it, and if, taking advantage of this alarm, the Jacobins mix with the crowd and propose to them the cessation of the bombardment at the price of the sacrifice of us all, you may be sure that this will be done, and that they will carry us dead or alive, according to our temperament, as a present to the regicides. This idea is not rose-coloured, but it is a sure and a true one, founded upon my knowledge of character and of our people, who would act thus, not out of hatred of us, nor friendship for the French, but to ward off misfortune from themselves.

We have had a well-organised Jacobin plot. The oath was to kill all kings and to destroy all sacerdotal and political authority. They swore it on the blade that they call their god—this has been discovered. They had already formed a revolutionary club, a sworn committee of public safety, &c.; nothing was wanting but the explosion. Branches of it have been discovered. I believe there are still many more, but what can we do, except fulfil our duty and await our destiny? I could say this calmly if I had no children, but my heart bleeds as I think of them. They say the little King is dead. I do not believe a word of it. It would, perhaps, be a blessed thing for him. As for the daughter, I dare not think of her; it is she for whom I am in torment. I would give all I have in the world to save her. No one will speak openly to me of her fate, and that is enough to show me that she has fallen into dishonour. In spite of that, I would take her with pleasure and try to reinstate her. But I do not wish to afflict you by telling you how much this affects me. . . .

Alas! talk to me of all that interests, concerns, and regards you. Let us, at any rate at a distance, keep up our correspondence and our memories. Give me your word that you reckon surely on finding in me a sincere, tender, and attached friend, who will be so in all times and circumstances. Adieu! I embrace you, and am yours for life.

October 8, 1794.

My very dear Friend,—

I owe you an answer for two of your dear letters, one of the 1st and the other of the 21st of June. They greatly touched and distressed me, by all that you tell me in them, and by the sadness that I find in your whole letter. The question of your health is particularly near to my heart. I should like to hope, and I flatter myself, that your troubles are dispersed, and I take an infinite interest in them. For God's sake do not carry despair to the point of letting your malady grow acute. There are excellent professors; consult them all. Go to London; and I conjure you not to have any false delicacy, but show me that you regard me as your friend, and that you make use of my small and limited propositions as a real friend to recover your health. If I could see you really well and free, not in mere words but in effect, from a malady which makes me shudder for your sensitive and delicate constitution, if by the consultations and the care of the cleverest doctors I could see you relieved, that would be a priceless happiness for me. But show me the confidence of friendship, and avail yourself of my offers. I beg you to write me details about your physical and moral state, your health of body and of soul, and that of your beautiful, amiable, and interesting Adèle. Write to me about your nice and clever boy and your estimable husband. On whatever horizon he is placed, your husband's talents, attainments, and brilliant qualities will come to light. There is too much need for such men not to be sure that he will be recognised. . . . My health is always weak. The shocks that my whole existence has experienced have been so great that I must feel them all my life, and never be well again. I cannot tell you the anguish that the death of the unhappy Child-King caused me. I am convinced, that it is a crime of the Convention and that he has swelled the number of victims sacrificed to their wickedness and to their iniquitous conduct, that knows no curb. I am told that they are going to make an exchange with the only surviving member of this unfortunate family, and that she is going to live at Vienna with Mme. de Tourzeel. I can hardly wait for the instant when I shall know her to be safe, and though I should have felt a sad satisfaction in having her near me, I believe that she will be more happy in every respect at Vienna, and, only desiring her real happiness, I submit to the privation of not seeing her. This messenger is going to London to speak about the strange and fatal peace of Spain. It was signed on the 20th at Basle and on the 28th at Madrid. They knew nothing of it, or pretended that no orders had been given, and that they were quite in the dark. All

the arrangements were made against their will, so it is very difficult to understand. Time will explain this riddle. . . . My dear
children are my sole consolation. If I had not them, I should
retire to live in a convent, ignored and buried away from the whole
world; but as it is they tie me. Adieu! my dear friend. Tell me
in full detail all that concerns you; I am so really and sincerely
interested in it. . . . Do not forget me, and believe me for life
your sincere and attached friend.

August 15, 1795.

Undated [*January* 1796]
MY VERY DEAR AND KIND FRIEND,—

Your letter touched me deeply. It is the interpreter of your
sentiments, but allow me to tell you that you grieved me by your
delicacy, though indeed I feared it. Do you then refuse absolutely
to admit a tender and sincere friendship? Silence on your part
would have indicated to me that you received as a friend from a
friend for whom in a similar case you would do the same. Silence
then, absolute and eternal, on this point and no painful resentment;
but show me that you esteem me as highly as Mme. d'Harcourt
and the Princesse de Tarente, if her situation were more favourable; in fact, eternal silence and friendship. Let me speak of
another subject . . . You are very kind to wish for my portrait:
I should like to have one that resembles me to remind you of me,
but what remains of self-respect makes me unwilling to give away
my old face. If I could put into the painting my heart, my soul,
my sentiments, it might pass, but my mere face is a little humiliat-
ing. . . . I am in despair about the delay in the fatal exchange of
all that is left of the family of my unfortunate sister. I am afraid
of some new rascality on the part of these wretches. I am in
veritable torments lest these scoundrels, having at their head such
criminals as the abominable Drouet, Sémonville, and such like,
may not pretend to hand over a young girl who is not the daughter
of my sister. The remoteness of Mme. de Tourzel and intrigues
of every kind give me cause for fear, and my mind is very much
disturbed. Indeed, the present time is most unhappy, and that
which we are expecting still more so. But I do not wish, my dear

friend, to communicate my dark mood to you. I will speak to you, then, of what alone binds me to life, namely, my dear children. My son is going to be married this year, and he is already a man, but not a corrupt young man. He is amiable and docile; although very quick and passionate, his heart and principles are good. My eldest daughter has been a mother three times already, and on the last occasion, thank God! very auspiciously. She lives in perfect harmony with her husband. My second daughter has two children, and is quite as happy in her marriage. My daughter Mimi is taller and stronger than I, but of a very praiseworthy piety, goodness, and affection for me. Her outward appearance is not to her advantage, but she gains infinitely by being known. Amélie, who has such a dear and mournful resemblance, is full of grace, wit, and amiability. Antoinette is still delicate, but very intelligent. They are all excessively attached to me, and to a point that gives me uneasiness about them. Leopold is handsome and good: he is nearly a man. Albert and Elisabeth are a little delicate, especially the girl, but full of intelligence. It is with so good a mother as you that I dare to speak of all which alone attaches me to the world. Otherwise what I have seen, tested, and known of men and governments, of injustice towards superiors, of deception practised on them deliberately, then dishonour and slander, of men's ingratitude . . . all this would make me shut myself off in a desert. If I could have one friend near me like you, that would reconcile me with the human race; but as things go, I desire nothing but solitude. Adieu! my charming friend. Take every care of your health, and give me a detailed account of it. Get better, regain your vigour, do justice to my feelings, remain my tender friend, and believe me for life your sincere friend, your most tender and attached friend,'

CHARLOTTE.

My very dear Friend,—

I received your very dear and kind letter of December 22, and I was very much touched by all that you tell me in it. So my poor niece is saved. They say that she is very amiable, interesting, pretty, very lively, but that, realising her birth, she

wears her sad mourning and lives in a kind of retreat suitable to
her dress. She has also to be examined. She is in no way
awkward, but inspires universal interest. She has already written
to me twice. I possess her portrait, which has been taken for
me and is said to be very like her. Indeed, all my letters from
Vienna only tell me of her, for every one knows how much I think
of her. Mme. Soucy was her hostess in the first instance, and she
is now under the charge of that very honourable and trustworthy
Mme. de Chanclos, whom I know and esteem highly. I speak to
you of all this, knowing your attachment to these unhappy relatives
of mine.

February 2, 1796.

. . . . The King of Sardinia, as we are informed is already
making his peace, and that will expose the whole of Italy. The
Venetians have just expelled the King of France in the most outrageous manner. He was living quietly at Verona. These examples make one shudder, and I confess to you that as mother
of a numerous and dear family my reflections are terribly sad.
For there are only two things for us: first, to await these villains
intrepidly, combat them, and repel them—in fact, to conquer
or die, but then we should have to see if the country would remain
calm, for corruption has made such progress and cowardice even
more; or, secondly, to lower oneself by making an infamous peace,
of which these scoundrels will dictate the terms, and to swallow
the poison of the humiliation and degradation which it means to
be in alliance and at peace with such monsters. I am myself,
and shall be all my life, for the first alternative, but you understand,
with seven children whom I love tenderly, how much thought and
reflection it needs. As for my unfortunate niece, she wishes to go
to Rome. She is restless and discontented. I have proposed
that we should all subscribe and give her a pension, marrying her
to the Duc d'Angoulême, which she wishes with all her heart.
This pension would last until the moment when this prince has his
revenues again, for I insist on hoping for an end to our miseries,
which cannot always go on like this. In this way the young

orphan would have an establishment according to her wishes and tastes, and all discussion would be finished. I believe it would be the best thing to do: and, for my part, in spite of the awful expenses into which the King runs, entirely on his own account and at his own risk, receiving nothing from any one, I will answer for it that he gives his consent. Adieu, my dear and kind friend! Be careful of your health. Do not give up the idea of coming to recover your forces in our beautiful climate. You will find here not a Queen, but a tender and sincere friend, who appreciates your merit and your heart, and who will seize every opportunity to be with such a sweet friend. Adieu! Believe me for life your very tender and sincerely attached friend

CHARLOTTE.

May 7, 1796.

August 20, 1796.

MY VERY DEAR AND CHARMING FRIEND,—

How touched I was with your letter of the 19th of July! You may not believe it, but I suffer to hear that you are still so unwell. . . . Our hopes, our fears, and our despair are beaten about like the waves of the sea. Wurmser has delivered Mantua, and taken Verona, Vicenza, and Ferrara. I imagined him to be already at Tortona, all the more so as he has 60,000 men, and these miserable, ragged Republicans only 35,000, and yet they have beaten them more than once, retaken all the places, and driven us back to the Tyrol. All this causes general discouragement. In the Empire also things are going pretty badly. Everything that happens is incomprehensible; indeed, we have to bow our heads, sigh, and hold our peace. My dear husband is at the frontier at the different encampments; and we continue by all means imaginable to increase the strength of our army, trusting neither to the armistice nor to negotiations of peace, when we have to deal with such men. Well, we are resolved, in spite of all the villanies, horrors, and rascalities which we see around us on every side, to conduct ourselves honourably and loyally, even if we have to suffer for it, and to die with our arms in our hands rather than be guilty of a base act. But all this makes my life one of torment.

. .. . Adieu, my charming friend! May Heaven assuage your pains of body and of mind, and may I see you happy and restored to health! Adieu! Believe me for all my life, with very sincere sentiments, your tender and attached friend

CHARLOTTE.

. . . I am going backwards and forwards between the army and the encampment on the frontier, where my dear husband is now. We have an armistice with the Republicans, but as their good faith and courtesy are known to us, we put no trust in them, and are augmenting our forces. All this makes me very sad, but be sure that the dear King of Naples will be consistent and loyal. . . .

September 22, 1796, MONTE CASINO.

November 10, 1796.

MY VERY DEAR FRIEND,—

I take advantage of a messenger of ours who is going to Paris to write you these few lines. As there is an English envoy, the couriers will be frequent, and I take advantage of them to give you my news and to assure you of my eternal friendship. . . . My health is ruined and destroyed; the vexations, cares, and anxieties of these times have killed me and undermined my health for ever. Thank God, the King and all my dear children are very well. The marriage of my young bride, who is to come to Naples, will take place as soon as the Austrians have cleared the road; I hope that will be soon. . . . You will already have heard, my dear friend, and you will have pitied me hearing it, that duty, prudence (considering how everything was turning out, the abandonment of Corsica, still worse the abandonment of the Mediterranean by the English squadron, our only support) all our misfortunes have compelled us to make peace on the honourable conditions on which it was offered. The Queen has done her duty in sparing the blood of her subjects and delivering them from this curse, but the Caroliner's heart bleeds. They are the assassins, the executioners of my sister and her family; they are the villains who have put the dagger into the hands of all nations to lead them on to destroy all authorities and thrones. In short, I cannot forget what they were, and are still, and my heart groans. I cannot think without shuddering of the moment when I shall see a tricolour, a cockade, a citizen. All my blood is turned, and I foresee what bitter pangs they will cause us, but the sacrifice is made; it has cost me much, and now I must submit to it. I desire keenly the continuation of brilliant successes, so that general peace may follow, and on that I set my only hope. Well, my sweet friend, how many things there are that I should like to tell you! But I fear to be indiscreet. Pity my position and situation, for they merit it. I am planning to go and bury myself in the country with my children and to live like a hermit longing for. . . .

November 21, 1796.

MY VERY DEAR FRIEND,—

As I can avail myself of an English courier, I do not want to miss writing to you, my dear friend, and to remind you of myself once more. I am sure that you will be thinking of me. Here we are at peace with those monsters that my heart detests so sincerely. The idea of a citizen makes me shudder. I shall never see in him anything but the representative of those who assassinated my dear, unhappy relatives, of those who put fire and confusion in place of peace and of the repose of the whole world, and particularly of all good order and government. Indeed, I doubt whether I can ever bow to circumstances, so I shall try to be in the country as much as possible and to avoid the sight of the fatal tricolour that my heart abhors.

My health is very precarious. . . . But all this comes from the vexations of every kind that I have experienced during these last years. My dear children are well, thank God! My daughter Mimi is taller than I am, and Amélie is nearly as tall as I am. Clever Antoinette does not grow, but she makes up in intelligence and heart for what is lacking in size. I am promising myself the visit of my daughter-in-law for the month of January. I shall do all I can to make the young pair happy. That will bring me consolation.

My dear Friend,—

I have been without your dear news for some time, and I am anxious for your dear health. . . . My heart, though far from you and torn by different anxieties, is interested, yes, keenly interested, in all that concerns you. We are now at so-called peace with the executioners of my sister and her family and the demolishers, at least in desire, of all thrones. This is very wretched but necessity admits of no discussion, and it would be long and very grievous and painful for me to give you in detail all that has placed us in this cruel necessity. It is better to try to forget it. My health is precarious; nerves, head, digestion are useless. My dear children, who are all that I love in the world, are very well, thank God! and are my sole consolation, for beside them I have nothing but anxieties now, and I foresee still more in the future. . . .

Believe me for life, your very tender, sincere, and attached friend

January 14, 1797. CHARLOTTE.

My dear Friend,—

Your letter touched me infinitely. I see in it the language of your heart and soul, and the touching interest that you show me flatters me infinitely and is very dear to me. But I am very far from satisfied with the news of your health. You suffer with a resignation and patience which humiliate me, for I have much less of these knowing you to be ill, my sweet friend. I really believe that a mild and warm climate might be beneficial to you, so take advantage of your first opportunities. Put aside all this false delicacy. Think that it is your duty to recover and preserve your life for your sweet and interesting children, for your husband and friends; and I hope that in spite of my rank, which is only a matter of circumstance, you will find my heart and soul worthy of this sentiment, and appreciating and venerating it as it deserves. Yes, believe me, it will be an infinite consolation to see you again, and the sentiments I have vowed to you are for life. My health continues precarious; my nerves torment me; but it is the political situation, rather than my physical condition, that causes my illness. My daughter-in-law is going on very satisfactorily towards her confinement; she is at the end of the fifth month. I have been a grandmother for seven years, but I have never yet seen my grandchildren. It will be a real joy and consolation for me. We live in perfect family union, and that is my comfort in my distress. My two daughters are both taller than I am, and very sensible young people. My third will not grow. My two little boys are charming, particularly Leopold. I had the misfortune to lose my youngest daughter suddenly in convulsions; it is the one who was born when you were at Naples. The time and the moment were too unhappy, so my beloved child never enjoyed good health. I tell you all this, knowing the interest that your friendship causes you to take in it. I do not speak to you about the sad condition of things in Europe. The capture of Malta, without a blow, makes one shudder. Impregnable fortresses and ports surrender at discretion, without even defending themselves. This makes one tremble and shudder; but I do not wish to distress you. Think of the re-establishment of your health, my dear friend. Come to our mild and healthy climate. Remember me cordially to your husband and to the dear and interesting children. Write to me sincerely and without ceremony. Be my friend always, and believe me for life your sincere and attached friend

CHARLOTTE.

June 20, 1798.

MY DEAR FRIEND,—

Your letter, dated June 5, has caused me a satisfaction and a joy which it is difficult to express, but which correspond to the tender and sincere friendship which I have vowed to you. At last, dear and sensitive friend, tender wife, excellent mother, you will have a moment of consolation. How I love and cherish the dear Adèle! How fortunate she is to be able to make her mother happy! How happy I shall be myself if this interesting family should come to Naples! Believe me that you will always find in me a real friend whose sentiments are invariable. I hope that this consolation, the source of which is dear Adèle, may have an effect upon your health so that you will be relieved and get well. This is what I am waiting most eagerly to hear. In a letter of congratulation and happiness I do not want to speak to you of us here and to give you sad jeremiads. I know so well what your friendship is, that I am sure of the sympathy you would take in all that concerns us, and I will not disturb your happiness, as I am too delighted that you should have any, all the more so as my lamentations are only sad anticipations and not yet realised. The fact that the Roman Republic, Corfu, the Islands, and now also Malta, are in the hands of these monsters, gives us much uneasiness especially with this great squadron and numerous transports of Bonaparte's roaming the seas, no one knows where, for the last two months, and Admiral Nelson not being able to find them, or indeed to know where they are. This cannot be otherwise than disquieting. However, we must hope that Providence will still save us: though as we are the only ones left untouched in Italy, and as we have not yet suffered spoliation, we have everything to fear from their cupidity. Precarious health, shattered nerves, sleeplessness, indigestion, all this is the result of these alarms: in spite of this I am not confined to my bed, but I am not all well, as a result of keen sorrow. I find all my consolation in my dear family, and also my greatest anxiety, for I should be very indifferent about myself. My two eldest daughters are tall and marriageable: the third remains small. All three are my dearest friends. Of my two little sons, the elder is my joy and hope on account of the affection, intelligence, and character he promises to have: the younger one is not so strong, but very intelligent. My eldest son is not very brilliant nor amiable, but an honest, strong young man. His young wife is kind, placid, and sweet. It is a pleasure to see how they love each other. The young wife is in the seventh month of a very satisfactory pregnancy, and a real patriarchal union reigns in the family. This is my only happiness. Many people would laugh at me for this, but I am speaking to a tender mother, and you will excuse and understand me. Adieu, my dear friend! I repeat my very sincere compliments and the assurance of my keen interest in this happy event. As a mother to a mother, and a friend to a very true friend, do give me more details of an event which I have so much at heart. Remember me to your worthy husband and your sweet children, and believe me heartily and for life your very sincere and attached friend

CHARLOTTE.[1]

August 12, 1798.

MY VERY DEAR FRIEND,—

When we are unhappy, and I feel myself very unhappy, we are all the more desirous to draw near to our friends. I count you among the number of my friends, and hope that you will not have forgotten me. My health holds out. I am older by a score of years, but I still live and exist, and I am astonished at that. All my dear family are well, thank God! My daughter-in-law, who is the best creature in the world, has given me some anxiety about her health, but she is, thank God, quite well again, and expecting to be a mother once more. We continue to live between hope and dread: the news varies every day. We are expecting help from Russia: if it comes it will be of the greatest service to us. The English render us the greatest services. Were it not for them both Sicilies would be democratised, I should be dead of grief or drowned in the sea, or else, with my dear family, imprisoned in a castle by our rebellious subjects. You can read in the gazettes, without my naming them to you, how many ungrateful subjects we have. It suffices to tell you that in their writings and their ingratitude they have surpassed their foster-mother France, but with us the classes are different. Here it is the class which has the most to lose which is the most violent; nobles, bishops, monks, ordinary lawyers, but not the high magistracy, nor the people. The latter are loyal, and show it on every occasion. In short, my dear friend, I suffer very much, but I should like to know how your health is and your maladies, how

[1] It is the marriage of Mlle. d'Osmond with General de Boigne to which reference is made in this letter.

dear Adèle is, if all those round you are happy, for I know how necessary that is for your peace of mind. Write or let me know all that concerns you and interests my heart so vividly. None of my ladies came with me or asked to come with me, although I proposed it to several of them. Two have gone with their husbands and families, Baroness Acton and Castelcigala. I have Sicilian ladies here. In short, all this gives me food for reflection, and all that I have experienced has disgusted me with the world for life. I hope to see my children firmly re-established in their patrimony, and then to be forgotten by the whole world, even to my very name. That is my wish. My dear children have behaved like angels in all our unfortunate circumstances. They suffer every kind of privation they did not know before, without complaining, out of love for me, so that I may notice nothing. They are always good-humoured, though they have no amusements. In fact, they make me blush; they have so many more virtues than I have. Adieu, my dear friend! Give me news of dear Adèle; of your son, of his father—in fact, of all that interests you; and believe that neither the seas that separate us, nor misfortunes, nor distance, nor anything will ever efface the impression of friendship with which you have inspired me, and that I shall be all my life your sincere friend

CHARLOTTE.

PALERMO, *May* 2, 1799.

I must reply, my dear friend, to your letter of November 14. Ah, how thoroughly I recognised your heart and soul in reading it, and how I should like to see you again! I am very much distressed that dear Adèle is not as happy as my heart would wish her to be, and as she deserves to be; but happiness does not always go with merit. You may fancy how affected I was by these fresh and fatal victories of the Republicans, seeing that I might have to take to flight again. At the present there is an armistice, but that does not tranquillise me at all, because of the bad faith of these monsters, and I fear some new treachery every day. I am still at Vienna with my children, who are very tall, and are my consolation and very sweet company. How many things my heart would have to say to you; it is so difficult to write to each other. Who knows if I shall have the comfort of seeing you again? I desire it most keenly, and should be delighted at that any time. Be very careful of your health; tell me about it, and about everything that concerns you. The Castelcigala family are my sincere friends, especially the husband; I count upon him entirely. Remember me to your husband and your children, and count upon the sincere and constant friendship of your sincere friend

CHARLOTTE.

VIENNA, *January* 2, 1801.

MY DEAR FRIEND,—

Your letter of August 17 and your constant remembrance have touched me very deeply. I have been nearly a month at Naples. On the 25th the wedding of my daughter with the Prince of the Asturias was celebrated; on September 12 the Spanish squadron arrived. In a few days it will deprive me of this dear child, probably for life. I confess that this separation costs me a great deal, especially considering this country. May God grant her happiness! I wanted to accompany her, but all that I found on my arrival makes it impossible for me, and I should never be comfortable if I left the three children here alone. Tell me in detail about your health, about your dear daughter, and all that concerns you. You know my keen and sincere interest in everything that touches you. Adieu! Do not forget me, and believe me for life your very attached friend

CHARLOTTE.

NAPLES, *September* 14, 1802.

VI

Letters from QUEEN CHARLOTTE OF NAPLES *to* MLLE. ADÈLE D'OSMOND.

MY DEAR ADÈLE,—

An unknown person who loves you and is a sincere friend of your mother sends you a trifle to pay your masters and to profit by their lessons, as well as your brother, and to give some comfort and consolation to your worthy parents. This little offering will be repeated as the circumstances of your unknown friends allow of it. I know you, and have not forgotten your sweet self. Your excellent parents, after all the misfortunes they have experienced, have only you and your brother, and your success, your destiny, and your tenderness alone can console them. Make it your entire study, therefore, to give them this joy. Accept this advice from the unknown person who, while remaining *incognito*, concludes by assuring you of her sincere love.

MY DEAR ADÈLE,—

Your letter touched me very much. Yes, you alone can be the consolation of your excellent parents. Give me details about the health of your good and loving mother. I hope and trust that she is getting well, but above all that her sufferings may cease and that Heaven may preserve her to you. You and your brother must try to comfort and console her. How I wish she were in Italy! I feel she would get some good from the mildness of the climate; but, however distant the country, my friendship follows you. Assure your tender and worthy mother that, attached to her as I am, I have the same sentiments for her children, who are a part of herself. Give me news, then, of your dear mother's health and of your success in giving her pleasure, and count upon my tender and sincere interest and friendship.

CHARLOTTE.

(No dates.)

VII

Marriage Certificate of MLLE. ADÈLE D'OSMOND *and* GENERAL DE BOIGNE.

Extract from the Marriage Register of the French Chapel in London.

In the year one thousand seven hundred and ninety-eight, on the eleventh day of the month of June, We, the undersigned, Antoine Eustache Osmond, Bishop of Cominges in France, at present residing in London, in virtue of the permission accorded to us by Monseigneur Douglas, Bishop of Centurie and Vicar Apostolic of London, have given the nuptial benediction, after having asked and received their mutual consent, to Messire Benoit de Boigne, originally of Chambéry in Savoy, elder son of M. Jean Baptiste de Boigne, and of Dlle. Elène de Cabet, absent, and to Demoiselle Louise Eléonore Charlotte Adélaide Osmond, younger daughter of Messire René Eustache Marquis d'Osmond and of Dame Eléonore Dillon, Marquise d'Osmond, present, and consenting to the said marriage, and in presence of Messire François Emmanuel Duc d'Uzès, of Messire Anne Joachim Montagu Marquis de Bouzoles, of Messire Charles Alexandre de Calonne and of General Daniel O'Connell, who have all signed this register with us.

Benoit de Boigne, L.C.E., Adèle Osmond de Boigne. Le Marquis d'Osmond, Dillon Marquise d'Osmond, Le Duc d'Uzès, Montagu de Bouzoles, de Calonne, Le Comte O'Connell, Arthur Richard Dillon, Arch. and Primate of Narbonne, Commander of the Order of the Holy Ghost, Ant. Eustache Osmond, Bishop of Cominges.

Fr. Emmanuel Bourret, priest, Director of the Seminary of St. Sulpice of Paris and Director of the French Catholic Chapel of Paddington Street.

VIII

Letter from ADMIRAL DE BRUIX, *commanding the fleet at Boulogne, written to* MADAME LA COMTESSE DE BOIGNE, *at the time of her return to France.*

BOULOGNE, *Vendémiaire* 25 (*October* 17).

How kind of you, my dear cousin, to have thought that it would be real happiness for me to learn of your arrival! How many people I shall charm by announcing a piece of such good news for us all! At this moment the old Bishop, Mlle. de Martainville, Joseph and his wife are together in my cottage of St. Gratien, three leagues from Paris. The Bishop of Nancy and M. et Mme. d'Argout are expected there every instant. You, my dear cousin, whom we did not expect, will fill the hearts of all there with joy and complete the happiness of a cousin who knows by heart all that Adèle promised at seven, and knows too how far she has at eighteen surpassed such hopes. Do not, then, turn aside from your road, my dear cousin; come as directly as you can to Paris, where all your friends will be counting the days until the moment of your arrival. But do not put down this advice to my credit. No, dear cousin, it is not out of generosity towards the good relatives of Paris that I dissuade you from the kind project that you had of coming through Boulogne. It is the hope of joining you myself in Paris, even more than the desire of sparing you some fatigue, which makes me persuade you to go there by the shortest way. This hope is founded on the approaching coronation of the Emperor, to which, if I can trust the constitutional Charter, I am to be summoned.

I recognise M. de Sémonville perfectly in the politeness he has

440

shown you, and I have such a good opinion of his kindness that I suppose he has received very strict instructions, since he has refused you a passport. Nevertheless, I am writing to him by this mail, and I hope to smooth away the difficulties that are an obstacle to his willingness. I am writing, too, to M. de Talleyrand, our Minister of Foreign Affairs, to ask him to send you a passport. So I think that if by ill luck what you expect does not arrive, the steps I am taking at this moment will supply your wants.

Accept, dear cousin, the assurance of the loving friendship of a cousin whom you will find very old, but whose heart is as young to-day as it was for Adèle in '88.

E. BRUIX.

I am addressing the copy of this scrawl to you to Antwerp, c/o M. David Barish, banker. Please send me just a word to tell me the date of your departure for Paris.

Address:
MADAME DE BOIGNE, *The Hague.*

IX

Letter from Adrien de Montmorency *to* Madame
la Comtesse de Boigne.

Grenoble, *September* 6, 1811.

Every kind of grace, kindness, and of elegant hospitality did you provide for us at Aix. This is no flattery; it is the truth that springs from the depths of my heart, and I feel the need of saying it to you and am anxious to persuade you of it, as I really felt it.

I found my poor cousin [1] in a deplorable state. However, she is said to be better than she was when you saw her at Geneva. The shower-baths ordered her by her doctor Odier did her much harm. The doctor here has changed his opinion: he is persuaded that it is the chest which is threatened. I myself have not the least doubt of it: I seem to recognise all the symptoms of this scourge of youth and of beauty. She suffers with a dry and frequent cough: talks quickly and excitedly. All her nights are sleepless, and in the morning she is feverish; and then at six o'clock in the evening she rises, dines, eats well, and suffers no more at all until midnight, when all her tortures recommence.

She is, however, most deeply touched by your interest and friendship. She would accept your kind offer to come and see her if she were in a state to enjoy it. It is one of her keenest regrets to have to refuse.

Then she is going away on Thursday the 12th. She has refused my offer to accompany her and look after her during this long and painful journey to Normandy.

You know that I am not afraid of the contagion of this malady

[1] The Duchesse de Chevreuse, at that time in exile.

442

(it is not that of the chest) which alarms so many people. I am going to prove to you how contagious it is. My companion received an order from the police general not to return to Paris, and not to come within forty leagues of the city. I make no reflections. But beware of the bomb! [1]

I pray you to keep this sad news secret until it is out. It is useless to make people to talk about it. Perhaps you know it already.

Adieu to you, whom I nursed in your childhood, and at whose knees I should like to kneel in your youth.

A thousand, thousand marks of tender homage and admiration.

ALFIN JÉRUSALEM.

A thousand greetings to Rainulphe. Juliette returned to Paris like an arrow, and you can imagine that it was the best thing to do.

Mathieu sends you his homage and gratitude.

I am going to you at Beauregard, and sing my gratitude for all that you have been to me.

[1] The bulletin of the police general, dated August 21, 1811, has on page 5, and under the heading "Ministerial Correspondence," the following notice: "The Minister has charged the prefect of Geneva to inform M. Mathieu de Montmorency that he cannot return to Paris, that he is free to go to Coppet or elsewhere, provided he remains forty leagues away from Paris." (National Archives, AF 4 1517.) Quoted by M. Edouard Herriot, *Madame Récamier*, English edition, vol. i. p. 237.

X

Letter from Madame la Comtesse de Boigne *to her husband,* General de Boigne.

Paris, *November* 24, 1812.

You always reply to me with such harshness, my dear friend, every time I speak to you of myself, and this harshness is so painful to me, that, although we are under the same roof, I prefer to write to you rather than expose myself to a discussion which always degenerates into offensive personalities and only serves to embitter us mutually one against the other, instead of fulfilling the object I have always set before myself, namely, to adjust as far as possible the differences that have arisen between us. At the time of your arrival I thought it my duty to inform you of what I desired you should do for me. It seemed to me that this simple and loyal fashion was the one to be employed between us, and was the best suited to our temperaments. Since that time you have agreed to some of my requests, while you have refused others. I will not speak of this again. I know perfectly well that I have no other claims except those of virtue and delicacy. To-day I see preparations for your departure, and, although I do not concur with the amiable desire you have expressed never to see me again, yet I feel that just now my presence at Buissonrond would be embarrassing for you as it would be for me. I cannot therefore fix a limit for this absence, which I shall not fail to curtail as soon as you express the faintest desire on the subject; but before this absence commences I should like to know what are your intentions relative to my pecuniary position. I do not mean to raise any difficulty, or even to enter into discussion with you, but you cannot think it extraordinary that I should wish to know your projects, and before

444

knowing them I submit to your judgment certain reflections. Although you always promised to improve my position on the sale of Beauregard, circumstances forbid me to ask for any increase of the sum at which you fixed my expenses fifteen months ago; but I will merely represent to you that if you suppress a part, not only will my lot not be ameliorated, but it will be made worse; and you will comprehend this easily if you will calculate that the maintenance and expenses of Châtenay, practising the strictest economy there, cannot be estimated at less than six thousand francs. Add to that the revenue of Beauregard, which you estimated in my income at eight thousand francs, and which may perhaps be calculated at six. Then there are the expenses of moving, which will amount at least to two thousand francs, and you will see that, even if you continue to allow me the sum of 50,000 francs which you had assigned to me for the charges of my establishment, I shall be much worse off this year than last, and it will be necessary for me even to find some means of economising, for on the 1st of October I had one hundred and ten francs in hand. It is true that the rent of this house is paid for six months, but there are other expenses, such as doctor, apothecary, etc., which must make up this difference. These then, my dear friend, are the reflections that I submit to you; but I beg you to weigh them with kindness and wisdom. I fancy that with the charges of the two houses, which come to at least 13,000 francs a month, you will think that the income I wish you to assure me, is not exaggerated. You judged it reasonable and fixed it yourself fifteen months ago. I do not see how I have deserved that it should be less, and as for your pecuniary position, it has rather improved since that time; first by the sale of Beauregard and then by the rate of exchange, which is somewhat better than at that epoch. However, my dear friend, I repeat that I submit to your pleasure. All I wish is to avoid a painful discussion. I hope that your decision may be such as I ask, and I believe it will; may straightforwardness and delicacy dictate it. I will willingly talk to you about this, if you will avoid offensive reflections and personalities so that a friendly discussion may not degenerate into a quarrel; but if you do not wish to make this effort, I beg you to reply to me by a few lines in writing.—

Good night, dear General! You imagine that you are surrounded by people who wish you well much more than I do, and you are greatly mistaken. Some day, and soon perhaps, those persons will show you what they are worth, and then, as always, you will come back to and judge perhaps with less injustice the woman who is and will always be your most faithful and your best friend.

INDEX

447

Lightning Source UK Ltd.
Milton Keynes UK
UKOW05f0202040217
293546UK00008B/230/P